Creative Teaching
of the Social Studies
in the
Elementary School

Creative Teaching of the Social Studies in the Elementary School

Second Edition

James A. Smith

Allyn and Bacon, Inc.
Boston   London   Sydney   Toronto

Library of Congress Cataloging in Publication Data

Smith, James A
    Creative teaching of the social studies in the elemen-
tary school.

    Includes bibliographies and index.
    1. Creative thinking (Education) 2. Social sciences—
Study and teaching (Elementary) I. Title.
LB1584.S62   1979   372.8′3′044   78-24552
ISBN 0-205-06049-8

Printed in the United States of America.

Cover art by Leslie Short, Jerry Dores,
and Scott Beckwith

To Lance Hunnicutt . . .

teacher and friend

Contents

Part II
The Nurture of Creativity Through
the Social Studies   75

3 Teaching for Creative Living   78

4 Developing Organizational Skills in Children: Pupil-
Teacher Planning   99

Foreword

Many fine books are presently available in which authors describe the whats, hows, and whys of teaching social studies. While reading several new ones each year, I frequently get the vague feeling that I have read these books before, though obviously this is not possible. I have come to realize that although these specific books are new, many of the ideas and techniques expressed in them are commonplace. Although nearly every author emphasizes some aspects of teaching social studies and gives minimal attention to others, there is a certain amount of sameness among most books about the teaching of social studies.

This book is different! It has a definite and distinct thrust that is paramount throughout it. James Smith believed in creativity. He understood creativity, creative teaching, social studies education, teachers, and children. Most important for the reader, he wrote creatively. This is one of the most readable books I have ever read and its important message—the development of creativity in all children—comes through clearly.

Creativity is one of the key humanizing forces, yet how many of us have said, "Oh, I'm not creative." I think James Smith would have replied, "Yes, you are creative!" His book not only offers guidelines and suggestions for helping children become more creative, it offers the reader ways to explore his or her own creativity, as a person and as a teacher.

I have never met James Smith. He passed away just before he was to finish revising this book. I know him only by his reputation. And yet, after reading what he wrote on these pages, I feel that I knew him personally. Certainly his views about children and social studies education reflect my own.

The publisher asked me to read the reviews of the manuscript and to make the few minor changes the reviewers suggested. That was the easy part. Much more difficult for me was fulfilling the publisher's request to shorten the book. Smith wrote well. He wrote important ideas to think about and practical strategies to apply. It is one thing to edit one's own writing; it is quite another to attempt to abbreviate someone else's ideas, especially when that other person has so much to say. After much deliberation I made the requested number of deletions. Dr. Smith might have made different deletions. The ideas expressed in this book, however, are his. I believe that they will be valuable to every teacher who is vitally interested in the development of the creative potential of every child. As interested as we may be, many of us just don't know how to facilitate the development of creativity. I am convinced that those who read this book will no longer have that problem.

One final word. I believe that James Smith would have wanted you to read this book creatively. He would, I am sure, have wanted you to use it as a springboard to unleash your own creative potential. He would not have wanted you to become locked into using just the ideas he shares here. He would have been delighted for you to use this book as a guide to generate your own creative teaching personality.

James Smith lives on—in the hearts and minds of teachers who share his unshakable belief that we are all potentially creative, and in the creative children whom we educate more fully, thanks to his help. Who could ask for a better legacy.

Buckley R. Barnes
Georgia State University

Foreword

In the Foreword of the first editions of the Creative Teaching series, E. Paul Torrance expressed concern that many exciting, meaningful, and potentially important ideas have died because no one has translated them into practical methods and that this could be the fate of the creative movement. Fortunately, this concern has not been realized. In the past ten years, educational literature has been flooded with reports of research studies, theories, and experimental programs that focus on the creative development of each child as a goal in modern education.

Including the development of creativity in each child as an educational objective is a staggering challenge for all school personnel. It calls for the invention of new materials and tools, the development of new time schedules and new patterns of organization, a new approach to child study, the invention of new testing methods, the devising of unique evaluation processes, and the creation of new textbooks and teaching procedures. And most of all the task calls for a commitment and dedication on the part of many people to take risks, to make choices and decisions, to push their own creative potential to new limits.

This has been done! In the past ten years the creative spark has caught fire. Thousands of people in all walks of life have found in the creative movement, self-realization and the challenge of making life meaningful for others. The educational scene in America has become peppered with experimental projects in the development of creative thinking.

No movement in education has swept the world as the creative movement has. The need for creative people across the globe today is tremendous. Developing the creative potential of each child has become an educational objective even unto the far corners of the world. The authors of the Creative Teaching series hope these volumes will contribute in some bold measure to producing the changes in teaching methods in the elementary school necessary to realize this objective.

James A. Smith

Preface

A pressing problem in today's world continues to be the inability of humans to live together and solve their problems in peace and harmony. The technological revolution has catapulted us into the space age before we have learned to cope with the problems that same technology has forced upon us. One thing is certain: nuclear warfare would mean genocide of the human race. Consequently, humans *must* learn to live with fellow humans. Never before in history has there been a mandate so strong or so compelling.

In the elementary schools, attempts have been made to meet this mandate through revisions and changes in the social studies programs, that area in the curriculum where children are supposedly taught the skills of living and working together. Examination of the "new" social studies programs, however, will show the changes consist largely of shifts in *emphasis* within the framework of previous social studies curricula, rather than any real revolution in structure, content, or strategy which prepares children to cope with the problems of the technological age.

One gross omission in the new programs is the area of creativity. In the past fifteen years, research in the area of creativity has developed to the degree that the myths have been exploded and its study as a human behavior has become commonplace. This new knowledge has been bypassed in planning social studies programs except for a meager attention provided more in the form of lip service than dramatic action.

The development of creativity as a common human behavior is essential in the social studies program as well as in all other programs in the elementary school. The solutions to the problems of the space age lie in the creative minds of humans. The creativity of the human mind will conjure the answers to the problems, if there are any answers. No longer can we effectively dip into history for answers because we now face problems that never before existed. New solutions are needed to meet them. In every aspect of human endeavor these problems exist—in politics, education, economics, sociology, psychology, industry, medicine, science.

Creativity, a behavior inherent in people, has become a precious commodity—because it has only been developed in a few. Throughout the world there is competition for the minds that possess it. The elementary school must play a more dominant role in developing this basic element of all problem-solving. Since the area of the social studies is that part of the curriculum which attempts to teach children the problems of humans and their relationships with other humans (the skills of living together, the methods of identifying, refining and solving problems, the skills of research, scientific investigation, and a scientific attitude toward life problems), the elementary school must play a vital part in developing the creativity of each child and in helping children find creative ways of living together.

This cannot be accomplished when creativity is restricted to the area of the creative arts. Through programs such as those described in this book, children will learn most directly how to take their places as participating, contributing citizens in a democratic society. And in a democratic society individuals and their individuality count!

This book has been written with the following convictions in mind: 1) The social studies is not a "pure" subject area. Because it deals with developing human relationships, it must be correlated, integrated or blended with other subject areas in order to fulfill its objectives. 2) The creativity of children can be developed through a social studies program when nurturing it becomes a normal, regular and vital part of the everyday classroom program rather than a separate element, treated only on specific occasions. 3) Elementary school social studies are taught today in a variety of ways. 4) To develop creativity through the social studies program prescribed in this book, teachers must have a working knowledge of the area of creativity, a knowledge of the objectives, plans, and strategies of the social studies, information about organizing for the teaching of social studies, and references for strategies and techniques for blending these bodies of knowledge. 5) There is no "correct" way to teach social studies: creative methods and objectives designed to develop creativity will result in creative thinking, but part of creative teaching is realized when teachers adjust methods to schools, classrooms, and individual children. 6) In order for the teacher to become creative, he or she must have practice in divergent thinking in each of the concepts presented here.

Not only does the fostering of creativity in each individual develop the greatest human resource we have as a community, it develops the greatest resource we have as individuals—our self-actualization.

The author is indebted to many people for the materials in this book. Among them are the many children with whom he has worked, the creative teacher-colleagues he has observed, his college students (especially his student teachers who dared to be creative in their teaching), and those special individuals who believe, as he does, that the fate of all of us is in the hands of our youth. The latter include: Miss Cecilia Linder of Great Neck School System, Great Neck, New York; Mr. Joseph Piteralli and his faculty of the elementary school in Brewerton, New York; Mrs. Martha Thompson of the Fitzhugh Park School in Oswego, New York; Mrs. Jan Greco and Mr. Paul Anderson of the Alden School in Baldwinsville, New York; Mr. Floyd Wallace and his faculty of the Lanigan Elementary School in Fulton, New York; Mr. Blaine Webb and his faculty of the Volney Elementary School of Volney, New York; Mr. George McDonald, Elementary Supervisor of the Fulton Public Schools, Fulton, New

York; Mrs. Beverly Gelwicks of the elementary school in Clarendon Hills, Illinois; Ms. Jeanne McCloskey and her co-workers from the Fravor Road School, Mexico, New York; Mrs. Holly Weller and her co-workers at the Palmer School, Baldwinsville, New York; Mr. Clarence Anderson of the Bureau of Cooperative Educational Services (BOCES) staff in Mexico, New York; Mrs. Elda M. Wight and Mrs. Betsy Sweeting of the elementary school in Minetto, New York; and Mr. John Ritson, State University College at Oswego, New York.

James A. Smith

I

The Nature of Creativity and the Nature of the Social Studies

1 The Art of Creative Teaching

The goal in education is not to increase the amount of knowledge, but to create the possibilities for a child to invent and discover.

RIPPLE AND ROCKCASTLE[1]

INTRODUCTION: CREATIVE TEACHERS IN ACTION

An intuitive sense seems to be at work when we observe some teachers and conclude, "This is a very creative teacher." Asked to define why the teacher observed is creative, we find ourselves in a difficult situation.

Let's look in on some creative teachers.

Teacher 1: A Middle East Bazaar

Here are some pictures taken at a Middle East bazaar held as part of a social studies unit in a modern rural elementary school.

One of the main objectives of the middle school teachers in planning their social studies curriculum was "to make understanding of the culture of other countries a reality through a study of the customs, food and dress of each country as evidenced by the children's ability to authentically reproduce a selected phase of the culture of that country and to role-play the lives of the people."

Mrs. Cline, the sixth grade teacher who headed the project, also had as an objective the development of the intellectual, social, emotional, physical and creative aspects of each child's personality.

1. Richard E. Ripple and Verne N. Rockcastle, *Piaget Rediscovered* (Ithaca, N.Y.: Cornell University Press, 1964).

2

Figure 1-1. *Middle school students and their teachers recreate a Middle East bazaar.*

Eight sixth grade classes, eight sixth grade teachers, and two student teachers worked together in groups of five or six to prepare for an open-air bazaar similar to those found in any large Middle East city.

Using an interdisciplinary approach in true unit fashion, students learned of Arabic numerals in their math classes. They learned about costumes, mosaics and Oriental art in their art classes, and in music classes they learned songs and played instruments of the Middle East. Much time was spent in listening to records of Middle East music. In language arts classes, some Arabic was learned and *Tales from the Arabian Nights* became very popular. In social studies classes the children learned a great deal about the oil problems of the Middle East and the economic problems of these countries. In fact, it was the concern regarding oil in the Middle East, brought into focus by the energy crisis, that aroused the curiosity of the children to study Arabia and other Middle Eastern countries in the first place.

The culminating activity of the several weeks of study was the Middle East bazaar, planned and carried out by the students.

Against a painted backdrop of an Arabian city, music, posters, models, product displays, and bright-colored costumes helped to create the aura of the bazaar. Students were transformed into exotic dancers, singers, snake charmers, public letter writers and water boys to capture the charm of these faraway countries.

Foods prepared by the children added an authentic aroma. They were sold in gay little booths or around hot coals. Various committees constructed stalls under a large tent on the school lawn for the display of Middle East realia, foods, items made by students and classroom projects. All 265 children and the teachers dressed in costume for the occasion.

A great deal of careful preparation contributed to the success of the project. Plans were painstakingly made with the children. Groups were formed to engage in the necessary background research. This activity alone consumed almost three weeks of time in social studies classes. As soon as the children learned about the Middle East by exploring magazines, textbooks, newspapers, films, filmstrips, phonograph records, maps, charts and television broadcasts, the teachers encouraged them to put this knowledge to use in a variety of ways. They reported their findings to each other and began to learn other things as their teachers correlated the art, music, mathematics, English, and social studies material. Even the gym teacher got in the act when she volunteered to teach belly dances and other Middle East folk dances.

Somewhere along the line the children saw pictures of the bazaars held in most cities. They were compared to the farmers' market held in a nearby city, which many of the children had visited with their parents. In a report period one day one child expressed the wish to go to a real bazaar. Mrs. Cline immediately said, "Well, Bob, I don't think we could visit one, but there's no reason why we couldn't have one of our own."

The children seized on the idea at once and from that point on plans were made on charts, committees were formed, meetings were held and activities planned to create a bazaar as near like a real one as possible.

The bazaar was given one sunny afternoon on the school lawn, and all the elementary school and middle school children and the parents were invited to it. On the following day, teachers and students evaluated the bazaar in terms of the objectives they had set up. All felt it had been a success. From the evidence they collected and from the discussions held with the children, the teachers felt the bazaar had contributed to the social, emotional, intellectual, physical and creative development of the children.

Here are some of the reasons why the teachers felt the bazaar had been a creative experience for the children.

1. In the development and in the finished product of the bazaar many new and unique experiences and products resulted. Many of these products were so creative they could not be anticipated by teachers in their planning.
2. Strong motivational tensions obviously led to the success of the bazaar. Concern over the Middle East oil crisis made the children eager to learn and understand about people in the Middle East.

3. Many open-ended situations were possible so the children were forced to engage in divergent thinking activities.

4. Children were daily challenged to generate and develop their own ideas. Their own differences, uniquenesses, and individualities were stressed. They were not expected to behave and produce alike.

5. Many new creative thinking processes and working processes were employed in developing the unit.

6. The evaluation at the end of the unit showed the unit to be successful. Each child felt he or she played an important part in developing and presenting the bazaar.

7. Most of the children went off to pursue learnings of their own interest and reported or demonstrated what they had learned to the rest of the class.

8. Children had many, many opportunities to manipulate and explore ideas and materials.

9. Some methods had been used which are unique to the development of creativity. The teachers had employed brainstorming, the use of deferred judgment, the processes of creative education; new uses, substitution, adaptation, rearrangement, and others. The teachers had also removed many barriers to creativity.

Teacher 2: Creating a Time Machine

How does a primary teacher develop a sense of time in children so they can better understand the meaning of history (past) and the meaning of time to come (the future)?

Mrs. Thompson created two excellent ideas, both of which served as methods of teaching and as evaluation devices to determine attainment of her objectives. She helped the children develop the concept of time through the teaching of a unit on *change*. As part of the unit she helped her second and third graders plan a series of questions to ask their parents and grandparents to help them understand that time extends into the past and that the passing of time brings about many changes.

Sample questions were:

1. Where did you go to school?
2. How did you get to school?
3. What was your school building like?
4. How did you dress for school on a cold winter's day?
5. What games did you play when you were my age?
6. What foods did you eat in the winter?
7. Where did you go to shop?
8. How did you travel to other towns?

A chart spanning three generations (the grandparents, parents, and children themselves) showed what sixty to eighty years of time had brought about. Two children in the class had great-grandparents and their interviews added substantially to the development of a time-line concept.

Each child made a list of all the important events in his life. One child's list looked like this:

1. I was born
2. We moved to Fairfax
3. I got my new puppy
4. My baby sister was born
5. I got a bicycle for Christmas
6. My daddy took us to a cowboy ranch in Arizona
7. Grandma came to live with us
8. I learned how to make knots
9. I joined the Cub Scouts
10. I went to New York City

Mrs. Thompson encouraged the children to copy their lists in chronological order. With the help of parents, dates were added. Then each child made a time-line chart plotting each event in sequence with a drawing and a brief note of explanation. The time-line charts developed a sense of chronology in the children and made a fascinating bulletin board display where children and teacher learned a great deal about each other.

It was then an easy step for Mrs. Thompson to help the children make a time-line spanning the eighty years covered by their interviews. When it was noted that father traveled by plane, train and car when he was a boy but grandfather traveled by horse and buggy, trolley car, bobsled, and on foot and that great-grandfather rode horseback, or traveled on foot, some serious questions arose as to what caused the changes. The children began to find such important dates as the year of the invention of the buggy, the automobile, the airplane, the steamboat, the super jets, etc. A shift in population at the turn of the century from rural areas to urban led the children into a study of the Industrial Revolution and its consequences.

The actual time-line developed by the children consisted of a stout cord stretched from one corner of the room to the other on which were suspended cut-outs made by the children: an airplane with the date of its invention, an automobile and its date, a gun bearing the dates of World War I, a tank bearing the dates of World War II, etc. The time-line developed more and more as the unit progressed. Each picture that was added had to be carefully located between other dates and events.

As a climax to the unit, the children built a time machine as shown in Figure 1-2. Each day for several weeks groups signed up on a schedule sheet to give a dramatization of something important which they had learned in their

Figure 1-2. *A time machine that takes children to many places at any time.*

studies. On the scheduled mornings, with improvised costumes and props, one group would go into the time machine. One member would spin a dial on the machine showing the time in which the event being dramatized occurred. Then the children would emerge from the time machine and dramatize the event, or present a slide show, film, scroll movie, or an original play or role-playing situation. Once in a while, it was an event not shown on the time-line such as a presentation by one group of their discovery of when nylon was invented. Another group focused on the use of buses as a means of public transportation. A third group discovered the date of the invention of the steamboat, which provided motivation for discovering many new dates.

This is, indeed, a description of a creative teaching situation. It is creative because it demonstrates the following principles of creative teaching:

1. Like Mrs. Cline, Mrs. Thompson worked to be sure that products new and unique for the children resulted from the study.
2. Strong motivational tensions were set up which were relevant to the children: they made their own time-lines—then one which spanned the generations with which they were familiar.
3. Open-ended situations were employed so the children were often engaged in divergent thinking.
4. Specific outcomes were not predictable.

5. Children were challenged to use all their experiences in making the presentations.
6. Children were encouraged to generate and develop their own ideas.
7. All knowledges and skills learned were put to use.
8. Self-initiated learning was encouraged.
9. Democratic processes were employed.

Teacher 3: An Open-Ended Situation

In Mr. Arnold's middle school group, the children studied the Constitution of the United States. This study grew from an interest in the activities being planned in West Haven to celebrate the Bicentennial. Questions set up by the children included, "How did the Constitution come to be?" and "What does it mean to each of us?"

In discussing human rights as stated in the Constitution, Mr. Arnold felt that he should encourage the children to apply the facts they were learning to an actual court case. He chose the film *The Law and the People* which is an excellent presentation of Muhammed Ali's Supreme Court fight for his right to box. Near the end of the film, Mr. Arnold shut off the projector and allowed the children to apply their knowledge to what they had seen and to make some decisions about the boxer's case. Later, the remainder of the film was played and another discussion was held.

This method is an excellent example of open-ended teaching which is the basis for divergent thinking, the core of all creative thinking. Mr. Arnold was also creative in his methodology in that he made provision for the children to learn many knowledges and skills, but he also made provision for the children to apply those knowledges and skills in new situations.

Teacher 4: A Puppet Sociodrama

Figure 1-3 is not a picture of an ordinary puppet show. It is a puppet sociodrama and was taken by Mrs. Jackson, a middle school teacher, while a group of her students were creating a role-playing situation.

One of the rules in Mrs. Jackson's school, as is true of many schools, is that there is to be no fighting on the playground. One beautiful spring day, immediately after lunch period, Mrs. Jackson decided it would be good for her students to spend some of their noon hour on the playground. The class voted to play dodge ball, so teams were quickly organized and the children burst out-of-doors to play in the new spring sunshine. It was a crisp day, one well suited to vigorous activity and the children enthusiastically went into their game.

Beth, one of Mrs. Jackson's students, had been out of school most of the week with a cold and soon felt too tired to continue the vigorous play required

Figure 1-3. *Learning to make decisions through the use of a puppet sociodrama.*

by the game. She and her friend Jill approached Mrs. Jackson and asked if they might walk around the playground, a less strenuous activity for Beth. Mrs. Jackson agreed and the girls went off on their walk.

In the partially melted snow surrounding the blacktop area on which the children were playing, Jill noticed a large brightly colored rubber ball. She seized upon it with delight and soon she and Jill were engaged in a gentle game of toss and catch.

Soon Betsy, one of their classmates, came running across the blacktop. "Oh, Jill," she cried, "where did you find my ball?"

It isn't your ball," said Jill. "I found it in the snow and Beth and I are going to play with it."

"It is so my ball," Betsy retorted. "I lost it just last week when my friends and I were over here playing after school one night."

"Tough luck!" said Jill. "You're just saying that. You haven't any proof! You just want to play catch with our ball."

"That's not so!" Betsy wailed. "It's my ball and I can prove it!"

"But you lost it," Beth chimed in. "And—finder's keepers, loser's weepers!"

Betsy was on the verge of tears. "It *is* my ball," she said. "It even has my initials written on one side! You look and you'll see!"

The three girls gathered around the ball while Jill, who held it, turned it around and around, seeking the coveted initials. Sure enough, finally she noticed some faded letters printed on one side of the ball—B.A.—Betsy Allen.

"There," said Betsy, "right there. I told you so!"

"That doesn't mean a thing," retorted Beth. "Lots of kids in this school have the initials B.A. Besides, you lost it and we found it, so it's ours."

Betsy was losing her temper. "You're mean, Beth Howard—and you, too, Jill Thomas! It is so my ball and you should give it to me!"

The two girls laughed at Betsy's outbreak of anger and pulled the ball away from her.

"Cry-baby, cry-baby—go ahead and cry like a big cry-baby," Beth smiled, grabbing the ball from Jill and holding it behind her.

This proved to be the last straw for Betsy. With frustration reaching the breaking point, she clenched her fists and plowed into the astonished Jill and Beth, who recovered quickly from their surprise and ran in different directions taunting Betsy and adding to her chagrin.

At this point, Mrs. Jackson, who had caught the last portion of the episode in the corner of her eye while enjoying the dodge ball game across the playground, approached the girls with

"What seems to be the trouble over here?"

All three of the girls accosted Mrs. Jackson—all talking at the same time. Mrs. Jackson finally placed her hands over her ears, then held up a hand for silence. "Wait a minute, wait a minute," she said firmly. "I can't hear any of you—now, one at a time. You, Betsy, you seem very upset, you tell me what happened."

Betsy began to pour out her tale between sobs—almost incoherently, but with enough sense so that Mrs. Jackson could take in the situation.

"O.K.," said Mrs. Jackson after listening for a few minutes. "I can see that you have a serious problem here. Now we need to discuss it and see if we can help you solve it, but I don't think we can discuss it now. For one reason, you are all too angry. For another reason, you need to think back on it so you can remember what has happened. I want Betsy to stay on this side of me, and Beth and Jill, you stay on this side and just cool off. When you are calm again, we will talk more. In trying to solve your problem you have broken a school rule and that is serious."

"If you think you can get along a few minutes without killing each other," she added in a joking manner, "we'll discuss this when we go in. Recess time is almost over. I think everyone should talk about this because breaking a school rule can be a serious thing for all of us."

Feeling somewhat sheepish, the three girls stayed with Mrs. Jackson who chatted with them as if the problem of the lost ball did not exist.

Soon the children were called in. After they had taken off their coats, Mrs. Jackson asked that they all be seated and listen to her.

"Boys and girls," she began. "We are going to take a few minutes to talk about a problem that came up on the playground which concerns all of us. Now, in order to see what the problem is, I am going to ask Betsy, Jill and Beth to act it out with puppets so we will know what happened. Each girl will play her own part and try to show us exactly what happened. I shall play my part and will try to come into the picture at the proper time. Girls, do you think you are calm enough now to play the scene with the puppets just as it happened? Try to remember all you said. I know you may feel ashamed about some of the things you said but remember, we all say things we don't mean when we are angry, so don't feel guilty about them now. We all want to see exactly what happened so we can help you with a solution to the problem. We cannot break school rules if we are all to live comfortably together, right? And you can't break laws when you grow up if we are to live safely and comfortably together, right? O.K., then, let's use your problem as an example and see if we can find a way to solve it without breaking a school rule."

Now, Mrs. Jackson had a reason for using puppets in reenacting this scene rather than role-playing it or using dramatization. Puppets allow the children to shield themselves behind a backdrop. As Mrs. Jackson implied, in the calm after the storm of emotions, children (and adults) are likely to feel guilty about things they have said and done. One of the advantages of using puppets is that the puppet says the words rather than the child and, with the child's face hidden, he or she is more likely to give a more accurate presentation of true feelings.

At the point in the presentation where Mrs. Jackson had stopped the fight on the playground, she also stopped the puppet show. She complimented the girls on their excellent portrayal, reminding them that she, too, now saw the whole picture, and consequently the whole problem for the first time. She asked the girls if they had anything to add to the presentation. Then she faced the class and said:

"Boys and girls, sometimes we allow our emotions to carry us away before we think a problem through. This is a good example of such a situation. Now you all can see what happened. Let's talk about it. Let's begin with these questions: 'Was it necessary for Beth, Jill, and Betsy to fight to solve their problem?' and 'Did the fight really solve the problem?'"

A lively discussion followed. The children went through all the stages that children generally go through in examining emotional conflict: they tried to place blame, they took sides with their friends, they asked the girls for more details, they passed judgment, they even became emotionally involved themselves.

After a while, Mrs. Jackson said, "My purpose in having the girls act out the playground problem was to make sure that we had all the facts and could see the entire problem. Does everyone think they have a good idea of what took place?"

The class agreed that they did. "Then," said Mrs. Jackson, "I am going to ask you to meet in your 'rap' groups and discuss a way you might solve the problem without breaking a school rule. We will report our solutions to each other in ten minutes if you need that much time."

The children broke up into their "rap" groups, or "buzz" groups as they are called in some schools. Mrs. Jackson walked from group to group. She appointed a capable discussion leader for each group and a person to take notes.

When the children came back to the large discussion group, they had five possible solutions to the problem. Briefly they were as follows:

1. Take the problem to Mrs. Jackson and present it to her. She is wiser and older and could help the children solve it. (What the children are really saying here is that one way to solve a problem is to take the case to an authority.)

2. Take the case to a lawyer. One of the girls had a father who was a lawyer so this group felt this was a logical solution. (What the children are saying here is that there are rules made for most social situations and a person trained to interpret these rules is another kind of authority who can determine the legality of the situation.)

3. Compromise. Inasmuch as Jill and Beth found the ball and Betsy claimed ownership, one solution would be for all of them to share it, or work out a way that each could take turns playing with it. (Here, the children are stressing that there are two sides to every question and "fairness" is of prime importance in making decisions.)

4. Compassion. Since both Jill and Beth are fairly certain that the ball belonged to Betsy, and since Betsy was apparently upset over losing it, Jill and Beth were in reality only "borrowing" the ball and should return it to Betsy. (Here the children are stressing permanency of ownership regardless of theft or loss, and are encouraging "fairness" and empathy.)

5. Take the ball away. Since neither side seems to be able to settle the problem, remove the ball from the scene. (Betsy had given it up for lost anyhow, and Jill and Beth had not purchased it in the first place) and give it to a worthy cause, such as the kindergarten play box, a children's ward in the hospital, etc. (In this situation the children are suggesting that common-law rules play a part in governing behavior and that an object lost is an object gone—an object found does not really belong to the finder.)

In this true account of a classroom incident, Mrs. Jackson placed her students in a very creative thinking and learning situation. In days of old it would not have been unusual for a teacher caught in Mrs. Jackson's situation to hustle the children who were fighting to the principal's office for punishment. Mrs. Jackson, who sees her social studies program as an attempt on her part to help children solve problems and function in a democracy, seized a social situation as a problem worthy of pursuing in order to demonstrate the discovery and application of principles and techniques utilized in a democratic society. Her approach was democratic and sensible. It was also creative because of the following reasons:

1. The situation was open-ended. Mrs. Jackson did not impose a solution on the children. She presented the facts and allowed the children to engage in divergent thinking to come up with many solutions rather than one "correct" solution. All solutions were logical and acceptable although the children had to place a priority on one solution for this particular case.

2. Knowledge was presented in a new form and then put to new uses. One of the major differences between creative and non-creative teaching is that in non-creative teaching knowledge is often memorized for its own sake. In creative teaching knowledge is a tool to be put to new uses in solving problems.

3. Mrs. Jackson's methodology was such that the outcomes were unpredictable. In creative teaching the exact outcomes are never completely predictable. Because creativity means invention and uniqueness, the outcomes of a creative lesson are, in themselves, unique and new to the individuals involved in the creative thinking process.

4. High motivational tensions were created. Mrs. Jackson used an actual situation in the lives of the children to help them discover new ways of living together. Emotion-packed and highly relevant situations are necessary for creative teaching.

5. Children faced the unknown. In the creative process there comes a time when the participants must face the unknown, that is, they must be placed in a situation which is foreign to them. They must rearrange former knowledges and skills into new patterns for dealing with the new situation and thus come up with new solutions. Mrs. Jackson gave the children all the knowledge they needed through the presentation of the puppet show and then left the children to face the unknown when she placed them in "buzz" groups to work out solutions to the problem.

6. Self-initiated learning was encouraged in this situation. This, too, is a characteristic of creative learning.

7. Mrs. Jackson encouraged deferred judgment. Deferred judgment is a technique employed in the creative process wherein no judgments are passed until all of the reasonably attainable facts and nuances of the situation are known. Then, a judgment is made.

A DEFINITION

Definitions are meaningfully formed as a result of experiences. Actually a definition is a verbal summary of an experience. One of the major fallacies of teaching methodology (especially in the past) has been that at the onset of a lesson or unit children have been forced to memorize definitions (a summary of *someone else's* experience) which are weighted with words that have little or no meaning to them. Actually, what many teachers think of as understanding is merely an ability to repeat the right answer to a question. But to comprehend is to invent, not just to repeat. Memorization is not learning. The parroting back of a group of words which someone else has arranged requires little ability. Meaning in definitions comes when the learner has had a direct or vicarious experience and creates his own arrangement of words to describe it.

The author has tried to help the reader experience some creative teaching situations in this chapter so that the reader may more fully understand the definition of creativity which follows: *Creativity is defined in this chapter as the ability to tap one's experiences and to come up with something new.* This new product need not be new to the world, but it *must* be new to the individual. This simple definition explains the kind of creativity most commonly shown by children. Because there are degrees of creativity, a higher degree of it would mean that the creator would produce something new to the world—a new math formula, a new technique for painting, a way to reach the moon. Because creativity is a process *and* a product, attention must be paid to the process if it is to be developed in children. The illustrations presented in this book show the creative process at work.

For research purposes, social scientists and psychologists use an expanded definition of creativity. E. Paul Torrance, for instance, asserts that all human processes can be stated in human behavior forms. He therefore defines creativity as *a process of becoming sensitive to problems, deficiencies, gaps in knowledge, missing elements, disharmonies, and so on; identifying the difficulty; searching for solutions, making guesses or formulating hypotheses about the deficiencies; testing and retesting these hypotheses and possibly modifying and retesting them; and finally communicating the results.*[2]

The process stated in Torrance's definition has been the process employed in his research.

For our purposes in this volume, the simpler definition is adequate.

CRITERIA FOR CREATIVE TEACHING

We have looked in on four creative teachers. Our intuition tells us that these are, indeed, excellent examples of creative teachers at work.

Although intuitive thinking has great value in human living, especially in the development of aesthetic senses, we cannot rely on it for purposes of scientific evaluation and judgment. We must more clearly extract those elements from a situation which provide sound criteria for judging creative performance and performance which results in creative growth.

Creative teaching is based on a cluster of principles.[3] These principles can form a set of criteria against which the performance of the classroom teacher may be checked. Or, they may be defined by a set of behaviors against which a teacher's performance may be assessed. Following is a criterion chart which enables an evaluator to identify creative behavior in teachers through the observation of their ability to apply creative principles in their teaching.

2. E. Paul Torrance, *Torrance Tests of Creative Thinking* (Princeton, New Jersey: Personnel Press, 1966).

3. James. A. Smith, *Setting Conditions for Creative Teaching in the Elementary School* (Boston: Allyn and Bacon, 1966).

CRITERION CHART FOR EVALUATING CREATIVE TEACHING BASED ON PRINCIPLES OF CREATIVITY

Teacher: Cline, Thompson, Arnold, Jackson, Walker
Situation: (Above)
Date: 4/23/76

Principle	Observations	Degree*
1. Something new, different or unique resulted.	**Cline:** The entire bazaar was a new experience for the children, created by them. Posters, booths, dances, costumes, entertainment and food products were all new experiences. Learning of Arabic, Arabic numerals, mosaics, music—all new experiences put to creative use.	1 2 3 4 ⑤
	Thompson: The time machine was a new product which provided a new way of dramatizing history.	1 2 3 4 ⑤
	Arnold: The children gained new insights into the meaning of human rights.	1 2 3 ④ 5
	Jackson: Five ways to solve a social problem resulted.	1 2 3 4 ⑤
2. Divergent thinking processes were stressed.	**Thompson:** Each dramatization required divergent thinking. Each time line was made up of divergent thinking.	1 2 3 4 ⑤
	Arnold: The use of the film provoked divergent thinking.	1 2 3 ④ 5
3. Strong motivational tensions were set up.	**Cline:** The concern over the energy crisis and the oil problem in the Middle East was a relevant problem to the children.	1 2 3 4 ⑤

* Key:
1-to some degree   4-to a high degree
2-to a fair degree   5-to a very high degree
3-to an average degree

Figure 1-4

Principle	Observations	Degree
	Thompson: The children were involved in making their own time-lines and in interviewing their own relatives. The time machine itself was a great motivational device for dramatization.	1 2 3 4 ⑤
	Arnold: The children's interest in the Bicentennial was used to motivate study of some important aspects of history.	1 2 3 4 ⑤
	Jackson: The breaking of a school rule provided excellent motivation for this activity.	1 2 3 4 ⑤
4. Open-ended situations were utilized.	**Thompson:** The children interviewed grandparents to list important events in their own lives.	1 2 3 4 ⑤
	Arnold: Mr. Arnold stopped the film and the children came up with solutions to the problem.	1 2 3 ④ 5
	Jackson: The class saw the problem dramatized, then were put in groups to discuss it.	1 2 3 4 ⑤
5. Specific outcomes were unpredictable.	**Cline:** Although a bazaar became the goal of the study, the actual parts of it could not be predicted until the children completed their products.	1 2 3 4 ⑤
	Thompson: All time-lines were different; all dramatizations were different.	1 2 3 4 ⑤
	Jackson: Although Mrs. Jackson felt some solutions were a result of her planned activity, she did not know what they would be.	1 2 3 ④ 5

Figure 1-4 (*continued*)

Principle	Observations	Degree
6. Conditions were set which made pre-conscious thinking possible.	**Thompson:** The time machine allowed the children to dip deep into their pasts and to imagine all sorts of things for their dramatizations.	1 2 3 ④ 5
	Jackson: Children were encouraged to use all their former experiences to help solve the problem presented by the puppets. Mrs. Jackson tried to remove guilt feelings and strong emotional reactions.	1 2 ③ 4 5
7. Children were encouraged to generate and develop their own ideas.	**Cline:** All children had an opportunity to develop their own ideas and to participate in the bazaar in a way that was comfortable for them.	1 2 3 4 ⑤
	Thompson: Every time-line and every dramatization was a product of the children's imagination.	1 2 3 4 ⑤
	Arnold: The open-ended use of the film made all contributions acceptable for discussion.	1 2 3 ④ 5
8. Differences, uniqueness, individuality, originality were stressed.	**Cline:** Children chose those activities in which they could be creative; singers created songs, artists painted, actors acted, etc.	1 2 3 4 ⑤
	Thompson: All products were unique to each individual.	1 2 3 4 ⑤
	Jackson: There were 5 solutions presented to solve the problem.	1 2 3 4 ⑤
9. The process as well as the product contained creative elements.	**Cline:** Careful acquisition of knowledge was made possible in meaningful ways.	1 2 3 4 ⑤
	Thompson: The interview technique and the making of the child's own time-line was creative as a process, and the products were creative.	1 2 3 4 ⑤

Principle	Observations	Degree
	Arnold: The facts of the case were presented to the children, then they were allowed to draw conclusions, make decisions, and pass judgments.	1 2 3 4 ⑤
10. Conditions were set so creative thinking could occur.	**Cline:** Children worked in large groups, small groups, "buzz" groups, and as individuals to create ideas for the bazaar.	1 2 3 4 ⑤
	Thompson: The time machine was a great stimulus for this.	1 2 3 4 ⑤
	Arnold: Stopping the film and challenging the children to conclude it was a challenge to their creative imagination.	1 2 3 ④ 5
11. Success rather than failure was emphasized.	**Thompson:** No child's ideas were rejected. Mistakes in presentations were corrected but all original ideas were accepted.	1 2 3 4 ⑤
12. Provision was made to learn knowledge and skills and also to put them to work in new problem-solving situations.	**Cline:** Knowledges gained through research were put to work to create atmosphere, booths, foods, music, dances, posters, and the backdrop.	1 2 3 4 ⑤
	Thompson: Knowledge was gained through self-inspection, interviews with relatives, books, magazines, etc., and used in the time machine.	1 2 3 4 ⑤
	Arnold: The film gave the children facts which they needed to apply specifically to what they had learned about the Constitution.	1 2 3 ④ 5
	Jackson: Knowledge was presented through and put to new uses in discussion.	1 2 3 4 ⑤

Figure 1-4 (*continued*)

Principle	Observations	Degree
13. Self-initiated learning was encouraged.	**Cline:** Every child was encouraged to pursue subjects of individual interest. Each contributed original work to the total bazaar.	1 2 3 4 ⑤
	Thompson: The dramatizations demanded research and factual material from the children making them.	1 2 ③ 4 5
	Jackson: The children learned from their own experiences.	1 2 3 ④ 5
14. Skills of constructive criticism and evaluation were developed.	**Cline:** After the bazaar was over, all those who participated in it sat down to evaluate each aspect of it.	1 2 3 4 ⑤
15. Ideas and objects were manipulated and explored.	**Cline:** These included the idea of the bazaar, realia from the Middle East, designing and constructing booths and scenery, sewing costumes, applying makeup, planning entertainment, role-playing, dramatizations, setting up exhibits, making posters, writing scripts, etc.	1 2 3 4 ⑤
	Thompson: Books, paper, interviews, materials, costumes, etc. were all used.	1 2 3 4 ⑤
	Arnold: Many ideas concerning civil rights were explored.	1 2 3 ④ 5
16. Democratic processes were employed.	**Cline:** Children helped in the planning. They were responsible for making decisions and passing judgments. They had a part in evaluating their own work.	1 2 3 4 ⑤
	Thompson: Children planned for their work each step of the way.	1 2 3 4 ⑤

Principle	Observations	Degree
	Arnold: Children learned more about democratic processes through the democratic manner in which the film was used.	1 2 3 ④ 5
17. Methods were used which are unique to the development of creativity.	**Cline:** Some of the special methods used in this unit were: • Deferred judgment • Brainstorming • New uses • Adaptation • Modification • Magnification • Minification • Substitution • Rearrangement • Reversing • Attribute listing	1 2 3 4 ⑤
	Arnold: Using the open-ended film is a unique method of developing creative thinking.	1 2 3 ④ 5
	Jackson: At one point in the process Mrs. Jackson's children were forced to face the unknown, a characteristic of all creative problem solving. Deferred judgment was also applied here.	1 2 3 ④ 5

Figure 1-4 (*continued*)

The chart has been used in this case to evaluate the vignettes taken from the work of the four teachers previously described. The principles listed are a summary of the comments made at the close of each verbal observation. These principles are derived from the results of current thinking and research in the area of creativity.

It is important for the reader to realize that no one lesson in creativity is likely to develop all the principles of creativity any more than any one reading lesson can teach all the many aspects and skills of reading. Because of this fact, four descriptions of creative teaching are presented earlier in this chapter to illustrate all the principles. Some of the experiences described *do* develop most of the principles; others concentrate on specific areas of creative development.

On the chart above the author has extracted some observations from the four teachers described in order to identify the principles as they are presented in context in the vignettes. Ordinarily a separate chart would be used for each teacher.

The reader may wish to extract other pieces of evidence from the verbal observations presented here to fill out the chart for each of the teachers. Our purpose in using the chart in this place is to present the principles for creative teaching and to illustrate each from a variety of situations.

ALTERNATE APPROACHES TO CREATIVE TEACHING

In recent years the concern for the development of creativity in children and adults has resulted in the promotion of diverse plans and schemes. Some of these plans have special significance for the elementary school teacher of social studies.

A Course: Parnes

One of the most popular and best-known of the early plans to develop creativity is a course taught at the Creative Education Foundation in Buffalo and recently expanded throughout the country. This course for adults is designed by Dr. Sidney Parnes, head of the Creative Education Center.

Dr. Parnes has designed an Instructors Manual and Student Workbook, recently revised, which is used as the core of his course.[4] Instructors are trained to teach the course and to follow a step-by-step process which develops creative thinking powers and creative production abilities in people. A great deal of follow-up research has been initiated to test the effectiveness of the course.[5] Recently, a graduate program in creativity was initiated at the University of Buffalo as a result of the success in developing creative abilities in an undergraduate experimental program.

The Parnes material is designed primarily to release creative power in adults. As such it seems to be highly successful, especially in jogging loose the creative powers which seem to lie dormant in the adult mind from lack of use.

Critics of the Parnes plan feel that the course calls for too rigid an adherence to the process: that it seems implausible that creativity can be developed by following one rigid plan. Creativity, they feel, can be developed many ways and the course should be designed to present more options to the learner. These critics assert that in the creative processes, the process is as important as

4. Sidney J. Parnes, *Instructors Manual for Semester Courses in Creative Problem-Solving.* rev. ed. (Buffalo: The Creative Education Foundation, 1975).

5. Sidney J. Parnes and Ruth B. Noller, "Applied Creativity: The Creative Studies Project. Part I: The Development," *Journal of Creative Behavior* 6, No. 1 (1972): 11-22.

Ibid., Part II: Results of the Two-Year Program, *Journal of Creative Behavior* 6, No. 3 (1972): 164-186.

Ibid., Part III: The Curriculum, *Journal of Creative Behavior* 6, No. 4 (1972): 275-294.

Parnes and Noller, *Toward Supersanity: Channeled Freedom* (Buffalo: DOK Publishers, 1973).

the product and that locking some people into one process may do little to release their creative powers.

Nonetheless, the Parnes materials have jarred the nation loose from its complacent concept that creativity is a vague, mythical concept that cannot be developed or measured. The materials, the library, and the program developed under the direction of Parnes at the University of Buffalo have given the study of creativity the respect needed to place it in the category of a behavioral discipline worthy of serious research.

Many of the Parnes materials are adaptable for use with children and should be mentioned here because they are used throughout this book as possible ways of developing creativity through the use of social studies.

Brainstorming

Founded in Osborn's book, the brainstorming technique can be used effectively with children.[6]

In brainstorming, a moderator (usually the teacher) poses the problem very specifically and sets a time limit for the session. A recorder (usually a child who is deft at notetaking) is appointed to list the ideas as they are given by members of the group. All ideas, no matter how inadequate or how foolish they may seem at the moment, are recorded. No judgment is passed on any idea until the end of the session (deferred judgment). The moderator can encourage the flow of ideas (creative ideation) by stopping the session and asking the recorder how many ideas have been recorded in the first ten minutes of brainstorming. He then says, "Let's see if we can double the number of ideas in the next ten minutes" (ideational fluency).

In order to keep similar ideas together on the recorder's list, the hitchhiking technique is used. If one person presents an idea that sets off a related idea in another person's mind, the latter snaps his fingers and the moderator calls on him next so his "hitchhiking" idea will come on the recorder's list immediately after the idea that prompted it.

After the session, a committee chosen from the group meets and evaluates the ideas that resulted from the large-group brainstorming session. All ideas are considered carefully. Some are discarded as impractical: too expensive, too time-consuming, too involved, or too difficult to carry out. The reduced list is often brought back to the large group for further discussion and decision making.

Creative Ideation

This process has been mentioned in the section on brainstorming. In creative ideation, various criteria are applied to a product in an attempt to make the

6. Alex F. Osborn, *Applied Imagination,* 3d rev. ed. (New York: Charles Scribner's Sons, 1963).

creative thinker see new uses for the product or to create in his mind a new solution to a problem. Examples of these criteria are: How can I put it to new uses? How can it be adapted to new purposes? Can it be modified to suit a new cause? Can it be magnified to change its use? Can it be "minimized," rearranged, reversed, or combined with something else? Can something be substituted for it?

For an example of the application of creative ideation in a social studies situation, see Figure 1-5.

The Principle of Deferred Judgment

Both Mrs. Jackson and Mrs. Cline used the principle of deferred judgment in the descriptions of their teaching included earlier in this chapter.

Research at the Creative Education Center has shown that excessive evaluation may be construed by children engaged in the creative act as disapproval and may check the creative thinking of the child. The work of researchers in the area of creativity indicates that evaluation and criticism of ideas be postponed until all ideas are out in the open. This concept is referred to as *deferred judgment*. Note how Mrs. Cline and her colleagues waited until all the ideas of the children were out before they evaluated the bazaar. Note how Mrs. Jackson

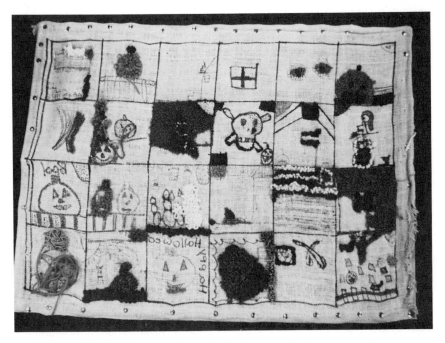

Figure 1-5. *Creative ideation: a hooked rug results from a brainstorming session exploring ideas to represent the United States.*

had the children play out the fight scene with puppets before she had them pass judgments or make decisions.

Since evaluation is part of the learning cycle of setting objectives, planning experiences to meet the objectives, evaluating by use of the objectives, and replanning, we are not suggesting here that *all* evaluation be postponed until the end of a project. This technique will be applied when the objective is to develop new and creative ideas.

Attribute Listing

Another technique suggested in the Parnes course to develop creative thinking is that of attribute listing. This is a type of checklist procedure. The problem solver lists all the various attributes of an object or an idea. Attention is then turned to each of the attributes, thinking of ways to improve it, or to duplicate it.

When Mrs. Cline was planning for the bazaar, she placed many pictures of people from the Middle East where the children could find them. From these pictures the children made generalizations about the everyday and special costumes of the people. The list looked like this:

Women:
- Heads covered: lace, cloth
- Most faces veiled
- Body covered—long robes
- Full pants
- Bare midriffs
- Jewelry: rings, necklaces
- Pointed sandals
- Brocade materials

Men:
- Flowing robes
- Heads covered—cloth held in place by band
- Hands and face exposed
- Beards and mustaches common
- Robes loose—some sashes
- Sandals on feet

Reasons for the use of this type of attire were discussed but the list served primarily as a guide for adapting modern western garments to the look and feel of the Middle East. The pictures of the bazaar best show how this was done.

The Williams Model for Creative Production

Another marked contribution to the development of creative processes is the work of Frank Williams at Portland State University.[7] Williams has devised a model for creative teaching. His model is designed on the premise that pupil-teacher interactions dealing particularly with both cognitive and affective behaviors are vitally responsible for releasing creative potential. He has, in his model, deliberately programmed the ongoing curriculum for developing those thinking and feeling abilities that contribute directly to the creative process. These are then measured by a combination of cognitive and affective instruments and gain scores to show each child's progress.

Williams believes in the training and measuring of teacher competencies and in the use of certain strategies that have been found to elicit those pupil behaviors which contribute to their creativeness. He feels that a measurement of teachers' understanding and performance of these strategies is necessary in order to discern how well they are doing in causing creativity to take place in the classroom. Williams has developed an interaction model for teaching and learning and new assessment instruments for measuring the effective installation of this model in the classroom. Williams indicates that although creativity tests allow for divergent thinking, they are, in actuality, cognitive since they are scored for how well a child can think fluently, flexibly, elaborately, or originally. His tests include those which measure children's feelings, attitudes and temperament factors of the affective domain. These aspects of personality are included because Williams, like many other scholars today, believes that children cannot become fully functioning, self-realized creative individuals until all their thinking powers have been aroused and used. Williams has also designed guidebooks and workbooks which give specific examples of the employment of the strategies and behavior changes demanded by the use of his model.

One of the outstanding qualities of the Williams model is that any teacher may use it to design his or her own lessons. Unlike some of the materials and plans developed by Parnes, the teacher who uses the Williams model is constantly having his or her own creative abilities challenged in designing new lessons and/or modules that fit in with his or her own teaching. The teaching of creative development becomes a creative act in itself with each new lesson developed—which seems much more appropriate to developing creative teachers than giving them a rapid plan to follow.

Because the Williams model is comparatively new, an evaluation of its effectiveness at this point is premature. A great deal of success in applying it to classroom use has been reported in current literature by people who are using it.

One benefit of the Williams model is that it classifies teaching strategies and methods employed by the teacher and thus organizes them into categories

---

7. Frank E. Williams, *Classroom Ideas for Encouraging Thinking and Feeling* (Buffalo: DOK Publishers, 1970).

for scientific study. Such a classification tends to appease the scientists who see creativity as a characteristic which is difficult to measure.

The Williams model bears significance to this volume because the social studies is one of the areas designated as subject matter where plans may be devised to develop creative thinking. In that sense, the Williams model supports the philosophy of this book in stating that the relationship between social studies and creativity is cyclic: creative processes beget creative products which in turn beget creative thought, which in turn, etc., etc.

A SAMPLE SOCIAL STUDIES LESSON PLAN
DESIGNED FROM THE WILLIAMS MODEL

To Encourage:	*Flexible thinking and imagination*
Through:	Social Studies
Using:	Strategies No. 5: Provocative questions
	No. 14: Evaluate situations

The teacher was planning to have the children study life in jungle areas. She asked the children to close their eyes and pretend they were in a plane flying over

A Model for Implementing Cognitive-Affective
Behaviors in the Classroom

D1 ⇔ D2 ⇒ D3

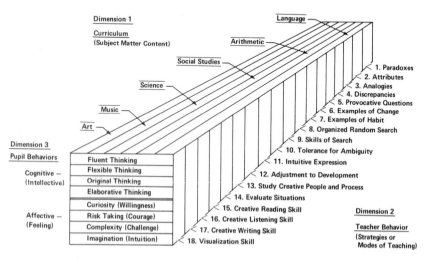

Figure 1-6. *The Williams model for creative teaching.* [8]

8. Ibid., *A Model for Implementing Cognitive-Affective Behavior in the Classroom*, p. ii.

a dense forest. "The engine begins to skip, the plane falters. Eventually the pilot finds a clear place in the jungle and the plane lands. We disembark from the plane but all we can see around us is trees; all we can feel is the dense heat of the tropical forest. All we can hear is the startled and raucous noises of the birds.[9]

"Now," says the teacher, "we are faced with the problem of keeping alive. What do we need to know about this place we have landed in order to live in it?"

From this situation, the children listed many questions which served as the base for their unit on a study of the jungle.

SAMPLE PLANS FROM THE WILLIAMS BOOK
ON ENCOURAGING THINKING AND FEELING[10]

To Encourage: *Flexible thinking and imagination*
Through: Social Studies
Using: Strategies No. 5: Provocative questions
    No. 14: Evaluate situations

The class brainstormed ideas about the meaning of the word "explosion." Then they discussed the meaning of "population." Once the concepts of population and explosion were understood, the teacher presented this problem "*Imagine what it would be like* if suddenly there were so many people that there was no more land anywhere on earth for them to live or to raise food. How and where could they live? *Think of as many different possibilities* as you can for ways which might solve this problem."

To Encourage: *Flexible thinking and imagination*
Through: Social Studies
Using: Strategies No. 5: Provocative questions
    No. 14: Evaluate situations

The teacher asked the class to pretend that "tomorrow a rocket ship will land on the playground and after a few hours it will take off for another planet. *Imagine that you are* responsible for selecting 100 persons who will board the ship and blast off to build a new world. Because only 100 persons will be allowed to go, you must carefully *decide on as many different ways as you can for selecting the most valuable people.* When you make your suggestions, also give the reason for your choice."

The activity was used in order to determine the class's concept of society and the teacher wanted the children to realize the value of social interdependence.

Williams' research on teaching creatively as well as teaching for creativity indicates that there are four predominant advantages for children involved in this type of learning:

9. Ibid., Idea No. 95, p. 64, and Idea No. 34, p. 34.
10. Ibid.

1. Children have more fun actively producing on their own rather than passively soaking up facts from the teacher or book. Actually the most fun comes when the child realizes he is really interacting with many things he already knows. Fun is what gives zest to learning. Providing encouragement and opportunities for children to learn in a fun-like atmosphere should not play a minor role in the classroom.

2. Children are provided opportunities to collect data on their own, organize and classify such data, make guesses and predict from that data, and test and verify according to their own individual criteria. Such learning encounters provide children with wide experiences in being imaginative, wondering, trying, playing around with discrepancies and questions calling for inquiry in and testing one's ideas, predictions or generated solutions against the facts. All of these thinking and feeling processes are ingredients of creativity.

3. By use of the idea lessons, teachers are able to direct the pupil's thinking and feeling processes across the regular substantive areas of an elementary school curriculum. No expensive or additional materials or equipment are needed. Teachers are not expected to stop the good things they have always been doing, but rather, to extend these practices by integrating them with the idea lessons contained herein, which help bring about the child's fullest emotional and intellectual development.

4. Everyone benefits; the gifted and talented, the underachiever and the slow learner. At one time creative thinking and feeling processes were viewed as being limited to only a very few children as expressed through art or music. Extensive research and study have proven that creative talents are found distributed throughout any group of normal children in some degree from more to less. Every child has some amount of creative talent which is just as likely to appear in science, arithmetic or woodworking, as in music or writing. The current viewpoint is that all normal children, if given a chance, can be creative. Some children will be creative in more ways or at higher levels than others, but all are capable of developing this potential. Children can learn how to be intuitive and expressive in their feeling, flexible and original in their thinking. A great advantage exists if this kind of learning starts with the young child and continues on throughout the years of formal education.[11]

The Purdue Model for Creative Production

Other models and plans for creative teaching have blossomed on the scene in recent years. One such plan is the Purdue Creativity Program.

The Purdue Creativity Program consists of twenty-eight audio tapes and a set of three or four printed exercises for each tape. The taped program consists of two parts: a three- to four-minute presentation designed to teach a principle or idea for improving creative thinking, and an eight- to ten-minute story about a famous American pioneer. The exercises for each program consist of printed directions, problems, or questions which are designed to provide practice in originality, flexibility, fluency and elaboration in thinking.

11. Ibid.

The process and principles of creative thinking are described to children at the beginning of each tape. In the research studies which have been conducted with these materials, it has been concluded that the total program is effective in facilitating the development of some creative abilities. The evidence leads strongly to the conclusion that the complex human cognitive abilities involved in creative thinking are amenable to influence by systematic instructional efforts.[12]

A study by Feldhusen, Treffinger and Bahlke showed that children's divergent thinking ability can be significantly enhanced through the use of the Purdue Creative Training Program.[13] The study also showed that the program developed superior performance by fifth grade pupils on several criteria of problem solving.

REMOVING BLOCKS TO CREATIVE PRODUCTION

Many scholars of creative thinking feel that one of the quickest ways to develop creative production in children (and adults) is to remove those blocks to creative production which have been identified through research studies.

Lack of knowledge.   As in all problem solving, complete knowledge of the problem and its components is necessary before a solution can be reached. Several weeks were spent, for instance, in Mrs. Cline's middle school situation in helping the children gather information about the customs, foods, history and current oil crisis in the Middle East. This knowledge was gleaned in several ways: by reading books, magazines, newspapers and pamphlets; by viewing films, filmstrips, television shows and pictures; by listening to cassette tapes, radio, lectures, guest speakers and discussions; by interviewing mechanics, service station attendants, a local politician and an authority on the Middle East. As knowledge was accumulated, it was put to use in many ways. One way it was used was in creative problem solving.

In Mrs. Thompson's situation, knowledge of the subject matter under study was gained primarily by interview.

In order to understand the problem presented by the Muhammed Ali film, Mr. Arnold made certain his students had a working background of the Constitution. Mrs. Jackson presented the required knowledge of a social problem through the medium of the puppet show. When all necessary facts are known, problems can be approached with assurance and a willingness to try unique solutions.

There are some authors of social studies texts who are firmly convinced that the major objective in teaching the social studies in the elementary school

12. John F. Feldhusen, Susan J. Bahlke, and Donald J. Treffinger, "Teaching Creative Thinking," *Elementary School Journal* 70 (1969): 48-53.
13. John F. Feldhusen, Donald J. Treffinger and Susan J. Bahlke, "Developing Creative Thinking: The Purdue Creativity Program," *Journal of Creative Behavior* 4, No. 2 (1970): 85-90.

is to teach children the importance and skill of making decisions. The ability to make decisions and to be willing to abide by the consequences of a decision is certainly a sign of maturity. But many skills are required before logical and effective decisions can be made. Acquiring necessary knowledge is only one, but a very important one. Further discussion on decision making appears in the next chapter.

Habit.   Researchers have found that habit is one of the greatest barriers to creative thinking. People become so accustomed to solving a problem in a specific way that they tend to automatically use the same technique, even though it may become less effective with the passage of time. Teachers, for instance, confronted with the problem of teaching history to a group of children may decide to present the material the way they did in previous years because it has worked fairly well, is easy to prepare, is economical in the use of time and is motivating to the children. They may forget that the children are not the same. This particular year one teacher has a slower group, or the class is larger, or there are many reading disabilities among the children. The situation may very well call for a new approach and a new methodology for teaching but habit may cause him or her to proceed in the old way with the ultimate result that more problems are created than are solved. Often a jolt of some type is necessary in order to free people from habit.

Attitudinal blocks.   "I tried this before and it didn't work!" "All this activity may be fine but you've got to teach them the fundamentals!" "I'd like to have more activity going on in my classroom, but I don't have time. I have to cover this material so the children will pass the test." These expressions and many like them are commonly heard in the teachers' rooms and at faculty meetings. They represent "sets" that form in the minds of teachers which often close their minds to imaginative thinking. Often they are the generalized thinking of one unfortunate experience or are based on some type of illogical rationalization— that is, the teachers know that "covering material" does not necessarily mean that they are really teaching and the children are really learning, but a syllabus has been imposed on them and the children are to be tested on the material outlined in it. They resort, then, to the memorization of the material as their method of teaching rather than real learning because if the children pass the tests, they feel this shows they were good teachers. Their training has shown them that lecture and memorization are not really the most effective ways of learning, but the threats and pressures of the job are most easily removed by resorting to such illogical rationalizations.

Other common attitudinal blocks are: lack of a positive outlook, excessive conformity to every rule and regulation, reliance on authority, and lack of effort towards positive thinking or positive problem-solving.

Alamshah summarizes the matter of blocks by stating that blockages to creativity may be identified as socioeconomic, psychological, and character-ological. Some of these are important to the teacher's own personal growth as well as to the children's. Some economic blockages consist of mistaken notions regarding choice of vocation, risk-taking, and human intelligence. Psychological blockages include: lack of inner quietude, feelings of inferiority, and mistaken estimates of talent. Characterological blockages include: lack of self-discipline, attachment, and absence of commitment.[14]

DIRECT TEACHING FOR CREATIVE DEVELOPMENT

E. Paul Torrance, a pioneer in the scientific study of creativity, attempted in the early stages of his studies to identify those characteristics of creative people that do not exist to a strong degree in uncreative people. Torrance found that qualities of fluency, flexibility, originality, and elaboration were four characteristics which appear in large measures in creative people. Torrance set about to devise a series of tests which would identify the degree of fluency, flexibility, originality and elaboration in individuals, believing that in doing so he could identify creative persons. The *Torrance Tests of Creative Thinking* which resulted were immediately controversial. Much bickering went on in the literature on creativity over the reliability and validity of these tests. As time passes and their use is more widespread, they are more readily accepted than they were formerly. Many researchers, however, have not yet accepted Torrance's premise that these four characteristics are equated with creative production. On the other hand, a large number of scholars engaged in creativity research support Torrance in his findings. These people, and others who are willing to accept their conclusions, have devised a series of courses, programs, workbooks, lessons, and gimmicks whose objectives are to develop creativity in children and/or adults through the development of the qualities identified by Torrance. The commercial markets of the country are currently flooded with such materials.

The model designed by Frank Williams, which has gained a great deal of respect among scholars and teachers, is based to a great degree on Torrance's work.

For many years, scholars have said that *creativity*, as such, cannot be taught. It was believed that certain conditions could be set in classrooms which would stimulate creative response in children and that, through reinforcement mainly given in the name of praise and acceptance, the teacher could encourage it to reappear again and again. Creative thinking is habit—and habit becomes habit when an act is reinforced to the degree that the student receives fulfillment each time he or she performs the act.

Teachers who believe the development of creative powers is an essential commodity for modern living have tried to develop creativity in their classrooms by setting those conditions which provoke creative behavior (see Chapter 3), by removing blocks to creativity and by planning lessons which place children in divergent thinking situations.

14. William H. Alamshah, "Blockages to Creativity," *Journal of Creative Behavior* 6, No. 2 (1972): 105-113.

More recently teachers have tried to design modules, lessons and/or units which focus on the development of fluency, flexibility, originality and elaboration based on the definitions given to each in E. Paul Torrance's work.

Creativity can be developed through these various approaches, according to the rise in scores on tests measuring creative thinking and creative ability. It is still too often viewed as a by-product, more or less, of other teaching acts and classroom conditions.

In his recent writings, Torrance has taken the position that creativity can be taught.[15] A study of his work indicates that he bases this conclusion on the fact that the subjects in his research have shown decided gains in test scores when submitted to exercises aimed at developing the four characteristics which the tests are designed to measure.

Consequently, much disagreement still exists as to whether or not creativity, as such, can be directly taught, like arithmetic or geography can be taught, or whether it results from environmental conditions, psychological settings, planned experiences in divergent thinking and a conscientious development of those characteristics which appear to be strong in creative people.

Much of the opposition to Torrance's work has come from professional artists, musicians, architects and dancers. Many of these people feel creativity cannot be defined: it is a God-given quality. They, along with others, feel that creativity is such a complex concept that it can never be, and should never be, broken down into its components, for it is the blending of the components in a variety of mixtures that makes each creative person creative. Because each creative person is creative in a unique way, they say that the mass production concept of producing creative people can never work. Creative ability is seen as such a vague blend of qualities and circumstances that to identify these qualities and circumstances would destroy the creativity itself.

There is much to be said for this argument. This author has visited several classrooms where he has observed teachers using some of the materials which are designed to "teach" creativity head on. In some instances the atmosphere of the classroom was charged with excitement. The children were delighted with the materials and responded enthusiastically to them: creative ideas practically gushed forth.

However, in other classrooms, the material was presented in such a way that the entire atmosphere was dull and boring—children plowed through the exercises in a mechanical, begrudging way and seemed relieved when the period was over. Only a few were challenged.

The variable here is, of course, the teacher. Care must be taken in using these devices to assure that the teacher is capable of properly administering them. It is difficult to believe that creativity is being developed in an atmosphere where everything is contrary to the type of setting and teaching noted in classrooms where Parnes' materials, Williams' modules or Smith's principles are being applied, many of which are described in this book.

---

15. E. Paul Torrance, and J. Pansy Torrance, *Is Creativity Teachable?* (Bloomington, Indiana: Phi Delta Kappa, 1973).

In the fetish of this era to measure *everything* by written responses or to discount it if it cannot be measured this way, it is important to remember that certain components of creativity described by researchers must be present in all creative learning situations and these components include high motivation, enthusiasm, cross-stimulation of ideas, a passion to complete a problem, external evidence of divergent thinking, free flow of ideas, development of ideas, and a host of other characteristics and qualities—very few of which are found in classrooms where teachers have children supposedly developing creativity in quiet, test-like situations.

Summary

Creative teaching is a special method of teaching: an art in itself. There is a decided difference in the methodology of creative teaching and in that of traditional teaching. Although creative teaching employs the principles of all good teaching, it requires an understanding of new principles and concepts which have emerged from studies focused on its development in the past twenty years.

Creative teaching is based on a cluster of principles which may be used as criteria against which the performances of a teacher may be checked to determine whether or not his or her teaching develops creativity in children.

Other plans for developing creative teachers and creative children have emerged in the past ten years besides use of the cluster of principles to guide creative development. Most notable and successful among these is Dr. Sidney Parnes' program and course in Creative Problem Solving at the State University of New York College at Buffalo, and a model designed by Dr. Frank Williams of Portland, Oregon. The Parnes material includes techniques for recapturing creative thinking processes in humans who have lost this ability and presents methodology unique to developing creative thinking. It is of primary benefit to teachers who wish to develop their creative thinking powers.

The Williams model is especially effective because it is a continual challenge to the teacher's own creative thought processes.

Another plan for developing creativity in children is the removal of those barriers to creative development which currently exist in the classroom.

Still other plans for developing creativity include the direct attack on creative thinking abilities through materials designed to develop within children the four components identified by E. Paul Torrance which are basic to creative thought: *flexibility* and *fluency* of thought, *originality*, and the power of *elaboration*. Controversy exists over the use of this material for the effectiveness of the results of its use seems to heavily rely on the ability of the teacher to present it in a stimulating, enthusiastic fashion.

The social studies content of the elementary school is uniquely suited to the challenge of developing creative thinking abilities in our youth. The objectives and content of social studies relate closely to the daily living of the child and to the role he or she must play as an adult in a democratic society. All teachers can develop their own creative powers through the application of the basic principles mentioned in this chapter to their own teaching. Creative teaching places children in unique, unusual, clever problem-solving situations so that their own creative powers develop. Creative teaching also means that teachers work specifically on developing those components of the intellect which contribute to the development of the total creative process. The teaching of the social studies can be a creative process for developing creative people.

To the College Student

1. View the film *Why Man Creates*. After you have seen the film, brainstorm ways you might use it as a motivational device for developing a social studies lesson for any chosen grade which will foster creative thinking in the children.

2. Reenact the situation described in this chapter in Mr. Arnold's class. View the film and hold a discussion. At the close of your discussion, try to identify the creative (divergent) thinking which came from your experience as well as some convergent thinking examples.

3. Keep a bulletin board in your classroom entitled "Creativity in the News." Collect newspaper and magazine articles for it. After you have done this for a few weeks, decide whether creativity is a popular news item. Note the type of papers and magazines publishing these articles. Would you say that research and news about creativity is reaching the lay public? What effect do you feel this will have on the school's part in the development of creativity?

4. Visit a school that has the reputation of being a good, modern school. Make notes of every way the school curriculum in social studies differs from the one you remember when you were in school. Back in your college classroom discuss why the changes have come about.

5. Visit a suburban school, a city school, and, if possible, a rural school. Note the differences and similarities in the social. studies program, in the classroom environments, in teaching methods, in resources and materials, in creative products and in children's behavior. Can you explain these similarities and differences?

6. What do you remember about social studies teaching when you went to school? Discuss this and then compare what you remember to the description of teaching in the classrooms described in this chapter.

7. Discuss the following problems:
   a. What is education?
   b. What is learning?
   c. What makes a good teacher?
   d. What makes a good school?
   e. Define creative teaching.

8. Make a list of the goals you believe your college instructors have in helping you to become a good teacher. Why do you believe certain courses you are taking are required?

9. Select a child in a classroom you are observing and keep an anecdotal record of all he or she does during your visit. After the observation, study your notes and identify the number of times the child uses creative thinking to solve daily problems.

To the Classroom Teacher

1. Observe the bulletin boards in your classroom. Do they reflect the creative ideas of your students, or are they filled with your own ideas? Think of ways you might develop creativity in your children through the use of bulletin boards.

2. Examine your own program and note the instances throughout the day when you organize your class or plan your lessons so that individual differences are considered. Do you tend to *meet* individual differences or *develop* them? Is there a difference? Do you develop them in any of the instances you have noted? Can you think of ways you could develop valuable differences that exist in your students?

3. Take half a class of children and demonstrate the use of a funnel to them by using colored water, a pitcher, a funnel, and a can with a narrow opening. After the experiment place the objects on a table before the group. Have the other half of the class return to the room, and ask *all* the children to write as many uses as they can think of for the objects on the table. Give them 3 minutes. Then compare the responses by *number* of items, *unusual uses* of responses and *variety* of items. If the group which did not see the demonstration has more responses and has come up with more ways to use the objects, you will have demonstrated the principle of functional fixedness.

4. Make a list of all the objections you can to the teaching strategies of the teachers described in this chapter. Examine your list carefully and indicate which items demonstrate your own version of 1) functional fixedness, 2) unnecessary blocks to creativity, 3) habit, 4) attitudinal blocks, 5) premature judgment, and 6) lack of new knowledge in the area of creativity.

5. Using the principles in the criterion chart, make a list of statements which will serve as evidence to show that you are engaged in creative teaching, consciously or unconsciously. Also, rate yourself on each statement by using the 1—5 scale.

6. Using the Williams model plan a lesson in social studies which also develops creative thinking as the examples in this chapter do.

To the College Student and the Classroom Teacher

1. Following is a lesson in social studies observed in a fourth grade classroom. Using the principles of creative teaching as they are defined in this chapter, replan the lesson so that divergent thinking processes will be employed and a creative lesson will result.

Miss Dee, a fourth grade teacher, has been teaching about foods. Here is a list of questions she has been asking for years:

   a. Where is the corn belt?
   b. What states are included in the corn belt?
   c. Why do we call this area the corn belt?
   d. What is the climate like in the corn belt?
   e. How is the corn planted on a large farm?
   f. How does it grow? How is it harvested?
   g. What products do we get from corn?
   h. Where is the corn sent?
   i. How does this country rank with the rest of the world in corn production?
   j. How does this compare with other countries, in quality as well as amount?

   Miss Dee's method is as follows: She puts the questions on the board. Under them she puts the page references where the answers can be found in the social studies text. The children are given a period of time to read. Then a signal is given, books are closed, and the class goes through the list of questions and answers each one by raising hands if the answer is known.

   Your problem: Using the principles of open-ended, divergent, and creative learning, redesign Miss Dee's lesson as follows:

   a. Plan a *method* of teaching based on principles of creativity.
   b. Using the same ideas, replan at least six questions so they provoke creative thinking.

2. Read Chapter 5 in Mary Lee Marksberry's book, *Foundation of Creativity,* pages 151–167, for a review of the concepts that may be developed in the creative teaching of the social studies.

3. Using Osborn's suggestions to develop creative ideation, think through the following problems and note how one creative idea, often built on another, has proven to be profitable to the creator. For example:

   a. *Object:* a bar of soap; *technique* how to put it in other forms.
      Sample answers: (using divergent thinking processes): soap flakes, soap chips, powdered detergent, liquid soap, cream soap, etc.
   b. *Object:* unsafe highway; *technique:* how to broaden it.
      Sample answer: wider highways with malls or cement walls in the middle make safer turnpike roads.
   c. *Object:* a coke bottle; *technique:* new uses.
   d. *Object:* a discarded antique butter churn; *technique:* adapt to new uses.
   e. *Object:* a picture on the wall; *technique:* substitute some decoration for it.
   f. *Object:* table for a Halloween party; *technique:* magnify it.

4. Observe a social studies lesson being taught in any school nearby. Using the criterion chart for evaluating creative teaching, try to identify creative behavior in the teacher.

Selected Bibliography

BIONDI, ANGELO M., ed. *The Creative Process.* Buffalo: DOK Publishers, 1972.
COLE, HENRY, and PARSONS, DENNIS E. "The Williams Total Creativity Program," *Journal of Creative Behavior* 8, No. 3 (Third Quarter 1974): 187–207.

EVANS, WILLIAM, ed. *The Creative Teacher*. New York: Bantam, 1971.

GETZELS, JACOB W., and JACKSON, PHILLIP W. *Creativity and Intelligence*. New York: John Wiley and Sons, 1962.

GILCHRIST, MARGARET. *The Psychology of Creativity*. Melbourne, Australia: Melbourne University Press, 1972.

GOODALE, ROBERT A. "Methods for Encouraging Creativity in the Classroom," *Journal of Creative Behavior* 4, No. 3 (Spring 1970): 91–102.

GORDON, W. J. "On Being Explicit about Creative Process," *Journal of Creative Behavior* 6, No. 4 (Fourth Quarter 1972): 295–300.

GOWAN, JOHN C. *Development of the Creative Individual*. San Diego: R. R. Knapp, 1972.

GUILFORD, J. P. "Factors That Aid and Hinder Creativity," *Teachers College Record* 63 (February 1962): 380–392.

————. "The Structure of the Intellect," *Psychological Bulletin* 53 (1956): 277–295.

MACLEOD, GORDON A. "Does Creativity Lead to Happiness and More Enjoyment of Life?" *Journal of Creative Behavior* 7, No. 4 (Fourth Quarter 1973): 227–230.

MARKSBERRY, MARY LEE. *Foundation of Creativity*. New York: Harper & Row, 1963.

MASSIALAS, BYRON G., and ZEVIN, JACK. *Creative Encounters in the Classroom: Teaching and Learning Through Discovery*. New York: John Wiley & Sons, 1967.

MAY, ROLLO. *The Courage to Create*. New York: Norton & Co., 1975.

MORRISON, HARRIET B. "The Creative Classroom," *Journal of Creative Behavior* 7, No. 3 (Third Quarter 1973): 196–200.

PARNES, SIDNEY. *Creativity: Unlocking Human Potential*. Buffalo: DOK Publishers, 1972.

————. *Student Workbook for Creative Problem–Solving Courses and Institutes*. Buffalo: State University Bookstore, 1963.

ROWETON, WILLIAM E. *Creativity: A Review of Theory and Research*. Buffalo: The Creative Education Foundation, 1973.

TAYLOR, IRVING A., and GETZELS, JACOB, eds. *Perspectives in Creativity*. Chicago: Aldine-Atherton, 1975.

TORRANCE, E. PAUL. *Encouraging Creativity in the Classroom*. Dubuque, Iowa: William C. Brown, 1970.

————. *Guiding Creative Talent*. Englewood Cliffs, N.J.: Prentice-Hall, 1962. Reprint, Krieger, 1976.

————, and MYERS, R. E. *Creative Learning and Teaching*. New York: Harper & Row, 1970.

TREFFINGER, D., and GOWAN, J. "An Updated Representative List of Methods and Educational Programs for Stimulating Creativity," *Journal of Creative Behavior* 5, No. 2 (Second Quarter 1971): 127–139.

UDELL, GERALD; BAKER, KENNETH G.; and ALBAUM, GERALD S. "Creativity: Necessary But Not Sufficient," *Journal of Creative Behavior* 10, No. 2 (Second Quarter 1976): 92–103.

WILLIAMS, FRANK E. *A Total Creativity Program for Individualizing and Humanizing the Learning Process*. Englewood Cliffs, N.J.: Educational Technology Publications, 1972.

The Art of Creative Living

The mounting evidence of fractionated, alienated, and "turned off" young people must not be ignored. Our schools have been so busy transmitting knowledge, developing skills, meeting college entrance requirements and preparing youth for making a living that they have often neglected questions on how to fashion a life worth living. Too many of our younger generation are becoming jobless strangers. . .

EWALD NYQUIST[1]

THE JOY OF LIVING

The three Rs are included in the elementary school curriculum for the purpose of teaching children those skills necessary for functioning as effective citizens in a democratic society.

But the social studies is included to attain other objectives—those that develop the skills of living and the art of developing human relationships. A good social studies program explores the problems of humans, ways those problems have been solved in the past, and ways they may be solved in contemporary cultures.

Learning to live together does not just happen with the act of growing up. We have come to realize more and more that training is needed to develop in humans those qualities and skills essential to successful life in a democratic society. Children must *practice* the act of sharing ideas; they must *practice* critical and creative thinking; they must *practice* decision-making; they must *learn* to listen to other people's viewpoints; they must *learn* to use democratic processes and group dynamics; they must *develop* empathy and understanding of people who are different from them.

1. Ewald Nyquist (Commissioner of Education, New York State), *The Age of Humanity* (Albany: University of the State of New York, Division of Humanities and Arts, 1970): 14.

Figure 2-1. *A direct attempt to study human emotions: a bulletin board designed by a middle school committee to explore the life and death of a president.*

The primary reason for the establishment of the public school was to take care of all those needs in the functioning of a democratic society which could not be left to chance. One of the first needs was literacy; today one need is learning to live together in peace and harmony. We are committed to developing these skills in children so that each child may function as an individual in a democratic country. In a democracy, and in a democracy alone, individuals count; their rights and freedoms are respected. Creativity functions best in a free society of free thinkers. Our social studies program should be the core for developing the creative thinkers of our republic.

HUMANISTIC OBJECTIVES FOR SOCIAL LIVING

"Humanistic" objectives are those which deal with the joy of living as a human being. Much thought has been given to them recently although the concept is not new to education. The fad for writing behavioral objectives (which are discussed later) and the many systems approaches to education (also defined

in this chapter) is so prevalent in educational programs today that many educators have become alarmed over the focus on *things* to the disregard of the
total individual. They have retaliated by reviving the child development studies
and insisting that teaching strategies be changed in order to develop the *whole*
child. No child is a worthy functioning citizen who is not a fully-operative
individual.

In the systems approaches to teaching, industrial processes are applied to
learning with little or no regard for the effects on teachers and children as
people. Because industrial success is easily measured in a product, the systems
approach guarantees to meet predetermined objectives in a product. But the
product in the school is a collection of human beings, and all humans are and
should be different. When certain aspects of the systems approach, along with
other aspects of modular methodology and the writing of behavioral objectives,
have been applied improperly or to the wrong learnings, the errors in process
and product have been colossal. Systems approaches and modular programs
emphasize efficiency: the economic expenditure of time, money, and human
resources. But the major problem of the world today is not lack of efficiency—
it is lack of humanity.

Humanistic objectives are those which emphasize three types of behavior:
1) *intelligent behavior,* which includes the development of the creative aspects
of the mind, the critical or decision-making aspects and the ability to apply skills
and knowledges to problem-solving; 2) the *affective aspects* of growth—deliberate attempts to help children develop value systems and an aesthetic sense;
and 3) behaviors dealing with human feelings and attitudes; those things which
make us happy, sad or indignant. Each of these types of behavior was seen in
the classroom accounts at the beginning of this volume: 1) all the teachers were
stimulating *intelligent behavior* to develop the creative aspects of the mind by
posing open-ended, divergent thinking problems for the children to solve, and
placing the children in situations where critical thinking and decision-making
were necessary in order to complete the task at hand; 2) Mrs. Jackson and Mr.
Arnold were each engaged in strategies to help the children develop value
systems; 3) each of these teachers was accomplishing his or her goal by using
human feelings and developing the habit of using feelings as an indicator of
intelligent action.

A sample of a written humanistic objective under 1) above is:

To help the children see both sides of the slavery problem and encourage
them to make a decision on the issues presented. This will be done by assigning
each child a book of facts or fiction on the War Between the States and then
having each play the role of a United States senator discussing the issue in a
role-playing situation of a meeting of Congress.

Mrs. Jackson's written objective for her sociodrama is an example for 2)
above:

To help children make logical decisions for living comfortably together.
This will be done by using the fight on the playground among three girls as a
role-playing situation using puppets. The class will then divide into five groups
to discuss the problem with the purpose of creating solutions acceptable to all.

An example of a written objective for 3) above is:

To provide an example of bigotry for the children to discuss as a basis for defining bigotry and its implications. This will be done by assigning the children the task of viewing a selected segment of the television program "All in the Family" and then discussing it to determine answers to the following key questions and others which the children will raise:

1. What is bigotry?
2. How is Archie Bunker shown as a bigot in this episode?
3. Have you seen examples of bigotry in your life?
4. What makes a bigot?
5. Do you know of any instances in history where a great catastrophe occurred because of bigotry?

Humanistic objectives are concerned under 3) above with the establishment of a strong self-concept in children. A self-concept is a system of beliefs which a child has about himself. Some psychologists state that a self-concept is really what a person thinks *other* people think about him. At any rate, that which a child believes about himself is learned and someone has taught it to him. Too often he has learned it incidentally, and he has learned the wrong thing. The teacher who is concerned about a child giving the proper answers in cognitive learnings may search his or her papers for mistakes and may criticize the work by the mistakes only. Actually, the paper may be very acceptable but because the teacher never says so, the child never comes to realize it. The child tries, harder and harder, and still can evoke only negative criticism from the person he or she likes, admires, and is trying to please. Finally the child begins to grow discouraged, sees his or her work as unworthy, sees failure impending, and directs the inevitable frustration at the person responsible for the feelings of unworthiness—the teacher.

Humanistic teachers do not leave the children's feelings about themselves to chance. They know children and understand the psychology of learning to the degree that they incorporate objectives—humanistic ones—which make learnings about self (often incidental as discussed above) a direct part of their planning. In addition, these same humanistic objectives make them aware of what is happening to the *students'* feelings every step of the way.

Once self-concepts are established they generally become very stable, that is, they set the behavior patterns for the children for the rest of their lives. Barring physical deficiencies, children who feel they can read, read. Children who feel they are confident become confident. Humanistic objectives dealing with ego development are important, then, at the earliest years of a child's schooling. A child's self-concept affects *every* aspect of his or her behavior and is closely related to all learnings. Positive feelings about self provide the joy of living.

Self-concepts strongly influence intelligent behavior. Intelligent behavior is the degree to which children behave effectively: the way people *feel* themselves and their ability to *feel* and think with others. Children who say they can't draw believe they cannot draw. Nor will they draw as long as they believe they cannot. Self-concept has a high relationship to creativity. Because so much emphasis has been placed on misconceptions of what creativity is and because methods have been and still are being used in many schools which impair a child's creativity, most people in our culture say that they are not creative and will make no attempt to create although it is the opinion of researchers in the area of creativity that everyone does, indeed, possess creative powers. The way one feels about himself or herself, therefore, has a great effect on that person's creative development.

Self-concept is strongly related to mental health. Children who have positive views of themselves have an inner sense of security. Consequently, they are more creative, act more intelligent, are less defensive, more productive, are more self-confident, are able to face defeat and failure as part of the learning process and relate well to most people around them.

Humanistic objectives provide people with the courage to take risks and try new things in an atmosphere that does not see mistake-making as failure or catastrophe. Labeling risk-taking experiences that do not work out as "failures" is detrimental to creative processes and to strong ego development.

Low grades are failure indicators. So is competition. So is grouping children by grade levels. Many humanists would abolish all as irrelevant to the learning process. They feel that the arguments in favor of sustaining these old practices are largely myths. For instance, one argument given for the use of all three devices is that we live in a world of competition and that children must compete all their lives. Therefore they must learn to do it from the beginning of their formal schooling.

Humanists disagree. They say that we really live in a highly cooperative society. In fact, our society could not exist if it were not cooperative. *Most of the time we compete only at comfortable levels.* For instance, Mr. Hall makes a specific income. He computes his consumer capabilities by his income. He selects other people with similar incomes (cooperation) among whom to live. He does not try to compete with the high income industrialists on Claghorn Drive because he knows he cannot. He knows he *can* build a house among his friends that is comfortable, acceptable and in line with his levels of aspiration. So he buys a lot in Melody Acres, builds his house and *lives happily* ever after. If he doesn't *live happily ever after,* he *moves!*

Nor is business really competitive to the degree that we flippantly say it is. Have you tried to buy a squeeze bottle of dishwashing liquid? Or a can of shaving cream? The brand name hardly matters—they are usually about the same price. Manufacturers dare not go too high above this price for fear of being undersold. Consequently, the consumer benefits—low prices pull other prices down. In like manner raising prices may bring other prices up as in the price freezes set by government in recent years. In either case, the act occurs because of *cooperation*, not competition.

Humanistic objectives, we have pointed out, have existed for a long time but they are general objectives and tend to be ignored. Because so much stress

is placed on competency in teaching these days and because teachers ar
evaluated on cognitive learnings, they work at those things on which th
be evaluated. Consequently, humanistic objectives, which are not neatl
precisely evaluated, are slighted in many schools.

Ways must be found to work with and to examine a child's self-concept
if evaluation of all teacher competencies is to take place. Barriers to understanding must be removed so teachers teach the right thing such as removing the
failure trauma mentioned previously. Different forms of evaluation must be
designed which evaluate all important aspects of learning. Forms of evaluation
which focus attention on picayune aspects of behavior must be broadened to
include all important learnings or abandoned. *Humanistic principles* of teaching
and learning are more important than the *details* of teaching and they must be
considered.

For example, the principle "A child learns best who enjoys his learning"
is a more important guide for creative and intelligent teaching than finding out
how many facts a child learned by counting correct answers on an objective
test. The principle focuses attention on the *process* and on what happens to
the child during it. The objective test focuses only on the *product* and pays little
attention to the child. Humanists insist that this is not education at all, that
children should be human and individual as a result of their education, not
memory tanks. Equality of opportunity in education means that *all* children are
entitled to learning, not solely those capable of developing strong self-concepts
(probably outside the school) who can survive the system. Humanistic teaching
means utilizing strategies to develop each child, and the whole child, and not
imposing *one system* or *one form* of teaching on all children.

Humanistic education can best be realized by using those methods of
teaching in which a strong self-concept is developed. The humanistic teacher
will consciously ask about each child, "I wonder how he or she *feels* about
that?" and "I wonder how he or she *feels* about what he or she just did to
learn that?" Then the teacher will seek for ways to make the child *feel* better.
The teacher will select methods where a child can build positive feelings about
self. Humanistic objectives are creative objectives because they are concerned
with the self actualization of each individual.

Looking at education from the humanistic viewpoint we conclude that
education must be affective or there is really no education at all!

CREATIVITY VS. ACCOUNTABILITY

Developing the creative aspects of the children's personality humanizes the
curriculum because the emphasis is placed on the individual and the development of his or her *inner resources and feelings*. Other things must be considered
which are compatible with the principles of creativity stated in the previous
chapter.

The emphasis on cognitive learnings has been brought about by the pressure on the schools by parents and other groups who do not feel the school is

doing its job. Parents, in particular, have become very finance conscious in a world of rising and exorbitant taxes and have demanded accountability. Administrators, pressured by parent groups and professional groups, have demanded accountability. State departments of education, pressured by parent groups, educators, legislators and other special interest groups have demanded accountability.

Accountability has come to mean, "Why can't my child read?" and "Why can't my child do math like my neighbor's child?" It has come to mean evaluation of teachers by the measurable results of their work, usually cognitive learning. In teacher education, accountability has come to mean performance-based evaluation of a student teacher as it has in the classrooms of the professional teacher. Often this performance evaluation is performed by peers, other teachers, who in most cases through some mystic system are suddenly capable of setting and using criteria in evaluating each other. Too frequently this is done without training or a full knowledge of *how* to evaluate. These teachers are often assigned to committees which set up the criteria for performance-based evaluations. Sometimes they receive professional help from specialists skilled in the art of evaluation, but often they do not, so the criteria evolve from a pooling of their own opinions as to what a good teacher is and how good teaching is manifested in the classroom. Little opportunity is left for changes in this procedure and often evaluation of this nature becomes inbred and provincial.

Consider the area of creativity, for instance. Until 1955 little research was done about it. Since 1960 the writing in the area and the research on creativity have reached staggering proportions. Part of that research has been to establish criteria to identify the behavior of creative teachers. A few educators have devised observation sheets for checking *creative* behavior of teachers, but these are, as yet, unresearched in terms of reliability and validity.

The creativity movement has swept the world. Each year the Creative Problem-Solving Institutes are enthusiastically attended by people from many countries and many professions. Creativity has become recognized in the literature as essential to full human development. Psychologists, educators, sociologists, anthropologists and philosophers have recognized it as necessary for the survival and self-actualization of the human species.

Many schools have tried to keep up with the new knowledge being accumulated in the area of creativity. Many have not. Few have tried to incorporate material in their competency-based and performance-based evaluations. Certainly in this age, for teachers to be competent, they must demonstrate their ability to develop the creative abilities of children! Yet, because of the inbred nature of peer evaluation of teachers, many evaluation systems contain false, little or no criteria for judging the ability of teachers to develop creativity in children. Judgments of success are too often considered by cognitive learnings resulting from a lesson, or a battery of tests, or the teacher's ability to change cognitive behavior as evidenced by behavioral objectives and which are often not real behavior changes at all. (See the discussion of behavioral objectives in this chapter.)

The pressure on teachers to become accountable so they can remain employed has placed them in a situation similar to that of students who must pass state examinations. They prepare for the test. With many teachers, performance criteria evaluation has caused them to emphasize those behaviors in their teaching which are used on the evaluation and to minimize or abandon those behaviors which are not rated or observed. The diversity and individuality in teaching, recommended so highly in this book for creative teaching, is discouraged, and teachers become depressingly alike in their teaching. Creative behavior, which is described as unique and individual, takes a beating in this type of evaluation and stands little chance of survival.

Typical accountability-oriented activities which are supposed to personalize learning for the children have led to a strong emphasis on cognitive learnings and little or no emphasis on the child and how he or she feels about these learnings. Some schools have taken comfort in operating like an industry and in declaring that they have taught certain knowledges and skills to children which they know the children have learned because they have the evidence to prove it.

But accountability should not be limited to simply measuring cognitive behaviors of children. Accountability in the social studies must answer the question, "Have I helped this child become a good citizen?" And good citizens are identified by the types of *values* they hold, the *feelings* they have toward other people, their *character, skills, abilities* and *concepts*. In the effective citizen many of the picayune learnings of the school may be irrelevant. Accountability, to many parents and educators, answers questions dealing with these problems which are currently popular: "Why does my child dislike school?", "Why are my child's abilities not recognized in the school when I know him to be very creative?", "How come my child dislikes books when he used to love them so before he came to school?" and "Why can't my child get along with other children?" The answers to these questions deal with the *feelings* of children and with their *relationships* to others. The answers lie in *affective* and *creative* teaching and cannot be measured as the result of one lesson. They deal with serious, long-range problems. The ability to become accountable for answers to questions such as these is the quality which takes teaching above the classification of industry and places it into the category of a profession.

Humanists fear that the teaching profession is becoming more and more like an industry. The good teacher, by some criteria in this pattern, could be a very poor one by other criteria. Inasmuch as competency-based teaching is supposed to produce better teachers, it would seem that common criteria designed by experts which include creativity teaching criteria as well as other criteria must be designed and receive widespread use. If not, the competency-based system can produce poorer teachers rather than better ones.

TEACHING THE ART AND JOY OF LIVING

Human beings come to grips with their abilities to live with one another when they deal in the world problems of economics, sociology, political science, geography, history, anthropology, civics, transportation, communication, education and safety. It seems appropriate, then, that children should be taught how to function as contributing individuals in the context of the above areas rather than memorize a multitude of irrelevant facts which are not applied to important problems. Knowledge is essential, but the way it is taught and the use to which it is put is what determines its relevance and hence its value.

SOCIAL STUDIES: THE CORE OF SOCIAL LIVING

In the forthcoming account of a middle school project in Glendale we see a social studies program developed through a highly humanistic approach. A humanistic approach was employed by Mrs. Cline in the account of the Middle East bazaar in Chapter 1. Mrs. Thompson also used a humanistic approach in her development of the time machine in that chapter. Helen Jackson solved a school social problem with the *feelings* of children in mind when she used puppets to help them direct their emotions to positive channels. Each of these verbal and pictorial observations has provided us with a view of a successful segment of a social studies program. Some, like Helen Jackson's, were contained in one lesson; others, like Mrs. Cline's, spanned many weeks.

From these examples we can see that the core of teaching the art and joy of living in the elementary school is the social studies program. We have identified the purpose and broad objectives of the social studies in terms of social content; now let us define the social studies in terms of intellectual content.

SOCIAL STUDIES: A DEFINITION

The term "social studies" has been derived from the more complex term "social sciences."

The *social sciences* are those bodies of knowledge which have accumulated from studies of economics, sociology, political science, history, geography, psychology and anthropology and the methodologies employed by the scholars in these disciplines.

Social studies is an integration of experience and knowledge concerning human relationships for the purpose of citizenship education.[2] The term *citizenship education* has often been substituted for *social studies*, especially when it is thought of in terms of social living.

Social living is the translation of the social studies into action in the classroom and the community. Social living is concerned with the building of sound, creative human relationships.

The teaching of social studies in the space age must incorporate the concept

---

2. Robert D. Barr, James L. Barth, and S. Samuel Shermis, *Defining the Social Studies* (Washington, D.C.: The National Council for the Social Studies, 1977): 69.

Figure 2-2. *A unit on economics for middle schoolers: candle-making.*

of social living. Children must learn diverse and complicated skills of living together and developing sound human relationships. Relationships may well be defined as the fourth R in the school curriculum. Conditions may be set in the classroom to provide children with opportunities to develop creative and aesthetic living, and objectives must be designed to promote the joy of living to the fullest possible extent.

Units, modules, projects, lessons and entire courses of study may deal with any of the areas of the social sciences. Or, these courses of study, projects, units or modules may be constructed around a general topic such as Mrs. Cline's Middle East bazaar or the environment with several of the social sciences contributing to the development of the unit.

If the social studies curriculum is to remain humanized, however, the skills of living together must be conscientiously developed and not left to chance.

The skills of living together cannot be learned exclusively from a textbook. In today's social studies program the textbook plays a different role than it has in the past. This new role is defined in Chapter 7 of this book.

The world today reflects a type of teaching that failed to show people how to live together. In pioneer societies much of the social development was naturally provided in family groups. Many families were large enough to provide companionship, status, and purpose for each child on varying age levels. Families often lived far apart and the need to know how to meet, to work with, and to play with large groups was not as necessary as it is now. Today people must learn to live next door to each other and to accept their neighbors' ideas and eccentricities. They must also learn to live with people of other cultural backgrounds. They must learn to overcome cultural and language barriers. They must, according to statistics, be prepared to be part of that 46.5 percent of the population which will be uprooted from the place of birth and moved as many as five times (or more) in their lifetimes.

Teaching the social studies is concerned with teaching children techniques, attitudes, values, understandings, concepts, and skills as well as facts. School becomes a place where children come to learn *how* to learn. The modern view of social studies teaching is directed as much at the change of behavior in individuals as at the accumulation of factual knowledge. The school attempts to help each child develop techniques for relating with the world and solving the problems that will be faced daily by providing practice appropriate for that level. The content of the social studies is concerned with the achievements and problems people have faced in all their civilizations—those of food, clothing, shelter, recreation, science, health, safety, transportation, communication, education, government, and family. Children face these situations in their culture at an early age, and the school can use them as the core of the subject matter it teaches. Each area has been accentuated by the process of grouping for better social living, and each one must, therefore, be resolved by a group rather than an individual. The school must encourage groups to interact and solve problems through the sound techniques of a humanized curriculum which utilizes knowledges from the social sciences, especially from the behavioral sciences.

The specific function, then, of the social studies is to teach youth about the various kinds of human relationships, and to provide opportunities in the daily curriculum through which they will develop the knowledge, values, skills and abilities necessary for their rational participation in human relationships.

SOCIAL STUDIES OBJECTIVES

A vast amount of material has been produced in the past fifteen years dealing with the purposes and objectives of the social studies in elementary education. An examination of this material indicates a decided concensus among many experts: the objectives for the teaching of social studies have been largely identified as developing the concepts and processes of *INQUIRY,* of *VALUING,* and *DECISION-MAKING.* In developing these processes, ways of gathering information, and formulating concepts and generalizations have been defined and techniques for helping children make choices have been advocated. Entire books have been written with the basic objective of developing one or all of these objectives.

The importance of this approach cannot be disputed. What *can* be disputed is whether or not such limited objectives can prepare the child in today's elementary school for the complex life he or she must lead *as a child* in today's society.

Where, in all the writing about social studies goals, are those which develop creative thinking in our children so they cannot only become gifted in the quest for knowledge, versed in the process of valuing, apt at decision-making, but also *inventive and adventurous* in the formulation of solutions? Where do we instill in the child the understanding that there is not already a worthy solution to a problem and *that a new solution must be invented?* Is not this the main reason that current social problems exist, that there are no workable solutions in history that can be used, and *that new solutions must be created?*

This book takes the broad view that the social studies is truly an interdisciplinary subject, and that, in the elementary school particularly, a broad view of what is taught and *why* it is taught must be taken. It has already explored the base for developing the divergent thinking processes in each child—that process in which his or her own creativity is rooted and brought out so the child may become inventive enough to decide whether or not an existing solution will deal with his or her problems and those of a group, or whether or not new solutions will need to be invented. Each of these ideas will be further developed on succeeding pages.

Many professional groups have organized definite, broad objectives for education in social living. Those established by the Educational Policies Commission in 1938 when the concept of social studies was a new one on the American scene, have withstood the test of time and appear below.

THE OBJECTIVES OF SELF-REALIZATION
The educated person:

- has an appetite for learning.
- can speak clearly.
- writes effectively.
- solves his problems of counting and calculating.
- is skilled in listening and observing.
- understands the basic facts concerning health and disease.
- protects his own health and that of his dependents.
- works to improve the health of the community.
- is participant and spectator in many sports and other pastimes.
- has mental resources for the use of leisure.
- appreciates beauty.
- gives responsible direction to his own life.

THE OBJECTIVES OF HUMAN RELATIONSHIPS
The educated person:

- puts human relationships first.
- enjoys a rich, sincere, and varied social life.

- can work and play with others.
- observes the amenities of social behavior.
- appreciates the family as a social institution.
- conserves family ideals.
- is skilled in homemaking.
- maintains democratic family relationships.

THE OBJECTIVES OF ECONOMIC EFFICIENCY

The educated person:
- knows the satisfaction of good workmanship.
- understands the requirements and opportunities for various jobs.
- has selected his occupation.
- succeeds in his chosen vocation.
- maintains and improves his efficiency.
- appreciates the social value of his work.

The educated consumer:
- plans the economics of his own life.
- develops standards for guiding his expenditures.
- is an informed and skillful buyer.
- takes appropriate measures to safeguard his interests.

THE OBJECTIVES OF CIVIC RESPONSIBILITY

The educated citizen:
- is sensitive to the disparities of human circumstances.
- acts to correct unsatisfactory conditions.
- seeks to understand social structures and social processes.
- has defenses against propaganda.
- respects honest differences of opinion.
- has a regard for the nation's resources.
- measures scientific advance by its contribution to the general welfare.
- respects the law.
- is economically literate.
- accepts his civic duties.
- acts upon an unswerving loyalty to democratic ideals[3]

These broad general objectives serve the purpose of guiding local groups in curriculum construction. Perhaps the best type of social studies curriculum is built when local communities, with expert guidance and help, establish their own objectives, plan the experiences which will accomplish the objectives, plan units and lessons from these broad experiences and devise a system of evaluation for each objective.

3. Educational Policies Commission, *The Purposes of Education in American Democracy* (Washington, D.C.: The National Education Association, 1938).

Let us examine how one school system went about planning objectives in the social studies for a five-year working period.

SETTING LONG-RANGE OBJECTIVES:
A REPORT FROM GLENDALE

Mrs. Rogers is an elementary education supervisor in Glendale. Her major job is to facilitate the teaching of her staff. As part of that job, she has committees set up to work on curriculum. These committees consist of teachers representing every age level from each of the ten schools in Glendale.

For two years Mrs. Rogers has been meeting with the Social Studies Committee for three hours on the first Monday of each month to plan a social studies program suitable to Glendale.

At the first meeting of her group, Mrs. Rogers asked the teachers to work together with her to help decide what their goals would be in teaching the social studies in Glendale and to make a composite list of those common knowledges and skills they hoped to develop in their children.

The teachers divided into smaller "buzz" groups and talked. Then they came together again and shared their discussions. From all the ideas given, they agreed on this one overall purpose for teaching the social studies:

> In teaching social studies we are trying to build certain characteristics, traits, values, knowledges, skills, abilities, appreciations and attitudes in each child to develop an effective citizen for a democratic society. . .

In the following weeks, the Glendale Social Studies Committee worked with the teachers in each elementary school trying to break down this goal into more specific objectives. Then they tried to define what knowledge, specific skills, abilities, characteristics, attitudes, appreciations and values needed to be developed in the children of Glendale. A consultant from a neighboring college was brought in to assist the group at this point.

Operating on the premise that schools in the United States were established in order to take care of those elements needed in a democratic society which cannot be left to chance, the Glendale teachers finally came up with an extensive list of objectives. Examples of their objectives follow:

Attitudes We Hope to Develop in Glendale Children

1. An attitude of open-mindedness: willingness to listen to the other person's viewpoint.
2. A concern for the rights and privileges of others.
3. A spirit of cooperation: a willingness to work with others.
4. Courtesy in working together.
5. Respect for each other's rights and privileges.
6. A respect for each other's integrity.

7. Acceptance of all races, religions and creeds.
8. An attitude of self-worth and a desire to contribute to society.
9. A sense of civic responsibility: environmental and conservation values.

Skills We Hope to Develop in Glendale Children

1. Skills in problem-solving.
2. Skill in self-evaluation.
3. Critical thinking.
4. Creative thinking.
5. Communication skills (listening, speaking, reading, handwriting, etc.).
6. Research skills.
7. Map skills.
8. Organizational skills (planning, outlining, etc.).
9. Study skills.
10. Skills in decision-making.
    valuing
    drawing inferences
    synthesizing
    making generalizations
11. Human relationship skills.

Values We Hope to Develop in Glendale Children

1. Moral values which help us in dealing with each other.
2. The value of democratic procedures and the democratic way of life: the value of individual decision making.
3. Aesthetic values: an appreciation of beauty and nature.
4. Human relationships: a respect for family and a desire to live peacefully together—guaranteed civil liberties.
5. A respect for natural resources.

Knowledges We Hope to Develop in Glendale Children

1. A knowledge of the democratic form of government and the democratic way of life.
2. The knowledge of our cultural heritage—the history of our country.
3. A knowledge of other cultures with emphasis on likenesses.
4. An understanding of world problems and why they exist.
5. A knowledge of the geography, weather, and climate of the world.
6. A knowledge of space, and the human exploration of it.
7. A knowledge of the sea and its importance in the future of the human species.

8. A knowledge of the problems of each culture in history and how those problems exist today (food, clothing, shelter, communications, etc.).
9. An understanding of the importance of group life.
10. An understanding of our own community.
11. A knowledge of the human struggle for freedom.
12. A knowledge of educational processes and the importance of education to human advancement.
13. A knowledge of technology and problems created by it (waste, economics, unemployment, etc.).
14. A knowledge of the research concerning drugs, alcohol and tobacco and their effect on human life and agencies created to deal with these problems.
15. A knowledge and understanding of the importance of a balanced environment and a study of ecology.
16. A knowledge of the problems of youth (unemployment, etc.) and of senior citizens (retirement, etc.) created by our society.
17. An understanding of the problems created by economic injustices (welfare costs, unemployment, taxation, etc.).
18. An understanding of the problems of minority groups.
19. A knowledge of social problems within the community (vandalism, crime, etc.) and agencies created to deal with these problems.

Appreciations We Hope to Develop in Glendale Children

1. A respect for all work.
2. An aesthetic sense.
3. An appreciation of the natural environment.
4. An appreciation for our way of life—our freedom.

Characteristics and Traits We Hope to Develop in Glendale Children

1. Self-direction.
2. Self-realization (creativeness).
3. Resourcefulness.
4. Initiative.
5. Open-mindedness.
6. A sense of humor.
7. Understanding.
8. Cooperation.
9. Honesty.
10. Sincerity.
11. Integrity.
12. Responsibility.

When the lists were completed, Mrs. Rogers asked that the teachers consider the list of *knowledges* first. In order to develop these objectives, the teachers began to list the topics they thought they should teach. After the topics were selected, the teachers used their knowledge of how children grow, how they learn, and their interests at various age levels to determine the sequence of the topics throughout the grades.

Once the topics had been placed, the teachers from each grade arranged these topics into a series of *units* and/or *modules* and developed them in great detail, pooling all the ideas they had for teaching each topic and accomplishing all the objectives. These were mimeographed and bound and served as *resource* units for each teacher in planning the work in his or her own individual classroom.

This is *long term school planning*. In order to build a democratic school situation, all the staff must engage in setting up goals and determining how they shall be met. This gives the total school program direction and purpose.

Developing a Classroom Curriculum

Once the overall school curriculum had been determined for each subject, each teacher was then confronted with the job of organizing the work of his particular classroom for the entire year.

Each teacher in Glendale roughed in the units to teach, determining the scope of the work and the sequence by using several guidelines:

1. The specific needs of the incoming class.
2. The difficulty of concepts to be developed.
3. An understanding of the children's previous experiences and learnings.
4. Knowledge of child development.
5. Knowledge of children's interests.
6. The available resources in the school and community.
7. A knowledge of each individual in the class.
8. Knowledge of how children learn.
9. Knowledge of the children's home environment.
10. Knowledge of child psychology.

Laying out the work of the year in this manner is also *long term planning:* from this overall planning comes a development of each unit which covers a shorter block of time. This short-term planning includes the setting of specific objectives, often written in behavioral terms.

SETTING SPECIFIC OBJECTIVES

Because of the increasing pressure that all teachers be held accountable for accomplishing acceptable and observable objectives, a great deal has been written about *behavioral objectives* and how to write them.

Behavioral Objectives

Behavioral objectives are so named because the task to be taught is stated simply and is followed by a description of the behavior which the child must exhibit to show the objective has been accomplished (terminal behavior).

In writing behavioral objectives, teachers are working toward common predetermined goals related to the children's eventual role in democratic society which values certain behavioral traits and actions. The writing of the objective calls for the objective to be attained and a definition of the trait and/or action.

Following are samples of some behavioral objectives taken from social studies units and lessons:

- As a result of this lesson each child will be able to read a bar graph as indicated by the test exercise on page 84 in the workbook, *Graphs and How to Read Them*. The child will be expected to have 80 percent of the responses correct.
- As a result of this lesson each child will be able to identify symbols on a physical map by making a minimum 85 percent grade on a prepared test of map symbols.

These are examples of logical behavioral objectives. It becomes a simple matter for the teacher to check a workbook exercise or a teacher-made test to see whether or not each was accomplished.

Mager, a pioneer in the behavioral objective movement, lists the following criteria for writing a behavioral objective:

1. It names a specific overt behavior.
2. It tells exactly what the behavior consists of.
3. It may need to exclude related but unwanted behaviors.
4. It describes the conditions under which the behavior must occur.
5. It specifies the criteria of acceptable performance.[4]

The term behavior refers to any visible activity displayed by a learner (student). Mager defines this as overt action. Terminal behavior refers to the behavior you would like your learner to be able to demonstrate at the time your influence over him ends.

McAshan says that the primary reasons for the current emphasis upon writing behavioral objectives are to: a) aid in curriculum planning, b) promote increased pupil achievement, c) improve the techniques and skills of program evaluation.[5]

In theory this concept seems valid. In practice it is difficult to achieve.

4. Robert F. Mager, *Preparing Objectives for Programmed Instruction* (Palo Alto, Calif.: Fearon, 1962).
   Robert F. Mager, *Preparing Instructional Objectives,* 2nd ed. (Palo Alto, Calif.: Fearon, 1975).
5. H. H. McAshan, *Writing Behavioral Objectives: A New Approach* (New York: Harper & Row, 1970).

The concept of behavioral objectives has not been fully accepted as logical or reasonable, especially in terms of creative teaching.

To state objectives in any form is not to achieve them. The methodology is still the important thing. Evaluation simply tells whether the method worked and what the teacher must reteach.

"Objectives" a teacher must have—clear and distinct. But there are many ways of being creative, many ways of measuring creativity, and many ways to develop it. And no teacher should feel forced to write objectives to fit a pre-conceived form. After all, objectives of any sort are only a guide to learning. There is still much to be said about capitalizing on teachable moments and changing objectives in mid-lesson; it is all permissible (and can be very creative) if the teacher keeps the goals of the program clearly in mind.

Instructional Objectives

Instructional objectives are those which are a serious statement of the school's purposes but which cannot be measured at the close of a lesson or even a series of lessons. Nor can they be measured by any single test or skill work-sheet—they require the gathering of a great deal of data and interpretation of it. Often the interpretation of such data is done in groups rather than by one teacher.

In the Glendale situation described previously, the teachers listed attitudes they hoped to develop in the children. *The attitude of open-mindedness— willingness to listen to the other person's viewpoint* was stated as a sensible instructional objective. This objective cannot be written so it can be accom-plished in any one lesson or in any one set of behaviors. The teachers discussed the type of behavior that was an evidence of open-mindedness. Then, over a long period of time, data were gathered and placed in each child's folder which showed growth in open-mindedness.

These data included: anecdotal reports by many teachers, attitude tests, participation charts, flo-graphs, observation anecdotes, personality tests, notes from parent conferences, etc. After a period of time a team of teachers met to evaluate the growth of each child in this objective.

To develop a sense of cooperation among the children is a legitimate objective. Listing the behavior that shows cooperation is but one device used to judge the attainment of the objective for each child, such as a check sheet for his or her folder something like Figure 2-3.

But other evidence is necessary before growth in an area as vague as cooperation can be determined: interviews with parents, attitudes and value testing, teacher-child interviews and lessons dealing with the topic of "cooper-ation" and "competition" with situations created wherein the child's values, concepts and abilities to act in a group are exposed. Teachers may observe the results of their teaching in puppet play, structured dramatization, role-playing, role-reversal, and a host of other simulated situations—and record the behavior changes from day to day.

CHECK SHEET

Social Behavior

Name _____ *Bob Miller — age 10* _____   **Date** _____

General Objective: To Develop a Sense of Cooperation

Behavior	Observations	Comment
1. Takes his turn in discussion.	Waits in planning circle for his turn—raises hand.	Good scores on social adjustment tests given by psychologist.
2. Shares his materials with others.	Excellent in making reports—made population graph for class.	
3. Seeks advice and help from others.	Good ideas about decorating candles.	
4. Shares his ideas and findings with others.	Excellent reports from his research—shared graph he found on Friday—"wax costs."	
5. Plays with others on the playground.	Shared playground equipment with team. Helps organize ball team each day. Volunteered one day to keep score.	
6. Is concerned about others.	Reported his buddy, Clark, had cut his finger; took Clark to nurse.	
7. Uses materials well.	Replaced borrowed materials where others could find them—cleans up his station every day after candle-making.	

Figure 2-3

SELECTING THE CONTENT OF THE SOCIAL STUDIES PROGRAM

What shall be taught in the social studies? With knowledge in the social sciences doubling every few years, how can teachers know what to teach?

A great deal is heard today about the "new" social studies, with the implication being that social studies teaching today has greatly changed from what it used to be. A reference to the four observations at the beginning of this book will indicate to some readers that social studies instruction has, indeed, changed since they were students in the elementary school.

But readers must not be mislead. It is true that new goals and the invention of "teaching" machines have changed some of the strategies and methods of teaching in many schools, but it is also true that the travelers across this great land who stop to visit schoolrooms will observe a great variance in the types of social studies programs they observe. In too many places they will see teaching which is very much like the teaching to which they were exposed when they were elementary school students.

Before the introduction of the social studies, classes were taught in given blocks of time and labeled history, geography and civics. Teachers drilled students to remember names, dates, places, products, and events. Most assignments were to read and memorize with the prospect of a test on the material studied an obvious part of the next day's teaching plan.

In the early part of the twentieth century the subjects having to do with the living relations of human beings were combined into a block called the social studies. Drastic changes resulted in many classrooms because of new objectives and a new philosophy which created this fusion.

History, geography and civics were still taught, but other areas of the social sciences were added so children could better understand the interrelatedness of the disciplines of the social sciences: anthropology, economics, sociology, and political science.

Students were encouraged to delve into human problems and to acquire knowledge in a way that would be meaningful to them. The textbook became a reference book and students sought out information from a variety of sources, often compiling their own reference files. Much of the "old" social studies content was included, but it was studied in a more relevant manner and with a different emphasis. The approach to studying cultures was through the achievements and problems of humans and how cultures contrasted. Emphasis was placed on the acquisition of knowledge which would help solve human problems of today, but problem-solving skills were also taught so children could function as citizens after they left school.

Topics were categorized into headings dealing with the social functions of humans: food, clothing, shelter, education, communication, transportation, economics, history, government, etc. (This social functions approach, as it was labeled, was designed under the leadership of Paul Hanna.)

Gradually emphasis in social studies changed from the learning of facts to the development of understandings, concepts and values, from the creation of student memory tanks and robots to the development of characteristics and behavior in students which appeared to be essential for a fruitful life in a democracy, from the parroting of information to the ability to synthesize knowledge in order to make decisions and pass judgments.

In the early 1960s, the National Science Foundation and the U.S. Office of Education set into motion some 50 curriculum development projects for the purpose of creating new materials and developing new teaching methods. Widespread reform was the general result of these projects.

Subject matter was updated and upgraded. New objectives, compatible with new life styles in the space age and the revolution in technology, were set up. Much irrelevant, outdated material was weeded from the social studies content and important principles, understandings and concepts were formed to help students better understand their heritage, as well as contemporary life. Innovative materials for children were designed and new machines of the technological world were employed. Children could now see on film in five minutes what it once took them an hour to read. Instead of reading *about* the oil crisis in the Middle East, they could view the problem on films or filmstrips. Instead of reading *about* a famous speech such as Lincoln's Gettysburg Address, they could hear it on a cassette tape, delivered by a great actor in much the same way that Lincoln himself might have delivered it. Instead of reading about the presidential campaign, students could be assigned to view the television debates of issues and national problems.

Up-to-the-minute issues are a part of the new social studies: international power plays, labor disputes, family life, poverty, racism, crises in education and government, ecology, democratic and human rights, and other world problems.

Because problems abound and the skills of problem-solving may be developed through solving *many* problems, emphasis in the new social studies is also on individual development. Classes sit together but not for the purpose of reading or reviewing the same material and being checked on knowledge they have memorized. The children come together for a variety of purposes: to report to each other on material they have found, to synthesize material, to work with the teacher on developing values or concepts, to present plays, reports, puppet shows, or films to each other, to do some role-playing with a problem, to work on a project together and occasionally to be tested or to evaluate learnings. It is not uncommon for students to be working in many small groups having heated discussions over some problem, or to be working alone on a series of contracts or modules, completing a unit of study by themselves in a carrel in the classroom, or to be working in the Learning Resources Center doing research on a group or individual project with the research being done not solely through the use of books but through the use of films, filmstrips, tapes, paperbacks, journals, pictures, instructional kits, workbooks, problem-solving puzzles, simulation games, maps, globes, reference books, and with almost every conceivable resource. (All of these resources and techniques are described or illustrated on later pages of this book.)

The four situations described at the opening of this volume are typical of the sights which a traveler might encounter should he drop in on a variety of schoolrooms. No one situation would be the same, yet many of the objectives for which the teachers were working might be the same. Many, however, would be very different, for local geography and history enter a great deal into the way that social studies may be taught in various communities, and current national and international happenings may or may not be used by the teacher to develop some of his or her objectives.

While it is obvious that Mrs. Cline was teaching a unit based on understanding the problem of Middle East oil distribution and consumption, thus putting meaning into our own national energy crisis, she was also concerned with many other things. For instance, she was very much concerned that her students would understand Middle Eastern cultures and appreciate the reasons why sudden world power might create political hassles. Poverty stricken countries that suddenly become rich and powerful find themselves in enviable positions which often change the behavior of their politicians. She was also concerned that the children develop values (such as, respect for other people's rights), that they develop generalizations (such as, natural resources may become exhausted and humans must invent other ways to provide energy), that they develop understandings (such as, humans the world over have the same emotions and react to power prestige in similar ways). Mrs. Cline was also concerned with building skills in the children (the ability to do research using a variety of resources, the ability to speak before a group, to write summaries and reports, to keep records, to use resources, to share ideas in discussion, the ability to synthesize, summarize, to pass judgment and to make decisions). She was also concerned that the children know various techniques for learning (by discovery, through inquiry and application of knowledges). And she was also concerned that the characteristics and traits of each individual in her group be developed to the fullest extent, especially the creative abilities of each child.

In our visit to Mrs. Thompson's room we saw a teacher engaged in developing an understanding of a sense of time, of the effects of change, a sense of history. Mrs. Thompson was helping her youngsters develop the concept of sequence. But many of her goals were the same as Mrs. Cline's. She was also building certain values, concepts and understandings. She was teaching, through her unit, many of the skills which Mrs. Cline was teaching through the bazaar: the ability to do research in a number of ways, the ability to speak before a group, to write summaries and keep records, to share ideas in discussion. Skills unique to Mrs. Thompson's current unit were: constructing a time-line and presenting original and unique reports. Mrs. Thompson also introduced various techniques for learning including inquiry, discovery, application of knowledge, interviews, etc.

In Mr. Arnold's class we saw a direct confrontation of a teacher and students with a relevant civil rights problem when children were attempting to understand the rights granted all citizens and how the law works to protect those rights. Mr. Arnold's presentation of the Muhammad Ali film showed the problem clearly; the discussion and role-playing which followed were his way of developing understandings, concepts, values, skills and methods of learning—many of which were similar to the skills being developed by the other teachers.

In the puppet sociodrama in Mrs. Jackson's classroom we can see how a teacher can use a local problem to develop some of the values, concepts and understandings which have been listed as targets in teaching the social studies. Many of the objectives are the same as those of Mr. Arnold, but the technique is very different. Both content and technique, however, are appropriate and relevant to the children.

A great deal of controversy still exists, however, on what the *content* of the new social studies should be. Since most of the content is now used as a means to an end, the end being to develop understandings, concepts, values, character and skills (particularly decision-making), what does it matter *what* is taught, some educators argue. It is *how* it is taught that matters. Opposing this viewpoint are educators who feel that there are certain bodies of knowledge which children must have in order to become effective citizens, and these bodies of knowledge should be used to teach the other aspects of the social studies program. Among these are: knowledge of the Constitution and the rights of citizens as designated in that document, the struggle for democracy, the struggle to maintain democracy with illustrations such as the War Between the States, the problems of natural resources and ecology, a knowledge of other cultures, a knowledge of the working of governments, the dangers of smoking, alcohol and drugs, the problems of the aged, welfare and education, to name a few.

In spite of the controversies which still exist over the content of the social studies, recent surveys of curriculum guides indicate that the elementary social studies curriculum content is similar throughout the country.[6] In the primary grades the following topics are most commonly studied: home, school, community workers, transportation, communication, food, shelter, clothing and American Indians. (This is basically an application of the social functions approach advocated years ago by Hanna.)

In the fourth grade the predominant topics are the regions of the world from a climatic point of view—largely contrasting cultures and how the climatic differences affect the lives of people.

In the upper grades the United States of America, Canada and Latin America (the Western Hemisphere) is taught first, then the rest of the world (Europe and the Eastern Hemisphere). This program is planned on the assumption that children build concepts and knowledges on known experiences. The study begins with the child in his or her home and school, branches out to the community, then to the state and country, and finally to other countries.

It would seem that these studies show that in spite of all the suggested changes in the social studies, *content*, as such, has not changed to a great degree from that taught earlier in the century. This may be true and is perhaps due to the fact that, in redesigning curriculum studies, it is not generally feasible to change the content topics because of the expense involved and the re-education necessary. The change might better be on *emphasis*—it is more economical and practical to use the same content but to identify different concepts and generalizations to be developed, values to be recognized, and decisions to be made as pointed out in the discussion of values in Chapter 8. Children can be taught the condition of life as it is, and to probe deeper into the *why* and *how* of these conditions.

In some of the British schools content is considered irrelevant, as a se-

6. Peter Martorella, *Elementary Social Studies As a Learning System* (New York: Harper & Row, 1976).

J. Bryan Moffett, *Teaching Elementary School Social Studies* (Boston: Little, Brown, 1977).

R. Murray Thomas and Dale L. Brubaker, *Curriculum Patterns in Elementary Social Studies* (Belmont, Calif.: Wadsworth, 1971).

quence, because all the generalizations, values, skills and knowledges which children need to understand and practice can be taught through *any* body of subject matter. Thus, the children pursue their interests and the sequence of events is placed in proper order when they reach the upper middle school or junior high ages where they are able to comprehend time and sequence and to develop concepts more rapidly than at any previous time in their lives.

Even if content has not changed much, the emphasis in recent years has shifted from the transmission of cultural knowledge to greater attention on current social problems, more attention on teaching the analytical skills of the social sciences and a stronger emphasis on teaching types of thinking and learning including creative thinking.

Among the social problems found in social studies curriculum guides are the following examples and some illustrations of how they have been used to develop other objectives of the social studies program.

- *Environmental studies:* including topics such as ecology, preservation of natural resources, waste disposal, beautification of environment, pollution.[7]
- *Drugs:* including harmful drugs, intelligent use of drugs.[8]
- *Taxes:* including how taxes are levied and collected, what benefits the taxpayer gets, etc.
- *Social problems:* including welfare costs, the problems of senior citizens, and costs of Medicare, health insurance, etc.
- *Labor unions:* including their purposes, operation, affect on prices, marketing, schools, etc.
- *Human rights:* including studies of discrimination laws, minority groups, women's rights, racism, etc.
- *Change:* including changes in family life, education, social customs, and values, technology, and how all change affects humans.
- *Economics:* including a study of the poor, of government aid programs, of the aged and social security, of pension plans and government-assist programs and grants, and how these programs affect citizens.
- *World problems:* including wars, distribution of goods necessary to human life everywhere, human rights.
- *Religion:* study of the various religions of the world.
- *Political ideology:* including a study of communism, socialism, democracy, and other forms of government.
- *Energy crisis:* including studies of fuel resources of the world, solar energy, gasoline substitutes, effects of change on the economic structure of the country.

The topics listed here represent only a few of the newer ones being dealt with in the elementary school. Others are listed elsewhere in this book where decision-making and value development are discussed.

7. Environmental Studies, Box 1559, Boulder, Colorado 80302.
8. *Drugs: Insights and Illusions: Contact,* 904 Sylvan Avenue, Englewood Cliffs, N.J. 07632.

Scope and Sequence

The scope and sequence of topics, so often the major problem of teaching in the social studies in the past, is still a relevant problem but not to the degree that it once was. At one time the depth of a study and its placement in sequence was the major task of the social studies curriculum designer; now both scope and sequence are influenced by objectives which do not deal as extensively with the acquisition of specific knowledge, but with the development of skills and values which can be applied to solving social problems. Since the development of values and the development of certain skills (such as the ability to make decisions) can be nurtured in almost all problem-solving situations, curriculum designers are more concerned with the selection and placement of topics which fit the criteria mentioned in the previous section. Sequence is determined by the child's ability to cope with the material, the child's developmental level, especially the ability to form understandings, develop concepts and to think critically and creatively.

CRITERIA FOR SELECTING CONTENT

Certain criteria may be applied in the selection of content for the social studies. Perhaps the first, already mentioned, is that *the content must be relevant to the children*. Content is relevant to children when they get meaning from it. Dropouts aren't dropouts because they weren't told or weren't able to memorize certain things. They are dropouts because *they didn't get meanings!* Meanings come for youth when what they study is important to them now—at this time in history. What was meaningful five years ago is not always meaningful now. We live in a world of fantastic *change*. Someone has said that the only thing we can be sure of in the future of our country is change. At a recent commencement address the president of a large university pointed out that most of the things which the graduating class had learned as freshmen were already obsolete. There is little assurance that current knowledge will be valid in the future. Nor can we be sure that the values we hold will remain constant.

This great flux in society has many implications in designing social studies programs. One is that we must expect continuous change and should educate boys and girls to the realization that change is a normal part of a technological world. Lack of creative development in the minds of young and old makes impossible the acceptance of the concept of change and the advantages which accompany it.

Another criterion, then, is that the content selected should help children understand *change*. Change in values, in life styles, in modes of governing, in thought processes, etc. Content must be realistic to the children and the world in which they live. It must be related to the lives of the children here and now—knowledge needs to be filtered in value so they may find out about things which help them settle current problems; it need not be assimilated for use in some far-off mystical time as was often the case in the traditional school. "Learn and apply" is a motto of the times. Anything learned exclusively for future use may never be used at all for knowledge may change before the time arrives when the particular piece of knowledge may be applied. Education is a continual process of learning and unlearning, and it is a process which continues throughout life.

Traditions may go. New life styles will emerge. The mobility of the population, for instance, in changing locations and jobs, cannot be emphasized enough as a major factor of modern life. Less and less does one drive through staid and settled little villages with old homes and unpaved streets: these give way to mobile home parks which accommodate society that is on the move. The stability of the family and family life has been shaken and will continue to be as children break away from old values and create new ones because of new influences on their lives.

Many educators today would incorporate one other criterion in the list for selection of content, and that is that the content must be of the nature which provides much opportunity for decision-making.

Decision-Making as the Ultimate Criterion for Content Selection

The factor that makes humans human is believed by many biologists to be the ability humans have to make decisions.

While many psychologists, such as B. F. Skinner, support the view that everything we do is determined by the way we have been shaped by the environment in early life, and that in essence we are not responsible for what we do and what we are, René Dubos, an eminent biologist, disagrees. He believes that an important characteristic of human beings is that we have freedom of choice and free will. We are human, states Dubos, not through our biological nature but through the choices that we make all along the course of our individual lives. The choices that humans have made for at least ten thousand years are the choices that have kept us human. The choices which we will make for the next ten thousand years will determine whether or not we remain human.

Dubos wrote:

> The most fundamental aspect for a biologist of the difference between the human species and the animal species is that everywhere [else] in the world of living things, adaptation means changes in the nature of the organism, in the nature of its needs, to fit the external circumstances. In the case of human beings, adaptation means changing the environment to make it fit man's nature, which as far as we can determine by any tests we know, has not changed throughout these hundred thousand years.[9]

Dr. Dubos believes that to be human means to proceed from purely instinctive reactions, which are animal, to willful creative activities which always

9. Rene Dubos, *So Human an Animal* (New York: Charles Scribner's Sons, 1968).
   Rene Dubos, *A God Within* (New York: Charles Scribner's Sons, 1973).

involve choices. Those choices are often painful. But humanity has always made choices, and because humanity has done it, humankind has become progressively different from animal kind and continues to increase these differences.

To be human is to be able to make choices. The ability to make choices is one of the most important skills to be developed in the social studies program.

Dr. Theodore Kaltsounis is one expert who sees the teaching of decision-making as the chief role of the social studies. He states:

> Teaching children how to make good decisions is becoming a very important, and most likely the ultimate, objective for the social studies. If social studies is to help children understand and find their place in society, and if the conditions in society continue to be as uncertain and threatening as they are at present, this new emphasis on [decision making] does make sense.
>
> Decision making has come into prominence to fill a vacuum in social studies. It is important to realize the existence of the vacuum, prior to analyzing and defining this significant process that could be considered the backbone of a democratic society.[10]

Kaltsounis offers a guide for the selection of content. He believes that emphasis should be placed on topics which examine the problems in any culture which involve human interaction, individual responsibility, organization and government, health and safety, conservation of our human and natural resources and similar areas of human concern.

Controversial issues in each topic should be explored because it is with these controversial issues that children gain their best practice making decisions.

Two other authors who define the main goal of the social studies as that of teaching children to make reflective decisions so that they can resolve personal problems and shape public policy by participating in intelligent social action are James A. Banks with Andrew A. Clegg, Jr. In their book *Teaching Strategies for the Social Studies* (Menlo Park, California: Addison-Wesley, 1973) they identify the main components of decision-making as 1) scientific knowledge, 2) value analysis and classification, and 3) the affirmation of a course of action by synthesizing one's knowledge and values.

These authors point out that people are not born with the capacity to make rational decisions and that decision-making is, therefore, a skill which must be taught and practiced with children. They identify the steps in decision-making as follows:

1) *The gathering of knowledge* which is relevant to the problem at hand. They use Kerlinger's four methods of knowing: tenacity, authority, *a priori* and the scientific method as the means of obtaining knowledge. Banks and Clegg differentiate between *inquiry* and *decision-making* as follows: the basic aim of social science inquiry is to derive social knowledge in the form of facts, analytical concepts, generalizations and theories. The goal is to accumulate as much knowledge as possible. In decision-making, the social actor (a name they use

10. Theodore Kaltsounis, "Swing toward Decision Making," *The Instructor* (April 1971).

to indicate the person making the decisions) is mainly interested in how the knowledge derived by social scientists can be used to help him solve problems and make decisions.

In their own words, "Social science inquiry produces knowledge; in decision-making, knowledge is selected, synthesized, and applied." [11] Knowledge from all the various social science disciplines is essential in solving personal and social problems in order to make wise and rational decisions. A social studies curriculum must therefore be interdisciplinary, and must incorporate key concepts and generalizations from all the social science disciplines.

2) *Valuing:* after the decision-maker has acquired higher level knowledge, he or she must attempt to relate the facts, concepts, generalizations and theories to his or her own value system before deciding to act. Valuing (or value-inquiry) should help the decision maker identify the source of his or her values, determine how they conflict, identify value alternatives, and choose freely from them. Conflicting and confusing values (both group and personal) must be clarified. Banks and Clegg believe that value inquiry and value classification is one of the most important phases of the decision-making process.

These authors believe that inquiry, valuing and decision making each consists of a cluster of interrelated skills which can be taught to children. They identify these skills and provide suggestions for systematic instruction in each. [12] Each skill is defined *behaviorally*. The synthesis of knowledge and values constitutes the process of decision-making.

Banks and Clegg identify the primary goal of social *inquiry* to be the building of social theory. They feel generic, theoretical knowledge will contribute more to the making of rational decisions than more specific and fragmented knowledge.

They caution:

> Elementary school students should be helped to understand both the strengths and limitations of the scientific process and of scientific knowledge. Children should learn in the earliest grades that social inquiry cannot be used to solve decision and value problems, but that scientific methods and knowledge can be used to help the social actor clarify his values and ascertain the means and methods necessary to attain the goals that he values, and to determine the possible consequences of different courses of action. [13]

In the examples of social studies settings described at the beginning of this book we saw teachers working with various stages of inquiry and decision making. In the unit on the Middle East bazaar, children were attempting to better understand Middle Eastern culture by obtaining knowledge which they shared with each other in many ways. This knowledge did not consist solely of

11. James A. Banks with Ambrose A. Clegg, Jr., *Teaching Strategies for the Social Studies* (Menlo Park, Calif.: Addison-Wesley, 1974): 19.
12. Ibid., 3–150, 444–518.
13. Ibid., 47.

facts, but of different ways of thinking and feeling and an exploration as to why Middle Easterners held concepts and values different from ours. All of this knowledge was used when the teachers and children later discussed the main problems which they had originally set out to explore such as: "Are the Middle East countries justified in demanding such high prices for their oil when the entire world needs it so badly?" and "Have other countries dealt fairly in sharing their products with the Middle East countries in the past?"

Mr. Arnold was using a film to impart knowledge and to identify values which might differ from those held by his students so they could determine how the Ali case might be resolved. Also, after seeing the remainder of the film, these children were better able to explore whether or not the Supreme Court decision was a just one, and to further explore the consequences of the decision.

In Mrs. Jackson's classroom, we are aware of a direct confrontation of young children in the valuing process, where knowledge was quickly presented, values were probed and discussed and five rational decisions were made.

Many of the problems of the world today exist because democratic rights are not afforded all people. Basic to the democratic idea is the belief that all people are worthy of equal opportunity and are therefore, worthy of respect and the dignity that comes with respect. Problems exist among people because some are not respected and, consequently, have not obtained the dignity worthy of the human being. Religion, race, creeds and traditions become facades behind which people cower in their inability to obtain self-actualization. Often a person's religion, race and laws become the weapons used in expressing a need for dignity and respect: the person's rights as an individual. In the framework of the democratic society the conditions exist (in theory at least) where each person, through legal freedoms, can obtain dignity and respect.

The basic freedom of all is the freedom to make decisions. The types of decisions people make eventually bring them respect or the loss of the respect of others. Some decisions that people are free to make are moral in nature. Moral issues deal with what is right or wrong for an individual or a culture. Making decisions about moral issues means that one must be willing to abide by the consequences of his or her decision. To expect others to change the circumstances of a problem in order to resolve the problem removes the moral aspect of the problem. An example of this is the student strikes on many of the college campuses some years back in protesting the Vietnam war. As part of the protest many students decided not to attend classes. In some instances their professors joined them. The question as to whether or not this was justifiable behavior to meet the desired result created a situation in the minds of many professors and students where a decision had to be made. Was the action right or wrong? It was a moral issue. The consequences for the student could be disastrous: loss of credit, loss of grades, expulsion from school, failure to graduate, etc. The losses for the professor could be equally disastrous: loss of job, loss of retirement benefits, rejection by co-workers, etc.

Some students tried to resolve the problem by asking the administration to sanction their act. In situations where this strategy worked, the moral issue concerning attending class was removed although the strike was held because of the morality of a larger issue: the Vietnam war.

In order to make decisions humans must also be literate in terms of their resources. These resources are political, physical, environmental, intellectual and historical. A social studies program should help children understand these resources.

In order to make decisions humans must also have a value system. Although one person's moral decisions may run counter to the values of another, nonetheless each must know the values of the other and must have established particular values of his or her own. What made students talk convincingly against the Vietnam war? They were able to do so because their own set of values regarding the rights of humans had been violated. Congress had never declared a war in Vietnam, so some felt that the conflict was contrary to the Constitution of the United States. Many students decided they would stand up and say they thought this was wrong. Many were willing to suffer the consequences of their decision and thousands hoped that a mass movement of students would create a change in government behavior and right a wrong, thus improving the world for all humans. Part of every social studies curriculum should be the exploration of values held by a society and the individuals within it. *Practice* in decision making is also essential to develop the skill in children.

Dr. Theodore Kaltsounis makes this statement about decision making:

> It should be made clear that decision making does not minimize the value of concepts, generalizations, inquiry, social sciencing, and the like. It simply shifts their position from ends to means.
>
> The student continues to analyze and explain social situations, and strives to discover and understand relationships, but he does not stop there. He uses them in order to be able to make rational decisions.
>
> Decision making involves three basic elements: knowledge, values, action.[14]

The role of the social studies in the elementary school curriculum becomes clear under Dr. Kaltsounis' description: 1) Knowledges which lead to generalizations and concept building must be taught; 2) values must be explored and developed (see Chapter 8); and 3) both knowledge and values must be applied in solving relevant classroom problems. This application should be done in a manner that makes social studies exciting and useful to the individual as well as to society. Kaltsounis states:

> Decision making takes social studies beyond simple intellectualization concerning the society and into the realm of positive social action.[15]

When decision making becomes the main thrust of social studies teaching, the social science disciplines become sources of information and value building. Children and their roles in society become the center of social studies education.

14. Kaltsounis, loc. cit.
15. Ibid.

Summary

The social studies are the understandings selected from the reservoir of knowledge in the social sciences. The social studies program is not simply a combination of geography, history and civics, as some schools propose. Nor is it a series of lessons in reading comprehension—a study of the accumulation of human experiences of the past with the intent of using this knowledge to solve the problems of the present. It is more than that; it means the opportunity for children to learn and practice the necessary knowledge and skills needed for them to take their places as effective individuals in their society—in making decisions both as children and as adults. The problems of the space age are new to the world and cannot always be solved in terms of the experiences of the past. Creative thinkers are needed now more than ever before. Therefore the new social studies program must assume the responsibility of developing citizens who can meet inevitable change with the ability to creatively solve the problems introduced by that change. The new social studies program also concerns itself with developing the joy of living in children. Content for the new social studies program will be chosen in terms of its relevancy to each child and the welfare of the group. Methology, a process of teaching, will be "humanized," that is, *children* will count above *things* if objectives for social living are to be accomplished.

Schools cannot become so carried away with the acquisition of knowledge and the evaluation of memory drills and skills that they do not take time to help children practice the art and joy of living. Some school schedules are so ridiculously tight, so much is jammed into the school day, and so much pressure is placed on the children that they leave school for a tiresome bus ride home exhausted and uptight. The child's school day, itself, must be one filled with the joy of living if each child is to fulfill his or her destiny as a human being.

To the College Student

1. Make a list of all the ways an autocratic classroom interferes with creative development.

2. Write a theme on the following topic: "Those Things I Would Be Willing to Die For." Share this in class and discuss those values young adults hold precious.

3. Discuss the following questions as objectively as possible:
   a. Is there prejudice on your college campus? Where?
   b. Is there religious prejudice?
   c. Is there racial intolerance?
   d. Is there unfair discrimination?

4. Here is a chance to do some creative thinking, and to see how many ideas you can use to prove your point. After discussing the above questions, discuss this one: Are prejudice and intolerance founded in any truth, and if so, what?

5. Check some of your own values by holding a debate on any of these topics and observe critical thinking processes in action as well as the values your classmates use in arriving at conclusions.

   a. In a democratic society anyone who enjoys pornography has a right to read it, print it and sell it without restriction.

   b. Nonviolent action will achieve more for Blacks in their fight for equal opportunity than any other tactic.

   c. All types of censorship are threats to basic democratic principles.

   d. Dictatorships can act more promptly in emergencies than democracies.

   e. Cold wars serve a purpose in that they often keep hot wars from breaking out.

6. View a currently controversial movie and discuss whether or not it should be banned for high schoolers. Prejudices are sometimes called "hang-ups." What hang-ups can you recognize in your classmates as they discuss this issue?

7. Compare John C. Calhoun's theory of states' rights with that of George Wallace, of Alabama.

8. Select an age level within the range of the elementary school and make a list of the topics you might teach to the children. Justify your selections.

9. Here is an exercise to bring out hang-ups, values and personal involvement in your classmates. Discuss these statements:

   a. Adults should exercise more control over young people rather than grant youth more freedom.

   b. The law should be revised so that all 18-year-olds can drink legally.

   c. Drug laws should be relaxed.

   Have a few nonparticipating "observers" note the values they observe during the discussion.

To the Classroom Teacher

1. Evaluate your social studies program and ask yourself what you are doing to develop characteristics, values, and appreciations mentioned in this chapter. What can you do to develop them or to improve them if you are already working with them? Chapters 8 and 12 will help you.

2. Education is the process that changes human behavior. Observe your children during a week and try to note in each child a behavior change which you have brought about through something you have taught him or her or something you have done for the child.

3. Examine your present social studies textbook, especially the section on Africa and determine if any of the facts recorded there might have lost their validity since the book was published. Think of ways teachers can help keep up-to-date facts before the children. How should textbooks that contain obsolete information be used?

4. Which of the values of living together can be taught through the use of divergent thinking processes? What about respect for property, freedom of speech and the

press, contributing to the welfare of others? Plan some lessons using divergent thinking processes which will help children develop these values and others.

5. What skills of living together can be developed through divergent thinking processes? What about skills relating to research, map reading, making decisions, and passing judgments? Plan some creative lessons that will help to develop these skills.

6. One way you can identify the values your students hold is to tape a discussion of the following situation and study it in private:
   Place a picture on the bulletin board of people involved in a variety of amusements. Scott-Foresman has one such poster for the bulletin board titled *Amusements in America*. You may send for it free of charge. Children can be alerted to the things people do or have done for amusements. Put such questions as these below the picture:
   a. What are your favorite amusements?
   b. Which of the amusements shown here do you like best?
   c. What were the favorite amusements of your parents? Your grandparents?
   d. How many of the amusements of your grandparents are still popular today?
   e. Why do people need amusement? Are amusements necessary for the well-being of humans?
   f. When there is work to be done, aren't amusements a waste of time and money?
   g. Should the government spend tax money on providing amusements for people?

To the College Student and the Classroom Teacher

1. Almost always, when a dictator rises to power, the first thing he does is to confiscate the school system. Discuss the reasons for this. Refer to the beginning of this chapter and decide whether or not the motivation for doing this is the same as that behind the establishment of public schools in the United States.

2. Make a list of all the things you can think of that cannot be left to chance if democracy is to survive. Is the school taking care of all of these functions? Should it?

3. The author remembers one of his elementary school teachers making the following statements:
   a. "Man's occupations are largely determined by the climate in which he lives."
   b. "Nevada is a desert state and will always be sparsely settled."
   c. "The South is agricultural; the North is largely industrial."
   d. "The shortest route from New York to Tokyo is through the Panama Canal."
   All these statements are now false, while a few years ago they were taught as fact. Discuss the circumstances which brought about the change in these one-time "facts." When children grow up with such misconceptions, often they operate for years in ignorance. How, in a good social studies program, can this sort of thing be avoided?

4. Hours are spent in many classrooms discussing the causes, important battles, terms of peace treaties, etc., of many wars. Those of the recent conflict in Vietnam were no exception. People are appalled at the useless waste of life. The reason for the inclusion of these topics into the social studies program is that some educators hope,

by teaching about wars, their causes and results, the useless waste of human life may
be avoided.

Yet, recent budget cuts in school aid throughout the nation have resulted in cutting
of many courses labeled as "frills." Driver education is one such course. Over 5,500
people are killed each year in auto accidents in the United States. Should driver
education be cut from the school curriculum and a study of wars be maintained?
Discuss this.

5. Collect magazine and newspaper accounts of new and interesting activities related to
   the social studies which are happening in schools today. Keep a bulletin board of
   these clippings and any pictures you may find. Discuss the merits of the articles. Can
   you discern the objectives behind each activity in the pictures you collect? Can you
   determine whether or not each school represented has a systematized or humanized
   curriculum?

6. Make a list of indications of change in our values as they have occurred in your
   lifetime. Examine them; are the changes for the good of society? If not, how do you
   suggest values be changed? Is there such a thing as a spoken value system and a
   behavioral value system? Are they different?

7. Identify ten of the most important values that seem necessary in order for people to
   live comfortably together. Then list as many creative ways as possible to develop
   these values in children.

8. List the things in your life which put joy into your living. Pool your list with those of
   other members of your class. How many of these things (topics, feelings or situations)
   are included somewhere as a goal for development in the elementary school
   curriculum?

Selected Bibliography

BEYER, BARRY K., and PENNA, ANTHONY N., eds. *Concepts in the Social Studies*.
Washington, D.C.: National Council for the Social Studies, 1971.

BLOOM, BENJAMIN S., ed. *Taxonomy of Educational Objectives: Cognitive Domain*.
New York: David McKay Co., 1956.

BROWN, GEORGE I. *Human Teaching for Human Learning*. New York: Viking Press,
1971.

BURNS, RICHARD W. *New Approaches to Behavioral Objectives*. Dubuque, Iowa:
William C. Brown, 1977.

CHASE, W. LINWOOD, and JOHN, MARTHA T. *A Guide for the Elementary Social
Studies Teacher*. 3rd ed. Boston: Allyn and Bacon, 1978.

DOLL, WILLIAM E. "A Methodology of Experience: An Alternate to Behavioral Objectives." *Educational Theory*, 1972.

DUNFEE, MAXINE. *Elementary School Social Studies: A Guide to Current Research*.
Washington, D.C.: Association for Supervision and Curriculum Development, 1970.

EHRMAN, HENRY W. *Teaching the Social Studies in the United States*. Westport,
Conn.: Greenwood Press, 1975.

FLANAGAN, JOHN C.; SHANNER, WILLIAM M.; and MAGER, ROBERT F. *Social
Studies Behavioral Objectives*. Palo Alto: Westinghouse Learning Press, 1971.

FRASER, DOROTHY M., ed. *Social Studies Curriculum Development* (39th Yearbook).
Washington, D.C.: National Council for the Social Studies, 1969.

GRONLUND, NORMAN E. *Stating Behavioral Objectives for Classroom Instruction*. New York: Macmillan, 1970.

HALLMAN, RALPH J. "Human Relations and Creativity," *Journal of Creative Behavior* 8, No. 3 (Third Quarter 1974); 157-65.

HANNA, L. *Dynamics of Elementary Social Studies*. 3rd ed. New York: Holt, Rinehart & Winston, 1973.

HAPLIN, GERALD; GOLDENBERG, RONALD; and HAPLIN, GLENNELLE. "Are Creative Teachers More Humanistic in Their Pupil Control Ideologies?" *Journal of Creative Behavior* 7, No. 4 (Fourth Quarter 1973); 282-86.

HOPKINS, LEE B., and ARENSTEIN, MISHA. *Partners in Learning: A Child-Centered Approach to Teaching the Social Studies*. New York: Citation Press, 1971.

KALTSOUNIS, THEODORE. *Teaching Elementary Social Studies*. Englewood Cliffs, N.J.: Prentice-Hall, 1969.

KRATHWOHL, DAVID R.; BLOOM, BENJAMIN S.; and MASIA, BERTRAM B. *Taxonomy of Educational Objectives: Affective Domain*. New York: David McKay Co., 1964.

LEE, JOHN R. *Teaching Social Studies in the Elementary School*. New York: Free Press, 1974.

MICHAELIS, JOHN, and JOHNSTON, A. M., eds. *The Social Sciences: Foundations of the Social Studies*. Boston: Allyn and Bacon, 1965.

POPHAM, JAMES, and BAKER, E. *Establishing Instructional Goals*. Englewood Cliffs, N.J.: Prentice-Hall, 1970.

SCOBEY, MARY MARGARET, and GRAHAM, GRACE, eds. *To Nurture Humaneness: Commitment for the Seventies*. Washington, D.C.: Association for Supervision and Curriculum Development, 1970.

WEINSTEIN, GERALD, and FANTINI, MARIO, eds. *Toward Humanistic Education: A Curriculum of Affect*. New York: Praeger Publishers, 1970.

ZAHORIK, JOHN A., and BRUBAKER, DALE L. *Toward More Humanistic Instruction*. Dubuque, Iowa: William C. Brown, 1972.

II

The Nurture of Creativity through the Social Studies

Writers such as Toffler (Future Shock) have predicted the world of tomorrow. In Toffler's world humans must be more adaptive and creative than ever in order to survive.[1] They must be able to make choices quickly, to pass judgments and to be self-motivated to constructively use the larger amounts of leisure time with which they will find themselves.

Strom and Englebrecht state:

> . . . the more crucial the mental health questions of leisure and "overchoice" become, the less ready our present schools apparently are to prepare us for our future. Some educational observers suggest that creative behavior can flourish if we reduce the public concern about grades and competition. Other less optimistic critics have abandoned hope that the school as an institution can meet its new imperative. The resulting proposal is to eliminate schools as we know them and begin anew. Obviously, futurists differ in their level of confidence in education; yet they are generally agreed that the creative ability of children must somehow be retained into adult life.[2]

Many writers agree that the development of creativity in our children is a crucial issue of our times, not only for the ability needed to render new and inspiring solutions to the problems of the age, but for the development and acceptance of independent thinking.

Hallman states:

> Strong, independent minds are always a risk. They do not fit easily into bureaucratic organizations. Their behavior may be unpredictable. They tend to remain true to their own insights rather than to established regulations. They expose themselves to uncertainties in preference to the safety of groups. Their motive is to produce new ideas, not to escape from group pressure. Society does not gracefully accept them. Governments dread them. Plato censored them. Napoleon controlled them. Hitler ejected them. Stalin destroyed them.
>
> This circumstance presents a continuous challenge to social institutions. Society is bedeviled by a host of complex problems: population pressures, pollution, urbanization, crime, war. The greatest promise we have for resolving these ills is the unlimited reservoir of creative capacity available. The new insights we need are best provided by the independent mind. We must find a way to accommodate such minds. Normally, though, we lag behind. We praise innovation only after it has been successful, that is, after it has been found to constitute no threat, or after it has been rendered harmless.[3]

1. Alvin Toffler, *Future Shock* (New York: Random House, 1970).
2. Robert D. Strom and Guillermina Englebrecht, "Creative Peer Teaching," *Journal of Creative Behavior* 8, No. 2 (Second Quarter, 1974): 93-108.
3. Ralph J. Hallman, "Human Relations and Creativity," *Journal of Creative Behavior* 8, No. 3, (1974): 161.

One major task of the educator today is to find ways to translate information such as that presented in Chapters 1 and 2 into action so that future adult citizens currently represented by the youngsters in our classrooms will be open-minded, creative, independent and happier thinkers. We have already seen some ways this may be done in the social studies by the verbal observations presented in the first chapter.

The social studies, more than any other subject area, represent the core of the elementary school curriculum as we shall see in the chapter on unit teaching which follows. The area named social studies deals with the changing of behavior in order to develop social adjustment, social completeness and social relationships. To the area of the social studies is delegated the responsibility of keeping people human. To be human is to develop all one's facilities to the highest of one's abilities.

To the behaviors already identified as worthy of development in a social studies program must be added the behavior of creative action. It will be developed by using a blend of knowledge and principles of creativity with knowledge and principles of social studies. Part II of this volume is the blender for reaching this end.

Teaching for Creative Living

Openness is not anarchy. In the kind of openness we talk about, you can do your thing, not in a vacuum, but in a rich seductive environment of resources that beg you to engage your mind in exploring the unknown. You look, touch, smell, and listen to it all. And soon . . . you begin to feel, value, and love. When all this happens you are swept up in a driving torrent that tumbles you past your first shallow findings into deeper more orderly ways of knowing. You become aware of order . . . you invent it . . . and compare what you have found to the exploration of others. Percy Bridgman's description of the Scientific Method *was only half the argument. He said that the scientific method was doing your damndest with your mind with no holds barred. To provide the other half one must engage his heart. Then it becomes the* Human Method. *Heart and Emotion provide the will . . . Mind and Rationality provide the way. Only in openness can both exist.*

ROBERT E. SAMPLES[1]

SETTING CONDITIONS FOR CREATIVE LIVING

Before the objectives of a creative social studies program can be attained, attention must be given to the environment in which the teacher and the children work. It is wishful thinking to believe that cooperation will develop as a quality in children when they have no opportunity during the day to practice cooperation. It is folly to leave the skills of group dynamics to chance by not producing situations in which group skills can function.

The teachers described in Chapter 1 knew the importance of setting the proper conditions for creative social development. Mrs. Cline's Middle School

1. Robert E. Samples, "Go Out and Learn," *Earth Science Educational Program Newsletter* (Boulder, Colorado, n.d.).

environment was very different in appearance from traditional classrooms. Each room in the Middle School was set up for the development of one segment of the Middle East bazaar. Each of the teachers mentioned in Chapter 1 worked hard at planning a social-emotional environment where children felt comfortable in acting out problems. They also kept unusual as well as standard materials available: films, filmstrips, puppets, boxes for making time machines, and all sorts of scraps. Yet intellectual stimulation was also present in large doses: children in these classrooms were so highly motivated to study that there was never enough time in the school day to do all they wanted to do.

THE APPROPRIATE PHYSICAL CONDITIONS

One of the plans involved in designing a classroom or school laboratory which now makes sense in terms of developing creativity was the idea of classroom centers. The schoolroom was divided into working spaces where the materials for various areas of the curriculum were kept in such a manner that they were easily accessible to children. This arrangement provided for grouping children for various activities so that they could use the materials and yet be somewhat isolated from other children. In such a classroom the tools children used in their work were readily available and the floor space was used economically, with opportunity for rearrangement of furniture to create large work and play areas. Materials could be easily manipulated and explored.

The environment for the open classroom was copied from the early "center of interest" plans of the Dewey Schools. Recently they have been enlarged upon to create the open school where the partitions between the rooms have been removed and entire areas are devoted to special interests or projects. Included in these special areas is a resource center well-equipped with multimedia components to encourage group and self learning.

A common denominator in all the "workshop" environments is movable furniture. If the children are to work in groups (both large and small), the furniture arrangement will vary from day to day, even from period to period. The children themselves should have a part in planning and rearranging their room.

Some teachers prefer to have their children enter a bare schoolroom or working area on the first day of school and begin from scratch to build a workable, functional, attractive schoolroom or total school environment. Others feel they miss the opportunity to study their children and discover their interests, needs, and individual differences by having them enter such a classroom; they plan a first-day program with definite objectives in mind, with the understanding that the classroom and/or work areas will be changed by the children as they have the experience of replanning it.

Considering that creative children are challenged to bring order out of disorder, the planning of the classroom as a working laboratory may well be one of the first planned experiences which teachers use to develop creative

Figure 3-1. *An open school environment with the resource center in the center of classroom cubicles.*

qualities in the children. The arrangement of the classroom or large working area will undergird the pattern of social living which is to take place in the school.

ESTABLISHING CENTERS OF LEARNING

Perhaps the most difficult job which falls on the shoulders of the teachers in setting conditions for learning in the open classroom is the setting up of centers. These centers require appropriate materials that will motivate the children to learn. They must also house equipment, including games, machines, books, devices and paraphernalia which make possible the learning itself. Each center should be carefully planned with specific objectives in mind and with specific children in mind. Each center should be planned to challenge the intellectually talented children as well as meet the particular needs of slow learners. This is one way the open classroom is able to meet individual differences. Centers are left only as long as they serve their purpose and should be changed frequently.

Following are the most important criteria to be considered in establishing a learning center:

1) *The center should be planned around specific objectives.* In some classrooms, centers are set up with general equipment available; that is, a social studies center may be established which houses equipment such as maps, globes, copies of textbooks, encyclopedias, books, graphs, etc. This material

which will be used the entire year is left in the center but topical equipment changes. For instance, many members of the class may be interested in advertising, so part of the social studies center will be labeled "Advertising" and will contain pamphlets and journals on advertising, trade journals, special graphs, charts and books, material to plan layouts, pictures of good and poor advertisements, art materials (if they are not already available in the art center) and an exhibit of materials collected by the class on a trip to the local newspaper. There is also a file of pictures and a file of project cards for individual and small-group assignments.

Another group, for reasons important to them, is studying ancient Greece because of the relationship of democratic principles to government. A portion of the social studies center is labeled *Ancient Greece*. It contains books and pamphlets on Greece, travel folders, a file of pictures of Greece, some small statues, a model of a Greek theatre borrowed from a local museum, and a small box of project cards for individual work by the children. Like the center on advertising, many of the cards in this file were planned and designed by the children and teachers working together. Predominately displayed in the center is a chart (Figure 3-2) outlining the problems posed by the group.

The cards in the project box (Figure 3-3) suggest ways children might go about finding answers to the questions they have listed. There cards were created after the teacher discussed with the children ways they could find the answers to their questions. Their ideas were included on the cards. Other teachers also offered suggestions. These cards dictate more or less which materials must be collected to put in the center.

In addition to the cards designed for specific aspects of Greek life, general

---

WHAT WE WANT TO KNOW

Ancient Greece

1. Did modern medicine begin in ancient Greece?
2. How did these people live?
3. What was their religion?
4. How did they travel?
5. Why do we find so many ruins of beautiful theaters in Greece?
6. How and why did they have such beautiful art work?
7. What did they do for a living?
8. What is a "city-state"?
9. Are those pictures of soldiers that we see on the vases?
10. What did the soldiers do?
11. What is the Acropolis—why are there so many pictures of it around?
12. Who were some famous men of ancient Greece?
13. What sports and games did the Greeks have?
14. Why is Greece called "the cradle of democracy"?

Figure 3-2

GREECE: GODS AND GODDESSES

Work Card 3

(Religion)

BOOKS (INFORMATION):

Caldwell, Helen. *Let's Visit Greece.* New York: John Day Co., 1961. (Photos and maps)

Darwin, Peter. *Years of Zeus.* New York: Ray Publishers, 1965. (Stories of all the gods and goddesses)

Estes, Peter. *The Art of Ancient Greece.* Itasca, Ill.: Peacock Publishers, 1973. (All aspects of Grecian art: sculpture, urns, paintings, icons, etc.)

Gregor, Arthur. *How the World's First Cities Began.* New York: Dutton, 1967. (Section on Athens)

Roberts, Charles. *The First Book of Ancient Greece.* New York: Franklin Watts, 1969.

Watson, Jill. *The Golden History of the World.* New York: Golden Press, 1965.

Werner, Leslie. *The Child's Geography.* New York: Franklin Watts, 1973. (Geography of the world—excellent pictures of Greece)

White, Arnold. *A Child's Book of Archeology.* New York: Random House, 1971. (Photos excellent—ancient Greece)

Young, Adele. *The Story of Telamachis.* New York: Crown Publishers, 1971. (Excellent account of the daily life of a young boy in Ancient Greece)

BOOKS (REFERENCE):

Encyclopædia Britannica, G, pages 1168–2000.
Children's Encylcopedia, G, pages 168–250.
Book of Knowledge, No. 7, pages 525–550.
Information Please, pages 98–206.

BOOKS (TEXTS):

Southland and Southland. *Ancient Worlds,* pp. 68–92.
Peters and Barnes. *Our Beginnings,* pp. 107–128.
Smith and Grambs. *Religions of Ancient Cultures,* pp. 63–90.

BOOKS (STORIES—FICTION):

Barnes, Lila. *Stories of Greece.* New York: Random House, 1972.
Carnes, Henry. *Homer's Iliad.* New York: Bantam, 1970.
Carnes, Henry. *Homer's Odyssey.* New York: Bantam, 1970.
Franz, Marjorie. *Legends of Greece.* Boston: Doubleday, 1968.
Geitner, Peter. *Zeus and Others.* Itasca, Ill.: Peacock Publishers, 1965.
Hale, Betsy. *The Golden Lamb.* New York: McGraw, 1972.
James, Edna. *The Story of Nickoli.* New York: Golden, 1976.
Lamb, Margaret. *Enchanted Islands.* New York: Friendly, 1973.

Figure 3-3

FILMS (LEARNING RESOURCE CENTER):

- *The Story of the Gods and Goddesses* (B and K)
- *Diana—Then and Now* (Arnold)
- *Legends of Ancient Greece* (Weston)
- *Religion of the Ancient Civilizations* (Dell)

FILMSTRIPS (LEARNING RESOURCE CENTER):

- *Thunder and Lightning! Rain and Sun!* (Weston)
- *Life in Ancient Greece* (McGraw)
- *Religions of the Ancient Worlds* (Jens)

PICTURE FILE:

1. Portfolio of Sketches of Greek Gods and Goddesses (Look under *Greece*)
2. Portfolio of Pictures of Ancient Greece (Look under *Greece*)
3. Odds and ends of pictures collected by librarian (Look under *Religions, Gods and Goddesses,* and *Legends, Greek*)

MULTIMEDIA:

Record and filmstrip: *The Glory of Greece* (Learning Resource Center)
Cassette tape and filmstrip: *Greek Gods and Goddesses* (Learning Resource Center)
Flip charts and cassettes: *A Visit to Ancient Cultures: Greece.* (Learning Resource Center)

MUSEUM:

Tate Museum, 106 Arnold St. Second floor: small exhibit of Grecian urns and file of Greek pictures, many of gods and goddesses

PEOPLE:

- Mrs. Armeney, primary school—took trip to Greece last summer.
- Mr. Paris, high school history teacher—lived in Greece one year.
- Mr. Thompson, middle school—has movies he took on his trip to Greece in summer of 1970.

ACTIVITIES:

1. Look up the Greek gods and goddesses using some of the above resources.
2. Plan a dramatization for the rest of the class which shows the human characteristics of the gods, such as rage, jealousy, etc.
3. Make a chart of the gods and goddesses and their jobs to show to the rest of the class.
4. Collect some Greek myths which tell stories about the gods and goddesses and read them to the class during assembly period.
5. Collect pictures of the Greek gods and goddesses as they appeared in various ways in paintings, in bas-relief on vases and buildings, in sculpture.

6. Problems to discuss in your group:
   (a) The Greeks' belief in gods and goddesses had an influence on:
       • how they built their homes?
       • how they educated their children?
       • how they built their theaters?
       • how they lived from day to day?
       • our own lives today?
   (b) Slavery in Ancient Greece was as bad as slavery in America in the middle nineteenth century:
       • slavery is a moral issue?
       • a political issue?
       • a social issue?
       • an emotional issue?
       • a democratic issue?
   (c) Greek gods and goddesses were probably an invention of the minds of early Greeks who sought to explain natural phenomena (such as thunder, lightning, night, etc.) which they could explain in no other way. The decline of such religious beliefs was probably due to the fact that science provided facts for the cause of these natural phenomena.

SUGGESTED PROJECTS:

1. Plan a dramatization for the rest of the class of the material you have found. You may also wish to dramatize your favorite myth.
2. View some of the films listed above and select the one you consider to be best and plan a showing for all the children in the class who are interested.
3. Share the material you have gathered with the group by planning an exhibit of the pictures you have collected and the charts you have made. Make a Greek frieze of the gods as a decorative background for your dramatizations. You may want to present your program wearing Greek costumes to represent the gods.

EVALUATION

How well have you learned what you have studied? Try the test on the next card. Correct your paper by checking it with the answers on the back of the card.

Figure 3-3 (continued)

cards were also designed with thought questions such as: What has happened to the medicinal practices of ancient Greece? Was slavery necessary to the economy of Ancient Greece? What has become of the Olympic Games of Ancient Greece?

The reader can see that the teachers in this open school have used the children's interests to meet general objectives such as: As a result of work in this area children will explore and come to develop many concepts and understandings as shown by the activities they present to the total group and the tests they take. They have also used these interests to develop specific objectives such as: As a result of this activity the children in this group will know the origins

and meanings of the Greek gods and goddesses as evidenced by their ability
to complete a pencil and paper test.

2) *The center must be well-equipped*. For instance, the following list indicates the equipment collected for the social studies center:

- encyclopedias
- reference books
- text books
- dictionary
- *Information Please*
- storybooks
- a classroom file
- a globe
- maps
- magazines
- pamphlets
- radio or TV set
- bookcase
- exhibit shelves
- films
- filmstrips
- tape recorder
- tapes
- box of puppets
- scroll movie
- puppet theater
- costume box with costumes
- social studies kits—commercial
- box of masks
- crafts books
- workbook samples
- file of duplicating masters
- bulletin board of packets for individual contracts
- box of working modules
- calendar of school events and special occasions
- *TV Guide*
- graph paper
- mural paper
- shelf paper
- magic light
- magic chalk and crayons

3) *The center should be attractive*. In some schools the author has visited the general tone of the classroom was one of general confusion and chaos. The rooms were so cluttered and covered with materials that children experienced difficulty in finding their way about. They were continually climbing over *things* and *people*.

Such a disorderly environment is unnecessary. It may even have a highly negative effect on the learning of the children. Too much clutter may void the objective for using centers. The overall impression children should have as they enter the classroom is one of attractiveness: the room should have cohesiveness and harmony. It should *look* as though it was organized so centers are easily identifiable and accessible. Much can be done to obtain this impression: children can help to plan and set up the centers. After a crude floor plan is drawn on the chalkboard, furniture and equipment may be arranged according to the floor plan to make each center functional.

In one classroom, after the arrangement of the room was determined and the materials listed, the aesthetic qualities of the room were discussed. Holding colored construction paper against the walls, the children chose color schemes. A survey of the material available led to a listing of furniture that could be painted and that which could not. Children agreed to bring bricks and planks for the centers where there were no bookcases. These could be painted to carry the color scheme around the room. The class decided to cover the bulletin boards with butcher's paper or old wallpaper and paint them over with water paint which harmonized with the room color scheme to make soft, pleasant backgrounds for mounting pictures and children's work. The possibility of making drapes for the windows and frames for the children's pictures was discussed. Next the class decided which jobs should be done at once and by whom; a list of necessary materials was made, and they formed committees to go to work the next day.

From such a first day's experience the children were well launched on the type of program that can lead them to respect one anothers' abilities, to

Figure 3-4. *A learning center set up for an economics unit.*

appreciate each other's ideas, to accept responsibility, to acquire working skills and new knowledge, to experience new organization techniques, and to create a pleasant working atmosphere. Highly creative children will thrive under such arrangements, and other children will learn skills that contribute to their creative development.

In such an environment children are given independence as soon as they can accept it. Committees are formed to care for the various centers and perform housekeeping and administrative duties. An accepting atmosphere, where children are free to make mistakes without developing guilt feelings, is developed. Teachers and children plan together, and together they solve the problems that arise. In this atmosphere, true democratic living is promoted, and the skills the children practice are those they will need for rich and intelligent living in adulthood.

When the children help to plan and organize their working environment, they make better use of it and can function more effectively in it.

4) *The center must be functional.* A functional classroom is one that is so arranged that the purposes of the program can be fulfilled. Obviously to be functional, centers must be well planned in keeping with general and specific objectives as stated above; they must be attractive enough to draw children, and they must contain proper supplies and equipment so that the children can learn when they work in them. But there are other things to consider in making the centers functional. .

5) *Each center should be easily accessible.* Watch the flow of traffic in the classroom during the first few days after the children come. Is there plenty of room for them to sit around tables when they need to sit? Is there open floor space where they need it? Is there a bottleneck somewhere in the classroom, that is, is there a place or places where children must line up continually and wait for others to pass? Is necessary equipment handy? For instance, do you have the art materials near the sink, the research material near the reading center? Have you considered the flow and type of activity for the daily program? Did you make allowance for quiet and seclusion in the reading center, or did you place that center next to a noisy shop center? Does each center contain materials for *all* children—the bright, the average, and the slow? Have you made allowances for small groups and for individuals?

The answers to these questions will determine to a large degree whether or not the learning centers are functional.

6) *The center must facilitate self-learning activities.* Often this is done by a card file of contracts, modules, projects, assignments, or units as shown previously under the title "Ancient Greece." Since self-learning is emphasized in the open school, curriculum committees concentrate on designing these contracts to help the individual child progress from one step to another.

7) *The center must be equipped with adequate writing materials so children can have at hand materials on which they may write notes, plan reports, or write creative impressions.*

The teacher's tasks in setting up centers are: 1) to provide and plan for ways to evaluate the learning of each individual; 2) to provide for variety and challenge to all age levels and all levels of ability; 3) to provide simple, understandable directions for procedures; 4) to provide an adequate number of manipulative materials to be used in learning; 5) to plot many open-ended "extension" tasks which will promote self-learning; and 6) to plot such a variety of contracts (or whatever) so that almost any need in the classroom can be met.

APPROPRIATE SOCIAL-EMOTIONAL CONDITIONS

Teachers not only must establish or operate within certain physical conditions in order to develop creativity through the teaching of the social studies, they must also be especially sensitive to the social-emotional atmosphere they are creating in their classrooms. A healthy social and emotional climate is necessary in order to develop certain social studies objectives. Special attention must be given to the social-emotional climate of the teaching-learning situation, as well.

There is some evidence available in the literature regarding the effect of the creative teacher on the social-emotional atmosphere of the classroom.

In a study by Haplin, Goldenberg and Haplin, measures of creativity correlated negatively with pupil control ideology. The more creative teacher is more of a humanist than the less creative teacher according to this study. Less creative potential teachers tend to be more authoritarian in their pupil control orientations. The study stresses the need to develop creativity in college students preparing to be teachers if we wish to develop more humane teachers.[2]

Creative behavior may be encouraged by the following practices:

1. Reward various kinds and varying degrees of creative achievement among children and encourage individuality, uniqueness, originality, and independence.

2. Develop an atmosphere in the classroom which is accepting and "expectant" to the extent that children feel free to manipulate, experiment with, and explore ideas and objects, and are not threatened with making mistakes or experiencing failure.

3. Help children recognize the value of their own and each other's creative powers and, in so doing, encourage all children to accept the creative child more fully.

4. Stress *both* convergent *and* divergent thinking processes by teaching knowledges that can be used for creative problem-solving; but place emphasis frequently on open-ended situations and develop creative acceptance of realistic limitations in a problem situation.

5. Plan high motivational procedures so that children become involved in

2. Gerald Haplin, Ronald Goldenberg, and Glennelle Haplin, "Are Creative Teachers More Humanistic in their Pupil Control Ideologies?" *Journal of Creative Behavior* 7, No. 4 (1973): 181–186.

Figure 3-5. *Individual differences are encouraged in a study of the Far East in a second grade self-contained classroom.*

their own learnings, and then employ the best techniques of discussion, questioning, and flexible thinking so that they are provided with the opportunity to talk about their ideas.

6. Teach directly for creative development by fostering those skills closely affiliated with it: outlining, summarizing, evaluating, synthesizing, critical thinking, making decisions, passing judgment, visual acuity, retention ability, fluency of thinking, flexibility of thinking, imagination and elaboration.

7. Help the children set reasonable goals that (because they are defined together) are recognized by the teacher, and then help the children arrive at basic principles rather than memorize excessive quantities of facts.

8. Make the curriculum experience-centered and use *all* areas of the curriculum to foster creative development.

9. Avoid unnecessary and excessive conformity.

10. Develop an appreciation of creativity in the classroom.
11. Keep the curriculum "humanized" as defined in Chapter 2.

A great deal of emphasis has been placed on the need for socialization in any social studies program. There are, however, some precautions which must be taken against oversocialization. Socialization can be overdone. Hall and Lindzey suggest the following:

> Socialization is not without its negative qualities. An individual may be over-socialized . . . conceivably an entire society may be exposed to socialization processes that are debilitating rather than preparatory for a fruitful life . . . it [socialization] may destroy the creative spontaneity and vigor which are essential to the most important kinds of human advances.[3]

Hall and Lindzey's quote bears special significance for the creative child. Hallman observes:

> . . . creative persons seem to prefer to work alone rather than with others. The more deeply they become involved with their particular interest, the more they withdraw from society. Hence, despite the high value that society places on creativity, it has not been able to take full advantage of its most innovative people—partly because of the tenuousness of the human relations involved.

Hallman states:

> . . . whereas most problem-solving operations are objective, externally oriented and guided by generally accepted laws, creative activity tends to be emotive, internally oriented and guided at least in part by individual aesthetic choices. These involvements produce a sense of personal worth, but they also affect the quality of one's relationships with other people.[4]

One job of the elementary school, it would seem, would be to determine where to strike a happy medium between independent work and sociability for each child, especially the creative child.

APPROPRIATE PSYCHOLOGICAL CONDITIONS

For creative social growth, certain psychological conditions must be set in the classroom. Certain securities must exist to make the child feel safe to venture forth into creative exploration. In addition to those mentioned under social-emotional conditions are the following:

3. Calvin S. Hall and Gardner Lindzey, *Theories of Personality* (New York: John Wiley & Sons, 1973).
4. Ralph J. Hallman, "Human Relations and Creativity," *Journal of Creative Behavior* 8, No. 3 (1974): 161.

1. An absence of threat to self.
2. Confidence that one has the necessary background and ability to face the problem ahead.
3. Self-awareness, the ability to keep in touch with one's feelings.
4. The willingness to be different because of lack of social threat.
5. The ability to accept the ideas of others.
6. The ability to meet failure experiences in social as well as intellectual relations.
7. A great deal of practice in creative thinking.
8. The use of democratic practices in the classroom.
9. The teacher's understanding of the developmental characteristics of children at each age level as well as each child's potential ability so that he or she will know what to expect from each child.
10. The development of strong self-concepts.

APPROPRIATE INTELLECTUAL CONDITIONS

A great deal of emphasis has been placed on divergent thinking processes to develop creativity. Teaching the social studies has long been regarded as helping children to understand the human problems through the problem-solving approach. This approach has been largely constructed of techniques that develop convergent thinking processes, collecting facts already known, and arriving at a solution to a problem that has already been solved by someone else. When we add the development of divergent processes to the convergent thinking processes, we add a new dimension. Social studies teaching will not be considered the teaching of facts and knowledge of the social sciences, but will present facts and knowledges to children with the intent of their applying them to possible solutions to current problems. This calls for skill on the part of the teacher in handling discussion, in phrasing questions, and in developing group abilities and group dynamics. Many of the older methods of teaching, such as the unit method (see Chapter 5 of this book), are especially adaptable to this plan and may be renewed with vigor because of their proven worth and their adaptiveness to the development of creativity.

In the creative teaching of the social studies it must be remembered that creativity cannot be identified by the current intelligence test, yet creativity is a kind of giftedness. Many children will be able to create sound ideas for good human relationships within the classroom. There is no instrument at this writing which will help the teacher predict this. He or she can only make certain that creative children are identified by listening to them and watching their behavior. The teacher must also be aware that all children are capable of creative production to some degree. The best way to identify creative talent is to look for originality in thought, ability to redefine, flexibility of thinking, associational fluency, ability to verbalize fluently, ideational fluency, and the ability to elaborate and evaluate. Children who seem to possess these qualities are probably more creative than other children.

These abilities may be developed in children through carefully planned lessons. They are all components of the creative act and can be developed separately. Setting the proper intellectual conditions for developing creative power means that teachers work at each of these abilities and that they make sure they are frequently used in creative problem-solving.

Another factor required for creative production is an understanding of the creative process. When teachers know how creative problem-solving takes place, they will not be tempted to force creativity. This knowledge can help the teacher understand the child who is in the process of creating, and will make a decided difference in the type of homework and school assignments which are given. It will also influence methodology in the classroom. Creative problem-solving requires a different set of skills than other types of problem-solving; it requires the whole of the individual—his or her experience, knowledge, skills, intellect, convergent thinking abilities, flexibility, personality, and a complete absorption in the problem.

In creative problem-solving the solution offers tremendous satisfaction—not only because a problem has been solved and a job completed, but because the product has aesthetic qualities and both the process and the product have been satisfying to the creator, who has given of himself or herself to the project. Something of the child has emerged in a form that he or she recognizes (and which others recognize) as his or her own unique contribution to the solution.

On the preceding pages we have discussed various organizational plans which make possible the individual development of children of varying abilities. In setting conditions for intellectual development in the social studies this becomes a prime factor. If all children are to learn, all must be motivated and all ability levels must be provided for.

Intellectual conditions for developing creative powers and social studies concepts follow:

1. Provision must be made for teaching all ability levels.
2. Provision must be made for developing a variety of interests.
3. Provision must be made for individualized instruction and for personalized teaching.
4. The material chosen for instruction must be *relevant* to the children. If it is not relevant but important for some reason, efforts to motivate the child must be doubled so the material does become relevant.
5. Topics for study should rise out of current interests and should be planned to develop many skills, characteristics, knowledges, values and appreciations (see the report from Glendale in Chapter 2).
6. Materials should be integrated and related and taught in large blocks of time so that achievement is possible.
7. The room should contain a great deal of intellectual stimuli: bulletin

boards, posters, graphs, charts, materials made by the children, books, workbooks, projects, etc.

8. Multiple resources must be available so children can learn and be stimulated: television sets, cassettes, films, filmstrips, pictures, books, magazines, slides, graphs, maps, charts, etc.

9. Both group and individual work assignments should be planned.

10. The child should have several options from which to choose his or her own learning experiences.

11. Topics must be presented in relation to the child's own experiences and contemporary life—knowledges should be put to work to solve current problems.

12. Accuracy in gleaning information should be stressed. The teacher will need to make certain that he or she is well aware of current problems as well as historical fact.

13. Both convergent and divergent thinking should be stressed.

14. Knowledge should be pursued in many instances simply for the joy of knowing; that is, there will be many instances when a child will discover a new fact and relay it enthusiastically to the rest of the class. Knowledge of one fact can sometimes change a child's behavior.

A PLAN FOR CURRICULUM ORGANIZATION

The physical environment of a classroom will be determined to a great degree by: 1) the objectives of the social studies and other curriculum areas, 2) the structure of the building, and 3) the available resources.

In curriculum planning, Ragan suggests the following steps:

1. The staff of a school *determines long-term and short-term objectives.* Once objectives have been determined, they serve as a goal for planning and teaching.

2. *Strategies for meeting the objectives are determined and experiences necessary to fulfill them are planned.*

3. *An organizational plan is then designed* which makes possible the attainment of the objectives and the execution of the experiences.

4. During and after each experience, it is *evaluated in terms of the appropriate objectives.*

5. This evaluation provides a basis for *setting new objectives, for determining which of the old objectives were not met* and for planning the next steps in each child's learning.[5]

5. William Ragan and G. D. Shepherd, *Modern Elementary Curriculum,* 5th ed. (New York: Holt, Rinehart & Winston, 1977).

Summary

Certain conditions may be set by the teacher in the classroom to bring creativity into the open where it can be used and reinforced. These conditions include the physical set-up of the environment, the social-emotional climate of the classroom, the psychological conditions established by school personnel, and the kind of intellectual stimulus planned by the teacher.

The key to the development of creative problem-solving and creative endeavor, however, lies almost entirely in the teacher's responsiveness to the child's creative efforts. Teachers can teach for creative development by engaging children in a sequence of experiences that give them practice in many of the skills of creative thinking, as later chapters in this book will demonstrate. In this sense the teacher can guide and hope to develop creative effort. But because the answers to the problems are not known at the onset of a lesson (indeed, the problems themselves may not all be known), the guidance and direction set by the teacher will result in behavior or processes or products which are not predetermined. In this sense they are not taught because they are discovered as the process develops.

Setting the proper conditions will draw out creativeness, and acceptance and reinforcement of the creative process or product will encourage its appearance again and again.

The setting required for developing creativity in children is also one which will enable the teacher to fulfill the objectives for social studies teaching as described in the previous chapter.

Organizational plans which appear to set conditions for development of creativity and social studies as they are described in this volume are: various forms of grouping, the non-graded school, the multi-graded school, some forms of team teaching, and the concept of the open classroom.

Departmentalization plans and strict personalized instruction plans tend to hinder the development of social studies as it is here described and creative thinking as well.

To the College Student

1. Frank Lloyd Wright once said, "A house is space enclosed for a purpose." Might this definition also be applied to a school? If so, what modifications in the plans of the traditional schoolroom would you advocate as a necessary change for the development of creativity?

2. Consider the conditions described in this chapter and use them as an evaluation of your college classrooms. Are some of your college classrooms better set up to develop creativity than others? Would you say that most college administrators consider the development of creativity to be one of their major objectives?

3. Plan a self-contained college classroom that will not only accomplish the objectives

of perpetuating knowledge in the subject matter area for which it is intended, but will develop creativity as well. Be sure to consider equipment, seating arrangement, facilities, etc.

4. Make a list of objectives you would have as a teacher for any grade level on the first day of school. Plan a classroom setup that will make it possible for you to accomplish these objectives.

5. Work out an organizational plan for a self-contained classroom on any grade level that is as ideal as possible for developing creative production in the children.

To the Classroom Teacher

1. Make a check list of factors necessary for the development of creative thinking and creative production as described in this chapter and use it to evaluate your own classroom. If you can recognize the deficiencies in current existing conditions, make plans to remedy them. Is your classroom really a working laboratory?

2. Look at the description of social-emotional conditions necessary for creative production in the classroom as described in this chapter. With these conditions in mind, consider the following questions:
   a. Can you as a teacher overpraise a child's work? What dangers are inherent in this?
   b. Is it possible for children to be creative under certain restrictions and pressures? When is this condition acceptable or even necessary?
   c. What parts of your school program are already devoted to developing many of the components of creativity identified in Chapters 1, 2 and 3?
   d. In one given situation a group of children were allowed to use any materials they chose from a large supply to design a poster. In another situation they were asked to construct a poster with only four basic materials. Which situation set the best conditions to challenge creative thinking and creative production?

3. In light of the information presented in this chapter, examine your plan of organization for the school day and consider this question: At what times during the school day does your plan best allow for creative development?

4. Educators have often been accused of negating one objective of education in attempting to accomplish another. If the development of creative thinking is to be an objective of the elementary school, what current accepted practices will need to be changed so that creativity will not be negated?

5. It is fairly certain that, if creative thinking is an objective of education, parents will need to understand this new concept. Plan an educational program for the parents of your school which will help them to understand the concepts of creativity and the manner in which you are attempting to implement these concepts. Do not overlook the use of popular current modes of communication, such as the P.T.O., the school visiting night, report cards, etc.

6. Does your school have a place on the report card for indicating the child's creative growth? Should it have? How would you measure the creative growth of children? How would you report it?

To the College Student and the Classroom Teacher

1. Teachers can provoke creativity in many ways. One is the manner by which they ask questions. For instance, when a teacher says, "What is that supposed to be?" when viewing a child's painting, he or she is practically demanding that the child answer with a definite label. "Tell me about your painting," allows the child to describe in his or her own creative way the creative product. Below is a list of questions the author recently heard in various classrooms. Reword them so they are more likely to evoke creative responses in the children:

   a. "I have placed on the chalkboard a list of the inventions resulting from Edison's invention of the electric light. Why is Thomas Edison an important man to remember?"

   b. "The firefighter is a community worker. In what ways does the firefighter help us?"

   c. "Read the next chapter in your social studies book and tell me the names of the main products of Argentina.

2. Which of the following projects, suggested by various textbooks, set conditions for creative activity, and which do not?

   a. "Draw a plan of a medieval castle as it is described in this chapter." (Grade 5)

   b. "Make three houses like this. Color one red, one blue, and one yellow." (Grade 1)

   c. "Make a list of the states and opposite each write its capital." (Grade 6)

   d. "Visit a supermarket and list all the ways you see foods being preserved today. Try to find out at what time on your time-line each way of preserving food was introduced." (Grades 4–6)

   e. "If you live near a library, visit it and ask to see some real old newspapers. Then look at the advertisements. Notice the differences in tools, clothes, materials, and services for sale. Notice, too, the difference in prices. What brought about all these changes?" (Grades 4–6)

   f. "Find a copy of a constitution to see just what it is that people believe in. The Constitution of the United States would be a good one for this purpose." (Grade 5)

   g. "Look at home to see if you have some articles made in the Lowland Countries. Do you perhaps have some Delft china or a Belgian rug? Make a list of all the things you can find that members of your class have from the Lowlands of Europe." (Grade 6)

   h. "After you have found some children to whom to write in England, make a tape-recording of your British program and mail it to them. Ask them if their teacher will send one to you for you to play in your class." (Grade 6)

   i. "List three causes of the War Between the States." (Grade 6)

3. All of the following people were considered to be eccentric or foolish at one time in their lives. Were they? How do you explain people's attitude toward them?

   Robert Fulton (Fulton's Folly)

   De Witt Clinton (Clinton's Ditch)

   The Wright Brothers

   Alexander Graham Bell

Sir Isaac Newton

Christopher Columbus

4. How does each of the beliefs of the above people demonstrate one or more principles of the creative process? *Example*: The concept that water does not run uphill is an example of the idea of functional fixedness and prevented many people from understanding Clinton's concept of the lock that could raise boats to higher levels.

5. Make a list of some of the characteristics of creative people and check those which you would like to see developed in all children because they are essential to creative and aesthetic living in a democratic society.

6. Maslow states that the status need comes before the creative need and that highly creative acts are performed generally by people who are comfortable with their status. Torrance states that creative children often cause tension within groups. Could it be that their creative ideas serve as a threat to other group members? Discuss this with your classmates.

Selected Bibliography

BERGER, EVELYN, and WINTERS, BONNIE. *Social Studies in the Open Classroom: A Practical Guide*. New York: Columbia University Teachers' College, 1973.

BLITZ, BARBARA. *The Open Classroom: Making It Work*. Boston: Allyn and Bacon, 1973.

CHRISTIE, T. "Environmental Factors in Creativity." *Journal of Creative Behavior* 2, No. 1 (Winter 1970), 13–31.

CHURCHILL, E. RICHARD, and CHURCHILL, LINDA R. *Enriched Social Studies Teaching*. Belmont, Calif.: Fearon, 1973.

GAGNE, ROBERT. *The Conditions of Learning*. 3rd ed. New York: Holt, Rinehart & Winston, 1977.

GOLDBERG, MIRIAM L.; PASSOW, A. HARRY; and JUSTMAN, JOSEPH. *The Effects of Ability Grouping*. New York: Teachers' College Press, 1966.

HOFFMAN, ALAN, and RYAN, THOMAS. *Social Studies and the Child's Expanding Self*. New York: Intext.

JOHNSTON, HIRAM, et al. *The Learning Center Ideabook*. Boston: Allyn and Bacon, 1978.

KENWORTHY, LEONARD S. *Social Studies for the Seventies*. 2nd ed. Lexington, Mass.: Xerox.

KOHL, HERBERT R. *The Open Classroom*. New York: Random House, 1970.

PRESTON, RALPH C., and HERMAN, WAYNE L. *Teaching Social Studies in the Elementary School*. 4th ed. New York: Holt, Rinehart & Winston, 1974.

RAGAN, WILLIAM B., and MCAULEY, J. D. *Social Studies for Today's Children*. 2nd ed. Englewood Cliffs, N.J.: Prentice-Hall, 1973.

SMITH, JAMES. *Setting Conditions for Creative Teaching in the Elementary School*. Boston: Allyn and Bacon, 1966.

TABA, HILDA; DURKIN, MARY C.; FRAENKEL, JACK R.; and MCNAUGHTON, ANTHONY H. *A Teacher's Handbook to Elementary Social Studies*. 2nd ed. Reading, Mass.: Addison-Wesley, 1971.

TAYLOR, JOY. *Organizing the Open Classroom: A Teacher's Guide to the Integrated Day*. New York: Schocken Books, 1974.

THOMAS, JOHN I. *Learning Centers: Opening Up the Classroom*. Boston: Holbrook Press, 1975.

THOMAS, R. MURRAY, and BRUBAKER, DALE, eds. *Teaching Elementary Social Studies: Readings*. Belmont, Calif.: Wadsworth, 1972.

WALBERG, HERBERT J., and THOMAS, SUSAN CHRISTIE. *Characteristics of Open Education: Toward an Operational Definition*. Newton, Mass.: Education Development Center, 1971.

4

Developing Organizational Skills in Children: Pupil-Teaching Planning

Throughout the development of civilization, man has been, above all, an orderer. Throughout time and in all places of the earth he has transformed wild hillsides into gardens of ordered beauty. Working his will upon the chaotic watershed of the Tennessee, he organized that huge area into a cultivated valley of farms and towns, with channels for production and distribution, transportation, communication, and markets. In the recurring episodes of Western history, creative men have transformed political anarchy into order, rebuilt disrupted economic systems, and stated the mood and the mind of the people in poems, songs, plays, paintings, dances. The creative task is always the same, whether it be in art, science or invention: that of reducing miscellany to order. This is the principle of form, variously called "Heaven's first law," the "first principle of the universe," "modern science's final explanation," and "the foundation of all art." It is the basis of the sciences and arts of man. Its synonyms are organization, organism, the unity of the whole.

HAROLD RUGG[1]

INTRODUCTION

In Chapter 3 the need for careful organization was discussed in some detail. As Harold Rugg pointed out in the opening quotation of this chapter, humans are naturally orderers. To be able to live life to its fullest, especially in these times, one must be able to organize. Among the many skills to be taught to children, perhaps the skills of organization are of top priority. A day in a modern elementary school affords an excellent, meaningful arena in which to work.

1. Harold Rugg, *Imagination: An Inquiry into the Source and Conditions that Stimulate Creativity* (New York: Harper & Row, 1963): 124–125.

A specific function of the social studies program is to inform youth about the many types of human relationships and to provide opportunities through which the citizen develops those capacities and qualities necessary for successful participation in human relationships. One of the greatest opportunities for developing the skills of organization and the capacity for successful participation in human relationships is through pupil-teaching planning. Teaching the skills of organization with complete personal involvement contributes to the development of creative powers. The idea of pupil-teaching planning, popular a few years ago, has fallen into disuse in many schools because of new organizational plans which neglect this important activity. As an aid to creative development, and as a curriculum "humanizer," pupil-teacher planning needs reviewing.

Berger, Guilford, and Christensen contend that planning must be broadly conceived as a term covering a number of classes of activities and entailing a number of separate abilities.[2] Their research in planning enabled them to isolate and define the following abilities as those involved in planning: verbal comprehension, numerical facility, visualization, general reasoning, logical evaluation, ideational fluency, education of conceptual relations, judgment, originality, and adaptive flexibility. Four new abilities were labeled by the researchers: ordering, elaboration, perceptual foresight, and conceptual foresight.

Many creative children are challenged by disorder; they enjoy creating order, seeing relationships, and setting goals. They thrive on independence and the ability to express themselves. Creative children often respond well to developing organizational plans.

Organization skills should be identified at each age level and taught throughout the day as a vital part of each social studies program. From the time that first graders begin by organizing their desks, their classroom and their materials up to the point where middle graders organize their own daily program, successively more difficult skills of organization should be developed.

Of the various organizational plans, it is clear that the open classroom plan offers the greatest opportunity for developing independent organizational skills in children. Organizational skills can be taught in all types of classroom structures, however.

OPENNESS VS. PERMISSIVENESS

Caution must be exercised in interpreting the concepts of *openness* and *permissiveness*. Openness and permissiveness are not necessarily the same. Openness is the term applied to the situation where the content of the children's learnings are not pre-determined and where they are in an environment where they may make many choices and decisions. Openness also means open-endedness: the ability to ask questions of children or to present the children with problems to be solved which have many answers rather than one, thus allowing them to develop critical thinking, logic and creativity in their learning.

2. R. M. Berger, J. P. Guilford, and P. R. Christensen, "A Factor-Analytic Study of Planning Abilities," *Psychological Monographs* 71, No. 6 (1957).

In this volume permissiveness means allowing the child to try his or her own ideas, to experiment and explore, often without the advice of an adult. It means to allow the child to make mistakes, to encourage the setting of individual learning patterns and codes of behavior.

Both openness and permissiveness have been interpreted to mean classrooms free from structures, but this is a misconception.

All children have some need for structure, for limits to be set, for goals which can be attained, and for an orderly process of reaching those goals. Children differ in their ways of expressing the need for this structure, but they all have the need. Often the obvious need is not the one that needs satisfying; because a child is uncomfortable in an open environment, for instance, does not mean that all of his or her learning should be structured. If the teacher does not set up a clear structure, the efforts of the learners are dissipated in attempting to create some sort of order by which they can learn. Children must have a great deal of experience with order, principles, and structure before they can create a structure of their own.

Creativity research is rich in data that testify to openness. These data are philosophically in conflict with the current practice of step-by-step organization which ends in closed problem solving. Robert Sample states:

> The researchers in creativity have found that divergent thinking is the most rewarding quality in the early stages of problem solutions. These same researchers do not discredit the convergent thinking that inevitably emerges in the final stages of solving problems. However, they voice concern about the pressure toward convergent thinking established in modern curricula as a result of the content and process biases.
>
> The research coming from models created to insure content integrity and cognitive integrity has biased the scene so that we are only currently becoming concerned with the qualities of divergence in creativity research. In the tradition of our Judeo-Christian heritage we have been coerced into believing that virtue lies within the tidy boundaries of logic and internal consistency. Psychologically, convergent thinking was most compatible with such a philosophical view. History, however, does not allow such an operational view to prevail. The great historical turning points were always accompanied by divergent production. The Renaissance, whether Arabic or Christian, was a refutation of convergent, internally consistent traditions of the contemporary scene. Bacon's break with Aristotelian precedents freed science from dogma and plunged it into an age of experimentation.
>
> In education there seems to be a tacit assumption that the greatness of an individual student will exceed the constraint of the times. To me, the urgent question of modern education is simple. . . . "Why wait?" Why should we as educators, in an effort to preserve the sanctity of precedent, wait for students to exceed our constraints *when by changing the constraints we could insure it*?[3]

In Sample's quotation lies the inherent danger of developing all organizational skills: the danger of over-organization at the expense of creative growth.

3. Robert Sample, "Go Out and Learn" (Boulder, Colorado: Earth Science Educational Program Newsletter, n.d.).

DEVELOPING ORGANIZATIONAL SKILLS
THROUGH PUPIL-TEACHER PLANNING

Those qualities which contribute to the development of creativity as mentioned by Guilford and others often appear in the planning process.

Aside from its contribution to the development of creative powers, pupil-teacher planning is important for many reasons. First, one learns to plan by having the experience of planning. Many adults do not know how to organize and plan because they have never learned. College students often must take courses in which they learn how to study and how to plan a school day because they waste hours of time in aimless activity and poor study techniques. This results in failing grades in spite of a high intelligence. Children should plan to learn how to organize with ease and skill.

Second, children should know the purpose behind the work they do. When children themselves have a part in planning, they are better motivated to their tasks and the work is meaningful to them. Learning is more effective when the learners participate in the planning of the learning act and in the carrying out of those plans.

Third, creativity is a way of living. The elements necessary to develop creative people are being promoted in helping children to organize, to see relationships, to make decisions, pass judgments, preplan, and use their imaginations. Careful planning does not mean overly-structured classrooms—in fact, it is only when the teacher and children have set goals together that they can fully take advantage of incidental learnings that arise and use them to accomplish predetermined objectives. Only through careful planning on the part of the teacher and then careful planning between each student and the teacher can an open classroom exist successfully.

Finally, pupil-teacher planning serves to motivate children to new learnings by helping them find opportunities each day when they can put known skills and knowledges to work in new experiences. It also gives relevance to new learnings because the child sees the need of the new learnings and relates them to his or her own needs.

Pupil-teacher planning places responsibility on the child. Each child has the opportunity to plan the day to some extent. This results in a great deal of independence and develops self-discipline, which is true discipline. It encourages the child to think critically and make important decisions. The learner becomes more self-directing.

Children who, with the guidance of teachers, help plan their own work soon learn the value of the communication of ideas. They see that ideas from many people are often better than ideas from one person. They experience group dynamics and true democratic processes. And their free time is used in fulfilling the work they have set out to accomplish as a group or as individuals. Goals become clearer to the child.

Pupil-teacher planning begins with the abilities of the children, anywhere, at any time. Many children come to kindergarten with a fine sense of organization and an ability to plan. These children have helped parents plan picnics, they have planned how to spend their allowance, they have had a share in planning their own parties and their holiday fun. They can plan with the teacher in the kindergarten. Generally, such planning takes place in several periods throughout the day, for the attention span is sometimes short, and the plans, if recorded on the board, cannot be read by children at this age.

not always true

Careful and beneficial pupil-teacher planning cannot be carried out unless the teachers themselves are masters at planning and organizing. They must make careful long-term plans to serve as guides. These plans are not fulfilled to the letter—to follow them rigidly would hinder creativity. They are often modified or changed, but they guide the group to goals and aims that give purposeful direction. Most of all, teachers must include plans on *how to plan with the students*. The teachers described in the classrooms in this volume up to this point are masters at setting up plans on how to plan with their students.

Often teachers formulate adequate plans for step-by-step planning but fail to provide plans for a physical set-up to carry them out. If the teacher is dividing the class into committees after a general discussion, it is well to give some children the responsibility of arranging the desks and chairs in groups before the general group disperses. When they are ready to go into committees, the teacher can say, "Let's let Bill's committee meet at this table, Anne's will meet here, and Joe's group will meet in the reading center." A set of placards with numbers is sometimes used as an economical way of keeping things moving. A placard is placed on each table or in each center, and Bill's group uses Table 1, for instance.

don't agree

The physical arrangement for each period must be anticipated if the daily program is to function smoothly and children are to keep out of each other's way. Centers can help in determining physical organization. Children working on art projects will use the art center; those doing research will use the reading center. If the teacher can keep a visual image of the children at work in mind as he or she plans the day's work, provisions for a variety of grouping can be made with a minimum of confusion.

An interplay of ideas is necessary if creativity is to be developed, and careful plans for various kinds of grouping make such interplay possible. Anticipating difficulty or hitches in *new* organizational patterns to be used with children often gives the teacher the foresight to deal with any problems that might arise. A country school teacher, for example, who was taking a group to a movie theater for the first time, helped the children dramatize these situations: buying the tickets, entering the dark theater, finding seats with the aid of an usher, watching the new medium they would see. This type of planning through role-playing gave the children security and helped to make the trip a successful one.

Procedures in planning, as in all good teaching, should be varied. The children's ideas should be used and are often as effective as those of the teacher. Skill in planning is developmental; the goal is to lead each child toward independence and to give each self-direction.

In the verbal observations which follow, taken from classrooms I have visited, I have used the plan of the teacher and students for the entire day so the reader can understand that, although the skill of planning can be a part of social studies objectives, it can be applied to the entire subject matter plan for the school day.

AN EXPERIENCE IN PUPIL-TEACHER PLANNING: SELF-CONTAINED SUBURBAN KINDERGARTEN

Miss Ellis is the kindergarten teacher in the Glendale school mentioned in Chapter 3. Hers is a self-contained classroom in an industrial suburb. Her students come largely from middle-middle, upper-middle, and lower-upper class families. Most of them have their own rooms at home and have access to books, television sets, phonograph or high-fidelity sets, automobiles, and toys. More of them have ridden on planes than on trains. The children are well dressed. The parents are very interested in school, and a strong P.T.O. (Parent-Teacher Organization) makes communication between home and school very effective.

The school staff is composed of forty classroom teachers, a part-time school psychologist, a principal, a secretary, an art teacher, a music teacher, a librarian, and a resource center person.

Although part of the school is designed for open classroom teaching, the kindergarten classrooms can be classified as "modified self-contained." The staff feels that the objectives they have set up for the kindergarten are best met in a self-contained setting.

Miss Ellis is a good teacher. She knows "fives" well. She plans her daily program to meet their needs and to capitalize on their interests.

On one particular bright October morning, she planned a day in keeping with her knowledge about them as a group, and about each as an individual. Her plans included plans to help the children to plan.

At 9:30 they began to arrive. Of the twenty children, only Billy Jones was still timid about coming into the room. Miss Ellis felt triumphant today, however. It was the first day that Billy did not cry! She credited this to the fact that today she finally managed to have something on hand that caught Billy's interest immediately, so quickly in fact that he did not have time to think of his mother watching hopefully from the automobile at the curb. The object that had done it was a real, soft, fuzzy rabbit which Billy could love. He sat with it now, in his lap, stroking it with gentle, tender pats of his chubby fingers.

By October all the children knew of the regular classroom routines. Miss Ellis greeted each at the door and engaged in small talk with them. They brought her the usual selection of offerings: a fistful of goldenrod plucked from the fields along the way, a red apple from the tree in someone's back yard, some pictures of farm animals and some pictures of babies collected from magazines, a few toys, and some bags holding secrets for "Sharing Time."

The children hung their jackets and sweaters and went to work and play with the many things available in the room. As soon as all were present, Miss Ellis flicked the light switch. The blinking lights signaled the class to come together for planning time. The children picked up chairs and formed a group around Miss Ellis.

Miss Ellis greeted them all. Today she would see if they were all here, she said, by singing their names. Would they sing back if they were here? After this came "Sharing Time." Brenda had a new doll to show. Peter had a new gun and holster. They talked about many things—a TV show from the evening before, some events that happened at home and on the way to school, a house that was being built next to the play yard. Miss Ellis even managed to get Billy to show the rabbit which he still held lovingly in his lap.

A short planning period followed when Miss Ellis told the group about the new things in the room on this day, and the children told her about the things they planned to do during work period.

"What are we going to do after work time?" asked Miss Ellis. She wanted at this time to put into effect her plans on how to plan. She had collected pictures of children engaged in various kindergarten activities and had mounted them on heavy colored poster paper. There were pictures of children running, singing, eating, going for a walk, and listening to a story. After a discussion of the pictures, Miss Ellis suggested they put the pictures on the chalk tray in the order in which they planned to participate in the pictured activities.

The first activity of the morning was to be the "work period" so the picture of children engaged in a variety of activities was placed on the chalk tray. Next to it a picture of children playing in a rhythm band was placed to show that music would follow the work period. These were followed by pictures of children dancing, eating a snack, resting, taking a walk, playing on the playground, and listening to a story.

As the morning progressed, Miss Ellis frequently suggested that the children "Look at the pictures to see what we are going to do next" or asked, "What do you need to do to get ready for the next activity?" In this way she developed a feeling for a time sequence and a sensitivity to planning and preparing for each period.

She also developed the children's concept of conceptual relations, making judgments, adaptive flexibility, putting events in order, elaboration, perceptual foresight and conceptual foresight mentioned by Berger, Guilford, and Christensen as necessary elements for creative endeavor.

After the short planning session, the children went to their work period. Each child went to his or her designated job except Billy who sat and patted the rabbit. Three children went to the corner of the room where Miss Ellis had set up paints and they fingerpainted on the large tables there. Four children worked at the easels. Four boys and girls went to construct a farm in the block corner. Three more played in the doll center where they immediately assumed roles of the family and acted out housekeeping tasks. Three boys went to the library table to look at the new picture books of farm animals. Two children went to the music center and played songs on the marimba and colored glasses of water.

As soon as Miss Ellis made sure all the children were busy, she went and sat by Billy. They talked about the rabbit. Miss Ellis told him that the rabbit must have a place to stay when they could not allow him to roam freely about the room. She suggested that Billy build him a hutch. Soon they were working together at the tool bench, sawing and pounding.

As soon as Billy could take over by himself, Miss Ellis visited all the groups, listening to the conversation for clues for vocabulary development, watching behavior patterns for clues of sound social growth, jotting down notes and anecdotes to help her plan for future periods, and discussing, suggesting, or intervening whenever necessary.

The groups soon began to change. Children left one activity for another. The hour went by quickly.

Then it was talk time. A flick of the lights and the children began to put away materials. Soon the group was seated on the floor around Miss Ellis. Here they talked about what they had done or were doing. Billy couldn't wait to tell about his rabbit hutch; Marjorie and Ellen showed their fingerpainting; Bob, Marie, Alvin and Russell talked about their easel painting; some children showed their collages made with paper and paste.

The next picture on the chalk tray showed that it was music time. The children chose action songs and sang happily. Miss Ellis then showed them a drum and drumsticks. Each child tried to make a different noise on the drum. Soon they were putting the noises together to make drum rhythms. Miss Ellis added a piano accompaniment. Then she asked Ellen to bring the colored glasses to the front of the room. Ellen had made up a melody during work period. She played it for the children. Miss Ellis also played it on the piano. They discussed the things Ellen's melody made them think of and soon had words to go with it.

> The leaves are falling
> To the ground;
> The wind is dancing
> All around.
> Fall fall fall fall
> Leaves!
> Dance, dance, dance, dance
> Wind!

Before long every child was trying to interpret Ellen's song with body movements. Other rhythmic music followed where the children played out the story of the falling of the October leaves. As children dramatized the story, Miss Ellis made up music to go with these rhythmics.

The next picture showed the children enjoying a mid-morning snack. The children handled this very well. One committee set napkins on the table, another set out the paper cups, another went to bring in the juice from the kitchen. There was a counting of noses, a counting of cups, a counting of chairs. While all took their seats Miss Ellis put a record on the record player. They carried on their small talk with music playing in the background.

As soon as juice time was finished, the children, checking with the "planning" pictures, went for their rugs or blankets for their rest period. Some went to a corner to quietly explore books. Miss Ellis knew that all five-year-olds did not need a mid-morning nap. Provision was made for those that did in one darkened section of the room; the rest understood they might engage in quiet activity. The soft music helped to keep the atmosphere restful.

When rest time was over, Miss Ellis brought the children together again to plan a morning walk. They were to walk to the grocery store at the end of the block to buy their juice and crackers for the next week. Miss Ellis planned to use the walk for other purposes as well: to notice the colors in the leaves, the sky and houses; to feel the air, to smell autumn smells. All of these experiences would be used later in vocabulary building or in creative music situations. The shopping trip was also the base for a short unit on economics.

The children planned how they would walk, who should do the buying, what the groceries should cost, and how they would cross the street. They discussed the things they would look for, the houses they would pass and the amount of time they would take. Jackets and sweaters were then put on and the shopping trip went off as planned.

There was even time left when the children returned to play for a while on the jungle gym, the swings, and the playground merry-go-round.

Back in the room the children talked about their trip. Miss Ellis read them a story about Peter Rabbit. Billy held the rabbit all during the story, but he volunteered to be Mr. MacGregor when the children dramatized it.

While they were getting ready to go home Miss Ellis started to sing the rabbit song. They all hopped to the door where the school bus was waiting. Here they waved goodbye.

Miss Ellis turned and faced the room. It was certainly quiet without the children. But it had been a good day—especially where Billy was concerned.

As the year progressed, little by little Miss Ellis led the children into more complicated forms of planning. For instance, as the children learned numbers, Miss Ellis numbered the pictures she used in planning the daily program. A few of the children showed definite signs of a readiness to read. For them she placed a symbolic verbal representation printed on a card by each picture, such as "We read," "We sing," and "We eat." Still later she put these phrases on a chart labeled OUR PLANS away from the pictures, and the advanced children in the class quickly learned to read the daily plans from the chart. By the time this group reached the first grade they were veterans at helping the teacher plan a daily schedule.

Notice these important things about the way Miss Ellis planned for her kindergarten in the self-contained classroom described here:

1. She planned only one or two periods at a time because five-year-olds grow restless if they are kept at one thing too long. Their attention span is not yet developed for long, "listening" periods and generally cannot be relied on for too long. Also, their memories are short, and they cannot remember for long what they are to do. At the same time she planned for the day so that advanced children could develop their skills in planning.

2. She planned a few new activities around some common fixed activities.

She planned a work period first because the children came from home well-rested and wanting a great deal of activity (five-year-olds work off their energy by spurts of movement). She planned some activities at the *same time* of day she always planned them since five-year-olds receive a great deal of security from fixed and routine periods during their day. Often they denote time from a familiar or fixed part of the day, such as, "I'll do that after my nap," or, "We took a walk to the grocery store after our juice." Fixed periods in a five-year-old's day give him a base from which to operate. Between these fixed periods there can be a great deal of flexibility and creativeness in planning.

3. She planned for many short, changing activities. In so doing she met the physical, social, and emotional needs of the five-year-olds.

4. Within her master plan there was a great deal of flexibility and allowance for children's ideas to be used in the planning of the short periods.

5. Her planning was concerned with the actions of people. She was child-oriented rather than things-oriented. All the children's ideas were used. She helped them to plan a balanced day.

6. She used symbols in her planning which all children could understand, namely pictures, then words.

7. She devised a system of planning wherein all ability levels were challenged—from pictures to simple reading charts.

8. Miss Ellis fulfilled her objectives for social studies by working on them throughout the day rather than isolating them to one block of time. She used the humanistic approach to teaching. Her concern for children and her ability to meet their needs and interests was apparent always. The children were developing many understandings and practicing many social skills. Because she used the planning time as a time when they engaged in decision-making, it was considered part of her social studies program. The trip to the grocery store was a part of her planned activity to meet social objectives, and the work period was her way of providing for follow-up activities. Billy was having his own special study with the rabbit. Even music time was a discussion of environment and the change of seasons. In her planning Miss Ellis used correlation, integration, and individual teaching to help children attain social studies objectives.

PUPIL-TEACHER PLANNING: FIRST GRADE LEVEL

Miss Angel is the first grade teacher in the Glendale School. Her classroom is a modified self-contained form of organization. Although one wing of the Glendale School is experimenting with open education, Miss Angel is working with three other first grade teachers in her wing on easing the children into an ungraded situation.

Most of the children in Miss Angel's room were in Miss Ellis's room last year so she is able to adapt and build on the work started by Miss Ellis in the kindergarten. Miss Angel believes strongly that the ability to plan is one organizational skill all children should learn at an early age. She feels it is a great step in building independence in children.

Miss Angel believes that children learn best when they participate in setting goals and in evaluating their own work. When she plans from day to day, Miss Angel does not tie up every period by writing lesson plans to cover every minute of the day. Rather, she organizes the jobs to be done into blocks of time so she can encourage and guide the children in their own planning. In her plans, she makes notes as to how she will plan with the children. She also makes detailed plans for the periods when she knows they will come together for instruction *and* for the times when they will be meeting in smaller groups.

Miss Angel began the day by reviewing the program printed on charts for the previous day and checking off the jobs completed. This established continuity from day to day in the children's work. Then, following up on Miss Ellis' excellent beginnings, she used both pictures and words on a pocket chart to plot the sequence of the daily program.

Within this daily schedule, Miss Angel helped the children plan from period to period so each child knew exactly what he or she was to accomplish. From the simple plan which follows Miss Angel developed her day.

PLANS FOR TUESDAY

Morning
- We work
- We plan
- We work
- We eat
- We talk
- We dance
- We sing

Afternoon
- We read
- We play outdoors
- We listen: arithmetic
- We go home

This daily schedule, when translated into action, went something like this:

8:45 We Work

The children arrived and hung up their coats. She greeted each one and helped each find an unfinished job from the day before, or some other activity to pursue.

9:00 We Plan

Miss Angel flicked the lights and the children brought their chairs to the front of the room in a semi-circle facing the empty pocket charts. One other chart hung on the wall. It was a chart to which the children added jobs at the end of each period. It said "Things We Need to Do" and under it were listed about 40 items. From this chart the children planned the day, putting the pictures and strips of cardboard in the pocket-chart to show the sequence of events. Then Miss Angel used her notes to discuss briefly what each child would do during the Work Period.

9:20 We Work

Many things were accomplished during the work period. The children were working on a farm unit for social studies. Last week they had visited a farm and they were now using the trip to develop skills and knowledge. Most of the children were pursuing jobs of their own interest which cut across subject matter lines. This is what took place during the Work Period:

Allen, Jimmy and Paula (who were excellent readers) were looking up the answers to some questions the children had asked since their return from the farm. Some sample questions were: 1) After the milk is put in the trucks at the farm, how does it get to us? 2) Why is the milk chilled? 3) How do people in cities get milk when there are no cows there?

There were four easels in the room so Dennis, Mary, Irene and Marsha were to have their turn at painting pictures of their trip to the farm. Dennis wanted many pictures because he was making a book which he wanted to illustrate.

Pete, Richie and Mark had been fascinated by the incubator so Miss Angel had obtained materials for them to construct a simple incubator where they would actually hatch some eggs for the rest of the class to watch.

Gladys, Cheryl, David and Esther chose block play for their work period. They wanted to construct a barn with stanchions for the cows.

Bill went to the construction center where he worked at making a milk truck.

Esther and Michael modeled clay cows, milk stools and farm equipment to go in the barn.

Lucy, Al, Isabel and Patty painted a mural about the farm on a huge sheet of paper fastened to the side wall.

Some of the children had odd jobs to do: Eileen figured the number of children absent so she could make out the attendance report. She used an abacus to help her. Dick, who had already learned to print, made a work chart for Miss Angel. Margie, who was on the housekeeping committee, watered the plants and took care of the rabbit in the hutch in one corner of the room. Ellen set up the puppet stage which was to be used later in the day.

Many children finished the jobs they had planned to do. At this point, they did one of two things. They came to Miss Angel to have her read the chart for other things to do, or they chose something they wanted to do themselves. Some read books, some painted, three children fingerpainted, some worked puzzles, others played house in the housekeeping center. Still others made a scrapbook cover for pictures collected on farms, some practiced writing their names or made charts for use during the day, and one pasted pictures on chart paper for Miss Angel for the afternoon reading group.

9:50

Miss Angel had been able to observe, help and guide during the work period. She took notes on each of the children. Ten minutes before the time for the period to end she flicked the lights and advised the children that it was time to clean up. Mary and Allen took this as a signal to set up the tables with napkins for the mid-morning snack. David and Michael went to the cafeteria at the end of the hall to get the chocolate and white milk. Esther put graham crackers in a basket.

10:00 We Eat

By 10:00 the work materials were put away and everyone was seated and ready to eat. Miss Angel played a recording softly while the children ate and talked.

10:15 We Talk

At 10:15 the tables were cleared and Miss Angel and the children talked about the Work Period. They discussed the good and bad points about it and decided on ways they might improve it on the following day.

Allen, Jimmy and Paula gave the answers to some of the questions they had read about.

Dennis, Mary, Irene and Marsha told about their pictures.

Gladys, Cheryl, David and Esther dramatized a farm story with the clay cows and props made by Esther and Michael for their block-made barn.

All the children evaluated the mural and decided it would take another day to finish it.

Miss Angel then asked, "What do each of you need to do next?" After each child told what he had accomplished during the period, the next steps were written down for planning the next day's program.

Those who finished their jobs chose other ones for the next day.

10:40 We Dance

Today the children had worked out rhythms of farm animals. The climax of the period had been the barnyard song they created, put to music and danced. Each child's individuality had been plainly demonstrated here in that they each imitated a different animal in the barnyard.

11:00 We Sing

Miss Angel then taught the children a few new farm songs. She also gave them a chance to sing their old favorites. She played a delightful record for them called, "A Trip to the Farm" which gave her the opportunity to introduce a violin and a drum for the children to explore.

Afternoon

1:00 We Read

After the children returned from lunch and a noon hour rest, Miss Angel had them participate in a short planning period and then divided them into five groups. She had planned and organized this part of the day so she could work with several groups and yet the children would not become too tired from sitting too long. For each Miss Angel had different objectives. The children were on different levels of reading ability, so Miss Angel grouped them at least once each day so she could help them with their reading progress. Later in the year Miss Angel would have a highly developed individualized reading program, but at this time she found this kind of grouping more efficient.

Her better readers made up one group of five. These were children who were already reading on a second or third grade level. For this group, Miss Angel had found advanced books. She had printed questions on cards and slipped the cards in the book in places where the answers could be found. Many of the questions were those asked by the children about the farm. After these children finished their assignment, they had a choice of reading other books on the library table or pursuing some quiet activity such as fingerpainting, coloring, clay modeling, doing puzzles, sewing or playing in the playhouse.

Group Two consisted of four children who were reading well in a first grade reader. They were far enough along so Miss Angel was working with them on word analysis and construction.

During the first twenty minutes of the reading period, while Miss Angel was working with Group Two, Group Three was working at their seats. There were nine children in Group Three. These were children who were reading at about the average reading level for this particular time of year. While they were waiting for Miss Angel they were engaged in some work she had planned to help them develop visual discrimination.

When Miss Angel joined the group they checked the work they had done, then put it away. They brought their chairs to the corner of the room where their chart holder was located. First, they chose several old charts about their trip to the farm and read them to each other. Then Miss Angel introduced a picture pasted on the top of a sheet of chart paper. One of the children had pasted the picture for her during the work period. The picture was one of a farmer having trouble with his tractor. Miss Angel was preparing this group to read in books soon. She was helping each child build a good sight vocabulary. She planned to use this picture to help her introduce new words and to use old words in a new context.

The children made up a delightful story called, "The Stubborn Tractor." Miss Angel printed the story on a chart as they dictated it. Then the children read it to each other. While they were doing this, Miss Angel printed the story once more on strips of paper. The children then matched these strips to the original story. Then they cut the strips into phrases and words and matched them to the original story or had fun making mixed-up stories.

After they had mastered this fairly well, Miss Angel gave each child an envelope in which there was a letter from her. This letter gave each child a job to do. The letters were illustrated and were made with words from old charts. John's letter said,

> Dear John,
> Draw a picture of a rabbit.
> We need a rabbit picture.
> We will need it tomorrow.
> Make it a white rabbit.
> Make it look like Peter.
>
> Thank you.
>
> Miss Angel

The children were told that they could engage in some quiet activity or look at their favorite books when their work was done.

Then Miss Angel moved on to the next group. This group was comprised of children who were only in the readiness stage of reading. They were just beginning to read words. While they were waiting for Miss Angel, they had been working on an assignment to help them develop keener auditory discrimination.

Miss Angel then checked Group Five. This group consisted of two children who were slow learners and were not yet ready to read. Miss Angel had allowed them to go to the play corner where they worked with blocks and puzzles to better see how shapes fit together. Then Paula, from the upper group, had been assigned to read them a story.

2:00 We Play Outdoors

The children went to the playground and for the first ten minutes were allowed to run and leap at will. Then Miss Angel called them together for an organized game. After the new game, they played an old favorite. Then they had time to swing, to use the see-saws and other playground equipment under Miss Angel's supervision.

2:30 We Listen

The children came into the classroom and settled down at once to listening period. They knew they would have a story and today Miss Angel had a delightful story about a farm dog. She also showed a short film, *Shep, the Farm Dog.* She used this film to lead into the development of some arithmetic concepts. On this day it was an exploration of the "four" family. They listed or drew all the places where they saw "four"—the dog's legs, the wheels of the automobiles, the window panes grouped by four's, etc. Miss Angel also used a flannel board where the children discovered different combinations of the "four" family. Some children drew these concepts on the chalkboard with colored chalk.

3:10 We Go Home

The children sang a song or two and then put on their coats to go home.

It had been a good day! As Miss Angel reviewed it, she planned the next day. She would have to make definite plans for: planning in the morning, for what each child might do during the work period, for the music and rhythm periods, for her reading groups and for her number work. She would have to select a good children's record and a good story before she went home. Twenty-three programs for twenty-three children, sometimes individual, sometimes joining and sometimes interweaving. She would prepare her materials and take care of the special periods. The children could help with the rest.

By the time children enter the first grade many have a good sense of the order of a school day. Children in Miss Angel's room were able to help organize a full day, but they had to have a ready source of reference to refresh their memories because they could not remember a whole day after they had planned it. Miss Angel, therefore, was using her planning period and chart to help her in the teaching of reading.

Notice that Miss Angel also had a master plan. Because she taught with the purpose of meeting individual needs and developing individual potential, her plans were very detailed. Miss Angel not only had planned the day's work; she had also provided many instances where she and the children would plan one period in greater detail.

The schedule she made out with the children helped them to know how the day would go from period to period. The plans Miss Angel made for herself told in detail what would take place during each period.

A survey of Miss Angel's plans shows she had taken the following into account:

1. She planned for the whole day in the form of a schedule. "Sixes" are able to plan for longer periods of time than "fives."

2. She planned around fixed periods in the day, such as the sharing time, lunch time, and recess time. "Sixes" still receive a great deal of security and comfort in routine.

3. She planned for short, changing activities. "Sixes" are still very active and often have short attention spans.

4. She planned a great deal of flexibility between the routine activities in her schedule. "Sixes" are very creative and energetic, and she wanted to make use of their ideas and their plans.

5. She made allowance for many short periods which the children planned in detail. Children need to develop a skill for organizing their day and to develop the quality of self-direction, but at the age of six they need a great deal of help in doing this.

6. Her planning was sequential. She felt children should learn that planning is continuous, and the completion of one job frees the way to attack another. She helped children to evaluate and to set new goals when she did this.

7. Within her larger plans, she allowed for individual planning. During the work period and several times during the day, children planned for their own work for a short period of time. Group planning is necessary for democratic living, as is individual planning.

8. For one period during the day she often made many plans. During the work period children were all working at different jobs. During the reading period, five groups were all busy. Good teaching does not mean all children do the same thing at the same time. Careful planning is needed to allow for individual abilities.

9. She knew her children well. To meet the individual needs and interests of children, the teacher *must* know them well so that she can plan those things they need most urgently.

10. Like Miss Ellis, Miss Angel has her social studies objectives in mind and provides opportunity to fulfill them in her planning throughout the day. In the planning period, the children learn organizational skills, learn how to make decisions and pass judgments on issues and to work independently. The work period allows them time to put their plans to work and to be individually independent. Their farm unit is the core of their social studies and from it they will learn facts, develop understandings and concepts, acquire new skills, and engage in many instances of problem-solving. Like Miss Ellis, Miss Angel uses a humanistic approach to teaching where the children's needs and interests are considered above programs and schedules. The work period provided the opportunity for

each child to pursue a follow-up activity of his or her own choice focussing on the trip to the farm which they all shared and evaluated. The afternoon was devoted to skills building, but the work was correlated to the farm unit so deeper meanings could result; the reading stories were all built around the farm so the children could practice reading and using the new vocabulary they were learning in the morning. All through the day, whenever possible, the creative talents of the children were used.

PUPIL-TEACHER PLANNING IN A MIDDLE SCHOOL

Mr. Martin is a teacher in the Glendale Middle School. In Glendale, the middle school is made up of the former sixth, seventh and eighth grades and is housed in a building by itself. As is the elementary school, the middle school is partly self-contained and partly open. One wing is also set up in a type of team-teaching departmentalized organization.

Mr. Martin teaches in one of the self-contained combinations of ten-, eleven-, and twelve-year-olds. He has capitalized to a high degree on the work of Miss Ellis, Miss Angel and other teachers who gave his students a good beginning in independent and group planning.

Mr. Martin's students are engaged in a social study of great importance to them. They are studying *What Makes People Human?* One segment of their study is *The Search for Freedom.*

This unit began when the children exhibited great concern over a local strike in the rug factory. During a discussion it became known that the parents of these children were working together for greater freedom by striking. This discussion resulted in a sharp interest in the origin of all freedoms. Soon the children had set up questions and objectives for a unit of work. These children were very independent. They had had many years of planning practice and were able to make many plans on their own.

First, the long-term plans for the unit were made. These were divided into plans for beginning the unit. Then followed plans for developing the unit, for committee work, for reporting, and for culminating activities. These plans were made for the month, the week, the day, and the period.

Mr. Martin's children learned to plan their daily program with their teacher a week in advance. Every Friday afternoon Mr. Martin gave his pupils a duplicated sheet with a rough schedule for each day of the coming week. On this sheet, large blocks of time were left each day for children to fill in their own activities as much as possible. Mr. Martin made a duplicate of this schedule on the chalkboard. On it he wrote in all the periods he would use during each day to 1) have the children together for instruction and 2) have specific groups meeting with him. The children filled in their own plan sheet with the times they would be meeting with Mr. Martin, and then filled in the remaining time with their own jobs. Each morning Mr. Martin had a short planning period at which time he checked each child's program for the day.

Following is a sample of one of the children's planning sheets for two days. All those periods in capital letters designate the time Mr. Martin put on the board for them to meet specific purposes. The items in lower case letters represent those plans written in by Kevin Edwards, a student in Mr. Martin's room.

MY PLANS

NAME:	Kevin Edwards		GRADE: 6
FROM:	Monday, May 3	TO	Friday: May 7

MONDAY—May 3

A.M.

9:00   PLANNING PERIOD—CONTRIBUTIONS

9:15   UNIT WORK AND OTHER WORK
ALL—LIST QUESTIONS FOR UNIT ON AFRICA
CLASSIFY QUESTIONS
CHOOSE COMMITTEES
MAP WORK—MR. MARTIN

10:15   CLEAN UP: PREPARE FOR REPORTS

10:30   REPORT PERIOD
Report on nations of Africa admitted to United Nations—my home-work. Show collection of pictures from newspaper on Africa to class.

10:50   BREAK: SNACK

11:00   LANGUAGE ARTS
PRETEST: SPELLING—MR. MARTIN
Make my spelling list.
Copy questions about Africa on chart.
Write letter to travel agency for African posters.

11:30   GRAMMAR: MR. MARTIN
Correct papers—from Friday

P.M.

1:00   READING GROUPS
1:00: My group—Mr. Martin will give us some workbook lessons.
1:40: With Mr. Martin—help in reading (to outline).

2:00   RECESS—OUTDOOR—play ball.

2:30   ARITHMETIC
DECIMAL FRACTIONS—MR. MARTIN
3:00: My group—work at seats on material from Mr. Martin

TUESDAY—May 4

A.M.

9:00   PLANNING PERIOD

9:15   UNIT WORK AND OTHER WORK
         SHORT COMMITTEE MEETINGS—ORGANIZE
         MAKE UP A PLAN FOR STUDY
         MAKE LISTS FOR REFERENCE-RESOURCES
         My committee will meet to organize.
         We will each take a job.

10:15   CLEAN UP: PREPARE FOR REPORTS

10:30   REPORT PERIOD
         Mary's group will report on their assignment—problems in
         Africa—"Africa's Fight for Freedom."

10:50   SNACK

11:00   LANGUAGE ARTS
         SPELLING WORDS—Study with Mr. Martin
         Write our reports for the school newspaper.
         Fix bulletin board of clippings in NEWS center.

         P.M.

1:00   READING GROUPS
         With Mr. Martin—new story—read for main ideas—"The
         African King," p. 187.
         1:20: Group planning—roll movie—list scenes—decide who
         will draw each.

2:00   GYM WITH MR. BUNDEE
         Plan May Day Festival.

2:30   ARITHMETIC
         With Mr. Martin—adding and subtracting decimal fractions—
         games.
         3:00: Practice sheets from Workbook, p. 86–87.

PUPIL-TEACHER PLANNING IN THE OPEN CLASSROOM

In the open classroom, pupil-teacher planning is essential—and the development of a high degree of independence in children is mandatory if the system is to work. Children engage in creative activities continually in that they make choices and decisions, and pass judgments in planning all through the day.

In the Glendale open classrooms the children were skilled at planning by the time they were seven-year-olds. In one wing of the Glendale school the rooms were built in hexagonal-shaped clusters so children could move easily from place to place. The clusters were all grouped around the learning resource center, the gymnasium, and the cafeteria, which also served as an auditorium. Even these utility rooms were divided from the clusters only with partial partitions so the physical open concept was still maintained.

Each child was assigned to a home cubicle where he or she began the day. The instructional program was set up in four-week units, and the days were divided into blocks of time. At the beginning of each four-week unit each child received help from the homeroom teacher in planning the skill subjects to be studied, the social studies units he or she chose to pursue, and the mini courses, based on each individual's interests. From then on it was up to each child to plan his or her own day each morning in the home cubicle. Even the lunch period was flexible, for lunch was served in the cafeteria from eleven o'clock to one o'clock. If a child was extremely interested in some math problem being worked on and lunch time came around, lunch could be put off until as late as twelve-thirty. It was interesting to this author to note that there were no traffic jams at lunch time, no horse play in the lines, the children were orderly and not excessively noisy, they ate comfortably and were eager to be on their way to other jobs which they had set for themselves.

Most of the cubicles were well equipped with a variety of self-instructing media. Along the walls of the skills building cubicles there were pockets containing cards or duplicating sheets of sequential modules carefully developed by the teachers so children could progress from one to the other after they had mastered any one module of learning. Much of the work could be self-corrected, but a teacher was always nearby to give a child a diagnostic test or to check individual progress at the conclusion of each module.

Options were offered the children. In the social studies cluster of cubicles were many of the materials mentioned in Chapter 3 as being part of the center in the self-contained classroom, except, of course, that there was more equipment to service more children. Slides and filmstrips were available on a variety of subjects and the children could sit in individual carrels to view them. Many of these had accompanying records to which the children could listen with head phones. Books, maps, charts, globes and games were easily accessible and their location and use was often referred to in the contracts or the modules. The children chose topics of interest and worked on them singly and in groups. One group of children, for instance, was very much interested in lumbering. The module from which they studied gave them non-fiction and story book references, encyclopedia references, and miscellaneous references. It also directed them to material on measuring board feet, uses for lumber, maps and pictures. The available filmstrips on lumbering were indicated in the contract and each child had viewed them. There were two films available on lumbering and the group had studied them together. At the end of the module were many suggested activities, some of which the children had carried out. Some samples follow:

- Kevin had made a map of the world showing the major lumbering areas.
- Susan had made a scrapbook of lumbering pictures, stories, charts and a list of lumber products.
- Jim had written a book called *Handy, the Story of a Cookie*. A cookie is a cook's assistant in a lumber camp.
- The group had labeled the trees on the school grounds with small signs cut from wood scraps which they varnished.
- They constructed a wooden shed to be taken outdoors to house the outdoor garden equipment one group was using in a science project. This activity was one of their own creation—the last activity on each worksheet

of the module was an open-ended one intended to develop the creativity of the children: *Design and carry out a project of your own which shows some of the things you have learned about lumber.*

Options were given to these children to encourage the making of decisions. Should a child choose to work in science over a four-week period, he or she reported to the teacher in the science cubicles, indicated what he or she would like to study from a wide variety of topics there, and then was given a project book similar to those distributed for social studies and went to work. Often one child joined with other children who had chosen the same topic and they worked together. Careful records were kept in each child's project book. Equipment was available in the cubicle center. After each project was complete, it was taken to the teacher and, using evaluation sheets in the project books, they evaluated it together. It must be remembered that the teacher was available to help any child at any time.

The mini-courses at the Glendale school were very interesting. If any child had a course that he or she wanted taught, it was reported to the homeroom teacher who made a list. Just before the close of each four-week period all of the teachers shared their lists. Then each teacher signed up to teach a mini-course, and the lists were distributed to the children at the beginning of the next four-week period. One list for mini-courses looked like this:

- Crafts
- Superstitions
- Airplane Making
- Cosmetics
- Photography
- Playing a Mouth Organ
- Baseball: The World Series
- The Life of Mark Twain

- Fairy Tales
- Monsters
- Moon Trips
- Clothes Designing
- Christmas Decorations
- Movies
- Gardening
- Traveling

At the first meeting of the mini-course, the children decided pretty much what they wanted to cover and how the course was to be run. In the course on crafts, for instance, they actually made crafts. This was also true of the course on Christmas decorations. In the course on superstitions, they decided to share all the superstitions they had heard, do some research on them, and report to each other with one report each class meeting. This group also decided to read some books on superstitions and read some ghost stories to each other. The group on Moon Trips decided to have open discussions with each person sharing his or her knowledge and readings and the teacher guiding the discussions. The group on The Life of Mark Twain decided that they would like the teacher to read some stories to them including *Dear, Dear Livy*, the story of Mrs. Mark Twain by Stoutenberg and Baker. And so it went: each group planned its own course, set up personal objectives indicating what it hoped to gain, and helped plan the strategies for running the course itself.

It will be interesting to follow one student through a school day in Mr. Frederick's classroom. Let's select Noel. Noel is one of Mr. Frederick's students;

that is, he reports to Mr. Frederick as his key teacher each day. Sometimes this report period is the only time he works with Mr. Frederick all day, however.

Noel: Noel arrives on the bus at eight o'clock. He likes school and is eager to get to work on some material Mr. Frederick was going to get for him on the space program. Some of his friends are going to rap this morning about making model rockets. Charlie is bringing a kit. They are all there, and they go to Mr. Frederick's cubicle to work because they are supposed to begin their day there at eight-thirty anyway.

By eight-thirty the school is humming with voices and laughter and Mr. Frederick has dropped by to listen to their discussion and to see Charlie demonstrate his model kit. Twenty-five students have assembled in the cubicle and Mr. Frederick welcomes them all and asks them to take out their individual planning cards for the day. He writes the "fixed" periods for the day on the chalkboard—the periods which everyone must remember are put in upper case letters so each may place them on their cards as follows:

   8:30 PLANNING
 10:00 ASSEMBLY—ALL PURPOSE ROOM
            DANCES—ERICKA's GROUP
 11:00 SPECIAL HELP
 12:00 LUNCH
            SELECTED ACTIVITIES
   3:00 MINI-COURSES

To this Mr. Frederick adds the special meetings he needs to have that day. He does this for two reasons: 1) it sets a time when everyone concerned can meet to accomplish the job at hand and 2) it keeps the other children informed of his whereabouts in case he is needed. Mr. Frederick's schedule looks like this:

   8:30 PLANNING
   9:00 Committee Meeting—Ericka's Group to plan Assembly
 10:00 ASSEMBLY—All purpose room
            DANCES—Ericka's group
 11:00 SPECIAL HELP PERIOD
            I need to see: Noel
                           Manuelo's group
                           Stella
                           Any others who need help
 12:00 LUNCH
            SELECTED ACTIVITIES (outdoors)
   1:00 Slum Clearance Committee—around my desk
   1:30 Reading: Bart
                  Consuelo
                  Christopher
                  Rodriquez
                  Sadie
   3:00 MINI-COURSES

Individual children are then to make out their own cards, entering on them the times Mr. Frederick can see them and then filling out the rest of the day with their own activities. There is a great deal of buzzing and regrouping as children who are working on special projects plan times when they can get together. Mr. Frederick checks each card.

Mr. Frederick draws attention to the fact that he has placed material for many groups on his desk or has a card there with references on it for them. Each child checks Mr. Frederick's desk for any personal or group messages before going off to begin the day.

Noel's card looked like this when Mr. Frederick checked it:

8:30	PLANNING
9:00	Committee Meeting—Space Program
	Make model rockets
10:00	ASSEMBLY
11:00	With Mr. Frederick—Math
11:30	Learning Resource Center
12:00	LUNCH with Eddie, Corky, Curt
	Baseball
1:00	Try math cards—contracts
1:30	Reading—Reading Center
2:00	Library—Research
2:30	Write my notebook
3:00	MINI-COURSE-Photography

Each child tries to tell Mr. Frederick on the planning card what he or she will be doing during each period of the day.

Noel went directly from planning period to Mr. Frederick's desk where the model rocket kits Mr. Frederick promised to get were waiting for his group. His committee met in a small cubicle with partial glass walls where they could close the door and not be distracted by other children. The partial glass walls made it possible to see that the cubicle was occupied yet few noises leaked out or in. Noel worked hard figuring how his kit went together. Charlie, who had had some experience in assembling kits, was a great help to Noel and the other three members of the group. While they worked they planned other topics they wanted to look up in the library and other activities they wanted to do. They also selected those things which they felt they might want to show or report to the other one hundred children in their wing. Charlie suggested they might want to put on some kind of show such as Ericka's group was presenting this particular morning.

At ten o'clock a buzzer rang as a reminder that it was time to go to Assembly. They had all agreed at planning period that Mr. Frederick would notify them in this manner. A messenger had been dispatched to the other teachers so everyone knew what the buzzer meant.

All the children sat on the floor of the all-purpose room in a large circle.

Ericka's group told about its study of dances. Some of the students wore costumes borrowed from their parents or friends. Ericka's committee showed maps, indicating the places where the dances originated. They told how Mr. Frederick had had some of the parents in to help teach some of the dances. The group of about sixteen children demonstrated many dances to the records on the record player. The last dance was a simple Hungarian folk dance, and everyone was taught how to do it in four smaller circles in the large all-purpose room. Ericka's group then showed how some of the current dance steps were taken from the old dances.

After the dances, Mr. Frederick read *John J. Plenty and Fiddler Dan* by John Ciardi. It was a good story and Mr. Frederick knew how to read it!

The children went back to their work around eleven o'clock. Noel met in Mr. Frederick's cubicle with ten other children who needed help in math.

Noel ate early with some friends so he could play baseball the rest of the noon hour. A large group of children had a series going, and baseball was his favorite sport.

At one o'clock he decided to try the math test that went with his last contract to see whether or not he had mastered long division. He missed only one problem and easily spotted a careless mistake so decided to try another card. So enthusiastic was he that he went through three cards and three tests before the period ended.

At one-thirty he reported to the Reading Center which he usually did each day. Noel was studying word attack skills to help him in decoding new words. He put on the earphones and operated a cassette tape which gave him instructions in the use of prefixes and suffixes.

Noel then went to the library which was next to the resource center where he found some good books on rockets, viewed the new tape recommended by Mr. Frederick, took some notes for his committee, and checked out a book to take home. He noted that the day was drawing to a close so he took out his notebook, one of which everybody kept, and wrote up his accomplishments for the day. He will leave this notebook with Mr. Frederick on Friday. He then went off to the mini-course he had chosen: one on photography which was taught by Mr. Whalen because it was one of Mr. Whalen's hobbies. Today they planned to take pictures of the Urban Renewal Project and Noel was excited about that.

GUIDES TO PUPIL-TEACHER PLANNING

Pupil-teaching planning has been described by citing teachers who are masters at planning and at helping children develop organizational skills. All teachers can develop this skill. They can begin by planning for single activities, single periods and/or single blocks of time and will gradually expand these plans until children take over the major responsibilities of planning for themselves.

From the illustrations above we can see pupil-teacher planning does not mean pupils decide they can do anything they please at any time. It does mean that children learn that the classroom is a place where each child may engage in activities that are of most personal value in relation to an entire peer group.

We can also see that pupil-teacher planning does not begin at any particular grade placement. It begins with the abilities of the children, anywhere at anytime.

As the ability to plan develops, more and more time responsibility can be placed on the pupil, thus giving the teacher more time to expend his or her energies where they are most needed.

The objectives for only a few of the activities described in these classrooms are given because others are obvious and because space is limited. The reader must remember that all the activities observed were designed to meet stated objectives.

Summary

The organizational skills children develop are essential and valuable for operating all classrooms and for use in life. Because creative people often develop a high ability to organize, creative development is fostered in the teaching of organization skills.

Pupil-teacher planning is important for many reasons as we have seen:

1. Children learn to plan and organize by experience.
2. Planning gives both teachers and children direction and a creative way to work towards the accomplishment of goals.
3. Children learn better when they are involved in the learning. Planning involves the children.
4. Problem behavior is reduced when children know how each part of the day is to be filled and do not waste time waiting to be told what to do next. Boredom is minimized.
5. Learning becomes more purposeful when children set their own goals and work out ways to reach them.
6. Learning is more creative when children have to think through ways of solving daily and long-term problems.
7. Pupil-teacher planning develops independence, responsibility, self-direction and other qualities essential to the citizen of a democratic society.
8. Pupil-teacher planning gives students an opportunity to experience group dynamics and democratic processes.
9. Pupil-teacher planning helps to develop the child's concept of worthwhile use of working and leisure time.
10. Pupil-teacher planning enables the children and their teacher to have more common goals and closer perceptions of common problems.
11. Pupil-teacher planning develops the skill of sequential organization and other good work habits.

12. Pupil-teacher planning is an open-ended experience and stimulates creative thinking.

13. Pupil-teacher planning provides children with maximum opportunity for making choices. Creative behavior is encouraged when choices, differences and flexibility are present.

14. The creative process is developed through sequential planning. In the creative process one idea leads to another and one decision creates new situations for making other decisions.

Pupil-teacher planning as we have reviewed it here presents the social studies not as a subject restricted to a portion of the day, but as the core of the elementary school curriculum. This idea will be further discussed in the chapter on unit teaching which follows.

To the College Student

1. In many schools you will visit, movable furniture is often kept in straight rows and children are not allowed to move about the classroom. What does this tell you about the teacher in terms of understanding the concept of the social studies? Are the children learning the skills of living together?

2. Many college students of adequate or superior ability flunk out of college or do not work up to their potential. One reason is that they do not adequately budget their time and leave too little time for required study. Many colleges teach courses such as "The Improvement of Learning" to help students learn to program a day and to develop study skills necessary on a college level. Can you see any relationship between this situation and the need to develop planning and study skills in the elementary grades?

3. Creative children are not annoyed by disorder. They are challenged by it. Many enjoy bringing order out of disorder. In what ways could you use this knowledge about creative children to put them to work in helping to plan a school day? Could this possibly suggest a way in which the creative child might be more active and accepted in the total group?

4. Examine some textbooks and workbooks in the social studies. How much attention is given to developing the skill of pupil-planning? Since this is such an important skill, why do you suppose it is so neglected?

To the Classroom Teacher

1. Try some of the following activities with your middle school students to develop planning and organization skills:
   a. Have the children make a list of all the things they have for breakfast or dinner. Then have them try to find out what part of the world all these things came from.

On a map of the world, have them color in the places where their meals come from.

b. In the encyclopedia, have the children look up Albania, Rumania, Greece, Yugoslavia, and Bulgaria. Do this in groups, and then let each group make a shoebox scene about each country. Place these scenes around a salt-and-flour map and pin a ribbon from the scene to the place where it would be seen on the map.

c. As you finish studying each area of Europe, you may divide your class in groups and have each group construct a diorama that most typically represents the region just studied.

d. After you read stories or a favorite piece of literature about a country you are studying, make a list of all the things that happened in the stories, scene by scene. Allow each member of the class to choose a scene and draw it. Two or three class members can cut a stage from a cardboard box to make a roll movie. After the pictures are drawn, label them, then have a committee paste them all on shelf paper. After the shelf paper has been put on rollers, someone can read the stories again while the roll movie is shown to the class.

e. Divide your class into committees. Assign each committee to make a chart on a large sheet of paper of one of the following topics:

(1) The food of the Ancient Egyptians

(2) The clothing of the Egyptians

(3) Homes of the Egyptians

(4) Transportation of the Egyptians

(5) The buildings of the Egyptians

(6) The life of the Egyptians

(7) Ceremonies of the Ancient Egyptians

Make your charts as attractive as possible. Use lettering, pictures and drawings. When they are finished, hold an exhibit and invite another grade.

2. Does your own classroom encourage children to develop organizational skills? Look at it objectively and make a list of ways you can improve the development of these skills.

To the College Student and the Classroom Teacher

1. Is it possible to tell what a teacher's philosophy of teaching and views toward creativity are simply by looking at his or her classroom organization, even when the children are not in the room? Visit a school after the children have been dismissed for the day, or visit some classrooms other than your own. Note the differences in seating arrangements, bulletin board displays, exhibits of student work, the materials and their accessibility. Can you tell what goes on during the day? If possible, return to the same classroom when the children are there to check your deductions.

2. Think of all the organizational skills required of you in your daily living. Many of these skills are automatic in your way of life. If all art and creativity grow from one's ability to organize his or her experiences into new arts, think of all the ways you can to make the skills necessary for living and creating automatic in children.

3. Mrs. Wylie is a fifth grade teacher. She believes children must know the facts presented in the social studies text. Her social studies periods consist of having the children open their books to the topic under study and then read to find answers to the questions she poses. Each day she gives a review test (written or oral) on the facts presented in the day's lesson. Mrs. Wylie's children know the names of the states and their capitals, the population of each state, the major rivers and watersheds of the United States, the countries of South America and a bookful of dates. What is commendable about Mrs. Wylie's teaching? What is poor about it?

4. Our government, our institutions and our organizations conduct their business through the use of committees. Make a list of the skills you need to work within a committee, such as the ability to say what you believe without feeling threatened. Take a poll of the class members to see where these skills were learned. Were you ever taught them or did you just pick them up through experience? How necessary is group work to you at this point in your life? Do you often wish you could function more effectively in a group than you do? How early in life do you remember working in some sort of group: high school dance committee? a yearbook committee? at summer camp? a school paper? doing homework? having birthday parties? church groups? When do you feel group dynamics should be taught in the elementary school?

5. "Preplanning for a school day can be overdone." In the light of what you have learned about creativity, discuss the pros and cons of this statement. Do you think Miss Angel overplanned her day? Why is preplanning necessary?

Selected Bibliography

AHERN, JOHN F., and LUCAS, NANCI D. *Ideas: A Handbook for Elementary Social Studies.* New York: Harper & Row, 1975.

GRAND, CAROLE, and GOLD, RAHLA. *Guiding the Learning Process: A Manual for Teachers of Young Children.* New York: Harper & Row, 1973.

HOWES, VIRGIL M. *Informal Teaching in the Open Classroom.* New York: Macmillan, 1974.

KELLER, CLAIR W. *Involving Students in the New Social Studies.* Boston: Little, Brown, 1974.

MARS, DAVID. *Organizational Climate for Creativity.* Buffalo: Creative Education Foundation, 1969.

PEPPER, WILLIAM F. *The Self-Managed Child.* New York: Harper & Row, 1973.

SABAROFF, ROSE, and HANNA, MARY ANN. *The Open Classroom.* Metuchen, N.J.: Scarecrow Press, 1974.

5 Creative Teaching through Units

Working with objects is active in and of itself if it is inspired by the spontaneous research of children but not if it comes only from the direction of the teacher.

JEAN PIAGET[1]

INTRODUCTION

One of the tried and tested strategies for teaching the social studies is the system of <u>unit teaching</u>, developed in the Dewey schools of the late 'twenties and early 'thirties. Extensive research and experimentation resulted from the unit concept and the "activity" movement (including the famous New York City Eight-Year Study of the 'thirties). At that time, the unit type of program and the activity program more closely fulfilled the objectives of the social studies in the elementary school and the objectives of schools in the United States than any other methodology and form of organization. The wealth of material which resulted from this experimentation and research was culminated in a book written by Lavone Hanna, Gladys L. Potter and Neva Hagaman called *Unit Teaching in the Elementary School* (New York: Rinehart and Company, 1955). This book remains a classic in describing the objectives and techniques of unit teaching and has yet to be surpassed.

Not only does the original unit plan stand up well today as a strategy for fulfilling the goals of a modern elementary school, it also stands up well in terms of meeting objectives for creative teaching and individual creative development.

DESCRIPTIONS OF UNIT TEACHING

The Hanna, Potter, and Hagaman book, recently revised, indicates that unit teaching and its many ramifications are still in a healthy state of practice in this

1. Jean Piaget, *Pedagogie et Psychologie* (Paris: Dunold Press, 1969): 120.

128

country.[2] Over the years the unit plan has been altered, modified, abused, glorified and made to fit new molds. Some of these changes have destroyed the meaning of the unit as it was originally conceived. Other changes have caused it to appear in new guises such as team teaching, or with new labels such as "projects," "modules" or "contracts."

In some of these forms the basic concept remains the same. In other guises the entire concept has been altered and what was once described as unit teaching has now become something else. Because of these changes, it is necessary to explore the many meanings of units as they are used in current literature on the social studies.

The Traditional Unit Plan

The original method of unit teaching was so named because of the concept of *unit*, meaning "one-ness," which is what the plan promoted: teaching so that knowledges and skills were related—they culminated in a one-ness.

Previous to the advent of the unit system, elementary schools in the United States went through a stage of breaking loose from the rigid schedules and the lock-step drill of the highly disciplined traditional classroom. This move away from traditional methods was accelerated by many new ideas on the education scene. Research in learning theory was responsible for innovations in methods of teaching. The separated subject matter curriculum was gradually replaced with broader types of objectives.

The subject matter approach focused primarily on giving children information. Providing children with knowledge is only one goal of a sound social studies program. The overall goal of the public school is to develop useful democratic citizens through a study of worthy human relationships in the social studies program. Information alone will not do this. Many skills are needed. These skills must be developed. Values and attitudes must also be developed. The subject matter approach is an unrealistic preparation for life in terms of the demands made on children and adults in democratic living.

Studies of the times reflected the flux of interest in the Gestalt of learning—the "wholeness" which stressed the interrelatedness of knowledge, the similarities in all learnings and the overlapping of skills. These studies revealed a strong correlation between children's ability to see relationships in their learning and their achievement and knowledge in those learnings.

Hanna, Potter and Hagaman have stated the principles of learning which apply in unit teaching as follows: 1) Learning results only from experiences; 2) Problem solving provides the most effective learning situation; 3) Drill is needed when the response must be "fixed"; 4) The objectives and activities of a unit must be defined in terms of individual behavior expected and must be formulated and accepted by the learner; 5) Instruction must be related to the actual life experiences of the child; 6) Learning experiences in the unit must be

2. L. Hanna, *Dynamics of Elementary Social Studies,* 3rd ed. (New York: Holt, Rinehart & Winston, 1973).

provided when the child is ready; 7) Fragmented learning is ineffective and isolated facts are soon forgotten; 8) Children should be helped to reach generalizations and to apply these to new situations; 9) Learning experiences organized into units are effective when the learner sees the relationship of one experience to another.[3]

The first break away from the compartmentalized day was the application of the concept of *correlation*.

The Correlation Concept

Gestalt psychologists maintained that isolated learnings were less effective to a child than integrated learnings. In other words, a child whose school day consisted of a half-hour's exposure to reading about Italy, followed by another half-hour's learning about how to carry numbers into the hundreds column in addition, followed by a practice period in handwriting for fifteen minutes, then a trip to the toilet and a pause to get a drink, then a study of the land of the Argentine gaucho for thirty minutes in geography, followed by reading about the Pilgrims for twenty minutes in a history book, was being bombarded with so many learnings that it was difficult to get much meaning from the piecemeal instruction to which he or she was subjected.

Experts of the time advocated that subject matter should be correlated so that a child would be faced with a more organized, related body of knowledge and that skills should be learned which would help in the application of these bodies of knowledge.

Instead of having the child hop from one subject to another all day, one topic, such as the gauchos of Argentina, served as the core for the day's learnings. During the reading lesson, stories were read about the South American cowboys. Geography for that day was a study of the terrain and climate of Argentina as it related to the life of the gaucho. The spelling lesson included the words necessary for use in written reports about the studies at hand. Language lessons were often built around the topic of the day: teachers taught the skills of composition by having the children write stories about their history and geography studies. Or, if a trip was planned to a nearby museum or theater, the grammar period was used to teach letter-writing so the children could write letters to museum directors or theater owners to make plans for the trip. Later the class letter was copied from the chalkboard for practice in handwriting and a neat and legible letter was sent.

The *correlated* curriculum had a great effect on changing methodology and content in the school program but had little effect on organization. Schedules became a little less rigid and the material from class to class became more related. At times, some teachers combined two classes such as grammar and handwriting and used a large block of time to compose letters, for instance, and had children copy them.

3. Ibid.

Figure 5-1. *A primary grade bulletin board made during a unit on Pilgrims: correlating art and social studies.*

The Integration Concept

The concept of integration was another step in the direction of blending the school day into a meaningful whole. Integrating the curriculum meant that the choppy little periods of the traditional school were abandoned and large blocks of time with correlated subject matter replaced them. Geography, history, economics, citizenship and civics became *social studies*, taught in an interrelated manner. Handwriting, spelling, word usage, grammar, creative writing, literature, listening, oral expression, punctuation and capitalization became the *language arts*. Art, music, dramatics and dance became the *creative arts*.

Reading, under this plan, was considered a language art but was deemed important enough to be allotted special periods. The large blocks of time used in the integrated approach was a dramatic change in organization. Instead of every member of the class being held responsible for accomplishing the same goals and for covering the same material, children were grouped (generally by ability) with different objectives and materials for each group.

Mathematics and science were allotted separate places in the daily schedule. The old schedule, which appeared outside the classroom door in the traditional school, took on a new look as large blocks of time were planned for the subject matter and small groups of children became involved in a variety of activities within each block.

The Unit

The *unit* method of teaching completed the cycle. Teaching by units meant that subject matter was organized by content into one complete whole—a body of related, integrated and correlated material with relevant experiences planned so that the intellectual, social, emotional and physical needs of children could be met on a highly individual basis. Although most schools were still organized by grades, in unit teaching age lines were blurred to a great extent and children were grouped in a variety of ways: by problems, by abilities, by interests, for skill development, and by instructional level.

The *method* of unit teaching is to this day a creative method of teaching and affords many opportunities for developing creative human relationships. Through unit teaching the teacher can develop group skills without sacrificing the development of each individual child. A unit is based on experience and provides the opportunity to meet the teacher's and children's objectives.

Because of the flexibility afforded in the organization of the school day in unit teaching, the humanistic philosophy of unit teaching, the extensive interaction among children in unit teaching, and because the major accent is on the maximum development of each individual child, many objectives regarding total development of individuals are achieved. A list of general objectives, which was taken from a curriculum guide of a suburban graded school, follows:

In teaching units, each teacher will:

1. Meet individual differences of children more realistically.
2. Foster good human relationships among students.
3. Provide a laboratory in which the skills for social living may be developed.
4. Foster self-discipline among students.
5. Develop concepts, understandings, and values among children.
6. Help each individual to live effectively in the world.
7. Develop an understanding and appreciation of other cultures in relation to the knowledge of the child's own culture.
8. Help children become aware of the problems of their society and their part in solving them.
9. Develop an appreciation of the work of others.
10. Give the child an historical perspective, a time-line concept.
11. Accentuate and use an appreciation of natural resources.

12. Foster democratic ideals and develop the democratic way of life.

13. Develop critical thinking on each level of the child's development.

14. Guide the child toward creative thinking and self-realization.

15. Give to each child the "tools" of culture in meaningful situations so that he or she learns to use them in practical applications.

16. Develop those characteristics of responsibility, independence, sharing, acceptance, cooperativeness, and other qualities necessary for living effectively in a democratic society.

17. Provide for open-ended experiences which afford children many opportunities to create.

The unit method of teaching is not the only one through which these objectives may be met, but it does seem to make allowance for more of the stated objectives than any other single method. Specifically, it sets conditions for creative development more than any other plan yet devised. It provides for self-development; it is a problem-solving method and, if properly used, will provide children with many open-ended situations. Through it children learn many knowledges, skills, and values which they may immediately apply to solving current social problems. Through unit teaching creative and critical thinking can well be developed; convergent and divergent thinking processes can be stressed. Unit teaching provides ample use of all the skills necessary for full creative development—decision-making, passing judgment, critical thinking, evaluation, visual acuity, and comprehension abilities.

The problem-solving approach of unit teaching provides high motivational tension and an opportunity to use many past experiences in new patterns. Children are encouraged to use their own ideas and individuality can be stressed. Ideas and objects are manipulated and explored, and the qualities and characteristics indicative of creative people are accepted as important.

Such outcomes imply the utilization of a variety of techniques and practices. The teacher is not only concerned with what the children learn, but with the *techniques* they learn for meeting the problems they face in their own lives *and* the changes the learning process makes on their own abilities and personalities. Learning of all kinds generally takes place best as a result of first-hand experience. A good unit provides opportunities for children to work together, to solve problems, to be creative, to think constructively, to develop skills, to make mistakes, and to learn from failures.

Even though the plan of unit teaching has been around a long time, there are many educators who misinterpret its original concept. The basic goal of public elementary education has been stated as promoting good citizenship, and it has been pointed out by some that the social studies plays only a part which is dictated by its specific function. Some writers state that social studies and citizenship education are not synonymous and they should not be used as such. The specific function of social studies is to inform the youth about the many types of human relationships and to provide opportunities through which the citizen will develop those capacities and qualities necessary for successful participation in human relationships. The development of other attributes of a good citizen, such as the ability to read and write, to create and to synthesize, to understand physical phenomena, to manipulate numbers and to be able to engage in research is the responsibility of other subjects.

The concept of unit teaching, as taught by this author and others of his vintage, and by Hanna, Potter and Hagaman[4] is that all learnings, when related and/or relevant, are more meaningful and easier for a child to master. Consequently, teachers should plan those topics which deal with human relationships in related bodies of subject matter content and experiences (social studies) but should teach along with such bodies of content those skills which reinforce the ability to learn and practice sound, effective human relationships. Human relationships cannot exist, for instance, without communication. Communication skills are the language arts. While children are engaged in studying conservation (a human concept girded with values, appreciations, understandings, facts, knowledges, and a necessary body of skills) it is only logical that they should learn those communication skills which will be of value to them the rest of their lives but which will be easily learned while the need is strong: the ability to read a unique vocabulary, for instance, the ability to write business letters to government agencies, the ability to do reading and research, to take effective notes, to write and present effective reports. Even the act of computing costs of reforesting a hillside or of mailing propaganda letters may be a useful part of the study.

The ability on the part of the teacher to plan large blocks of time during a day around a chosen topic is the original, intended concept of a unit.

The goals must be clearly stated, and the activities carefully chosen so that each contributes to the accomplishment of the objectives. Evaluation must be considered an on-going process and the results of each unit and all its aspects must be carefully appraised. A great deal of dust is raised about categorizing that which is social studies and that which is language arts. In a true unit plan none of this matters.

Under the Dewey unit plan, as a matter of fact, units are built around any topic and yet social studies objectives are realized. A teacher may, for instance, develop a unit on Communications, or on Outer Space, or on Great Paintings and fulfill many of the objectives of sound human relationships even though the unit is not primarily social studies oriented.

Beginning a Unit

In a modern, humanized curriculum, the topics of a unit are based on current relevant problems of contemporary society or the world. In teaching any unit the topic must be carefully defined, such as "Newspapers and their value as a mass medium in modern times." Some curriculum guides state their unit topics this way: "Is the modern newspaper necessary as a means of communication?"

4. Ibid.

Often a question is raised in a classroom because it is a specific, practical problem of society adjusted to a relevant school level, such as "What can we do in Freeport to decrease vandalism in our school?" (personalizing the fact that vandalism exists almost everywhere). On the other hand, the problem may be concerned with the *local* community such as "What can we do at school to develop an ecology awareness in our home town?" or "How can the people in Freeport conserve energy?" Or the problem may be confronted directly as a world-community problem such as "Why is the Panama Canal so important?" "Who should control it?" "Why are the Arab nations becoming so powerful in the world today?" The problem may be an interplanetary one such as "How will our government's space program affect our lives in the years to come?" At the intermediate grade level, children are generally interested in *contrasting* cultures and may simply ask, "Why are the roofs of the houses flat in northern Mexico?" or "What is communism?"

These are not simply surface questions—each requires in-depth exploration and discussion in order to develop the understandings necessary to give the answers meaning. Each is concerned with the development of types of human relationships.

The understandings necessary to arrive at logical answers to each of these problems require much more than information, although information is necessary. They require an exploration of the feelings of people, a study of facts as they exist, knowledge of the psychology of human beings, an awareness of how values, appreciations and character are developed in people, a sensitivity to the emotions of people in general and sub-cultures and minority groups specifically, the ability to empathize so problems can be seen and felt from many viewpoints, the ability to be objective, to synthesize materials (facts *and* feelings), to make decisions, pass judgments and draw conclusions. Thus the process of solving the problem becomes as important as the solution to the problem itself for it is in the *process* that children encounter those situations where they explore feelings, learn to empathize, come to understand how other children think and feel, develop values and appreciations, develop sensitivity to others, understand other people's viewpoints, learn to make decisions, pass judgments and draw conclusions and develop much of their own character; in short, they learn how to live and cope with other human beings.

The system of unit teaching encompasses all the processes which create situations for this type of problem solving. This is not to say that other methods of social studies teaching do not place children in similar types of situations, for they do. Many conscientious plans and strategies have been designed recently for the purpose of making the development of each of these processes a direct target for instruction, but the system of unit teaching described in this section is the most natural and, consequently, the most realistic and practical application of an *organizational plan* and a *method of teaching* yet devised to accomplish the general objectives of the social studies.

In beginning a unit the major task of the teacher is motivating all the children in the group to the study of the unit. Motivation in unit teaching is more than an act of arousing interest or of salesmanship—it also involves the act of establishing purpose that will require cooperative effort on the part of the teacher and pupils over a sustained period of time. The system serves as a vital strategy for involving *all* children in a vital problem. This type of involvement is not only essential to the successful development of a unit, it is also the first step of the creative process.

Parts of a Unit

Most curriculum guides consider the following steps necessary for developing a unit:

I. The topic: The topic is generally stated as a problem, a concept or a generalization as described above.

II. A statement of general objectives: These statements are made in terms of the generalizations and basic controversial issues. Example (a generalization): Newspapers perform different functions than they once did; (a controversial issue): Newspapers could easily be replaced by different types of radio and television programming.

III. Specific objectives: General objectives must be translated into specific objectives. These are specific statements of facts, skills, concepts, knowledges and understandings to be learned by the children. One of the tasks of the teacher designing the unit will be to determine which of these objectives can be defined in *cognitive* learnings resolving themselves in behavioral changes. For these learnings they will write behavioral objectives. But these teachers also list those learnings which belong to the *affective* domain which cannot be easily measured by pencil and paper tests. Some behavior changes will be observed as teachers collect evidence in the form of anecdotal records over a period of time. Such an objective might be: As a result of this unit the children will be better able to *assume responsibilities* for their own learnings as evidenced by any or all of the following behaviors and others:

1. They will do reading research more often by themselves.
2. They will take over responsibility for their own discussions.
3. They will assume roles of leadership such as serving as chairperson of committees, giving reports, volunteering for key jobs, etc.
4. They will volunteer for school tasks, i.e., responsibilities outside their own classrooms.
5. They will care for their own materials in the classroom, replacing tools and supplies on shelves and maintaining orderly work centers where supplies can be easily located.
6. They will assume increasing responsibility for their classroom planning.
7. They will assume increasing responsibility for working independently.

8. They will assume increasing responsibility for evaluating their own work and the work of their class groups or class as a whole.

These objectives will be evaluated as evidenced by the following records:

1. written reports of their reading research collected in folders (outlines, notes and sample essays)
2. records of committee constituency
3. records of volunteer work
4. host and hostess charts
5. weekly plans for committees to care for classroom center with teacher comments on plans
6. individual daily and weekly planning records placed in file folder (see Chapter 4)
7. individual conferences with the teacher
8. notes of class evaluation of trips, projects, etc., placed in individual folders
9. tests on attitudes, interests, competencies (specific tests are listed)

For other objectives they will expect no specific evidence other than empirical observation, but will plan their work so that conditions are set with the hope that changes will occur in the children. These teachers realize that the time required for creating change will take longer than the weeks of the unit and may extend through several units or even over the entire year. An example of such an objective would be: As a result of the units of the school year children will develop an appreciation of beauty in their environment as observed in the following behaviors:

1. There will be little or no vandalism in the school.
2. Children will express a desire to make parts of the school attractive.
3. Children will take the initiative to keep the school yard and the school building clean.
4. Children will discuss their concerns about pollution problems in the community.
5. Children will participate in environmental plans for improving the community through scout groups, 4-H groups, church groups, etc.

Sometimes objectives are stated as *outcomes*. This is a list of the anticipated learnings the teacher expects the children to get from the unit. Some teachers use them more as a summary or as a guide to an evaluation of the effectiveness of the unit. They are important in keeping the teacher directed toward his or her goals.

IV. Content: The content of the unit can be stated in a variety of forms. While many curriculum guides have abandoned the outline of subject matter which once served as a guide to the teacher, others include an outline for two basic purposes: 1) a teacher needs to know the material which the children will seek out. Knowledge is accumulating so fast from year to year that the teacher must read and outline new material which can be used in making decisions in order to keep up-to-date; and 2) teachers must be aware of the reference material available to children and help them develop accuracy in reporting, help them to summarize, and to conceptualize.

The outline of the content is the subject matter of the unit. It includes the knowledge and facts that the children are expected to learn. From these facts the children develop concepts and generalizations. This outline is the result of a teacher's research and accumulated knowledge about the subject of the unit. It is *not* included in the unit so the teacher can give all the answers to the children's problems. It is there so the teacher can give the children direction and so the validity of facts presented by the children can be checked. Unless some sort of check is made in this manner, children may report things that are not true and thereby cause other children to form misconceptions. If the teacher outlines the subject matter, limits of the unit can more easily be set and directed toward desired goals. Some units are so broad that children can wander far from the central theme unless the teacher thinks through the content and materials which help accomplish the aims most directly.

In some social studies units, content is stated in terms of questions which are designed to stimulate children to discover relationships, to assess values, to analyze and synthesize, to challenge positions on issues and to come face-to-face with decision-making situations. Examples:

1. Now that the Alaskan pipeline for oil is built, what problems might develop between the United States and Canada?
2. How is the ecology of Alaska being affected by the pipeline? What studies have been made of the ecology problems of Alaska that influenced the decision of Congress?
3. What effect is the pipeline having on the gasoline supply in our country?

Some teachers feel that information which bears on discussions of questions of this nature should be outlined as the content of such units. Certainly such information saves the teacher many hours of library research and reading once the unit is underway.

Other social studies units are written so they are geared to the development of generalizations and concepts rather than to attack a specific problem. An adaptation of one such list of generalizations follows:

Topic: Greece Advances Civilization
Generalizations and Concepts:

1. People make adaptations to their physical environments.
2. Interdependence is inherent in all types of social organization.
3. All societies must accept certain values to succeed.
4. Some form of education is essential to the maintenance of a culture.

5. People strive to widen and deepen their abilities to live more richly and meaningfully.

6. Each age produces people and ideas that influence the culture of succeeding ages.[5]

In this curriculum outline each topic is chosen because of the effect or contribution it has made on life today.

The listed understandings are each followed by suggested activities that will help children arrive at the understanding, with key questions to ask during discussions and references for the teacher. Spaces are left for the teacher to write in anticipated behaviors, procedures to follow and evaluation techniques.

V. Activities and correlations: In order to answer the questions and fulfill the objectives such as those stated above, the teacher and children will discuss and plan activities specifically directed to the questions. These activities are fully planned and are used as the procedure or method of teaching for the unit. Example: To answer the question, "How is the newspaper organized?" one teacher arranged for the children to visit a newspaper plant and to talk with editors and reporters. The children further met the objective by deciding to publish a newspaper of their own.

In a unit on transportation, the children in a primary school were encouraged to ask their parents about ways they traveled when they were in primary school. Grandparents were then interviewed; and, in a few cases, great-grandparents. The summarizing of this information on a large graph led to increased understanding of the growth and changes in transportation as well as about time.

In both of the instances given here as examples, it must be remembered that the activities carried out and the information gleaned is always with the intent of helping the child gain information and establish values so he or she can make decisions regarding the major problems of the unit.

A great deal of caution must be exercised in selecting activities. It must be remembered that each activity should be selected for the purpose of imparting some knowledge, developing insights, promoting a concept, teaching or applying a skill, exposing a value, promoting empathy or feeling, fostering creativity or stimulating understanding. Activities are *not* selected for such reasons as keeping children busy or filling in time. Nor should they negate the above reasons for their inclusion in the unit. Building igloos from sugar cubes can give young, impressionable children a complete misconception of how traveling Eskimos house themselves unless the children understand completely that they are using materials to simulate a scene rather than to reproduce it accurately.

It is also a fact, however, that in most classrooms, far more time is spent on experiences which provide for intake (reading, studying pictures, maps and graphs, listening to films and tapes, looking at filmstrips, TV or films) than on the expressive and accommodative experiences (drawing pictures, making

5. Montgomery County Public Schools, *Scope and Sequence with Illustrative Units: Grades K-6, Bulletin No. 175K.* (Rockville, Maryland: Montgomery County Public Schools, Sept. 1964).

maps, graphs, models, dioramas, and murals, dramatizing, making films or applying knowledge to solve new problems). The teacher must remember that it is these expressive and accommodative experiences which require application or utilization of knowledge that guarantee internalization of learning, produce uses of learning and develop the children's creative powers as they seek new ways to express their understandings or to teach others what they have learned.

Creative thinking can be developed when children brainstorm ways they can reproduce a scene of Hawaii for the backdrop for a play, or when they come up with the idea that they can use tissue or crepe paper to simulate flowers in the leis for their luau, but the children must understand completely that real flowers are used in the actual situation. One of the greatest criticisms leveled against unit teaching has been the unwise selection of activities approved by teachers which have caused children to be confused in their understandings rather than edified.

VI. Culminating activity: The culminating activity of a unit pulls together all the information gathered, summarizes the activities and synthesizes the knowledge obtained so the children can make some worthy decisions and come up with answers regarding the main problems of the unit.

VII. Evaluation: Evaluation is not something to be done at the end of the unit, although this is certainly one place where evaluation is logical. Evaluation goes on all the time the unit is in action as part of the learning process. Objectives are set, an activity takes place, and the results are evaluated immediately to determine whether or not the objectives were met. Inasmuch as many of the specific objectives of the unit are written in behavioral terms, many of the objectives can be met simply by administering the exercises proposed in those objectives.

Objectives which cannot be easily evaluated by pen and paper exercises, such as those in the affective domain and the creative behaviors, will need to be evaluated in other ways. Long-term objectives will need to be evaluated by observations, discussions, checklists, anecdotal records, project results, written work, attitude tests, self-concept tests, various ability tests and many self-evaluation devices (see Chapter 11).

The culminating activity provides one means of evaluation. There are other means which the teacher will want to include in the unit plans. In order to evaluate the unit fully, the teacher will need to study the objectives of the unit once more. Did it accomplish what was intended? Ways to measure achievement of each of the objectives must be devised. These types of measurement are generally stated in the objective at the beginning of the unit.

Knowledge is easily tested through the use of teacher-made tests or standard achievement tests. This testing should be a valuable experience for both teacher and student. They should be interested in knowing what has been learned from the unit. Sometimes teachers can find out a great deal about what the children have learned by letting them help construct the test.

It is not as easy to measure the social growth of children as it is to measure their knowledge. Neither is it easy to measure the acquisition of certain values and skills. But, it can be done.

Here is how Mr. Howard did it:

1. Mr. Howard kept cards in a file in his top drawer on each child. These cards could be carried during the day in his coat pocket, for him to jot down notes on them and slip them into the files in his desk each evening. On these cards he listed the child's problems and his ideas for helping him. He kept anecdotal reports of the child's behavior in significant situations during the day.

2. Mr. Howard prepared sociograms of his group (see Chapter 11) at the beginning of his unit and at the end of it. From these sociograms he was able to study the interaction of children as the unit progressed. He watched to see if rejected children were more accepted. Were shy children participating more? Were the aggressive children learning to listen and wait their turn?

3. Mr. Howard kept a check on the objectives of the unit as he went along to be sure he was not omitting any particular phase of the children's learning.

4. Mr. Howard gave some skills tests to see if his children were developing essential map skills, research skills and communications skills. (see Chapter 11).

5. Mr. Howard constantly checked the social interaction and the group dynamics in his room by using flo-graphs, participation charts, self-evaluation sheets, and other sociometrics (see Chapter 11).

Unit Teaching: Verbal Observations

Classrooms have been used often in this volume for the purpose of "verbal observations." In each observation one phase of a unit was described in some detail.

The process by which teachers arrive at objectives was described in Chapter 2 with the work of Mrs. Rogers and the teachers of Glendale. These broad objectives are translated into unit problems and topics.

The manner by which content is determined and worthwhile activities are selected was described in Mrs. Thompson's unit on the time machine in Chapter 1.

An excellent example of a valuable culminating activity was described in Chapter 1 in the account of Mrs. Cline's Middle East bazaar. In the culmination of this unit, the knowledges and facts learned by the children were synthesized and applied to show the understandings, concepts and skills the children had learned.

While the culminating activity serves as a cursory type of evaluation in a unit, a more specific evaluation is needed of each unit objective. Various types of evaluation appropriate for various unit objectives were described in Chapter 2, and evaluation will be discussed in Chapter 11.

Fragmentary accounts of the unit system of teaching, using a variety of topics, have served to describe the manner by which many social studies objectives are met. A more detailed concept of the unit system of teaching may be developed by following one teacher through his planning and execution of a unit.

UNIT TEACHING: A CASE REPORT

Launching a Unit

Because of the strong interest in the United States' Bicentennial, Mr. Kranz, a teacher in a small city open school, believed that his students (ranging in age from eight through twelve) were ready and anxious to develop an understanding of the problems of a modern America and the relationships necessary to promote a democratic form of government.

Resources in United States history abounded in the community because of interest in the Bicentennial, and Mr. Kranz felt that much of the material available from the past could be studied as a means of better understanding the present.

Mr. Kranz encouraged the children to bring in press clippings and realia from home related to the Bicentennial and post them on a bulletin board designated for this purpose in the large central area of the open classroom. Soon they were asking many relevant questions which he encouraged them to discuss and which he wrote on a large chart. A few were:

1. Why are we celebrating the Bicentennial and what is a Bicentennial?
2. What has happened in this country in two hundred years? What was life like when this country began?
3. How did our schools get started? Our system of roads? Our mail system?
4. Why are there so many strikes in our town?
5. Why are there some people who are not happy about being citizens of the United States?
6. What do we mean by civil rights?
7. What is welfare and how does it affect us?
8. Why do our parents sometimes groan about taxes? How are taxes paid and why?
9. Who builds our roads?
10. Who pays for our schools and teachers salaries?
11. How are people chosen to be our government officials?
12. What is a democracy?

Stating the Problems

This random selection of questions from the chart reflected the degree to which these children were becoming aware of current problems in the community—problems which held national implications. Like all teachers, Mr. Kranz was faced with the task of helping the children cluster the questions around one central problem and then to organize the questions into specific categories for study. After several discussions the general problem agreed on was as follows:

To what degree has the United States been successful as a democracy after two hundred years?

The children decided they would study this large problem by breaking it down into sub-topics. These sub-topics were to be expanded and studied by committees. Once the problem of the unit had been stated and the main topics for study had been established, the children felt they should list all the questions they could think of under each topic, the answers to which would be an aid in solving the major problem. They would also list all the ideas they could think of to find answers to their questions.

Discovering What We Already Know

One period of time was spent in a discussion of what the children already knew about the history of the United States. As the children volunteered information, Mr. Kranz jotted a summary statement of each child's contribution on the chalkboard and then tried to arrange them in chronological order. He found, for instance, that all the children had a good background of the explorers because they had studied them in school at an earlier age.

He also found out that his students knew a great deal of accurate information about the Pilgrims and how they had come to America. Many students also knew *why* they had come. The children knew about George Washington, that there had been a war for freedom with Great Britain and many had fragmented pieces of information about colonial wars and colonial life. Several knew a great deal about the settling of the west from cowboy movies and television series such as "Little House on the Prairie." Almost all knew there had once been a war between the states. Most of the children had seen *Gone with the Wind* and other Civil War movies.

The children knew a great deal about the products raised in various parts of the United States. They knew about Abraham Lincoln and the underground railroad. They had many bits of information about famous men and their contributions, namely, Thomas Edison, the Wright brothers, Marconi, Robert Fulton, Paul Revere, John Hancock, Jonas Salk, Henry Ford and Martin Luther King.

Part of Mr. Kranz's job in this discussion period was to judge whether or not the children's knowledge was sound fact, hearsay or whimsy, and to help them to determine whether or not a topic should be added or omitted from the list of questions.

The Planning Periods

The next day the total group studying the Bicentennial met with Mr. Kranz for a planning period. At this time Mr. Kranz hoped to help the children make plans on how to plan for their unit. Several such periods took place in the following few days.

On the chalkboard Mr. Kranz listed all the questions asked by the children. Each question was recorded regardless of its outward importance, though some were reworded for clarity. After a total of seventy questions had been listed, Mr. Kranz said, "These are good questions and they are important, and if we can answer them I am sure we will know what a democracy is and how successful the United States is as a democracy. As our questions now stand, however, they are not easy to work with. What can we do to them so that we can work better with them?"

A discussion of the questions showed that they appeared to be clustered around certain topics, with some overlapping, such as history, geography, government, education, food, transportation, communication, and the like. The main topics for classifying the questions were placed on chart paper to be used later to list all questions belonging under that topic. A partial outline of the topic headings prepared by Mr. Kranz appeared as follows:

I. History
  A. Beginnings of the United States
  B. Development of the United States
  C. People Who Settled Here: Reasons for Settling
  D. Forces Interfering with Democratic Dreams
  E. Important People of the Past
  F. Important People of Today

II. Government
  A. Beginnings
  B. Problems
  C. Taxes

III. Development of Resources
  A. Natural Resources
  B. Transportation
  C. Communication
  D. Geography—Exploitation
  E. Human Resources

IV. Rights of People
  A. Food
  B. Clothing
  C. Shelter

       D. Political Rights

       E. Education

       F. Protection (from War and Poverty)

       G. Freedom of Speech

       H. Freedom of the Press

        I. Work

  V. Life Styles

       A. Ethnic Groups

       B. Religious Groups

       C. Economic Groups (levels of wealth)

       D. Political Groups

       E. Geographical Groups

          1. Slums—deprived

          2. Suburban groups

          3. Rural groups

          4. Urban groups

Using colored chalk, different children took turns going to the chalkboard and circling the questions which fit under the various headings. Meanwhile, "secretaries" were appointed who copied the questions from the chalkboard onto charts, one for Government, one for Resources, one for Life Styles, and one for History. After all the questions had been classified in this manner, the groups decided they would put the questions on duplicating masters so each child would have a copy of all the questions of the unit. Committees were appointed to type, duplicate, and staple the questions into a booklet. A sample of one of the charts follows:

History of America

   1. Why did people come to the United States?

   2. Where did the people come from? Why?

   3. Who were the first settlers after the Pilgrims?

   4. Where did they settle and why?

   5. How did the colonies get to be a nation?

   6. How were the first laws made?

   7. Who were the officials in the first government?

   8. Why did the colonies have a war with England?

   9. How was the country settled?

  10. What important people lived then who helped in the making of the United States?

  11. How was our first government different from other governments of that time?

12. What did *democracy* mean?
13. What were some of the problems of settling a big country? Were there other wars?
14. How did our government pay for the wars?
15. How did people get the right to vote?
16. Why did so many young men leave the United States for Canada during the Vietnam war?

The next day each child was given a copy of all the questions and was able to see the problems of the unit classified by topics. Plenty of room had been left under each category so children could add new questions.

How to Study

"Now that we know what we are going to study," said Mr. Kranz, "let's talk a while on *how* we are going to study. For instance, are we going to have a different committee work on each topic, or are we all going to work on each topic together?" A good discussion led to the conclusion that since the Bicentennial was important to all and that since a knowledge of history would be a good background for a discussion and pursuit of the other categories, the class would study the history chart first.

A chart (Figure 5-2) for guiding the steps for study emerged.

Setting Up Committees

Mr. Kranz then led the class into considering the various ideas that could be used to answer the questions about the history of the United States. The class decided that they would cluster the questions into logical categories and that each person would sign up to work on one committee. The sign up chart looked like Figure 5-3.

Listing Sources of Information

"Our committees have been formed, and we know some ways they can plan to do their work," said Mr. Kranz, "but before we have our committee meetings, let's make a list together of all the places where we can go to get information to help us find the answers to our questions."

As a result of this experience, another chart (Figure 5-4) was made.

Work Begins

"Now our committees can meet," said the teacher. "Let's review what they are going to do at their first meeting."

STEPS FOR STUDYING OUR UNIT

1. We list our questions.
2. We classify them.
3. We choose committees to do research.
4. We decide on sources of information.
5. The committees:
   a. Do research on their topics.
   b. Plan an interesting report.
   c. Present the report to the class.
6. We evaluate reports.
7. We file reports.
8. We do activities together:
   a. We will have a Bicentennial Birthday Party.
   b. We will have an exhibit of all our work.
   c. We will take a field trip to Fort Niagara.
   d. We will see some historical movies.
   e. We will go to the Museum of the National Historical Society.
   f. We will attend the Bicentennial celebration in our town on June 15th.
   g. We will attend the play *The Great Rope* at the college.

Figure 5-2. *A criterion chart developed by Mr. Kranz and his pupils.*

On the board he listed the specific duties to be accomplished in this first committee meeting.

Each committee will:

1. Choose a chairperson.
2. Choose a secretary.
3. Decide what they will do to answer the questions.
4. Suggest ideas for a final report to the class.
5. Tell the class their plans.

The committees then were assigned meeting-places in the room and met in "buzz" groups to fulfill their duties. The teacher went from group to group suggesting ideas; giving information about films, books, and people each committee might use; and making notes about groups or individuals within the groups. Each group gave a brief report of its plans at the end of the period.

The groups were then ready to go ahead. The next day, the librarian was asked to come to the room and the children and Mr. Kranz planned with her how they could find materials in the library. The children learned new library techniques by going to the library with the librarian and learning how to use the card catalog and the call cards. Then the children gathered material from far and near. Letters were written to historical societies, to state museums and government agencies. The committees met daily and research began—infor-

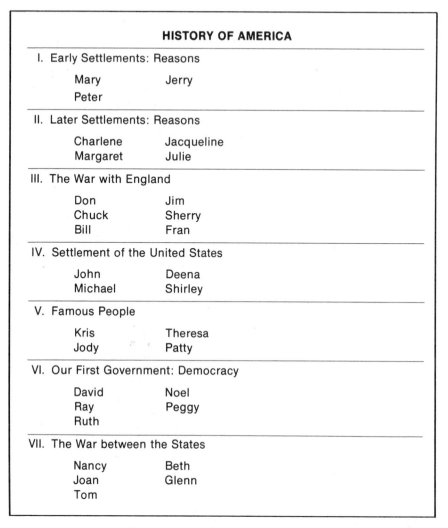

HISTORY OF AMERICA

I. Early Settlements: Reasons

      Mary   Jerry

      Peter

II. Later Settlements: Reasons

      Charlene   Jacqueline

      Margaret   Julie

III. The War with England

      Don   Jim

      Chuck   Sherry

      Bill   Fran

IV. Settlement of the United States

      John   Deena

      Michael   Shirley

V. Famous People

      Kris   Theresa

      Jody   Patty

VI. Our First Government: Democracy

      David   Noel

      Ray   Peggy

      Ruth

VII. The War between the States

      Nancy   Beth

      Joan   Glenn

      Tom

Figure 5-3. *Mr. Kranz's sign-up chart.*

mation was "dug out" of the most remote corners. Each day a short report period was held so the committees were kept informed on each other's progress.

Many times committees desired to take trips which the whole class felt would be valuable: trips to see homes and buildings of colonial architecture, to commercial movie theaters to see motion pictures of historical value, to museums, and to parks commemorating historical events.

Finally the committees began to feel they were ready to report their findings, so reports were presented. In this particular unit, each group wanted to contribute something for a culminating activity. After all the reports were made, the whole group participated in a variety of worthwhile experiences which helped draw the entire unit together.

OUR SOURCES OF INFORMATION

1. Textbooks
2. Reading books
3. Story books
4. Music books
5. Encyclopedias (World Book, Compton's)
6. "Information, Please"
7. Dictionary
8. Childcraft
9. Radio programs
10. Television programs
11. Films
12. Our school library
13. Our town library
14. Filmstrips
15. Slides
16. Pictures
17. People
18. Museums
19. School learning resource center
20. Cassette tapes
21. Multi-media kits
22. Forts
23. Bicentennial Barge; other traveling exhibits
24. Town programs
25. Town historians
26. Maps
27. Filmstrips
28. Workbooks

Figure 5-4

Culminating Activities

They made a scrapbook of their written reports, poems, original stories, and assimilated news items. In this book, too, were lists of their questions and copies of their planning charts. They made an exhibit in an empty room in the school of all the realia they had collected, the charts, graphs and pictures they had made and the creative stories and poems they had written.

They held a Bicentennial program for the rest of the school as a culminating activity. One of the best learning experiences was a visit carefully planned by the class to the Bicentennial Barge which docked at a port in a neighboring town. Children gleaned information from all the resources they had listed but found other sources of information as well. The town librarian proved to be a local history buff and came in to the classroom several times to serve as a consultant. The history department at the local college proved to be an invaluable resource. History majors enjoyed visiting Mr. Kranz's room and talking to the children—often leading the children in a discussion of political and historical issues.

The children planned and took a field trip to a local fort; they went as a group to the college theater to see a special performance of *The Great Rope*, a play of local history by Rosemary Nesbitt and later went backstage to meet the author and see how a play is produced. They planned a float which they entered in the June 15th Bicentennial Parade which was part of the town's celebration.

Learnings in Human Relationships

All of these activities were not only information gathering or synthesizing experiences—they provided the children with new experiences in human relationships: how to work with older and younger people, how to properly request and thank people for favors, how to hold a discussion with a consultant, the type of questions to ask, how to organize and categorize information, and a host of other skills identified by Mr. Kranz as objectives at the onset of the unit.

Development of Skills

Many other skills were developed. As part of their contribution to the school Bicentennial celebration, the children learned to write plays, then proceeded to write and produce a pageant of the history of the United States. This play was later put on television tape by the Educational Communications Department. The art, music and physical education departments all cooperated in this production.

Among the skills developed were those of map making. The children made maps of all types including salt and flour terrain maps, physical maps, political maps, and campaign maps. They made charts of all types of information, and even some models (such as one created by Chris and Jimmy of a canal lock demonstrating how boats are raised from one level to another).

Concepts and Understandings Developed

Throughout all the activity when the children were engaged in information gathering and synthesizing the material, Mr. Kranz acted as a guide for planning each step of the unit, for suggesting new ideas and materials, and *for helping the children draw together the concepts and understandings they were developing.* These were checked against an original list the teacher had made and were largely concepts and understandings that can result only as the outcome of experience, such as:

1. All people are interdependent.
2. All countries are now interdependent.
3. Climate has an effect on the way people live.
4. Rainfall has an effect on the way people live.
5. Each country of the world has common problems (food, clothing, shelter, education) and unique problems (struggle for independence, etc.).
6. The struggle for a democratic form of government in the United States was an experiment quite unlike any other in the world.
7. We are not, even yet, a full democracy—we are still working to perfect our form of government.

8. In a democratic society where much is left to the individual because each individual counts, human nature may cause much graft and corruption.

9. In a democratic society a sense of values is very important in order for people to live successfully together.

10. The Constitution provides rights for everyone—there are no privileged groups in a democratic society except by circumstance.

11. "All men are born free and equal" means equality of opportunity should be available for all people in a democracy. It does not mean each person has equal ability.

12. In a free society individuals are important, more important even than the government.

Weighing Evidence and Making Decisions

One of Mr. Kranz's greatest tasks was to make children aware of the controversial issues of each question or problem discussed, making certain the children weighed available evidence, encouraging discussion on both sides of the question and encouraging the children to make decisions about the controversies. His technique was simple: after each report which gave the children the necessary background of knowledge, he held a discussion asking for any other knowledge individual children might possess, or he added needed information to the report, or he helped the children identify gaps in their knowledge which needed filling and he sent them off to do further research. When sufficient knowledge was assimilated, Mr. Kranz presented the controversial issues or guided the children in identifying them. Often they were identified and discussed through puppet plays or role-playing. The children were encouraged to make decisions on the issues with evidence to back their decisions. When they were historical decisions, it was exciting to read further to see how each issue was resolved, and to note why or why not the resolution agreed or disagreed with the ones made by individuals in Mr. Kranz's group. When the decision was made on a current problem, the children had the experience of putting the decision to a vote, applying it to the classroom program and learning to take the consequences of their decisions.

Individual Differences Met

Not only were the children learning to work together but they were learning to think critically, to accept responsibility, to become more independent, to become appreciative and understanding, to learn their specific contribution to group living. They were constantly developing new understandings and arriving at new concepts. Also, such a plan afforded the teacher the opportunity to help individuals. Bill, who was shy and retiring at the beginning of the unit, volunteered for the part of George Washington in the play; the teacher had used every possible experience within the unit itself to help Bill gain poise and status with the group. The rewards of his work were forthcoming in the changes in Bill's behavior.

Careful records kept on each child helped the teacher in knowing that Nancy's excessive reading activity was her way of escaping life's realities in an attempt to avoid failure experiences. Nancy's self-concept was low; her home life was such that the child was constantly belittled and everlastingly told she didn't know how to do anything right. The teacher made sure Nancy had many opportunities to do things "right" and rediscover her capabilities. Nancy's failure experiences were carefully resolved, and the teacher's anecdotal record cards toward the end of the unit read:

> Nancy volunteered to figure up the milk bill today. She said, "I don't know if I can do it, but you will help me if I can't, won't you?" I assured her I would and she set to work. When she brought the bill to the class to report, several of the children checked it and found she was right. One said, "Boy, Nancy's a good figurer—I wish I could add like that." Nancy beamed and said, "I'll help you anytime, Mary." It was a wonderful success experience for Nancy, and she did not run to her corner to read once all day.

As in all good teaching, the success of a unit depends largely on the careful planning of the teacher for group and individual experiences. Some samples from the notebook of this teacher give ideas on how a unit may be carefully planned so that every experience may be used to help meet the teacher's objectives, and yet free her or him to take advantage of each child's creative contribution and develop each child's creative abilities.

Teacher's Plans

Some Pages from Mr. Kranz's Plan Book

I. BROAD GOALS

    A. To develop in the boys and girls an appreciation and understanding of the early historical and geographical backgrounds of their own culture.

    B. To stimulate an interest in current problems of their country.

    C. To foster an understanding of people from different cultural backgrounds than their own.

    D. To develop the concept of the democratic form of government.

    E. To help children appreciate the great sacrifices made in attaining the Bill of Rights.

    F. To help children form concepts and understandings of the influences of climate and geography on the mode of life, the type of people, the food, shelter, and clothing of a culture.

G. To help them appreciate the contributions of the early settlers to our mode of living today.

H. To help them understand that people are interdependent.

I. To show how transportation and communication developments have caused the world to shrink.

J. To show how the geography of a nation has influenced its history.

K. To develop an appreciation for the literature, music, art, and type of living in their own country.

L. To integrate the group and solve certain group problems:

1. Integrate new children in classroom so they work and play well together.

2. Give the girls status in important jobs.

3. Develop an appreciation of each other's work, etc.

II. SPECIFIC UNDERSTANDINGS TO BE DEVELOPED

Main Problem: To what degree has the United States been successful as a democracy after two hundred years?

A. Democracy was an ideal dream. No other country had ever conceived it as our forefathers did. A dream is something all must work for. We are still working for democracy. Each year we develop a better understanding of how a democracy must function in order to be successful.

B. As a complete democracy as stated in the Bill of Rights, the United States has not, as yet, reached its goal. But we have come a long way.

C. Americans are impatient. We are often ashamed of our lack of progress in the development of civil rights. Yet no country in the entire world has reached the standard of living and the equality of opportunity for minority groups that has developed in the United States in the short span of two hundred years.

D. America has many problems to face, both internally and in dealing with other countries of the world. Some of our major internal problems are: energy and how to produce and control it, welfare costs, unemployment, problems of the aged, national health insurance, food distribution, ecology and conservation, educational opportunities for all, reestablishment of railroads, graft in government (and other problems which Mr. Kranz listed). Some international problems listed were: trade, the storage of plutonium, world pollution, international peace organizations (such as the United Nations), establishing rights to the seas and to outer space, distribution of products, world poverty and hunger, conflicts in political ideologies, and many others.

This is but a sample of a long list developed by Mr. Kranz and used by him as a guide for discussions and planning class experiences.

III. FIRST STEPS IN DEVELOPING UNIT (His Plans for Planning):

    A. The children will list questions about things they want to know. Categorize questions.

    B. They will determine *how* they are going to study their unit and make a chart.

    C. Divide in committees—voluntary.

    D. List resources.

    E. Give instruction on use of resources.

    F. Discuss how to make a report.

    G. Practice making a report.

    H. Brainstorm ways of making creative reports.

    I. List committee functions.

    J. Practice committee meetings.

    K. When they are ready, turn kids loose on materials.

IV. SOME ACTIVITIES TO CONTINUE THROUGHOUT THE ENTIRE UNIT

    A. Keep a list of new words at front of room—a vocabulary chart. These will be used in part for the spelling words.

    B. Keep a "unit" bulletin board where new materials may be posted daily.

    C. Clip news bulletins, radio and television programs, and theater ads from the paper each week so these may be utilized in the unit.

    D. Listen to these radio and television programs; have committees attend movies (if whole class can not go) and report.

    E. Keep a file of all materials used on bulletin boards—teach child to use the file early in the game.

    F. Keep a list of all stories, books, and materials used in the unit which are available in the school.

    G. Map work—repeatedly.

There are many ways of plotting a unit on paper so it is usable and functional. Most teachers will study various plans and evolve one of their own. Mr. Kranz used a self-designed form. It was easy for him to keep his plan book on his desk and flip it open for immediate reference. By using columns he is able to see at a glance: 1) the content he feels a specific committee should be researching; 2) many ideas for learning activities which he can use with each committee in case the children do not have some of their own (in giving reports to the remainder of the class, for instance); 3) the references and resources available in the school which are on the children's instructional level; and 4) the references which he can use for his own information or for helping the children (such as information check sheets in workbooks, radio and television programs, etc).

Mr. Kranz can make easy reference to his objectives at the top of each page and to his evaluation strategies for each objective on the opposite side of the page.

The examples shown previously from Mr. Kranz's notebook demonstrate how carefully he planned his unit before he went to work on it with the children. Much of his initial work was done in the first days of planning while the children were forming questions, etc. He left room on all pages so new ideas by the children and new resources discovered by him could be added.

In many schools today, teachers work by committees, design the units for the year, print them and make them available to all teachers. This plan provides a rich variety of ideas as all teachers pool their work and points up to each teacher all the resources available in the school system. Units organized in this manner are properly called Resource Units. Because resource units are not developed with specific children in mind, they must be adapted by each teacher to fit the needs, interests and ability levels of the children in each class.

The last few pages of Mr. Kranz's plan book contained lists of ideas for culminating activities for the unit. These appeared on the children's "Steps for Studying Our Unit" chart (Figure 5-2).

This first phase of Mr. Kranz's unit provided an excellent background of information, concepts, understandings and appreciations for the next sub-unit which followed, all a part of the children's original plan.

The children felt they were ready to carry out their sub-unit on Government next inasmuch as they had already made a study of the constitutional convention and the first government of the United States. Carefully planned activities led to an in-depth understanding of how the United States government works, how taxes are levied, how the economy of the country is managed, the purposes and benefits of social services (including welfare, social security, medicaid, medicare and government sponsored projects), and how the government fulfills its obligations to a democratic population. Such matters as defense, international relations, election systems, interstate and international commerce, tariffs, treaties and how laws are made were all explored and learned through a variety of worthwhile activities. Many trips were taken, consultants were called in, films and television programs were viewed, a great deal of role-playing and dramatics were employed, and the learning resource center was in constant use.

All of this was a natural lead into the third sub-unit: The Rights of People, a natural follow-up to a study of the Bill of Rights and this in turn prepared the children for a study of the violation of rights of minority groups. The strikes of the early '70s were explored; methods of obtaining rights (unions and organized lobbying) were discussed, along with all the other civil rights problems of the past decade.

When all the sub-units had been developed, the children were gradually guided into discussions and role-playing situations where they were encouraged to use the experiences and the knowledge they gleaned to make decisions on their original unit problem: To what degree has America been successful as a democracy after two hundred years?

The children held many discussions on this. One activity that evolved was a large chart where the children listed successes of the new democracy in one column, failures of the new democracy in another column, and areas where progress was being made toward a true democracy in still another column. A small portion of that chart appears in Figure 5-5. It is a dramatic example of children applying the decision-making process where each contributed knowledge and values to arrive at a group decision.

One item on this chart is of special interest: the placement of "Recognition of minority groups." In the discussion of the Black revolution (and the revolutions by other minority groups), the children read or heard about the fight of

THE NEW DEMOCRACY: THE UNITED STATES

1776—1976

Successes	Failures	Progress
Establishment of the Bill of Rights.		Fulfillment of the Bill of Rights. Court cases still interpreting.
Establishment of government of the people, by the people, and for the people.	Corruption in government, lack of strict moral code.	
Economic independence.	Unequal economy— poor, underprivileged.	
Protection from enemies.		Disarmament conferences; maintaining of Army, Navy, Coast Guard, Marines.
Development of natural resources.	Uncontrolled development; pollution.	Ecology studies and control of natural resources.
Recognition of minority groups.	Needs of minority groups to gain rights granted by Constitution by means of "civil disobedience."	Great gains for minority groups in past 10 yrs. Legislation of civil rights.
Technological revolution.	Pollution.	Controls over pollution; national drives for beautification.
Air/space program.		Landing on Mars.

Figure 5-5

Blacks for their rights and the activities of the 1960s including the tragic death of Dr. Martin Luther King, Jr. After a great deal of discussion, the children suggested that the recognition of minority groups should serve as one criterion for judging America's success as a democracy. Mr. Kranz was surprised when the children placed the concept in the "Success" column. The children agreed quite readily that since the United States had been in existence as a nation only two hundred years and had been attempting to establish a democratic govern-ment in a true sense in that span of time, and since the country started with a conglomerate of people of all backgrounds and creeds, all of which had to be fused into common understandings, two hundred years was not a very long time and that the United States government had been very successul in estab-lishing the concept of equal rights for all, especially when the other countries of the world were considered. With such reasoning, Mr. Kranz agreed to leave the minority groups statement in the "Success" column.

We have seen a large-scale traditional unit in operation in Mr. Kranz's room. We can see how all goals are established and built around the major topic for study. Mr. Kranz's unit was a long one—actually it was composed of five sub-units, each of which lasted from three to five weeks—a half-year's work. Through his unit he was able to develop a sound social studies program, develop many important communication skills (language arts) and map skills for the semester, incorporate much of his art, music and other creative activities for the semester, reinforce and extend a good reading skills program, and incorporate realistic and relevant math lessons.

Some learnings were taught outside the unit, such as other specific reading skills, math skills and some art and music skills. These were taught, often on an individual basis, in one of the centers set up for it in the open classroom situation. Basically, however, most subjects in the traditional concept of the unit are integrated into one theme.

THE LESSON PLAN

After goals have been established for a year's work, they are generally translated into manageable units of work, and eventually into lesson plans.

A lesson plan is a sub-division of a unit: it generally is designed to last only one period while a unit stretches over a large block of time.

Lesson plans are generally written to be used with a group, or a class, within a definite period of time for the purpose of accomplishing certain specific objectives. Modifications of lesson plan forms are often used for individual study in modules, in workbook exercises or on task cards.

A lesson plan has certain essential parts and they ordinarily fall under: 1) a statement of the objectives for the lesson, with evaluation statements to measure the accomplishment of the objective if possible; 2) a list of concepts, understandings, outcomes or skills to be developed; 3) a specific form of motivation if one is needed; 4) an outline of the procedure the teacher plans to take—this is often a result of the creative thinking of the teacher; 5) an outline of any content the teacher needs; 6) a method of evaluation; 7) a list of materials needed for the lesson; and 8) individual or group assignments and follow-up.

While most lesson plans contain these parts, the teacher must not assume that lesson plans are all alike. Among the many criteria for writing lesson plans is the criterion of economy—each teacher will devise a quick and efficient way of planning so that time is gainfully spent. Many teachers do not write detailed lesson plans—they need only a few notes. Others need to plan in detail.

As in other planning, the basic element in a lesson plan is the objectives. The content and its presentation and the techniques of evaluation are designed to help students attain the objectives. The objectives of each lesson plan are not different from the objectives of the unit in which the lesson is taught except that they may be more limited or developed in more detail. Only a few objectives should be planned for each lesson.

The main purpose of writing lesson plans is to give the teacher a guide in directing his or her energies toward the accomplishment of specific objectives in a unit. The plan should not be rigidly adhered to, though. This might preclude taking advantage of better ideas. These ideas might come from the students or might occur to the teacher while the lesson is in progress. Such subsequent ideas sometimes make lessons richer or more relevant.

A good example of a lesson plan being developed in actual classroom practice is described earlier in this chapter where Mr. Kranz is teaching his students how to work in committees.

UNITS ON THE PRIMARY LEVELS

Application of Unit Method

In modified form traditional unit teaching is applicable to older children. In simplified form it can be used with younger children. Many teachers of primary-grade children utilize unit techniques in the kindergarten, first, second, and third grades, but the subject matter is planned differently. Recognizing the inability of children to read extensively for information, other resources are used to answer questions. The teacher may record questions in the kindergarten, for instance, and then, in planning for a trip to the fire station, may give each child the responsibility of finding out the answer to one question.

In a first grade where a group was reading at various levels, the teacher printed on the board each question that was asked, and the child copied his or her own question on a 3 × 5 card. Then the child was responsible for reading that card to find the answer to the question when the group went on the trip.

Primary-grade teachers who have their objectives clearly in mind fulfill these objectives by a series of experiences rather than through a detailed subject matter unit. These teachers often plan their work by listing objectives vertically on a large sheet of paper and then horizontally blocking off experiences which they will plan with their children to fulfill these objectives throughout the semester. In this fashion, the short interest span of many young children is considered, and each experience provides a contribution toward developing activities to meet the objectives. The objectives provide purpose for the various experiences of the year.

An idea of the planning an early primary teacher can do is obtained from this sample sheet of a kindergarten teacher's plan.

EXAMPLES—KINDERGARTEN TEACHER'S PLAN BOOK

I. GENERAL KINDERGARTEN GOALS FOR THE YEAR

A. Help children to solve their problems.
B. Increase their knowledge.
C. Improve skills.

Through a wide variety of experiences.

D. Develop desirable habits and attitudes.
  1. Responsibility.
  2. Independence.
  3. Social awareness, cooperation.
  4. Creativity.
  5. Self-discipline.
E. Develop in each child a sense of happiness and security.
F. Help develop readiness for skills and knowledge to come later.

II. OBJECTIVES TO BE ACCOMPLISHED

As a result of the units planned for these first ten weeks of school, each child will:

A. Develop the realization that people are interdependent and that people need each other in order to live effectively.
  1. The child will understand that each person has freedoms and responsibilities to perform in order to make life good for all, as evidenced by his or her growth record on anecdotal reports, observation of increasing ability to share and do his or her part of a job, records of the child's willingness to work with others and to do acts of kindness and help others, records from weekly sharing charts and responsibility charts.
  2. The child will understand that it is important to be helpful and considerate of people and that living together is more pleasant when certain accepted social courtesies are observed as evidenced by empirical observation (records on anecdotal reports), and a check sheet on social courtesies.
B. Be able to work effectively in a group, as evidenced by:
  1. Teacher observation, anecdotal records.
  2. Participation charts.
  3. Flo-graphs.
  4. Responsibility and work check sheets.
C. Develop basic concepts of quality and quantity: to give each child a meaningful base in numbers as evidenced by application of

Figure 5-6

knowledge of numbers to classroom situations (counting for chocolate milk and white milk, etc.), anecdotal records of teachers, pen
and pencil tests.

D. Develop oral language skills:
  1. To help the child to be comfortable in speaking before a group
     as evidenced by actual performance and growth in the anecdotal
     record kept by the teacher.
  2. To provide opportunity for the child to express his or her own
     ideas, as evidenced by lists of each individual's contributions in
     individual folders.
  3. To guide the child in developing clear, colorful and correct
     expression as evidenced by speech in class (recorded in anec-
     dotal records), and samples of creative speaking, painting and
     writing.

E. Develop an appreciation and love for music:
  1. By teaching the child many songs suitable for his or her age
     level and noting reactions to singing these songs on anecdotal
     records.
  2. By providing experiences with musical instruments and noting
     the child's reaction on anecdotal records.
  3. By helping the child to develop his or her body through the use
     of rhythms and noting creative reactions, motor reactions, and
     psychological actions.

Figure 5-6 (*continued*)

THE SCIENTIFIC METHOD: CREATIVE SOCIAL LEARNING

In unit teaching the approach has been based on a scientific method. This is
the unique contribution of science to the social studies and to creative thinking.
No longer are children expected to accept dogmatic statements made by a
teacher or a textbook author. Critical and creative thinking do not result if such
techniques are overused.

A scientist has a creative, exploratory mind. He or she learns to observe
carefully and to examine critically; beliefs are tested. These qualities are also
possessed by the creative person.

Although the area of science has its own body of knowledge, the main
purpose for teaching science in the elementary school is to develop creative
minds by using the scientific approach to problems.

This scientific method is not confined to the subject matter of the physical
sciences alone. In the discussion on unit teaching, the scientific approach was
used in a cultural-social problem. The basic steps in the use of the scientific
method might be listed as follows:

1. A problem is presented.
2. An hypothesis is formed concerning the problem.

3. Data are collected to prove or disprove the hypothesis.
4. Material is classified.
5. The hypothesis is tested in light of the data collected.
6. Conclusions are drawn; understandings are developed.

Children who are taught to study by use of this procedure are working creatively and constructively toward solutions to their problems. Some of the specific objectives which may be met through using the scientific method might appear to be something like this:

Through use of the scientific method—

1. Children learn to think creatively and critically.
2. Children learn to become more observing—observation becomes a habit.
3. Curiosity about the environment is aroused.
4. A healthy thirst for knowledge results.
5. Children are equipped with techniques for finding out answers to their own problems independently.
6. Experimentation is encouraged as a means of learning "why" and "how."
7. New interests are constantly being developed.
8. Children learn to differentiate between fact and fancy; superstition is dispelled.
9. The joy of exploration and the thrill of discovery are encouraged.
10. Children learn to appreciate and enjoy the works of others.
11. Children develop the ability to see relationships.
12. Children acquire the habit of basing judgment on fact.
13. Children develop open-mindedness.
14. Children develop good social attitudes.
15. Children obtain practice in logical, convergent-thinking problem solving, and in divergent, creative problem solving.

DURATION OF UNITS

How long should a unit last? This is determined by three factors: 1) the amount of time it takes to accomplish the objectives; 2) the age and interest span of the children; and 3) the amount of motivation the teacher is able to sustain.

Kindergarten teachers develop their work around short units. First graders would not generally be able to sustain interest over too long a period on any one theme. Studies of children at this age level reveal that children do not pay attention for more than ten to fifteen minutes to any one thing unless highly motivated. Consequently, they also jump easily from one activity or one topic of interest to another. Within the unit a teacher should plan many changing activities in order not to violate the biology of the children.

By the third grade children's attention spans are longer. They can sustain interest in a topic over a longer period of time. One unit on transportation was designed to last about six weeks; however, in that unit there were many topics to study: boats, trains, planes, trucks, buses, and cars.

Children in the fourth grade can stick to one topic for a longer period of time. One teacher's unit was designed to last six weeks, and it was built all around one general topic: foods.

Mr. Kranz's total unit was planned to last the entire semester, but it was sub-divided into topics designed to last from two to three weeks each.

Each teacher realizes, however, that each unit may last longer than is planned should the material have to be adjusted to the children because of its difficulty, or if the objectives are not accomplished as quickly as the teacher hopes. Sustained enthusiasm on the part of children may also lead a teacher to extend the time spent on a unit.

In like manner, the unit may not last as long as the teacher plans because of many reasons. The children may be so highly motivated that they speed through the unit wholeheartedly, or the teacher may have anticipated the needs of the group so well that the children accomplish their objectives with little distraction. Occasionally, children are just not interested, thus causing a unit to end earlier than planned. In any case, it is wise for a teacher to have a succeeding unit planned so the children can move gracefully and efficiently into it.

The allotment of time to a unit depends on the teacher's objectives and the children's interests and abilities. If good learning is in progress, the length of the unit is not of major importance.

Summary

The effects of a sound social studies program in the elementary school is expressed in the social living of the children from day to day in the regular classroom. The social studies program contributes to behavior changes which result in more creative and constructive human relationships.

The unit method of teaching contributes directly to the development of creativity in the following ways:

1. It allows children to be inventive, original, and imaginative.
2. It gives the opportunity to develop fluency of thought.
3. It provides for evaluation, necessary for the total creative act.
4. It provides for concentration.
5. It makes provision for putting knowledges and facts into divergent thinking situations—to apply them to new situations.

6. It is based on integration—the ability to see unity and to perceive structure and new design, the ability to relate and connect experiences.
7. The unit is flexible and allows for spontaneity and individuality.
8. Opportunities are afforded for children to analyze, abstract, and synthesize.
9. All types of experiences (verbal, symbolic, evaluative, figural, etc.) are provided to place children in situations where creative thinking and doing is at a premium.
10. Creative acts are guided by a goal or purpose.

Unit teaching is valuable and provides a good method of teaching for several reasons:

1. It possesses cohesion or wholeness.
2. It is based on the personal-social needs of children.
3. It cuts across subject lines.
4. It is based on modern concepts of learning.
5. It requires a large block of time so that jobs can be completed.
6. It is life-centered.
7. It utilizes the normal drive of children.
8. It takes into account the maturational level of the pupils.
9. It emphasizes problem solving and decision-making.
10. It develops a scientific attitude in children.
11. It helps children develop scientific techniques in problem-solving.
12. It provides opportunities for the social development of the children.
13. It is planned cooperatively by teacher and pupils.
14. It helps develop values and attitudes.
15. It helps develop skills.
16. Through its use teachers can develop knowledges, understandings and concepts.
17. It encourages creativity in teachers and pupils.[6]

To the College Student

1. Poll your class to see if any of the students remember being taught by the unit method. If so, have them tell what they remember about any given topic. Compare this with the memories the rest of the class have about learning the same topic. Did the experience approach help minimize forgetting?

2. Review the unit described in this chapter and consider the following:
   a. How many ways did the teacher use different media to develop creativity?
   b. How did the teacher meet individual differences?

6. Lavonne Hanna, Gladys L. Potter, and Neva Hagaman, *Unit Teaching in the Elementary School* (New York: Rinehart and Co., 1955).

   c. Think of all the ways the children showed evidence of developing creative human relationships.

   d. Did you feel the teacher was creative? Did he set conditions so children could be creative? Discuss the total role of the teacher as shown in this unit.

3. Planning a unit of work is essential before teaching it. Some reasons are listed below:

   a. Education is a selective process. The teacher must know what (from all the information available on each topic) is suitable for use with her or his particular group.

   b. The teacher must have adequate knowledge of the subject matter of the unit so children can be guided in finding information and so that the authenticity of their findings can be checked.

   c. The teacher must have goals and objectives in mind for the class and for individual students. This does not mean that the children will not help set their own goals. It does mean that the teacher will have a plan for helping them set these goals.

   d. The teacher must know the resources available in the school and in the community which can help meet the unit objectives.

   e. The teacher must be able to organize a large body of material into a workable form.

List some other reasons why planning ahead of time is necessary. Try planning a unit to teach to a classroom of children you have recently observed, or, better yet, one you plan to do your student teaching with.

4. Describe the difference between a *teaching* unit and a *resource* unit.

5. Visit a suburban school, a city school, and, if possible, a rural school. Notice the differences and similarities in classroom environment, teaching methods for the social studies, resources and children's behavior.

To the Classroom Teacher

1. Review your school objectives and note which ones can be met by content and which by method. Check your own program to determine how many of these objectives you are working on. How can you expand your program to meet more of them?

2. In terms of the objectives of a good social studies program as outlined in the last two chapters, can you justify the following practices, which were observed by the author in a recent school survey on which he worked?

   a. Class schedules were posted outside each door and each teacher stopped teaching one subject at the end of each scheduled time and began another, *even though logical stopping-places seldom occurred at the designated times.*

   b. A school that was totally subject-centered.

   c. All the children were reading from the same social studies textbook.

   d. Only the bright children were allowed to work on activities.

   e. The only form of measurement used was teacher-made tests administered every Friday.

3. In what ways does a unit provide for open-ended experiences that a subject matter curriculum does not?

4. Check yourself for a few days on each of the following questions to see if your teaching leans toward creative or conservative styles?

   a. Do I give more answers than the children do?

   b. Does my room reflect the children's work or my own (bulletin boards, exhibits, etc.)?

   c. Does the furniture in my room get rearranged into new patterns during the day?

   d. Do my children have the opportunity to talk or do they spend most of their time listening to me?

   e. Do the children's creative products appear daily on my desk or on the bulletin boards (poems, stories, paintings, etc.)?

   f. Am I tolerant of mistakes and do I help children turn their mistakes into successes?

   g. Did I help *each* child in some way each day?

   h. Did I learn something from the children each day?

To the College Student and the Classroom Teacher

1. Review the purposes of unit-teaching shown in this chapter and decide how the teacher who taught the unit on the Bicentennial fulfilled these purposes.

2. In a rural community, an intelligent but uneducated farmer came to school at the invitation of his fifth-grade son to attend the culminating activity of a unit that was a dramatization and exhibit of Alaska. In the exhibit was a great deal of art work painted by the children. He made this comment, "I don't see why Harry has to spend so much time in school foolin' around with paint—he ain't ever goin' to be no artist—he's goin' to work on my farm. Seems to me you folks waste a lot of time and tax money lettin' kids fool around with all this art stuff."

   How would you defend your program to this taxpayer? Does his comment indicate the need for an adult education program?

3. Of the following plans of organization, which are more likely by their very nature to foster creative teaching situations?

   a. The ungraded school.

   b. The self-contained classroom.

   c. The multigraded school.

   d. Team teaching.

   e. Machine teaching.

   f. Homogeneous grouping (for reading and other areas of the curriculum).

   g. Segregated classes for the bright or slow students.

   h. Television teaching.

4. Go to your curriculum library and examine some courses of study and some commercial units. Note the objectives of each and criticize each as to whether or not provision is made to meet each objective.

5. Using Mr. Kranz's lesson for developing committee work with his students as described in this chapter, see if you can reconstruct his original lesson plan. What were his objectives (behavioral and otherwise)? What concepts, understandings, outcomes or skills did he hope to develop? What motivation did he use? Outline his procedure: what content did he teach, how did he evaluate his lesson, what materials were needed, and what follow-up did he employ?

Selected Bibliography

ENGLE, SHIRLEY, and LONGSTREET, WILMA S. *A Design for Social Education in the Open Curriculum*. New York: Harper & Row, 1972.

GILLESPIE, MARGARET C., and THOMPSON, A. GRAY. *Social Studies for Living in a Multi-Ethnic Society: A Unit Approach*. Columbus: Charles E. Merrill, 1973.

HANNA, L. *Dynamics of Elementary Social Studies*. 3rd ed. New York: Holt, Rinehart & Winston, 1973.

MEYEN, EDWARD T. *Instructional Units: Applications for the Exceptional Child*. 2nd ed. Dubuque, Iowa: William C. Brown, 1976.

MICHAELIS, JOHN U. *Social Studies for Children in a Democracy*. 6th ed. Englewood Cliffs, N.J.: Prentice-Hall, 1976.

6 Creativity Is Individualism: Providing for Individual Differences

We were all born with a gift of wonder. Some of us retain the child's belief that creation is fabulous.

... when we praise the rose for its scent, the bird for its song, the sun for its radiance, the moon for its glow, nature gets credit which should go to ourselves. In reality nature is soundless, scentless, colorless, merely the hurrying of material, endless, meaningless.

We, not nature, create from the jumble of external physical phenomena the sounds, the scents, the colors and meanings which make up our emotional and intellectual lives.

RENE DU BOS[1]

INDIVIDUALITY: A DEMOCRATIC RIGHT

Every major organizational change in the public schools of the United States in the past two decades has stemmed from one goal: *to give each child an education that is commensurate with his or her ability.* As a democratic nation and a free society we are committed to this cause. We are the first group of people in all of history to be concerned with the development and education of *every* individual. Our political ideology is designed around this concept: in a free society individuals count but they don't count for much if they do not remain individual.

PLANNING FOR INDIVIDUAL DIFFERENCES

To foster the concept of developing individual differences among our children, creative people have frequently designed new plans of instructional organization

1. Rene DuBos, *A God Within* (New York: Charles Scribner's Sons, 1973).

167

or new methods of teaching, as we have seen in the previous chapters. We have adjusted materials to the child, impoverished or enriched the curriculum, altered promotion policies and changed grade standards, homogenized children by ability levels and other criteria, introduced the Joplin Plan, the Denver Plan, the Amidon Plan, and a score of others, ungraded and multi-graded our schools, employed television-teaching and programmed learning, utilized core curriculum and unit teaching, departmentalized our elementary schools, teamed our teachers, mechanized our syllabi, used self-instruction, individualized reading, pre-designed contracts, and have developed the concepts of the open classroom and open schools. The degree to which some of these plans have made individualization of teaching possible is related in the last chapter.

Each of these plans has been successful when used in a situation where it was carefully applied and evaluated. Many have been disastrous in communities where they were applied simply because change was held to be important for change's sake and was necessary so that a particular school could claim it was innovative. One fact is evident, however—the traditional forms of instruction, where all the students are taught the same thing at the same time, are no longer defensible. In their place environments are being created in which individuals proceed at a self-determined pace, often on self-selected subjects, to achieve self-satisfying goals.

The changes brought about by these organizational plans and different philosophies have, in many cases, been encouraging, and often startling. Changes have been recorded in teacher and pupil behavior. Discipline problems, drop-out problems and truancy have diminished; attendance in these schools has improved; teachers report being more satisfied with their work. The *human relationship* aspect of teaching, when cherished, appears to bring about a strengthening of self-concept and more pleasant human exchange.

DEVELOPING INDIVIDUAL CREATIVITY

With all our attempts to meet individual differences and to develop individual potential, much remains to be accomplished. The reason may very well be that the basic way to help each person to become an individual is through the development of his or her *creative* powers. In developing the children's creative powers, we may find that they are able to meet many of their own needs without all the organizational plans and the gadgets and gimmicks of modern education. For if children have their creative powers developed from pre-school times, even little children will be inventive enough to help themselves more than they presently do. Rigid conformity to an organizational plan may be as detrimental to the development of creativity as conformity to traditional teaching methods. The socialization process of every child is accomplished largely within the existing structure of the school. The structure will have a decided effect on each individual's creativity as well as other social abilities. That we have not been as successful as we had hoped to be is evidenced by the continued rise in the number of drop-outs from our traditional schools; the rise in delinquency and vandalism; the number of school failures, including nonreaders; and the failure of many pupils to be motivated to learn.

The social studies is the curriculum area in which democratic concepts are developed and which prepares boys and girls for their *child and adult* roles in a democratic society. While much attention has been given to individual differences (largely in ability) in reading, spelling, and arithmetic in the elementary classroom, little attention has been directed toward *developing the uniqueness of individuals* in the social studies program.

Research on group processes in their relation to creative development shows that groups have tremendous influence on individuals, and individuals often conform to the opinion of group majority—even when the individuals are right and the groups are wrong.[2] Ability to be independent seems to be less possible under group pressures.[3] Yet independence in human beings is essential for creative production. Part of the teacher's job will be to help individuals who have unusual or different beliefs to stand their ground until proven incorrect. On the other hand, the teacher will help all group members to be accepting of any one person's ideas until they are proven to be incorrect or impractical for application to the situation. These goals are social studies goals as well as creative ones.

Figure 6-1. *Individuals count when their own individuality is activated.*

2. S. E. Asch, "Studies of Independence and Conformity: A Minority of One Against a Unanimous Majority," *Psychological Monographs* 71, No. 416 (1956).
3. G. Moeller and M. J. Applezig, "A Motivational Factor in Conformity," *Journal of Abnormal Psychology* 55 (1957): 114–120.

Research also shows that we may expect greater descriptive social stress when classroom groups are divided heterogeneously than when they are divided homogeneously. Creative thinking is stimulated by social stress. It would seem then that heterogeneous grouping in a classroom might be more productive than homogeneous grouping.[4]

Teaching for the development of individuality in the social studies curriculum means helping children understand and be at peace with self. Much of this can be accomplished through creative activity.

The value of creative activity and its effect on the development of the human personality cannot be underestimated. Creative activity can do a great deal to help individuals find peace within self. It can replace boredom and apathy with a zest for life. A *doer* experiences expectations and hope instead of despair; deep involvement and interest instead of fear; enjoyment of being and of producing instead of concern about physical and psychological self; a feeling of meaningfulness instead of uselessness; a respect for oneself instead of self-pity; and an optimistic friendliness toward others instead of a pessimistic upsetting of others.[5]

It has been pointed out in this volume that over-emphasis on social participation of any sort, regardless of personal gain or loss, can result in discontented, unhappy adults who cannot adjust to group living to the degree that they, themselves, are happy people. Often in seeking contentment, adjustment or happiness, they can create waves which violate the ethics and standards of their peer group, thus bringing more discontent and unhappiness on themselves.

Czurles has put it well in his article "Art Creativity vs. Spectatoritis." He states:

> If man does not have creative outlets, he tends to turn more and more into an unsatisfied, uncreative *spectator*, instead of an ever enriched *doer*.
>
> In our society we have developed more and more efficient ways of training people to "do with things," but we have not done well in helping them "do with self." We prepare them more "for sale" than "for self." Thus many are almost incapable of creating their own satisfying activities or of finding lasting *meaning* in what they do. They cannot see, hear, or feel beyond what can be bought and struggle to obtain meaningful experiences through watching others. They contract the stifling disease of "spectatoritis" . . .[6]

Involvement in anything leads to understanding and a sense of "taking part," of "doing your share." These are worthwhile feelings to cultivate for group living in a democratic society. Since creative people are eager and willing to become involved in most projects, the conscientious development of creativity in the classroom and the fostering of creative characteristics in children may well be one way to combat "spectatoritis" in a society which really needs more

---

4. E. Paul Torrance, "Can Grouping Control Social Stress in Creative Activities?" *Elementary School Journal* LXII (December 1961): 139–145.

5. Stanley A. Czurles, "Art Creativity vs. Spectatoritis," *Journal of Creative Behavior* X, No. 2 (1976): 104–107.

6. Ibid.

"doers" and fewer "lookers." Democracy is dependent to a great extent on the degree to which individuals become involved in its functioning.

Czurles further states:

> Because man is both a feeling and a doing creature, he not only does, but he constantly responds with feeling to what he does and to what happens around him. Human meaning and feeling about objects and events, as distinguished from the purely impersonal physical and historic facts, are the essence of what man strives and lives for.[7]

INDIVIDUALIZATION VS. INDIVIDUAL DEVELOPMENT

Although this volume pleads for the development of individuality and uniqueness in humans as a great personal and national asset, it does not advocate independence or self-indulgence to the point where any individual becomes disinterested or unconcerned about fellow humans.

The respect for individuals and the rights of individuals must be taught even in the elementary school: it cannot be left to chance. Because it has been left to chance in the past, many changes have come about in society which may or may not be of value. Young people have heard many times from many sources that it is the day and age to "do your own thing" and many have done so without considering the consequences to others. When teachers do not serve as guides to individual teaching, learning and development, they are forsaking their professional reason for being in the classroom. It is the teacher's job to develop the individual abilities of each child, to try to develop that natural sincerity in human relations which all children have and to avoid the current superficiality predominant in many adult groups. The teacher must develop in each child a sense of responsibility toward others and an understanding of the need for one another that is as strong and lasting as is knowledge of space flights.

The school systems of the United States need to mature in their use of affluence and technology so that they facilitate the forces which draw people together and help develop a total national unity. At the same time, they need to plan for the growth of each student so that his or her own talents and capabilities are developed in relation to the environment and the people in it, thus making happiness as a member of a congenial group possible.

PROVIDING FOR INDIVIDUAL DIFFERENCE IN THE CLASSROOM THROUGH GROUPING

When we consider the facts mentioned in Chapter 1 of this book—that all children are creative, that there are degrees of creativity, that creativity is related

7. Ibid.: 105–106.

to intelligence, that creativity is individualism, that creativity is a process and a product, that creativity is a series of characteristics and traits—we have as sound a set of criteria for grouping within a classroom as the criteria currently used for many of our grouping plans.

Effective grouping to develop precious individualism calls for a change in the attitude of teachers. Teachers, too, must be individual—their roles must change from mimetic ones to creative ones. Objectives for teaching the various curriculum areas must also change in keeping with the philosophy of the times; the past objective for developing *correct* communication in the language arts, for instance, must change to that of developing *effective* communication.

Effective grouping also means that developing individual differences must be considered from the standpoint of each individual rather than as a form of curriculum modification, or as an organizational plan, or as giving teachers more free time. It means that sometimes a child will be taught alone, sometimes in a small group, and sometimes in a large group. Sometimes he or she will be in a group based on interest or ability, or with the children who live on the same street. But *the plan must suit the child*—it is not the child who must be manipulated to make possible the successful working of the plan.

This calls for new concepts and creative ways of grouping. Why not, for instance, group together for certain lessons children who respond to certain ways of teaching better than to others? Recent studies indicate that some children respond and learn best in situations where there is considerable structure and many rules and directions, while others learn best in a less structured, more open situation. Some children learn better in a creative situation while others are threatened by it. And some children can be more creative in a structured situation than in another type.

Meeting individual differences in the classroom is not accomplished simply by teaching each child individually. The physical, the social-emotional, the intellectual needs of a child cannot be fully met in a tutoring type of situation. Group or class interaction is needed to achieve the creative and social objectives of a social studies program.

Many teachers have not been as successful in meeting individual needs as some of the teachers described in this book.

Fallacies of Grouping

Before the problem of grouping for individualized instruction can be attacked meaningfully, an examination of some of the common fallacies of most grouping plans is in order:

1. Individual differences are still regarded in many schools, and by many teachers, as a nuisance rather than an asset to the schoolroom society. Planning for individual differences requires a great deal of time, as we can see by the accounts in the last chapter, which many teachers are reluctant to give. Until individuality is seen as an *asset* to a free society, and until the attitude of the teacher is changed so that he or she regards

it as a precious commodity and as a base for the operations of free people in a free society, *no organizational plan for meeting individual differences has a chance of being effective*, not even the open school which is designed specifically to develop individuals.

2. All the organizational plans for grouping have one basic fault. They assume that there are enough likenesses in an assortment of children so that the children can be grouped to enhance their differences rather than develop them through individual help. Often there is little allowance made for individual differences within the smaller groups.

3. Grouping for individual differences has taken place without clear-cut objectives. When a teacher asks, "Shall I have three or four reading groups?" a lack of understanding regarding the purposes of grouping is revealed. The only purpose in grouping is *to help each child learn in harmony with his ability to learn.* Often grouping is used simply because it is easier for the teacher and not because it is more beneficial to the child! Grouping is a form of segregation, which, if done improperly, may create more problems over a long period of time than it solves. Some educators find it difficult to see much difference between segregation by intellect (ability groups) and segregation by color of skin. They wonder if democratic understandings are being developed in *any* kind of segregation.

4. Every grouping plan except the open school plan interprets meeting individual needs to mean, "How can we arrange, organize, and teach our children so they can learn what *we* think they must know, or develop the skills *we* believe they must master?" *Only a few of these plans attempt to get to the inner personality or unique learning patterns of each child and develop the individual as he or she is.* Instead, we try to make the child over so that he or she will conform to our stereotype of the acceptable student. Consequently, many children often feel rejected because of their individuality. Every human being on the face of this earth must bring of himself or herself to learning, and it is the *whole* self, not just the mind, which changes as a result of learning. *We need to talk less about and do more to develop individual differences.*

5. The concept of meeting individual differences *or* developing individual differences has been regarded almost totally as an individual or a small group process. One important element of individuality has gone unheeded: *individuality only shows when it displays itself in a group.* In a good social studies program, there will be many opportunities to develop individuality and to meet individual differences *in a large group situation.*

   By their very nature, some of the new organizational plans (the Individually Prescribed Instruction plan, for instance) prohibit this type of grouping and therefore deny the child the challenge of creative thinking "on his feet" before an audience.

6. The concept of individualization as it relates to individual freedoms is often misinterpreted and misunderstood, sometimes to a harmful degree. In this volume the main thrust of the plea for individualizing the curriculum

is that of finding the learning pattern of each child, making plans to develop his or her own creative ways of learning, teaching each child in accordance with that individual's own learning patterns by offering many options for learning, leading the child toward self-actualization with the result that he or she can lead a happy full life and will contribute to the welfare of others in society.

The concept of individualization is not to be interpreted to mean that any individual in a given society shall have the privilege and right to "do his thing" at the expense of other members of society. With all liberty comes responsibility. Cooperation is necessary among people just as it is among nations.

Successful Grouping

So far we have seen many evidences of teachers successfully meeting the needs of children through grouping by ability, by interest or by problem area. To refresh the reader's memory, he or she may wish to refer to the following instances.

Chapter 1: Mrs. Cline's Middle East bazaar is a general description of how one group of teachers created a social atmosphere to meet the social, creative and intellectual needs of the children of a middle school.

Also in Chapter 1 is the account of Mrs. Thompson's Time Machine which shows how another teacher met the intellectual, creative and social needs of a group of primary children.

In Chapter 4 we read a more detailed account of a kindergarten teacher grouping her children to meet individual needs. We can go through an entire day in Miss Ellis' room noting that she seems to have designed a plan whereby every child is working in groups according to his or her own ability, interest or social level. So it is with Miss Angel, a first grade teacher whose program is also described.

By reading the weekly schedule planned by Kevin Edwards in Chapter 4 we can see how Mr. Martin made detailed plans for meeting individual differences in his open school situation.

The Slow Learner and Grouping

The degree to which a total grouping plan can be successful is exemplified by Michael in Miss Angel's room. Let's focus again on Miss Angel's classroom and follow Michael, a first-grader, through the day. We chose Michael because he is a slow learner and Miss Angel has done a masterful job in keeping him a part of his normal society while meeting his individual needs through a variety of types of grouping which are explored below.

At 8:50 Michael entered the room and went to work on some odd jobs which he had left unfinished from the day before. At 9:00 Miss Angel flicked the lights and Michael took his chair to the front of the room to show a game he had brought and to help in the planning period. He was able to take part in planning the program because the teacher used pictures which he could read easily. As soon as the planning period was over, Michael went to work with Esther making clay animals, milk stools and farm equipment for the model farm the children were building. He finished his work before the period was up so Miss Angel gave him a job to do: she taught him to use a heavy marking pen and asked him to reproduce a chart for her.

At 9:50 Michael helped clean up. He and David were on the Milk Committee so they went down to the cafeteria to bring the milk to the classroom. Then they helped Esther and Cheryl set the tables for the mid-morning snack. At 10:00 Michael enjoyed sitting with his friends for a mid-morning snack while Miss Angel played some soft music on the record player.

At 10:15 Michael and David took the empty cartons back to the cafeteria while other children cleared the tables. As soon as they returned, they joined the group at the front of the room to listen to reports. Michael learned some things about the farm when Allen, Jimmy and Paula gave their report. Some of the children showed their pictures. One group gave a play of a farm story and they used the clay cows and props Michael and Esther had made.

At 10:40 they played music and acted like farm animals. Miss Angel liked the way Michael waddled like a duck.

At 11:00 Miss Angel taught a new farm song. In it there was a duck so Michael showed his interpretation of the duck again. He liked the record Miss Angel played that had ducks in it.

When Michael returned from lunch at 1:00 he met with the class while Miss Angel told the children what they were going to do for reading. Miss Angel put Michael and the rest of his group in a corner of the room where she had set up an easy-to-operate tape recorder. He listened to the tape with earphones and followed some simple directions Miss Angel had recorded on the tape.

After Michael had done all the things Miss Angel's voice told him to do, he opened the envelope she had given him. In it was a puzzle for him to do. Before he finished it, Miss Angel called his group together. She looked at the papers on which they had drawn and she talked about them. She told Michael his was very nice. Then they played a game with their names.

At 2:00 they all went outdoors to play. Michael and Dennis played on the see-saws for a while. Then Miss Angel let them all play "Bombardment." She taught them a new game, "Caboose." It was fun. Michael got to be the caboose twice.

When they returned to the classroom, Miss Angel read them a story about *Shep, the Farm Dog*. Michael loved dogs. He had one at home. His dog's name was Gabby. The story was nice—it made him think of Gabby. Miss Angel had a real surprise after the story. She showed a film of Shep. It showed all the things a farm dog does to help the farmer.

After the film Miss Angel told them all about "four" and they tried to remember all the places they had seen four. Michael remembered four wheels on the tractor, and the four stars on the dairy truck. Miss Angel told him he had good eyes to see "four" so well. He remembered his cat had four legs so he drew a picture of his cat and put it up on the bulletin board under a big "four" before he went home. It had been a good day for Michael.

The fact that handicapped children can benefit from creative techniques of teaching has already been established. Evidence continues to mount concerning the advantages of creative programs for handicapped children.

Sharpe conducted a study with intermediate grade educationally handicapped children to determine the effects of a creative thinking skills program on their thinking ability. The results of his study seem to support the use of brainstorming as a method for developing creative thinking in handicapped children: the children showed significant improvement in figural creative abilities, in figural fluency, flexibility, originality and elaboration.[8]

Sharpe's work was consistent with the findings of Torrance,[9] Buchanan and Lindgren[10] who found similar results to be true when brainstorming was used with normal children.

The Bright Child and Grouping

Now let's follow Allen through the day. Allen is one of the brightest boys in the class. He could read when he was in kindergarten.

Like Michael, Allen came in at 8:50 and went about completing jobs that were left from the day before. He, too, joined the planning group at 9:00 but he had fun reading the words in the pocket chart which showed the day's plans.

In the work period Allen worked with Jimmy and Paula. They looked through books they had obtained at the library to find the answers to the questions listed by the children on the charts in the front of the room. When they found answers, they shared the book and took turns reading it together so they could report to the class. Miss Angel came by once in a while to see how everything was going.

At 9:50 they put away their books and joined their friends for a mid-morning snack while Miss Angel played soft music. David helped him clear the tables. At 10:15 he and his committee stood before the class and gave their reports on the questions they had looked up. Then Allen listened to reports from the other children and they all discussed their Work Period. One group dramatized a play which Allen enjoyed very much.

8. Lawrence Wesley Sharpe, "The Effects of a Creative Thinking Skills Program on Intermediate Grade Educationally Handicapped Children," *Journal of Creative Behavior* X, No. 2 (1976): 138-145.

9. E. Paul Torrance and P. Torrance, "Combining Creative Problem Solving with Creative Expressive Activities in the Education of Disadvantaged Young People," *Journal of Creative Behavior* VI, No. 1 (1972).

10. L. J. Buchanan and H. C. Lindgren, "Brainstorming in Large Groups as a Facilitator of Children's Creative Responses," *Journal of Psychology,* 83 (1973): 117-122.

At 10:40 the children all did rhythms of things they had seen on the farm. Allen pretended he was driving a tractor. Then he was the turkey gobbler. Finally, he showed the farmer chopping wood. Miss Angel made up music to go with each of his dances.

At 11:00 the children learned some new farm songs. Allen liked the one about the tractor best. He also liked the record Miss Angel played about the trip to the farm.

In the afternoon, Allen was in the advanced reading group. Miss Angel gave him a good book and some cards with questions on them. Allen read the questions and then hunted for the answers in the book. The pictures helped him a great deal.

When he finished he found some good books on the reading table and read some stories. Then he put together some puzzles that were on the play table.

At 2:00 Miss Angel told the children to put away their work and they all went outdoors to play. Allen loved the slide and for ten minutes he climbed up and slid down. Then they played an old favorite of his, "Bombardment," and Miss Angel taught them a new game called "Caboose." He was the caboose four times; he liked the new game very much!

Back in school Miss Angel read a story about *Shep, the Farm Dog*, and the children then saw a film, which he really enjoyed. Then Miss Angel asked the children to think of all the places they had seen "four" in the film. Allen remembered all these ways:

- four dog's legs
- four wheels on the car
- four wheels on the truck
- four slats in the gate
- four wheels on the wagon

- four stalls in the barn
- four horses in the stalls
- four wheels on the tractor
- four boys at the table

Allen was able to show the four family four different ways on the flannel board: 3+1, 2+2, 1+3, and four ones. It was then time to go home. Allen liked school!

It is possible, in a self-contained classroom, to group children in such a way that they work academically up to their potential and at the same time grow to physical, social and emotional maturity.

In Miss Angel's room children meet in groups for different purposes. Each child contributes to the best of his or her ability; the group dynamics of the class are planned so that each child may progress at his or her own rate and yet each is challenged.

Let's study the charted plan of Miss Angel's day. Notice the different *kinds* of grouping each child experienced during the day.

Types of Grouping

8:45   *Heterogeneous* grouping (each group includes children of various abilities).

9:00   *Family* grouping (all children assembled to work on one common project).

9:20   *Interest* grouping: the children chose jobs they wanted to do or signed up for committees that appealed to them.

10:00   *Heterogeneous* grouping: children ate lunch with anyone they wanted to.

10:15   *Heterogeneous* grouping: chiildren evaluated the school day and listened to reports.

10:40   *Heterogeneous* grouping: the children danced.

11:00   *Heterogeneous* grouping: they sang and listened to records.

1:00   *Ability* grouping: reading groups.

2:00   *Heterogeneous* grouping: outdoor play.

2:30   *Heterogeneous* grouping: story, film, and number concepts.

3:10   Dismissal

Planning the school day so that good human relationships are developed is part of a good social studies program. This is social living—the application of social studies objectives to classroom operation.

In a program where teachers and pupils plan their work together, all the reading groups or all the arithmetic groups do not necessarily meet at the same time. Other activities may be in progress while the teacher meets with one group just as there were many reading activities going on when Miss Angel met with each reading group, or as her committees engaged in many activities during the work period. Each child knows what he or she is supposed to be doing at any given time of the day.

Grouping children by ability may attach stigmas to the child, and this tends to create a negative social structure in the classroom if it is not done carefully and sensitively. As we have seen, each of the children participated in many kinds of grouping, and group membership changed with each period, weaving in and out like the colors in a beautiful tapestry.

Both Michael and Allen had these group experiences during the day: they met

- seven times in a heterogeneous group
- two times in a family group
- two times in an interest group
- one time in an ability group (reading)
- They also met two times for individual work.

Grouping need not be confined to classroom activities alone. Inter-grade groups give children new social contacts and new experiences in human relationships. Inter-grade groups can be formed for assembly programs, producing school newspapers, for school dances, garden clubs, school government activities, paper drives, UNICEF help at Halloween, and for a variety of other purposes.

Grouping and committee work have become the technique for getting the work of a democratic society done. Children cannot begin to learn these skills too soon.

PROVIDING FOR INDIVIDUAL DIFFERENCES IN THE OPEN SCHOOL

One of the main goals of the open school is to encourage each child to develop according to individual abilities and interests. The strategy of self-learning is employed to a great extent. The entire plan is designed so that each child is challenged to learn, receives help in learning, and learns to evaluate his or her own learnings.

In the open classroom organization, children are less likely to meet in classes although some teachers conduct open classrooms similar to the self-contained classrooms described previously. In these classrooms the children meet, plan, go off to work, meet again and report or replan. The teacher is not burdened, however, with planning so many "classes" for groups. His or her responsibilities lie more in planning and keeping records on each individual child.

If we follow Noel, the boy in the open classroom described in Chapter 4, we can see that his individual needs and interests were well met and developed during the day. At the same time Allen was learning to be responsible and independent by assuming responsibility for his own behavior and working independently all day.

MEETING INDIVIDUAL DIFFERENCES THROUGH MODIFIED PLANS OF UNIT TEACHING

The traditional and original unit plan as described in Chapter 5 was both a *method* of teaching and an organizational plan. It made possible the meeting of individual differences, the development of the interests and creative talents of individual children, an adjustment of ability to subject matter, and the use of a variety of resource material. The unit plan paved the way for other teaching strategies and organizational plans. The breaking down of grade barriers and the sharp focus on developing individual differences in children has brought into use many alternate plans and strategies for meeting the objectives for which unit teaching was developed.

Modified unit programs have replaced the traditional unit structure in many schools. Some of the more common ones are described as follows.

Modified Unit Program

Correlated Units

The word "unit" is often used in referring to a body of related experiences planned around two subjects such as social studies and English in a departmentalized middle school. "We are going to study a unit on Communication," says the teacher, and it means that the children will study the history, present uses and the future of communication and transportation, and while they are at it they will learn many communication skills. Generally, this unit is studied during one period of the day or one block of time with little or nothing during the remainder of the day related to it. It is really a throwback to the correlation plan. In non-departmentalized schools the correlation units are also used. In an open school the author recently visited, the children referred to their ecology unit which they studied during a specific period when two teachers worked with them in a team-teaching situation.

Integrated Units

The integration concept is often referred to as a unit of work in modern schools. This type of unit is generally built around one topic where many subjects are included, such as in a unit on safety where children study safety and incorporate such activities as signmaking and poster design for art, writing plays and stories for language arts, creating safety songs for music, etc. The unit is again restricted to a period of time during the day. Some schools have more than one such unit running in a classroom simultaneously. For instance, the children may tell you they are going to work on their safety unit in the morning and on their science unit in the late afternoon.

Work Units

Textbooks are often divided into UNITS OF WORK. In this instance a unit is a body of material about a specific topic such as *Freedom* which supplies the subject matter necessary to understand the concept of freedom and suggested activities or problems which will challenge the learner to put his or her new knowledges to work. Many teachers arrange these units on cards or in workbooks.

When the unit is arranged on cards, several cards are needed to complete it. Each card requires an allotted amount of work to be completed in one sitting. The objectives for the lesson are stated, information and directions are given, activities are suggested, some type of evaluation is stated (often a self-checking test) and the student is told to go on to the next card once the first one is completed correctly. Completion of all the cards is the completion of the "unit."

Contracts

Similar procedures are used in completing contracts, such as described in Noel's classroom in the last chapter. A contract or a set of contracts is written which develops a theme such as *Welfare*. This set of papers is often referred to as a unit. The sheets of paper on which these contracts are written are often posted on a wall in pockets with the contracts clearly labeled in sequence so a child can begin independently with contract No. 1. The teacher is consulted only when the child needs help, or to share the evaluation form which is filled out at the end of each contract, whether it is a test, an activity or some type of record. When the first contract is completed, the child goes on to the second, then on to the others until the unit is complete. Generally at this time some type of final evaluation meeting is held with the teacher.

Modules

A module has been described as a selected unit of measure, varying in length and used as a basis for planning and standardizing. The term was applied to educational teaching strategies with the advent of the interest in developing the talents and skills of children in relation to their abilities rather than by grade level. The curriculum for a year in any subject matter is divided into logical segments, and a series of lessons is designed so a child may work step-by-step through each segment, mainly individually, so that each successive segment is mastered. Each segment is called a module. Thus the old meaning of the word module is maintained because each lesson of the module becomes a unit of measure used as a basis for determining readiness for beginning the next lesson and for measuring each child's progress toward the ultimate fulfillment of the goals of the total module.

Units vs. Individualized Study Plans

Basically, the traditional unit plan is designed to place children in those circumstances where they learn to practice group skills and to foster worthy human relationships. The individualized study plans, on the other hand, help a child to be independent and develop independent work skills. When used for social studies teaching, the individualized plans can contribute only in a limited way to developing the basic objective of the social studies—to foster sound human relationships, and to be concerned with democratic interaction among groups.

Creativity

In each of the modified unit forms, creativity can be developed providing the teacher is aware of the need to develop it. Many "card units" or modules of teaching, in fact, contain a list of activities which are designed to develop the divergent thinking abilities of young people. Some focus directly on developing flexibility, fluency, originality, and elaboration in thinking—the basis of creative ideation.

OTHER INDIVIDUALIZED PLANS

In addition to modified unit plans of teaching, other plans of teaching and organizing have been made available to teachers.

Learning Activity Packets and Kits

Learning activity packets and kits are one such invention. They are instructional modules that contain one or more specific instructional objectives (generally stated in behavioral terms), sample test items which suggest how the behavior will be measured, and a complete listing of references to all instructional materials available to aid learners in developing the specific behavior.

An example is the I.P.I. (Individually Prescribed Instruction) packets which contain carefully sequenced and detailed objectives stated in behavioral terms, empirically developed materials which help students to proceed independently to learn prescribed behaviors, material for diagnosing pupils' progress, written prescriptions for each learner, continuing teacher diagnosis, and frequent feedback to the learner.

Tutorial Plans

Tutorial plans use the children as tutors to improve learning and then evaluate the long-term effects of tutoring both for the tutor *and* the learner. Although tutors often are children who are in the same class as the learners, cross-age tutoring has also been quite successful.

Resource Center Plans

All materials are housed in a resource center with schoolrooms often opening directly into it. Students are afforded facilities and opportunities to learn and conduct experiments which are not possible when materials are divided among many classrooms. Commercial materials kept in these centers are often of the self-instruction type such as those produced by Innovative Resources Incorporated, which has a drug education program designed for children from kindergarten through the third grade. It contains a thirty-frame color filmstrip where children meet Tat and Tot, two turtles who encounter some "friends" in a forest and are faced with a decision concerning drugs. The color filmstrip is accompanied by a teacher's manual.

PROVIDING FOR INDIVIDUAL DIFFERENCES THROUGH PERSONALIZED INSTRUCTION

Most educators see the I.P.I. program, previously referred to, at the opposite end of a continuum which begins with the old traditional classroom in which the teacher lectured and the children recited all day with no attention given to individual abilities, interests, or learning patterns. The I.P.I. type of program, when developed to the extreme, focuses on the intellectual development of children often at the expense of their social, emotional and creative development.

In order to fulfill the objectives of the sound social studies program as described in this volume, the meeting of individual needs and the development of individual differences requires a sensitive balance of large and small group work, some total class work, a generous portion of individualized instruction and guidance, and a large chunk of independent work.

Summary

The American dream and the democratic commitment has always been to provide each child with an education commensurate with his or her abilities and interests. Such an education was rarely provided in the old traditional school. It was inevitable that educators would abandon the lock-step, autocratic set-up of the traditional school for a more democratic, individualized approach to learning.

In this chapter we have explored how teachers and administrators provide for individual differences in children through a variety of grouping processes, through open schooling, through personalized instruction, through contracts, modules and other plans.

Basic to all creative, aesthetic living is the recognition of the worth of every individual child and an acceptance of his or her contributions. Individual differences in children are the greatest natural resource we have in this nation today. The development of these individual differences is a basic necessity of creative growth. The great ideas of all cultures of all times have come from a relatively few men or women in each culture who dared to break away from the accepted mores and concepts of the culture and think differently. Making all children think and act alike is a sure way of destroying progress and committing genocide of a democratic nation. Individual differences in children are a precious commodity and deserve to be developed and accepted by other members of society, but always within a framework where the rights and differences of other members are not violated.

In classrooms such as those described in the first four chapters of this book, teachers are teaching facts as well as developing attitudes, building skills, establishing values, instilling appreciations, promoting abilities and forming character. Within the creative organization of a classroom, creative methodology also helps the teacher to meet the goals for social living.

Creative development is fostered when children have the opportunity to explore and manipulate ideas and materials. Some degree of stress and tension is essential for creative thinking. Too much homogeneity lessens this stress and tension. The reproduction of the total society of mixed abilities, races, ideas, religions, and creeds may do more to create the necessary tensions for creative thinking and creative living than the placement of children in groups that are too much alike.

To the College Student

1. Discuss these statements:
   a. All children in the same city should follow the same curriculum.
   b. Teaching the principles of democracy through rote memory was a successful way of producing democratic citizens.
   c. Good courses of study are those which follow a textbook written by experts.
   d. Social studies and social living mean the same thing.
2. Try this in class: Spill a little paint or ink on the center of a few sheets of paper. Fold the paper to make ink or paint blots. Make five such blots. Put them before the class one at a time and have each class member tell what the blots remind them of. Categorize the answers (a committee may do this). Then analyze them—which ones seem to be unique or different from the others? Do you think the people who wrote these answers are more creative than others? Why?
3. List the merits of self-instruction as it pertains to the development of a child's creative ability. What specific group of children are most benefited by self-instruction devices?
4. Teachers need materials in their classrooms which are appropriate for *all* ability levels. Each individual brings something different to these materials and uses them according to the dictate of his or her own creative ability. Paint, clay, and colored paper are examples of such materials in art. Make a list of the materials that might fulfill this criterion in social studies.
5. Many research studies have been conducted on children's interests at various age levels. Consult such a list and note how many of these interests are touched on by the teachers described in this and previous chapters.
6. Knowledge of child growth and development can be applied to all learning experiences, both in and out of school. When the natural growth characteristics of children are considered, successful parties can be planned for children. Plan a good party for any age level, using your knowledge about children and individual differences. Then, check your party plans against *The Gesell Institute Party Book* by Ilg,

Ames, Goodenough and Anderson. Did you make ample provision for individual differences so all children might have a good time?

7. Following is a list of fictitious names of books and stories. From what you have learned about children in all your classes, try to classify them by age level, remembering the children's interests:

    a. Man and Machines
    b. The Little Lost Rabbit
    c. Mary Sears, Airline Hostess
    d. The First Date
    e. Baseball Joe on the Big Diamond
    f. Steamy, the Steamshovel
    g. The Book of American Indians
    h. Happy the Hoptoad
    i. How to Make a Rocket
    j. Homes in Other Lands

8. One good way to observe the differences in various age levels is to visit a nursery school, then a kindergarten, then a first grade and on up through the sixth grade. This technique will enable you to see how children change from year to year in their growth patterns.

9. Work out a series of questions to ask a child. Ask them of a five-year-old; then ask them of a ten-year-old. Tape the answers. Play them back in class. Notice the differences in the type of answers, the use of vocabulary in the answers, the sentence structure, the difference in understanding of concepts and the abilities to communicate. Some samples of good questions are:

    a. What are your favorite interests? (to get the child to talk of self)
    b. Who is your favorite friend? Tell me about him or her. (a social question)
    c. Who is your favorite adult? Tell me about him or her. (a social question)
    d. What is fear? Anger? (emotionally packed questions)
    e. What is an astronaut? (a check of knowledge)
    f. What does "curious" mean to you? (a concept question)

10. Bring a child to visit your college, or your home, or your sorority or fraternity house. Make a list of all the questions he or she asks. Post them in class.

11. In the comic strip "Peanuts," one of the characters, Linus, carries a blanket wherever he goes. Why do you think he does this? Collect the cartoons of Linus and study them. Does the cartoonist know children well? Does he capture the individuality of each character in his comic strip?

12. Collect some creative writing of children of various ages and compare them for content, form and style. Have each member of your class write a letter to a child asking the child to answer. Put the answers on a bulletin board in order of age. Compare the letters in relation to:

    • form
    • content
    • tone
    • handwriting
    • punctuation

- means of expression
- apparent like or dislike of writing letters
- relatedness to the letter you wrote the child
- Do letters show individuality in children?

13. Discuss these statements, taking a stand for or against each one:
    a. Gold stars are good motivators for learning.
    b. We live in a competitive world, therefore competition is good for children.
    c. A kindergarten program is just a play session.
    d. Primary children are too young to make decisions.
    e. Primary children should learn "The Star Spangled Banner."
    f. Some good games for the nursery school level would be "Farmer in the Dell" and "Dodgeball."
    g. Children should not be passed to the second grade until they can read.
    h. Reading is the most important part of a first grade curriculum.
    i. In a case where a school rule is broken, all fifth grade children should be kept after school until someone tells who the offender is.
    j. All children should use the same workbooks.

To the Classroom Teacher

1. Various psychologists have observed these traits in creative children: a willingness to take a calculated risk, an ability to sense and question the implicit, a capacity to be puzzled, an openness to the seemingly irrational in himself, considerable sensitivity and exuberance, and a greater acceptance of himself than is the norm. How do you regard the children in your class who possess these traits? Do you value them or consider them problems?

2. Sound human relationships are among the most creative of all acts. In our many ways of grouping, we have not put children together geographically—that is, grouped them by neighborhood when they come on the bus. This might be a good way to group children because the relationships made in school would be reinforced outside of school in the neighborhoods. Discuss this as a creative idea. Is it a practical one?

3. School personnel generally have a list of objectives they hope to meet, then they determine a method of teaching to meet their objectives. To this they add the necessary tools, supplies, and resources to enhance the methodology. Then they set up an organizational plan whereby the determined methodology may function. Does your school plan its organization as carefully as this, or has it adopted some of the new plans without first defining goals and methods? Has the effect of your total school organization ever been evaluated in terms of the goals and objectives of the school? Should it be? How would you go about it?

4. If you could wave a magic wand and have what you want, what sort of organizational plan would you want in your school? Your classroom? Why?

5. What things about your school would you like to change? What do you regard as valuable and would like to keep? How can change be instigated? Think of plans that might rouse the faculty to make some needed changes.

To the College Student and the Classroom Teacher

1. Make a list of instances you can think of where creativity develops best in solitude. Make a list of those where it develops best in a group situation.

2. "Some things are better taught individually, such as reading, handwriting, and grammar usage. Other things cannot be taught individually or they are ineffective because they are basically concerned with relationships among people; for example, oral expression, listening, and social studies." Consider this statement and decide what implications it has for teaching the social studies. Does it mean we do not take individual differences into account in the social studies?

3. Rigid schedules in a school can be a detriment to creativity. How? Devise an organizational plan that would best help you meet the objectives you set up for a classroom of your own.

4. Here are some suggested topics to investigate and report to the class:
   a. Hobbies of Intermediate Children
   b. Favorite Songs of Children
   c. Play and Its Importance in Learning
   d. Block Play and Its Relation to Learning
   e. Building Values in Children
   f. Using Television in the Classroom
   g. Field Trips as an Educational Device
   h. Left-Handedness in Children
   i. The Wetzel Grid
   j. Using Projective Techniques with Children

5. What sort of homework assignments should Miss Angel give to the children in Glendale's first grade? Would they be the same as those given in a school that has culturally different children?

6. Make a collection of report cards from many school systems. Compare them. What does each really tell a parent? Is there any consistency among them? Any great differences? Do report cards tell parents anything about the individuality of their children? Can you find even one that promotes the concept of individuality? How can individualism best be reported to parents?

7. *Behavior modification* is a concept currently in vogue. Actually it is the old psychology of stimulus-response with minor alterations. Study *behavior modification* and discuss whether or not it develops or blocks creative development in normal children.

Selected Bibliography

BANKS, JAMES A., and JOYCE, WILLIAM W. *Teaching Social Studies to Culturally Different Children.* Reading, Mass.: Addison-Wesley, 1971.

BARCLAY, J. R. *Appraising Individual Differences in the Elementary Classroom: A User's Manual of the Barclay Classroom Climate Inventory.* 3rd ed. Lexington, Ky.: Educational Skills Development, 1974.

BECHTEL, WILLIAM M., and CONTE, ANTHONY E. *Individually Guided Social Studies.* Reading, Mass.: Addison-Wesley, 1976.

BERMAN, LOUISE M., and RODERICK, JESSIE A., eds. *Feeling Valuing, and the Art of Growing*. Washington, D.C.: Association for Supervision and Curriculum Development, 1977.

COMBS, ARTHUR W., et al. *Perceiving, Behaving, Becoming*. Chap. X. Washington, D.C.: Association for Supervision and Curriculum Development, 1962.

ESBENSEN, THORWALD. *Working with Individualized Instruction: The Duluth Experience*. Belmont, Calif.: Fearon, 1968.

GOODALE, ROBERT A. "Methods for Encouraging Creativity in the Classroom." *Journal of Creative Behavior* 4, No. 3 (Spring 1970): 91-102.

GOWAN, JOHN C. *Development of the Creative Individual*. San Diego: R. R. Knapp, 1972.

HAUCK, BARBARA B., and FREEHILL, MAURICE F. *The Gifted: Case Studies*. Dubuque: William C. Brown, 1972.

HOLLIFIELD, JOHN H. "The Gold Star Kid." *Learning* (October 1973): 36-37.

HOWES, VIRGIL M., ed. *Individualizing Instruction in Reading and Social Studies*. New York: Macmillan Co., 1970.

MORRISON, HARRIET B. "The Creative Classroom." *Journal of Creative Behavior* 7, No. 3 (Third Quarter 1973): 196-200.

SAMPLES, ROBERT E. *The Metaphoric Mind*. Reading, Mass.: Addison-Wesley, 1976.

SUCHMAN, J. RICHARD. "Diagnostic Teaching." *The Instructor* 86, No. 8 (April 1967): 62.

TALBERT, GENE E., and FRASE, LARRY. *Individualized Instruction: A Book of Readings*. Columbus: Charles E. Merrill, 1972.

WILLIAMS, FRANK E. *A Total Creativity Program for Individualizing and Humanizing the Learning Process*. Englewood Cliffs, N.J.: Educational Technology Publications, 1972.

7

Using Textbooks and Printed Materials to Develop Creativity

The teacher . . . gives not of his wisdom but
rather of his faith and his lovingness.
If he is indeed wise he does not bid you enter
the house of his wisdom, but rather
Leads you to the threshold of your own mind.

KAHLIL GIBRAN[1]

INTRODUCTION: DECISION MAKING AND INQUIRY

The gathering of data and amassing of knowledge is a necessary step in the making of decisions. Without adequate inquiry, decision making is impulsive. It is just as important for children to learn the techniques and skills of gathering information as it is to gather the knowledge itself. These skills (such as the ability to do reading research, take notes, summarize, etc.) must be identified and taught to children, preferably in the context of units.

Teaching by inquiry simply means that the teaching and learning in any classroom is based on involvement and investigation on the part of the child. Inquiry teaching develops such skills as observing, classifying, analyzing, inferring, hypothesizing, generalizing, drawing conclusions, synthesizing, critical and creative reading.

Traditionally, textbooks have been used largely for the purpose of providing information. Recently, however, there has been a shift in the emphasis of social studies textbooks to develop the skills of inquiry as stated above. Much more could be done by textbook writers to further a multi-purpose use of the textbook than is currently done.

Current textbooks, as a rule, do little to develop creativity. Overuse and

1. Kahlil Gibran, *The Prophet* (New York: Alfred A. Knopf, 1964): 56.

189

incorrect use of the contemporary textbook was even found by researchers to be one of the barriers to creative development.

Until recently, textbooks in the social studies have been more descriptive than analytical. They presented the rosy aspects of society: all the people in the United States were presented as happy and prosperous. Rarely, if ever, were problems presented or pictures of minority group children used. As such, they performed a disservice. Although social studies focuses on human relationships, the problems of those relationships were not discussed or mentioned. Social studies books presented (many still do) factual matter on economics, civics, history, geography, and some anthropology. Children who used such books were due for a jolt when discovering the facts of life later in their high school or college years.

Some social studies texts are beginning to place emphasis on the problems of society. Good social studies texts in the elementary school should teach the skills of inquiry, problem solving and creating. They should lead the child to the ultimate goal of the citizen in a democracy—the ability to make his or her own decisions.

Children need practice in functioning in their complicated society. Many of the skills needed to function wisely are best taught in the elementary years. Decision-making is one of them. Children can practice decision making by participating in the social behavior of their own classrooms and their community. A good textbook will be relevant in that it supplies children with information necessary for decision making, helps them to formulate values through situations and information and suggests activities and projects which involve children in decision-making, examples of which we will see on the pages which follow.

TEXTBOOK TEACHING

Textbook teaching has never completely fulfilled the objectives of the educational system in the United States, particularly in the social studies program. In many subject matter areas, including social studies, new knowledge is being amassed so quickly that parts of textbooks become obsolete between the time they are written and the time they leave the printing press. One popular sixth-grade social studies series printed in September and released the following February contained no mention of nine African nations that had been formed within that period of time, nor were any of the maps of Africa up-to-date. This puts great responsibility on the shoulders of the teacher, where it has rightfully belonged all along. Too many courses of study in schools have been determined from textbooks and not from the needs of the children or of any particular community.

Teachers can use textbooks creatively and many do. But it is not an easy task when most textbooks in themselves are so unrelated to diverse types of learning and uncreative in their presentations.

Can textbooks be creative? This author believes they can. George Stoddard says this about textbook teaching:

. . . Now we know that memory has a part to play in learning: speaking any language, including our own, involves a vast number of correlated impressions on call. The trouble is that in textbooks far removed from original sources, we are fed fragments that conform neither to the logical demands of an intellectual discipline nor to the psychological needs of the learner. Devoid of form, many a textbook renders its authors wholly unexciting. Our search for creativity therefore demands a new role for the textbook—a lesser one in the totality of the school day, but a deeper one. Its main purpose should be introductory. It should stir the student to ask, and find answers for, key questions. It should send him to original readings, experiments and experiences not otherwise occurring to him; it should transport him across the barrier of words to sights, sounds, feeling, and emotions. Such a work viewed as a map, ticket, or guidebook is defensible; not itself creative, a good textbook can show the way to creativeness.[2]

This author believes that the textbook of the future *must* be guided by the concept stated above by Stoddard. It is his firm belief that textbooks (and so-called workbooks) *can* be designed to take an active part in the creative development of teachers *and* children. Creative uses for textbooks as they now exist and suggestions for changes in their design follow in the hope that teachers will supplement the textbooks used in their classrooms with their own intelligent, creative ideas.

Social studies textbooks are primarily a summary of facts intended to impart knowledge and build concepts. We have learned that communication on the conceptual level is difficult without the common experiences which underlie these concepts. For this reason, children encounter too many concept words in the social studies books which they do not readily understand, and communication often breaks down.

The imparting of information is *one* aspect of the social studies program, but it is only one aspect. Children who have difficulty in reading can obtain information in many ways: through films, filmstrips, still pictures, interviews with people, observation, field trip experiences, and sharing with other children.

The textbook can generally be used with children of average or above-average abilities to gather information for reports, for checking factual knowledge, to read for specific items, and for developing research skills.

Used as an aid to the social studies program rather than the core of it, the textbook takes on new dimensions. It can help in developing many skills in children. It becomes a springboard for creative learning.

THE TEXTBOOK AS A RESOURCE MATERIAL

Textbooks have their primary value in serving as resource material for children. As sources of information they can be used in the following ways:

1. To gather material for a debate, a discussion, or a report.

2. George Stoddard, "Creativity in Education," in Harold H. Anderson, ed., *Creativity and Its Cultivation* (New York: Harper and Brothers, 1959): 182.

2. To provide information for children doing research in order to report to the rest of the class.

3. To summarize and culminate a unit of work. Often textbooks help organize the material the children have presented and pull it together. The textbook also fills in gaps in the children's information.

4. As a check for material gleaned from less reliable sources.

5. As instruments for testing children's knowledge.

6. To provide material for details—such as making scenery for dramatizations set in a foreign locale, for determining correct props, etc.

7. As a resource to gain ideas for worthwhile activities and thought-provoking questions and study skills.

8. As an overview of an organized body of knowledge.

9. To develop map skills.

10. To develop graph and chart skills.

11. They can contribute to critical thinking.

12. The suggested activities in some texts *could* develop *social* skills in children.

13. To save the teacher endless hours of research.

14. To provide continuity in studies; help develop time-line sequences.

15. To provide visual aids.

16. To develop basic values in children if the materials are properly used.

All of this can be summarized by the statement: social studies textbooks provide children with information to help them in making decisions.

Figure 7-1. *The textbook serves as a resource material.*

PICTURES IN TEXTBOOKS

Pictures, carefully selected, can perform a variety of functions when used in a social studies textbook:

1. They can enhance the text in several ways. One of the most common is to supplement the printed word and in so doing make the written vocabulary of the textbook visible. This is illustrated by a textbook which introduces such words as koala bear, kangaroo, and coral to a reader and presents a picture of each to show the reader the meaning of the word.

2. They can add depth to the knowledge being transmitted to the reader by providing a vicarious experience. This is illustrated by a text which describes George Washington's winter at Valley Forge. The text may simply state the wretched conditions under which the soldiers lived, but a picture shows not only the conditions and the suffering, but the type of clothing worn, the type of fire the soldiers built, the material used, the kind of country which comprises Valley Forge, the difference between an officer's and enlisted man's uniform, etc.

3. They can further develop the generalizations being presented by the written text. A textbook may, for instance, be developing the generalization that people are interdependent. An accompanying page may show a series of pictures tying the basic idea into the everyday life of a child such as one picture which shows a mail carrier delivering mail, another showing a waitress or waiter serving a family in a restaurant, another showing construction workers building a house and still another showing a mechanic repairing an automobile. A simple caption at the top of the page reads *We Need Each Other*.

4. They can extend the text by supplying information or concepts not in the printed word. This is illustrated by a textbook which is describing the importance of conserving gasoline because of the energy crisis. The text gives figures and facts about current gasoline consumption and may show graphs and charts to clarify the points being made. A picture of an electric automobile appears on the page with this information in the caption: Long ago electricity was stored in batteries and used to run cars like these. Some modern engineers believe that using electric automobiles may be one solution to the present gasoline shortage problem.

5. They can promote both convergent (critical) and divergent (creative) thinking. Convergent thinking is well shown in a composite picture of various scenes that depict how a bill becomes a law. Divergent thinking is fostered by a picture or a cartoon of strikers picketing a building with the statement under the picture which directs, "Write slogans that might appear on the signs the picketers are carrying."

6. They serve as a means of developing competencies and skills. A verbal

text gives the directions for construction of a log cabin. The accompanying picture shows how it should look after the directions are followed.

7. They help present situations in a manner so clear that without them children could not completely understand the problem being discussed. In a chapter on equal rights, for instance, one social studies text approaches the concept through equality of opportunity—the constitutional right of every person to an education. A page of pictures under the caption *"Are these children having equal opportunity?"* shows a school in the country, a beautiful city school, a lovely central school, a suburban school, a school in a deprived area in a large city, a poor village school, and a one-room school. The discussion guide accompanying the text helps the teacher bring out the advantages and disadvantages of each type of school shown and leads the children into a deeper discussion of what makes an equal opportunity school.

8. They can help the teacher in the development of values, traits and character. A picture of a war refugee child left starving and crying in a pile of rubble can do a great deal in developing empathy and can involve the child emotionally in the horrors of war; a picture of the Marines raising the flag at Iwo Jima can help a child understand the values of valor, courage and integrity.

9. They can develop appreciation and an aesthetic sense. Pictures in a text on any country, when carefully chosen, can show the glory of a panorama, the art value of a totem pole, the artistry of a Navajo sand painting, the majesty of a skyscraper, the sensitivity and skill of the sculptor, the value of color, the creativeness of the artist, the mastery of the architect, and the beauty of dance and drama.

10. They are invaluable in developing time-line sequences and a sense of history in children. Pictures of the Smithsonian Institute's inaugural gowns of the Presidents' wives show a careful sequential development of women's fashions of one segment of our culture.

CREATIVE USES OF THE TEXTBOOK

The textbook can be put to creative use. A few current textbooks are not concerned solely with imparting factual knowledge; they attempt to develop creativity by posing open-ended problems and learning situations that set conditions for creative thinking and creative doing by putting the knowledge to work.

On the pages that follow are types of materials that could be developed in textbooks or are being used in current textbooks to pursue the following objectives:

1. To put acquired knowledge to work.
2. To stimulate various creative kinds of research.

3. To provide supplementary material rather than serve as the core of the unit.
4. To build understandings through creative thinking and experiences.
5. Help children in making choices and in passing judgments.
6. Help children with problem-solving.
7. Help to promote creative thinking.
8. Help to develop critical thinking.
9. Help to develop aesthetic appreciation.

Each of these objectives has been identified in Chapter 1 as contributing to the development of creative problem solving.

If the textbooks which you are using do not provide exercises and suggest experiences such as those which follow, you as the teacher are afforded a great opportunity to use your own creativity to design task cards or modules which do incorporate material such as the following and which supplements the unit in the textbook.

Put Knowledge to Work: *Textbook Activities—1*

Objective: *to provide experiences for children where acquired knowledge will be put to work*

It is an essential element of creative development that 1) children acquire a great deal of knowledge, and 2) that this knowledge be put to new uses in problem-solving. Some of the illustrations in this chapter show how knowledge gleaned from textbooks can be put to work. They also show ways that textbooks can suggest experiences for children which will help them put knowledge to work.

Primary Grades (Ages 6—8)

1. In the picture book you are using which shows how children can help to be good members of a family, you see pictures of boys and girls doing many things. Now tell the teacher all the things you can do to help at home. Your teacher will print them on the chalkboard. The teacher will give you strips of paper. Copy from the chalkboard one job you can do for each day and write each on a separate strip of paper. Put these strips in an envelope. Decorate the envelope with pretty designs. Print the words TO MOTHER on the front of the envelope and give it to your mother for a Mother's Day gift.
2. Take a trip to your local museum to find out:
   a. What did the early people who lived in your town wear?
   b. What did they use to eat with?
   c. What kinds of houses did they live in?
   d. How did they travel?

Figure 7-2. *Putting acquired knowledge to work: a result of the creative use of textbooks in a primary grade.*

   e. What materials did they use to build furniture?

   f. How did they make cloth?

Find words that these words have taken the place of:

zipper   _____

furnace   _____

chalkboard   _____

margarine   _____

carpeting   _____

3. Take a visit to your town or school library and ask to see some really old newspapers. Then look at the advertisements. Notice the differences in tools, clothes, materials and services for sale. Notice, too, the difference in prices. What brought about all these changes?

Middle Elementary Ages (Ages 7—10)

1. You have just finished reading many stories about Indians. All of these stories did not happen at the same time. The Incas, for instance, lived many hundreds of years after the Mayas. With your teacher's help, arrange the stories in order so that you will know which happened first, which happened second, and so on. Putting things in order is called a sequence. You are making a sequence chart.

2. The Apache and the Hopi Indians were both desert tribes but they were very different. Make a list like the following and include ways they were different.

Hopis	*Apaches*
Farmers	Wanderers
Peaceful	Warlike

Then make a chart of the ways they were alike.

3. Below are some words which tell the methods used for travel in the early days of this country. Opposite each word write what mode of travel today has replaced each of them.

horseback	stagecoach
wagon	surrey
foot	canoe
flatboat	sleigh
raft	covered wagon

Upper Elementary Grades (Ages 9—12)

1. Watch your newspapers for headlines and for advertisements that are propaganda. Collect propaganda material and make three charts: "Propaganda for Good," "Propaganda for Bad," and "Propaganda that Has Little Effect." Paste the headlines and advertisements on the proper charts.

2. Some things people must do in order to live together comfortably are: 1) make rules to protect each other's freedom, 2) work out ways to give people equal rights, 3) work out ways so each family can have enough food, 4) plan a way so all families have a place to live, 5) agree on some ways to communicate, 6) decide who will be a good leader. What are some other things people must do in order to live together? Find parts from the story of Red Hawk to show how his people took care of these things. Then discuss how these things are taken care of in your community today. Also discuss this question: Did you consider these topics when you made plans to live together as a class this year?

Stimulate Creative Research Activities: *Textbook Activities—2*

Objective: *to stimulate creative research activities*

A characteristic of creative children is that their learning is often self-initiated. One way to develop creativity in all children is to encourage them to learn for themselves by providing stimulating problems and by teaching them skills for seeking out the answers in many ways. The following types of exercises suggest a need for many kinds of research skills and a motivation to research for many children. Often research leads to discovery, and discovery is a great impetus to creativity.

Many sources for research are suggested in the following examples and in other chapters of this book. Many types of research are implied, all of which can be used comfortably by children. Among them are historical research, research through experimentation, action research, analytical research, and applied research.

Primary Ages

1. Ask your grandparents or other older people these questions and then discuss how their lives were different from yours:
   a. What kind of school did you go to when you were my age?
   b. How did you get to school?

Figure 7-3. *The textbook can stimulate creative research activities.*

c. What amusements did you have then?

d. How was your dinner cooked?

e. Where did your parents shop?

f. How did you learn the news each day?

g. How did you heat your houses?

h. Where did you get most of your food in the winter?

i. In what kind of house did you live?

2. Collect old photographs from home and make an exhibit in your classroom. Notice the changes in clothing, hair styles, automobiles, homes and recreation. Try to explain why these changes came about by telling your teacher and classmates some of your ideas, such as: clothing is lighter and less bulky because 1) houses are better heated, 2) vehicles which take us from place to place are better heated, 3) new fabrics are warmer, 4) some new fabrics are cooler, 5) fabrics are easier to wash and do not need to be ironed to look fresh.

Middle Elementary Ages

1. Visit a supermarket and list all the ways you see foods being preserved today. Try to find out at what time on your time-line each way of preserving food was introduced.

2. Make a list of all the things you ate for breakfast, or dinner. Try to find out from what part of the world all these things come. On a map of the world color in the places where your meals come from.

Upper Elementary Ages

1. If you live in a part of the country where maple trees grow, try to locate a farm where the trees are tapped and maple syrup is made. Plan a visit to this place. If possible, tap trees and boil some maple syrup.

2. If you are interested in life as it was lived in ancient Egypt, read the following books and share them with each other:

   Bright and Morning Star by Rosemary Harris. (New York: Macmillan Co., 1972).
   The Golden Goblet by Eloise Jarvis McGraw. (New York: Coward McCann, 1961).
   Wrapped for Eternity by Mildred Mastin Pace. (New York: McGraw-Hill Inc., 1974).

3. The Bicentennial celebrated in America in 1976 was a tribute to our two hundred years as a country. Many communities did special things to celebrate the Bicentennial. Below is a list taken from newspaper articles. Why did these communities do these things? Why were they important to United States history?

   • The city of Rome, New York, rebuilt old Fort Stanwix and held a gala festival at the opening of the restored fort in May 1976.

   • In Lexington and Concord, Massachusetts, the citizens gathered together and acted out several events from the Revolutionary War, such as the Battle of Bunker Hill, Paul Revere's Ride, etc.

- In the small city of Oswego, New York, the community Bicentennial was started with a beautiful dramatization of a children's book, *The Great Rope* by Rosemary Nesbitt.
- In Washington, D.C., all the patriotic buildings and statues were cleaned and special events were planned for tourists.
- In Philadelphia the Liberty Bell was put on display in Independence Hall, and the month of July was set aside for special celebrations.
- A copy of the Magna Carta was loaned by the British government to be displayed in Washington, D.C.

Provide Supplementary Information: *Textbook Activities—3*

Objective: *to provide supplementary information rather than serve as a core to a unit*

Textbooks may be used effectively as supplementary material. After a teacher has launched a unit and the children are gathering information, the teacher may want the children to first gain a unique "feel" for a country or place. Literature contributes greatly to the feeling about a country. Children's literature today contains stories about every country in the world which paint delightful word pictures and use illustrations that give vigor and reality to the countries being studied. A teacher may prefer to use literature (or a film or filmstrip) as the principal way to introduce the factual material or a feeling for a country. The textbook is used to fill out the details of the overall impressions the children get after their original exposure to the topic. Teachers who use this approach to unit teaching prefer to have many different textbooks available in the classroom rather than thirty copies of one book.

When social studies texts are used with good pieces of children's literature, a new world opens to children! Compare the passage from *Secret of the Andes* to those found in most texts. Can there be any doubt as to which will arouse the feelings and free the imagination of any child?

Children's literature passage from *The Secret of the Andes* by Ann Nolan Clark

Copyright 1952 by Ann Nolan Clark
Reprinted by permission of The Viking Press
Pp. 24-26

The minstrel went on talking. It seemed that he knew as much about llamas as he did about songs. He knew how to use the llama slingshot. He knew how to turn the llamas' heads inward in a circle before one began to put the loads on their backs. He knew why father llamas were never sheared—so that the long hair on their backs would make matted pads for their loads.

"Did a llama ever sit down and refuse to move for you?" Cusi asked him.

The minstrel said, "No, I myself have never owned a llama. But I have seen them sit down when they were displeased about something." Both he and Cusi laughed at this. There is nothing funnier than to see a string of llamas sitting down on the trail and refusing to move. "Just because one of them has been over-loaded," Cusi said.

Chuto called to them. The old Indian was satisfied that all was well with each and every member of his flock. He was ready to return to the hut and finish weaving the mat he had been working on. He was making it of tortoru reeds and twisted grass. It would be good to sleep on when he traveled. Cusi also had work to do. They needed new rope to tie their bundles. Yesterday the boy had gathered armfuls of long grass and had put them to soak in water overnight. Now he pounded the water-soaked grass with a rounded wooden club. When he had mashed it into a pulp, he rolled it into long strands between his hands. Next he braided the strands into even, strong rope lengths.

While he and Chuto worked, the minstrel sang to them. This morning his songs were about the Inca Kings of long ago, when Peru belonged to them and not to the Spaniards who conquered them.

The minstrel played softly at first on his Panpipes, and the grazing llamas stopped to listen. Then, as the music continued, they folded their feet beneath them and rested. They began humming. No music is more beautiful than llama-humming. It sounds like wind over the water. It sounds like water rippling over moss-covered stones. It is wind-and-water music. It made a moving background for the sweet crying of the minstrel's pipes. Cusi stopped braiding the grass strands to listen. Chuto stopped twisting tortoru reeds and long grass to listen. Suncca crouched by his young master and forgot to whine and forgot to be afraid in beauty of the music. The minstrel began to sing, softly at first, then louder and louder to the music of the Panpipes and the llama-humming.

He sang:

> "Long ago they made it,
>   the world.
> It was young.
> The people in it,
>   the world,
> They were new.
>
> "Then the Sun Father
>   in kindness
>   sent Topa,
>   grandfather of the Inca,
>   sent Coya,
>   queen mother of the Inca,
>   to teach them,
>   the people.
>
> "Sun Father sent them,
>   Topa and Coya,
>   saying,
>   'Take you this golden staff
>   and walk with it

across the new-made world,
walk with it
until by its own desire
it sinks itself
into the heart of the earth.
There then is your new home.'

'They did as they were told,
Topa and Coya,
and the staff sank itself
into the soft earth
of the place that is known
as Peru,
Four Quarters of the World,
to become home of the Inca.''

The minstrel finished his song. The music stopped. Only the llamas kept on
humming.
The echo:

"In—ca
Home—of—the—Inca
Home—of—the—Inca
In—ca
In——ca''

kept bounding from mountain peak to mountain peak.
The song was finished.
The llamas kept humming.

In this instance it is obvious that a piece of literature teaches much more
than the textbook. The textbook can best serve as a summary after the children
and the teacher have read many stories such as this.

The teacher who read *Secret of the Andes* to the children held a discussion
on all they had learned about the Incas from the book. They checked the
original questions of their unit to see how much knowledge they had gained.
The textbook then served to help them summarize their findings and as a
resource to find answers to questions which they had not found in the story.

Build Concepts and Generalizations through
Creative Thinking: *Textbook Activities—4*

Objective: *to build concepts and generalizations in children by stimulating
creative thinking*

Concepts are built after many specific experiences; they stay with children
after specific facts are forgotten. Some words in themselves are concepts. Some
geographic concepts are "hot," "region," "area," "desert" and "range." Concepts are built as a result of many experiences. Conceptual understandings

Figure 7-4. *The textbook serves as a source for building concepts and stimulating creative thinking.*

continue to grow and change throughout an individual's entire lifetime as new experiences are encountered. Often the same word may have a different meaning to two people because their experiences have not been the same.

Textbooks give children many specific facts and information. Often the teacher is left to develop concepts and generalizations from these facts. A creative teacher will set conditions for new ideas to recur in new situations to promote the development of concepts and generalizations.

Generalizations are statements that reflect relationships among concepts. The generalization "Values, technology and the natural environment influence the culture of a society" includes the concepts: values, technology, natural environment, culture and society. The broader the generalization's ability to explain the world—throughout space and time—the more useful it is. Statements about specific people, countries or events are not generalizations.

The development of concepts and generalizations is a long-term goal and is affected by the intelligence, experimental background, social-emotional adjustment and reading ability of each child as well as access to mass media and a host of other factors.

Many recently published textbooks focus directly on the development of concepts and generalizations rather than on the memorization of facts. Such textbooks make a major contribution to creative learning in the classroom.

Following are some activities suggested by textbooks which teachers can use to set conditions for teaching concepts and generalizations in the classroom.

Primary Ages

1. After the children read the story about life on the farm, divide your class into five groups. Have each group make a bulletin board. One group will make a bulletin board about FOODS ON THE FARM; another group will make one on WORK ON THE FARM; another group will do one on FUN ON THE FARM; another on ANIMALS ON THE FARM; and another on BUILDINGS ON THE FARM. When the children tell each other stories about their bulletin boards, add other things that they know about each bulletin board topic that they did not read here. Also have them tell how their bulletin board topic is important to all the people in your town.

2. Have each child draw a cut-out picture of each member of his or her family. Have them string the figures to a coat hanger to make *family mobiles* which are something like family trees. Hang all the mobiles from the ceiling of your classroom and have each child tell an interesting story that happened to his or her family.

Middle Elementary Ages

1. Collect pictures of several recent inventions. At the top of a large sheet of paper draw or place a picture of each of the inventions mentioned that started others. For example: on one sheet of paper you might paste an electric light. Under that would come neon lights, the radio tube, television tubes, etc.

2. Following are some activities which were carried on in many communities long ago. What do they mean? Find out by viewing films, using books or looking in encyclopedias.

people *churned* butter	women *quilted*
farmers *dried* apples	pioneers *boiled* soap
blacksmiths *shod* horses	mothers *dipped* candles
men *cured* leather	fathers *tapped* their children's shoes

   Are these words ever used anymore? Do they mean the same thing as they did then, or have the meanings changed? Make lists of other words that have changed in meaning over the years.

3. Below are some words taken from the vocabulary of Laura Ingalls Wilder

from "Little House on the Prairie" and some taken from an eight-year-old schoolgirl today. How are these words related?

lye	gasoline
quilting bee	freeway
candles	air conditioner
dishwasher	mill wheel
dances	corduroy road
furnace	skateboard
slate	television
cornhusking	neon lights
fireplace	

Upper Elementary Ages

1. Collect pictures of all kinds of weather and landscapes. A book says, "Almost all kinds of climate can be found on the great continent of South America." Place a map of South America on your bulletin board and pin your pictures around it. Now with colored string or ribbon, make a path to the place where that scene or weather picture might be found. You will have to use what you learned about geography and climate to figure out some places. Your teacher can help you with others.

2. Draw a picture of a computer on a large sheet of paper and put it in a conspicuous place in the classroom. Then draw a vertical line through the center of the page dividing it into two equal parts. On the left side of the paper, have everyone list jobs that formerly men and women held, but now are handled by computer; on the right side, list jobs that now exist because of the invention of the computer.

   Do the same thing with the telephone, the automobile, and airplane.

3. A "united" country does not mean that everyone always agrees with everyone else. It does mean that the people are united in their beliefs. One of these beliefs may be that people have a right to disagree. Because people are united in their fundamental beliefs, the country is strong in the sense that it cannot be divided. The Constitution of the United States states our fundamental beliefs. Read the part called *The Bill of Rights* and think of all the ways different groups in the country have come to argument, to demonstration and even to violence because of disagreement on what the Bill of Rights means. When people do not read a document such as the Bill of Rights in the same way, it is called a difference in "interpretation." Some of the violence and action was over the "interpretation" of the rights of people. Their belief that they have the right to disagree is accepted and therefore "interpretation" problems are often solved. From clippings and magazines find instances where controversy over "interpretation" of the law is now going on.

Opportunities for Making Decisions and Judgments:
Textbook Activities—5

Objective: *to provide the student with experiences in making decisions and passing judgments*

The ability to make decisions and pass judgments are two skills that are a necessary part of the creative process. The artist must make decisions continually in choosing the right color for the right space. The poet must be concerned with using the right word in the right place, the architect, with the right material or design in the right place. All creativity relies on these two skills. The social studies program offers unlimited opportunities to develop these skills which are also essential for democratic living. People must choose jobs, decide on school-bond issues, vote for political candidates, and judge persons on trial.

There are many small ways children naturally make decisions in a modern classroom all through the day:

Decision-making Situations

- Painting
- Creative writing
- Choosing games
- Map study
- Modeling
- Dramatizations
- Planning trips, parties, programs, etc.
- Working contracts
- Doing worksheets
- Arranging exhibits
- Engaging in projects such as the Middle East bazaar, the time machine, the food unit
- Planning the daily program

- Solving arithmetic problems
- Evaluation of each class period
- Construction activities
- Choosing committees
- Scheduling time for various activities
- Working through modules
- Arranging conferences with teachers
- Planning posters, announcements, letters, invitations, etc.
- Working through sociodramas and other sociometric techniques

The elements in decision making may be defined as follows:

1. The student encounters a problem.
2. The student "feels" that a problem exists that he or she wants to solve.
3. The student faces the problem, defines it and begins to hypothesize possible solutions. This is where creativity plays an important part in the thinking process. Actually, the student is engaging in some private brainstorming in thinking about possible solutions to his or her problem.
4. The student studies the problem by relating it to past experiences, through reading and/or field explorations.
5. The student sees and considers a variety of solutions—all of which are

possible. Creativity again plays an important part in the thinking process but so does critical thinking for the student must intellectually weigh the consequences of any decision he or she might make.

6. The student makes a decision. It may differ from the decisions of others but it should help him or her feel again in equilibrium for having acted.
7. The student takes action on the decision.
8. The consequences of the decision must be accepted by the student.

One interesting approach in teaching decision making is to have a unit which meets the entire problem head-on. To show how all people must constantly make careful decisions, Mr. Allen used the MEDIA MATERIALS tapes and accompanying materials to show children in his middle school group how great decisions were made in the past and how the people who made them bore the consequences of their choices. These topics bear the titles of: *Thomas Jefferson and the Louisiana Purchase, William McKinley and the Spanish-American War, Abraham Lincoln and the Emancipation Proclamation,* and *Woodrow Wilson and the League of Nations.*

Following are some examples of contrived experiences which put children in decision-making situations. They could be incorporated into textbooks to develop critical thinking.

Primary Ages

1. All your life your parents and teachers have been telling you to *share* your things. But there are some things we do not share. We do not share a toothbrush, for instance. We do not always share a new bike, or a lollipop. Make a picture chart of *Things We Share* and *Things We Do Not Share.* Have good reasons for drawing each picture and for placing it where you do.
2. Here is a story for you to act out:

    School begins at nine o'clock. Every morning at nine o'clock Miss Murphy, the teacher, calls the boys and girls to the front of the room to begin planning for the day. Every day, about five minutes after the children begin, the door opens and Beverly comes in. Beverly is always late. She slides quietly into her seat, puts her books away, and then brings her chair to join the planning group. It is breaking a school rule to be late. Miss Murphy speaks to Beverly quietly at first and Beverly, who lives only a block from school, promises to do better. The very next day, however, Beverly is again late for school. If you were Miss Murphy, what would you do?
3. One of the things we all have to learn in order to become adults is how to make judgments. Making judgments means making a decision. But it means more than that because it means trying to make the wisest decision. Below are four sets of statements. Using the last four chapters in this book, decide which one you think shows the best judgment for the people about whom you read.

Statement 1. Chapter 11

Brave Hawk was foolish to believe that the rain dance would bring rain.

or

Brave Hawk helped his people believe in their gods by believing in the rain dance.

Statement 2. Chapter 12

Fleetfoot was unwise to live in a wigwam in the winter.

or

Fleetfoot's parents made the best use of materials they had to make a warm winter shelter.

Statement 3. Chapter 13

Aztec's father was foolish to work for the Lord Serpent for one whole day every once in a while when he needed the time for his own cornfields.

or

Aztec's father was wise to work for the Lord Serpent.

Upper Elementary Ages

1. Children: Here is a problem for you to think about!

CHILDREN SHOULD HELP TO MAKE SCHOOL RULES!

This is a problem about which all people do not agree. We call it a "controversial" problem. That *big word* means you could have a dispute or a controversy over it.

Let's see how you can share ideas. Can you listen to other people's ideas and opinions? Can you wait for your turn to talk?

To see that everyone gets a chance, divide your class into small groups of about six people in each group. If your chairs are in rows, face each other. If you sit around tables, group them. Choose a chairperson to call on people. Choose a secretary to write down your ideas. Have the secretary keep a list of ideas *for* the argument and a list *against* the argument. Discuss this for ten minutes. Then let the chairperson from each group report to the whole class.

2. This activity gives you a chance to make a special kind of chart. Write "Things We Think We Know" along the left side of a sheet of paper. Across from each thing we think we know write why we think we know it.

Things We Think We Know	*Why We Know It*
Examples:	
We think the Mayas were serpent-worshippers.	All their carvings are full of serpents.
We know the Mayas had ball courts, good roads, and great temples.	They can be seen today.

We know the Mayas made beautiful jewelry and had religious customs.	A great deal of jewelry and realia were found deep in the Mayan well of sacrifice and can be seen today in museums in Mexico City.
We know about the Mayan number system.	Mayan customs were described in a book written by a Spanish priest in 1566. All but three books written by the Mayans were burned by the Spanish.

3. *A Problem for You to Think about: A Controversial Issue*

In a democracy the majority of the people rule. That means that if *all* the people do not want a law it is put to a vote. If *most* of the people vote for it then it is passed. "Most" of the people is a majority. Another way to say it is that a majority is at least one more than half the votes.

Some people feel this is unfair. They say that when a vote is very close a majority is not enough. A law needs support of the people, and if nearly half the people in a country do not want it, then it will not work. There will be too many people who do not support it. They feel it is more democratic to get what is called a "consensus." A consensus means that people work on a law together and change it until nearly all are satisfied with the change. What do you think about this?

> PROBLEM: If the rights of nearly half the individuals in a country are suppressed by a small majority vote, is this really democratic?

Divide your class into groups and talk about this. Then come together and share your opinions.

The group that is not the majority is called the minority. In a real democracy the rights of the minority are also considered. Can you think of some ways minority groups might secure *their* rights also? Discuss this problem, and share your ideas about it.

4. *An Illustration: A Controversial Issue*

Foster Problem-Solving: *Textbook*
Activities—6

Objective: *to provide the student with experiences in problem-solving*

Textbooks can help in the solution of social problems. Recently textbook authors recognize that social studies programs must involve those learnings which help children to understand and deal with social problems.

Many textbooks suggest the following as steps in problem-solving:

1. Initial stage, in which a person becomes aware of a problem requiring a solution.
2. Data-gathering phase, in which the person becomes familiar with the problem and seeks materials for solution.

3. Hypothesis formation state, in which the person formulates tentative solutions.

4. Hypothesis testing phase, in which solutions are tested.

Many basic textbooks in the teaching of social studies advocate similar steps in the method of problem-solving. It will be noted that these are essentially the same steps as John Dewey lists as steps in critical thinking.[3]

Following are some of the ways textbooks help teachers set conditions for creative problem-solving.

Middle Elementary Ages

1. Many of the problems we now have about energy are due to the fact that people were trying to save energy at one time and invented ways to do it. Then, supplies ran out or new ideas were invented and other problems about energy were created. Show how some simple tools help to save energy. For instance, try to drag one of your classmates across the floor in a flat-bottomed wooden box. How many children does it take—how hard do they have to work? Now put some dowels under the box. Keep putting dowels in front of the box as you move it across the floor. How many children are needed now to push or pull the box? How difficult is it? You can see that a simple roller can move heavy objects more easily than a strong push. The Egyptians knew this. Where did they use this knowledge?

2. List several ways you can think of that people invented to save energy. Some examples are: the mill wheel to save people the job of grinding, by hand, the bicycle to save people the effort of walking, automobiles to save people time and effort. Now list all the problems we have because of these inventions.

3. Try this. Fasten a strong rubber band on the front of a heavy toy truck. Lift the truck and measure the length of the rubber band as it stretches. Now lean a board against a chair and pull the toy truck up the board by the rubber band. Again measure the stretch of the rubber band. What do you notice? The tilted board makes it easier to lift the truck, doesn't it? It makes the weight of the truck less so the stretch of the rubber band is less than when you lifted the truck directly. The Egyptians knew this, too. Where did they use this idea?

Upper Elementary Ages

1. Some techniques are used in propaganda which appeal to the values of certain groups or to their sentiment. Here is a list of some techniques. Add to the list and find illustrations in magazines, newspapers or on television of each technique.

3. John Dewey, *Democracy and Education* (New York: Macmillan Co., 1916): 192.

    a. Use of bad names.

    b. Using respect, admiration, love to build up a person or an idea. Making it possible for people to transfer feelings.

    c. Using testimonials.

    d. Stressing only good values ("card-stacking").

    e. Using the "band wagon" approach.

    f. Using good names.

    g. Appealing to youth, or just "plain folks."

    h. Using beauty as a come-on.

    i. Using popularity and/or acceptance as a come-on.

    j. Keeping youth.

    k. Maintaining good health.

Plan some ways to use these techniques in a class election or to sell your class newspaper.

2. Is it election time in your city or town? Who would you elect as mayor if you were old enough to vote?

    Make a list of all the problems your community faces. Some samples might be: roads are not well paved, parks are neglected, welfare costs are high, etc. Discuss your list of problems for possible solutions. Take your list home and talk over the problems with your parents. Also add their ideas of other city problems.

    Discuss in class what you think makes a good mayor and how a mayor at this time should respond to some of the problems you have listed. What is the role of the mayor, what kind of speech gets him or her elected, how is a mayor elected?

    Nominate candidates among your classmates for mayor. Hold elections allowing each of the candidates to run a campaign, give speeches, hand out buttons, etc. Pay careful attention to how each candidate plans to solve the community's problems. Then hold elections just as they are held in your town. It will also be helpful to ask the real mayor or candidates for mayor to talk to your class about the problems you have listed.

Experience Creative Thinking: *Textbook Activities—7*

Objective: *to provide the student with experiences in creative thinking*

    Creative thinking was defined as that thinking which involves the production of new ideas. Creative production depends upon a background of related experiences. It comes from the growth of an urge to express one's self, the accessibility of a variety of materials, time, and an accepting atmosphere for creative work.

    Setting conditions for creative thinking in social studies means providing all the kinds of experiences mentioned in this book. Criteria for problems in creative thinking are: 1) the problem must be open-ended; 2) many solutions for the problem are possible and may be acceptable rather than *one* solution; 3) deferred judgment must be employed; 4) flexibility and fluency of thought are encouraged; 5) originality and uniqueness are stressed; and 6) elaboration of ideas is encouraged.

Textbooks can make giant steps in stimulating creative thinking through a variety of suggested activities. Some suggestions follow:

Primary Ages

1. Fold a paper in half then turn it and fold it in half the other way. Open it and you will have four boxes. In each box draw something you saw on the way to school this morning that taught you something new. Share your drawings with each other.
2. Write or tell a story about several jobs you might like to have when you grow up.
3. Make a list of all the things you can do for amusement inside on a rainy day.
4. Make a model of a farm. What can you use in your model to show (the process of substitution):

a brick house	asphalt
growing wheat	grass
animals	fences
a silo	furniture
a barn	farm equipment
stones	hay

Middle Elementary Ages

1. Can you think of any reasons why the first roads to a town were not good enough after the town became a big town? Can you find out what the roads of long ago were made of? How were they built? Compare them to the way we build roads today. Name several inventions that have made the differences possible.
2. How did your town get its name? Find out about the first settlers to come into your town. Perhaps you can start making a picture history of your town.

Upper Elementary Ages

1. Take the theme COLOR IN MOTION and see how many ways you can show color moving. Divide your class into five groups. Allow each group fifteen minutes to brainstorm all the ways they can show color in motion. Then let them plan a five-minute presentation of their ideas for the rest of the class. Suggestion: use films, filmstrips, slide machines, overhead projectors, opaque projectors, water colors, tempera paint, colored paper, confetti, etc.

2. *Let's Pretend*: Pretend you planned an outdoor party and it rained. What substitutes such as the following could you suggest for each activity that would be just as much fun?

Outdoor Party	*Substitutes*
a. Cook hotdogs outdoors	a. Cook hotdogs on the fireplace indoors
b. Play hide and seek	b. Make party hats from junk box
c. Play croquet	c.
d. Play beanbag-toss	d.
e. Have a relay race	e.
f. Toast marshmallows	f.
g. Have groups put on skits for entertainment	g.
h. Hold a treasure hunt	h.
i. Eat in a tent	i.
j. Play baseball	j.

Stimulate Critical Thinking: *Textbook Activities—8*

Objective: *to provide the student with experiences in critical thinking*

Critical thinking is generally defined as being more objective than creative thinking. It is problem-solving, as is creative thinking, but it is more directed toward some goal. It is taking a group of facts, making decisions, and passing judgment consistent with those facts.

Critical thinking can be stimulated by situations in which children find themselves forced to pass judgments or make decisions. Sometimes the motivation for critical thinking comes from the questions teachers ask or those listed in a textbook.

Many questions asked by teachers and textbooks serve the sole purpose of checking comprehension. The answers can be found simply by rereading parts of the text. This is not to be confused with critical thinking.

The following questions were taken from the plans of two teachers who were concerned that their students have experience in critical thinking. The answers to the following questions *may* be found in some textbooks, but this is unlikely. Each requires the weighing of evidence and arriving at a judgment.

Questions that Provoke Critical Thinking

1. What effect has the opening of the St. Lawrence Seaway had upon our country?
2. Why were a desert state (Arizona) and a cold state (Alaska) two of the fastest growing states in population since 1975?
3. What were some of the differences and similarities of settlers in Virginia in 1607 and in California in 1849?

Figure 7-5. *Textbooks encourage critical thinking.*

4. Do you suppose Russia regrets selling Alaska to the United States? Why?
5. What has happened which makes it possible for people to live comfortably in the desert now?

Primary Ages

1. Do you have crossing guards at your school who stop traffic and help you cross the road safely? If so, who puts them there? Who pays their salaries? Who trains them in their job? Who hires them? How are they hired? What do they have to know to get the job? What hours do they work? Invite a crossing guard into your classroom and ask him or her these questions.
2. Billy and Alice both wanted to look at some pictures in a library book. Alice grabbed the book and Billy tried to get it away from her. In fighting for it, the book was torn. What should Billy and Alice do about it?

Middle Elementary Ages

1. The Great Wall of China is considered one of the seven great wonders of the world of the Middle Ages. What are the other six? The Pyramids are considered one of the seven wonders of the Ancient World. What are the other six? Make a list of what you consider to be the seven wonders of the Modern World. Give your reasons.
2. Here are some statements. Using this chapter, see if you can find information that shows if these statements are true.
   a. People work to bring order to their world.

    b. People depend on each other for a living.

    c. In order to live in harmony, people must develop a common set of values.

    d. Most people have religious beliefs.

3. Changes are often brought about in our living by:

- inventions
- discoveries
- changing attitudes
- new knowledge
- accidents
- creativity

Discuss changes that have been brought about by each of these means in your lifetime. Then find a great change in the past which changed the whole world for each of these words. Example:

- inventions—the invention of the wheel
- discovery—the discovery of America
- changing attitudes—women's rights
- new knowledge—research in the relationship between cigarette smoking and cancer
- accidents—Goodyear spilling sulphur into his mixture to create rubber
- creativity—using ground peanut shucks for mulch

Upper Elementary Ages

1. There are many forms of propaganda. Some are: magazine and newspaper advertisements, television and radio commercials, political cartoons, polls, slogans, newspaper and magazine editorials and political speeches. List others. Collect and classify pictures which demonstrate each type of propaganda on this list.

2. "Liberty and justice for all" is a phrase from the pledge of allegiance to the United States flag which applies to all citizens of the United States. What is the difference between liberty and justice? Divide a large sheet of paper by drawing a line down the middle. At the top of the left hand column write the word LIBERTY. At the top of the right hand column write the word JUSTICE. Now fill in the columns like the sample below until you have many illustrations to show the difference between the words.

Liberty	Justice
a. All children can play ball on the playground.	a. Punishing or penalizing children who play in forbidden areas or where other children may be hurt

b. All people are encouraged to use public parks

b. People who destroy public property and spoil it for others are not allowed to use public parks

c. Schools exist for all children and are made possible by taxpayers' money

c. Vandals who destroy buildings and materials are made to pay for the damage they cause

d. People are allowed the freedom to say what they feel is important

d. People who do things to keep other people from disagreeing are punished

e. Children are free to go to the movies on Saturday afternoon

e. The manager should ask them to leave if they run around, throw things, or bother other patrons

3. In the front of this textbook you learned much about geography. Geography helps us to understand why people throughout the world are alike and why they are different. You have already seen many pictures, films, and television shows of people from other places doing things differently than you do.

Here is a big problem for you:

a. Collect all the pictures you can of people who are doing things differently than you do in your town. Also collect pictures of people who dress differently than you do. Make a big bulletin-board display of these pictures. Then see if you can answer these questions about the people in your pictures.

   (1) If they are working, why are they doing the work they are doing? Is it because the land where they live is different from the land where you live? Is it because the weather or climate is different?

   (2) Can you tell from your pictures what part of the world these people come from?

   (3) Can you guess what temperature zone they might live in?

   (4) Can you tell which places are hot all the time, which are cold all the time, and which are in-between?

   (5) If people in your pictures are playing, can you tell if the climate and geography determine how they shall play?

   (6) See if you can make lists of facts that are *sometimes* true of cold countries but not always (such as: These is generally ice there), of hot countries (such as: They generally do not have snow), of temperate countries (such as: They generally have cool or cold winters and warm or hot summers), of high countries (such as: They are generally cooler than low countries), of low countries (such as: They are generally near the seacoast).

b. Do the above activities, this time focusing on similarities.

c. Here is another problem that will make you think. Arrange a bulletin board or a chalkboard with signs as follows:

Found *only* in hot countries	Found *only* in cold countries	Found *only* in temperate countries
Found *sometimes* in hot countries	**Found *sometimes* in cold countries**	**Found *sometimes* in temperate countries**
Never found in hot countries	**Never found in cold countries**	**Never found in temperate countries**

Figure 7-6

d. Now take the following list of words and fit them in the proper spaces. After you have done this, make up lists of words of your own and put them in the proper spaces:

- mining
- roses
- clouds
- palm trees
- jungles
- the equator
- cactus
- icebergs
- seaweed
- igloos
- hurricanes
- cowboys
- apple trees
- maple syrup
- evergreen trees
- pelicans
- koala bears
- pineapples
- oyster fishing
- coal mining
- bamboo
- equatorial forests
- terraced fields
- bananas
- oil
- sharks
- lakes
- pearl divers
- corn
- rice
- whales
- sailboats
- ice caps
- westerly winds
- glaciers
- fishing
- bathing beaches
- dates and figs
- dairy farming
- sunburns
- blizzards
- airplanes

- oranges
- doldrums
- hailstones
- sponge fishing
- alligators
- wheat

- nutmeg
- papaya
- lemons
- polar bears
- sugar cane
- chocolate

Develop Aesthetic Appreciations: *Textbook Activities—9*

Objective: *to provide experiences which will encourage children to develop aesthetic appreciations*

All Grade Levels

1. There are many stories about Spain and Portugal which you will enjoy reading. Here is a list of some you might get from your library:
   - *Ferdinand the Bull* by Robert Lawson and Munro Leaf
   - *The Talking Tree: Fairy Tales from Fifteen Lands* by Augusta Baker
   - *Goya: A Biography* by Elizabeth Ripley
   - *The Land and People of Spain* by Loder
2. Spanish music has a rhythm all its own. A French composer, Georges Bizet, caught the beauty of this music and put it in an opera about a girl in Spain. It is called *Carmen*. You may enjoy reading about *Carmen* in the *Children's Book of Operas* and then listening to the music.
3. In the story time you read some books that were very interesting. People who worked in Committee II read *Anna and the King of Siam*. A motion picture called *The King and I* was made from this story. The music from this movie was put on records. You probably will enjoy this music, particularly "The March of the Siamese Children" which captures the charm of the music of Thailand, once called Siam.

Summary

Within the framework of unit teaching it is possible for teachers to be creative and to develop creativity with the academic materials they use. Chief among these materials is the textbook. The role of the textbook in the modern school is changing. This changing role calls for a more creative use of the textbook and a more creative outlook on the part of the teacher.

Social studies textbooks should be selected for the contribution they make to developing the objectives of the social studies program and the creative development of boys and girls. Special attention should be given to the pictures used in textbooks.

Figure 7-7. *The textbook provided the motivation for this aesthetic experience.*

Creative uses to which the textbook may be put are: 1) putting acquired knowledge to work; 2) stimulating various creative kinds of research; 3) providing supplementary material for classroom studies; 4) building concepts through creative experiences; 5) helping children make choices and pass judgments; 6) problem-solving; 7) developing creative and critical thinking and 8) aesthetic appreciation.

To the College Student

1. Which of the suggestions in this chapter on using a textbook creatively might apply to the use of textbooks in your college classes? To this textbook?

2. Your author once taught a fifth-grade class of children, each of whom made his or her own social studies textbook. At the beginning of the year these children bound

books of blank pages and then, through research, discovery and experimentation, filled the books with pictures, graphs, maps and written material about the units they studied. In terms of the criteria for a creative experience, how does this stack up? What sorts of resources did the teacher need in order to be able to carry out a project of this kind?

3. Many modern social studies textbooks contain information that is outdated by the time the teacher gets it. Appoint a committee to explore resources which can supplement the textbooks in the classroom.

4. Which of your college textbooks do you enjoy? Analyze the reasons.

5. Here are two questions taken from two different sixth grade social studies textbooks:
   a. Why was the Battle of New Orleans fought *after* the end of the War of 1812?
   b. Why did Vermont lose population in 1961 while a desert state, Nevada, and a swamp state, Florida, became the two fastest growing states in the U.S.?

   Which of these two questions is more likely to result in a lesson of critical thinking? Why?

6. Check out some social studies textbooks from your curriculum library. Read a chapter or a unit in each and decide whether or not they develop the objectives listed on pages 194 and 195. If not, create some task cards to supplement them.

To the Classroom Teacher

1. Ask your children to do some creative writing on the topic of textbooks; they may write poems, essays, criticisms, plays, or stories about how they feel about their textbooks. Analyze the writing to see if you can detect their attitudes about these texts. Then ask yourself whether or not they learn much from them if they do not like them. What could you do to supplement the textbooks you use to make them more attractive, or how could you supplement them to make them more useful to children who like them?

2. What materials, other than textbooks, do you use as sources of information for the children?

3. Textbooks in the United States generally are the most attractive and best-planned books on the market. Children should like them. Do they? If not, it is the use of them that has built a negative attitude. Check your use of textbooks and decide whether or not you are using them to the best advantage.

4. Hold a discussion with the children on textbooks. Ask them to suggest ways they feel the textbook might be used in interesting ways.

To the College Student and the Classroom Teacher

1. List all the ways you can use television and radio creatively to help your students obtain current information.

2. Make a survey of children's literature that can be used to supplement each unit of the social studies program.

3. Take the questions with answers from any chapter of any teacher's manual that accompanies a social studies textbook and think of creative ways for children to apply this knowledge.

4. Study the activities suggested in the teacher's manual of a social studies book and analyze them. Which ones provide for creative development and critical and creative thinking? Which ones help children to grow in their ability to make decisions or pass judgments? Which ones appear to be just busy work?

5. Make a list of skills, attitudes, values, and appreciations which *may* develop when a teacher uses more than one resource book in teaching a unit rather than a single textbook.

6. Which of the following statements can be answered by a textbook and which require a gathering of information, the use of values and the weighing of evidence in order to make a decision?
   a. The Civil War could and should have been avoided.
   b. The War Between the States did not really free Blacks.
   c. The individual in a democracy is sometimes justified in breaking laws.
   d. Smoking marijuana should be legalized.
   e. Prisons should re-educate and re-orient inmates for social living and should not be regarded as houses of punishment.
   f. Cigarette smoking should be allowed only in designated areas. Non-smokers are discriminated against when smokers fill the air with cigarette smoke.

7. A fifth-grade teacher recently said to me, "I follow the social studies textbook and teacher's manual religiously. After all, the people who wrote it are experts in their field and know a lot more about social studies than I do." What is the fallacy in this teacher's reasoning?

8. Review the list of functions for pictures in textbooks and check the pictures in this text against the list.

9. Following are some college-level examples of textbook exercises which may be used to develop the same objectives for you as the exercises in this chapter do for children.
   a. *to gain knowledge and apply it to new uses:* Set up some evaluation criteria against which you can rate yourself as a teacher. Use it from time to time. Does an awareness of the objectives of good teaching as you have spelled them out on the evaluation sheet tend to improve your teaching?
   b. *to stimulate creative research activities:* Make a study of violence on television by creating a criteria chart of what violence is, degrees of violence and what constitutes a violent act for a child. Divide your class into committees and have each committee watch a favorite TV show scheduled during family viewing time, and rate it according to the violence presented. Pool your data, decide if there is excessive violence on TV and discuss this question: Should programs with high violence scores be censored?
   c. *to provide supplementary material rather than serving as the core to a unit:* Choose some students in your class to read *The Man* by Wallace or *Seven Days in May* by Knebel and Bailey and report on these books from the standpoint of presidential power. Check out the facts with your own class textbook.

d. *to build concepts by stimulating creative thinking:* Write a real estate ad for your house as though your family were going to sell it. Write about all the good points. Include a description of the yard and the neighborhood.

e. *to provide experiences in making decisions and passing judgments:* Debate the following questions and statements by choosing teams to represent each side of the question:

(1) In any war, hot or cold, civilian dissent must be silenced in the interest of victory.

(2) In a democracy, students have the right to control their own education even if it leads to protest and disruption.

f. *to provide experiences in problem-solving:* Demonstrate the concept of creative dramatics to each other. Divide the class into groups and have each group work out a plan for presenting a creative dramatization, i.e., one that puts them in a situation where they must come up with the solution to a problem by forcing relationships among unrelated things.

Example: Collect a variety of hats and distribute them to the group (a Boy Scout hat, a cap, a scuba diver's helmet, a top hat, a bonnet, a cook's hat, etc.). Each person is to assume the characteristics of the person who would wear such a hat. The dramatization comes in when the group is challenged to present a play showing how all these characters might come together in a rational situation. After each group has presented its play, discuss how each technique or situation used might be applied to a situation in the elementary classroom.

g. *to provide experiences in creative thinking:* Brainstorm the following topics:

(1) Ways I can make history interesting to my fifth and sixth grade students.

(2) Ideas I can use to develop creativity in a unit on Canada.

(3) Field trips I can take in my town to build necessary concepts of man's interdependence in the second grade.

h. *to provide experiences in critical thinking:* Find migrant workers in your community and tape interviews with them for use in the classroom. Ask them to talk on such topics as:

(1) Their acceptance or non-acceptance into communities.

(2) The yearly life of a migrant.

(3) Problems in a migrant camp.

(4) Social life in a migrant camp.

(5) Living facilities within a migrant camp.

(6) Their aspirations for their children—for the future.

Use these tapes in class when studying sub-cultures.

i. *to develop aesthetic appreciations:* Read *Island of the Blue Dolphin* by Scott O'Dell, a Newbery Award book, and discuss all the ways you can think of in which it could be used in the classroom in connection with various areas of the teaching of social studies.

Selected Bibliography

BANKS, JAMES A. with CLEGG, AMBROSE A. *Teaching Strategies for the Social Studies: Inquiry, Valuing and Decision-Making.* Reading, Mass.: Addison-Wesley, 1977.

BERRYMAN, CHARLES, "One Hundred Ideas for Using the Newspaper in Courses in Social Science and History." *Social Education* 38, No. 4, 1975: 318–320.

CLEMENTS, MILLARD H.; FIELDER, WILLIAM R.; and TABACHNICK, ROBERT B. *Social Study: Inquiry in Elementary Classrooms.* Indianapolis: Bobbs-Merrill Co., 1966.

FELDHUSEN, JOHN F. and TREFFINGER, DONALD J. *Teaching Creative Thinking and Problem Solving.* Dubuque, Iowa: Kendall-Hunt, 1977.

HANNA, L. *Dynamics of Elementary Social Studies*, 3rd ed. New York: Holt, Rinehart & Winston, 1973.

KENWORTHY, LEONARD S., ed. *Social Studies for the Seventies.* 2nd ed. New York: John C. Wiley, 1973.

LEE, JOHN R. *Teaching Social Studies in the Elementary School.* New York: Free Press, 1974.

MALLAN, JOHN T., and HERSCH, RICHARD. *No G.O.D.s in the Classroom* (3 vols.: *Inquiry into Inquiry, Inquiry and Elementary Social Studies, Inquiry and Secondary Social Studies*). Philadelphia: W. B. Saunders, 1972.

MARTORELLA, PETER. *Concept Learning in the Social Studies.* Scranton, Pa.: Intext Publishers, 1971.

POPHAM, W. JAMES. *Systematic Instructional Decision-Making.* Los Angeles: Vimcet Associates, 1965.

THOMAS, R. MURRAY, and BRUBAKER, DALE. *Decisions in Teaching Elementary Social Studies.* Belmont, Calif.: Wadsworth, 1971.

8 Values, Attitudes and Character Development

Every society creates ideal images of what the behavior in thought and action of its members should be. When taken together, these images express the vision of the good life that the people of the society have achieved. . . . Because values are beliefs, they serve to inspire the members of the society to act in the approved ways. Because values are ideal pictures, they provide a means of judging the quality of actual behavior.

RALPH H. GABRIEL[1]

INTRODUCTION

Children can learn to understand and appreciate differences in human behavior. They learn why people know and believe different things. They also understand why people value different things. When people value different things they behave differently. A person who values money excessively, for instance, may become ruthless and cruel in his or her efforts to get it. By comparing people, children learn about the differences in them and the effects of different value systems. By comparing them children also learn about the ways all people are alike, the values all hold precious and the underlying unities of the human species.

These are necessary understandings to develop if children are to build healthy human relationships as part of their own lives. Common values are the cement of society.

In the early schools in the United States, little was done to help children explore their own value systems. Values were imposed on children in much the same manner that knowledge was imposed. Children were told the proper way

1. Ralph H. Gabriel, *Traditional Values in American Life* (New York: Harcourt, Brace, Jovanovich, 1963).

224

Figure 8-1. *A middle school bulletin board that illustrates children's values.*

to act and feel without understanding why, or why they felt guilty when they did *not* act as they were told.

A modern social studies program must help children identify and develop their own values. Values are often the basis for decision-making, in some cases even more than knowledge. Children need to explore their own values and to understand the values held by society. They need to understand the values which are changing and to understand why. They need also to understand that their own values will change with age and with the realignment of their own lives during the maturing process. The emphasis is on *teaching the valuing process* as well as *transferring some specific values* themselves.

Equally important as listing concepts and generalizations in developing units and lessons is listing the values which prompt them, such as these humanistic ones:

1. Because humans care for other humans, they know they must share natural and manufactured products with others. No one person or group deserves control over the limited resources found on the earth.

2. Because the balance of nature is so important, humans must learn to respect it.

3. The physical needs of humans are basic to all other drives.

4. Because conditions on the earth change, other changes must be accepted and adjustments made if life is to continue.

5. People need other people and it is a human act to cultivate friendship.
6. The same basic social functions are necessary to human life everywhere.
7. Freedom and the freedom of choice is a human's most precious possession. With freedom comes increasing responsibility.

What Are Values?

Kaltsounis defines values as follows:

> Values are those unseen forces which influence an individual to behave the way he does and make him strive for whatever he wants to achieve in life.[2]

Kaltsounis outlines the valuing process as having the following steps:

1. The students are presented with an unresolved controversial issue. *Example:* What should be done about poverty as we find it in the United States?
2. Students suggest as many alternative solutions as possible. *Examples:* Provide everyone with a basic annual income; let the government create jobs for the poor; encourage private industry to make an effort to develop jobs in poverty areas; move the poor out of poverty areas; find out which qualifications for employment poor people lack and provide educational opportunities to overcome these handicaps; and many others.
3. The students then consider the consequences of each alternative.
4. The children are given the opportunity to express their feelings about each alternative. This requires an open atmosphere so that everyone in the class can say what he is really thinking.
5. At this point each student should be encouraged to reach one or more decisions about solutions to the problem of overcoming poverty in this country. In the future, it would be hoped that he would support or modify his decisions as he obtained more information and experience in solving this problem.[3]

We observed the valuing process in operation in a slightly modified form in Chapter 1 when we saw Mrs. Jackson using the puppet show in order to help the children develop values of living together, and Mr. Arnold using a film to develop values about equal opportunity and human rights.

Many of the units and lessons described in this volume take the children through the valuing steps described by Kaltsounis. Engagement in inquiry and the resulting activities is bound to result in the formation of values.

Value Judgments

Decision-making is always a result of knowledge plus values. Often we hear someone say to someone else, "That is a value judgment." Sometimes this is

2. Theodore Kaltsounis, "Swing toward Decision Making," *The Instructor,* April 1971.
3. Ibid.

said in a derogatory manner as if any decision based on a value is unworthy and not of the same status as a decision based on knowledge. As a matter of fact, almost all decisions are based on values—and all in a sense are therefore value judgments. The real difference lies in the fact that some decisions are made on values held worthy by society as a whole and are based on the experiences of society as a group. Others are built on values held worthy by an individual and not necessarily by society as a whole and are based on the experiences of that individual.

Selecting Values

Some values are cherished by society as a whole and are fairly obvious, others are cherished by most members of society, some are cherished by some members, others by only a few members. Some differ from community to community.

The obvious values are those which should be passed along to children as part of a social studies program because they are the core of all human relations. Those not held by all members of society should be dealt with as controversial, and children should learn that they will need to decide for themselves those values they will need in decision-making in these instances.

Some of the obvious values held by society which should be incorporated into a social studies program in the manner that the teachers of Glendale planned are stated here as samples:

1. All people have specified rights in a democracy.
2. In a democracy the individual is important.
3. Each person has the right to own property.
4. A citizen in a democracy has the right to freedom of speech, religion and thought.
5. All citizens have the right to engage in free enterprise.
6. All citizens are entitled to equal administration of justice.
7. Opportunity should be equal for all persons.
8. Citizens in a democratic society are concerned for the welfare of other citizens.
9. Citizens deserve protection from violence, theft and vandalism.
10. Each person has the right to pursue his or her own interests and talents in society.

Each of these stated values, and probably many which are unstated, require responsibility on the part of the individual to bring them about. To respect the personality of others one must respect oneself and must assume the responsibility of learning techniques with which to deal with people of differing opinions.

Many values, such as those stated above, have many meanings. Freedom, for instance, means freedom to work, freedom of speech, freedom of access to knowledge, freedom of choice and freedom of religion.

The values people develop and hold precious become the basis for the traits they develop which constitute their character.

Clarifying Values

Children can have experiences in social studies which will help them clarify their values. These experiences may be used by the teacher to demonstrate that knowledge (and other forces) serve as instruments for helping us to value. An example follows:

A group of middle school children living in a new housing development and attending a new suburban school became interested in housing because they now lived in a new upper-class community. The architecture of the development was largely colonial. One new family wished to build an A-frame and there was a great deal of resistance to this idea on the part of the other residents because they felt it would "spoil" the charm of the neighborhood. In studying this situation, the children got into discussions on constitutional rights and other aspects of individual rights. One value which they stated unanimously was that it was the constitutional right of each individual to live in the type of house he or she preferred. This was a verbally stated value. Did the children really believe it? They had the opportunity to test their belief when, not much later, a young couple bought a lot on which they hoped to place a mobile home. To the dismay of many homeowners in the development, the township had no zoning laws to restrict this type of dwelling. The children, in this case, were in a position to really examine their own values.

An example of understanding the values of society may be seen in Mr. Arnold's study of "Migration in the United States Today." The children had studied migration in the country, the Westward movement, then migration from the city to the suburbs, and the more recent trend of migration back to the cities. One value statement to come from this study was: If cities are to survive, they must be made comfortable and attractive to live in.

The old system of studying "what is" needs to be changed to help children understand the "reasons for what is," and value judgments which brought about changes or which helped make decisions in the past need to be examined and frankly discussed if a humanistic curriculum is to result, for every decision in a democratic government is determined by the existing set of values held by the citizens of the society which that government represents.

Teaching Values

Certain values and appreciations must be taught—their development cannot be left to chance. Appreciation of freedom and an understanding of the rights of people are examples. Teachers can employ many sociodynamic devises to help children build the character traits that are necessary to the perpetuation of human rights.

That attitudes and values can be changed when they become a target for direct teaching has been proven by many research studies in psychology and education.

Dr. David Zodikoff has designed some materials on building basic attitudes in children.[4] He points out that, by the age of five, the basic attitudes of the child are set. Any change in attitudes after this time calls for a deliberate, conscious attempt on the part of someone (generally the teacher). Dr. Zodikoff points out that content is not likely to change attitudes unless deliberate plans are made to use it for this purpose.

Zodikoff cautions the teacher that the first step in attitude development is to determine those attitudes which need changing and those attitudes which you would like to develop. He has devised some materials which help teachers inventory the attitudes of children. Zodikoff presents a list of behavioral areas with related attitude statements such as:

> *Group cooperation:* The desire for the individual to work actively in a group. A sample attitude statement here is: *I would usually prefer to work with others than to work alone. Group work is more interesting than working alone.*

Once the inventory is taken, the teacher can plot attitudes about group cooperation, empathy, independent thinking, social responsibility and democratic living on an attitude model which will help in planning for the development of attitudes. Dr. Zodikoff has designed module forms which will help the teacher to build consistently on the development of attitudes.

STRATEGIES FOR DEVELOPING VALUES, ATTITUDES AND CHARACTER CREATIVELY

Some techniques which have been used successfully by teachers to develop or change attitudes and values are discussed below.

Dramatization

Dramatization can be used in many ways to help teachers build values and attitudes in children. Any social eruption taking place within the classroom (which is a group problem) can be dramatized in order to give the class a first-hand experience with the situation. Once the group *sees* the problem presented by the dramatization, a discussion of the facts of the situation (which are clearly known) can take place.

In a sixth grade the children were trying to decide which was the best of

4. David Zodikoff, *The Use of Comprehensive Models in Social Studies Education* (Dubuque, Iowa: Kendall Hunt, 1973).

two different plans. One group felt they would like to go to the school library to look up material for their unit each day during their room work period. The other group felt the library rules would cramp their style and would kill the opportunity to discuss their findings among themselves, to move freely about, to get materials, etc. They felt that books kept in the classroom would afford a much better opportunity to accomplish their goals.

The teacher suggested that a committee from each group dramatize the scene which they did *not* want to happen. This was done, and in the discussion that followed the children immediately agreed that the library situation offered too many restrictions for accomplishing their goals, so a library was set up in the room.

Dramatizations help children prepare for trips taken in the social studies program. Miss Marsden, a first-grade teacher, was taking her children to a small circus. Since many children had never been to a circus, the children arranged their chairs as they would find them arranged at the circus and then dramatized buying their tickets and taking their seats. Later, at the circus, they performed with all the poise and security of veteran circus-goers.

Miss Rockwell, a second-grade teacher, used dramatization to help evaluate a trip to a pony farm. In spite of careful planning and excellent preparations, the trip had not gone well. Some of the children had not carried out their responsibilities at the farm, and the bus ride home had been noisy and unruly.

Miss Rockwell talked to the children about the trip on the following day. First they discussed all the good parts of the trip. Then Miss Rockwell asked them if there were any parts of the trip which they felt had not gone so well. Immediately, many of the children said they felt some of the children had not done what they were supposed to do, nor had they behaved well on the bus. Miss Rockwell said she had felt this too.

"I wonder what happened," she asked. "We planned well, we talked about problems that might come up, we talked about how we should behave, and still we had trouble. I wonder what went wrong?"

One of the youngsters who had been responsible for the trouble on the bus was the first to volunteer. He felt some other child had "picked on" him. Soon a discussion was going on as to what happened to bring about the disorder on the bus. Miss Rockwell suggested the children dramatize the bus scene to see whether or not the class could find out why their plans had failed, and what they might do to make them better next time.

Chairs were lined up to resemble a school bus and the scene unfolded. Children were quite free about reconstructing their roles. Soon the trouble center was spotted; four children had set it off.

Miss Rockwell stopped the dramatization and held a discussion. The four students who began the trouble were allowed to talk first. Almost at once it came to light that they had been terribly bored and were just trying to relieve their boredom. Gerry gave the clue to the problem when he said, "I've been to that old pony farm so many times I'm sick of it anyway."

"Why," said Miss Rockwell, "I thought no one in the class had ever been to the pony farm. Have others of you been there, too?"

The four who had created the problem had all been there many times before. Further discussion brought the class (and the teacher) to the realization that this had been an oversight in their planning. The class decided that the next time they planned to go on a trip they would find out at the very beginning who had been there before.

"Once we know this, what will we do about it?" asked Miss Rockwell.

"Well," said Charlie, one of the troublemakers, "you could have given us sumpthin' to do besides look at all that old stuff again."

"A very good idea," agreed Miss Rockwell. "Charlie, Gerry, Joan, and Hank could all have been guides for our small groups. Even when I've seen something many times I get a thrill out of showing it to people who have never seen it before. How do you feel about that idea?"

They felt fine about it. It was agreed by the class that one weakness in planning their trip was in making proper assignments to individuals and that the next time they would be more careful about it.

In each of the instances cited above, the children were faced with a natural or contrived, but unresolved, controversial or problem issue. Suggestions were made for a solution to the problem, consequences of decisions were considered, and decisions were made—all steps in the valuing process.

Role-playing and Role-reversal

Other forms of dramatization also provide opportunity to develop understandings. Most popular among these is role-playing.

Role-playing is a conscientious attempt on the part of the teacher to use these natural tendencies of empathy for constructing natural group relations.

In the fourth grade a child feels he has been treated unfairly at home and comes to school with a chip on his shoulder. He is angry and cross. Finally, when confronted with the need to account for his actions, he spews forth his ill-feelings concerning his father who was overdemanding of him before school time. By being encouraged to play the role of the father while another child plays his role, he may be able to understand more readily his father's actions—to identify the true reasons behind them. Thus he learns through empathy plus analytical discussion that what appears to be malice toward him is really his father's own bitter feeling coming out, which may have been caused by his father's boss's overdemands of him. Thus a feeling of understanding replaces one of hostility.

Role-playing differs from straight dramatization of a problem in one major respect. In role-playing children are placed in a situation where they must see (and defend) a viewpoint different from their own. Through this technique they learn to project themselves through empathy. Often they are able to understand why there is disagreement between themselves and other people.

In a fourth grade two boys were arguing. Ivan thought that Carl had taken his pen. Carl flatly denied this and said he had just received the pen as a gift from his father. It was just like Ivan's because he liked Ivan's pen and had asked his father to get one just like it.

Miss Kelly, the teacher, said she *could* settle the problem, but first would the boys mind changing roles? Carl was to accuse Ivan of stealing a pen. Miss Kelly did not know or care at this point whether or not Carl had stolen the pen. She wanted to build better relationships among her students by having them realize that it was damaging to friendships to accuse someone of taking something without being sure first.

In changing roles, Carl let loose on Ivan. Ivan had to defend himself. Considerable emotional tension was drained out of the situation in the process. Without prompting from the teacher, Ivan drew in his fangs and apologized to Carl.

Shortly after, Ivan's pen was found on the floor under the piano. Ivan was especially sorry after his pen was found, but Miss Kelly pointed out that this was not really important. The important thing about a situation of this nature was never to infringe on anyone's rights or character before making certain about any given situation.

Role-playing can be combined with problem stories, problem pictures and dramatization to make effective social situations in which children develop values and understandings.

Some suggestions for the creative use of role-playing are:

Lower Grades

1. A playground fight over the swings—sharing.
2. A safety hazard, such as fighting over a turn on the slide.
3. One child blaming another for an accident, such as spilling the milk at snack-time.
4. Helping one child feel better by developing understanding among the others in a situation as when a child is tardy for school.
5. Children do not understand why certain school rules must exist, so the teacher and the children exchange roles to better realize each other's situation.

Intermediate Grades

1. Children are careless about cutting across the corner of a neighbor's lawn on the way to school.
2. Children are resentful about some regulations passed by the school principal.
3. Children choose the same team all the time making the teams uneven.
4. Some children use certain materials all the time depriving other children of their use.
5. Children cause the janitor unwarranted work by being careless about cleaning up their room.
6. Children do not cooperate with the safety patrol.

The Sociodrama

The sociodrama is a type of role-playing which deals with a social problem. The *general* plot of a sociodrama may be planned. The actors experience the situation they are role-playing in the very creative sense that they make up the plot as they go along. In this situation, children bring past experiences to a new problem and use both reproductive and productive thinking to solve the problem at hand.

The children in Miss Hire's sixth grade were very concerned over the fact that some parents would not allow them to attend a seventh-grade dance to which they had been invited because the dance was to be held on the evening of a school night. Miss Hire felt the children were not understanding of the parents' viewpoint, so she set a series of scenes as follows:

Scene I: Sally Peters' (a fictitious girl) home—the kitchen. Sally comes home to tell mother about the invitation.

Scene II: Living room of the Peters' home. Sally, her mother and father talk over the dance.

The scenes were played impromptu. In this case Miss Hire allowed two casts to play it two different ways. A better understanding of the parents' attitude resulted from the discussion that followed.

Children then directed their energies toward a possible solution to the problem. Some brain-storming resulted. A committee was finally organized and sent to the seventh-grade room to discuss the problem. The seventh-graders could not change the night because the gym was to be used for other functions, but they did set the dance for an hour earlier so that the sixth-graders could attend the first hour and still be home early. The teachers cooperated by assigning no homework on that night.

The Structured Dramatization

The structured dramatization differs from role-playing in that it has been written beforehand. Children memorize the lines or simply read the lines and "walk out" the play.

Generally teachers use a structured drama in the classroom when they are having problems in social behavior which are founded in a lack of a sense of values or appreciations. They find (or write) a play built around a theme that shows a lack of a sense of the same values or appreciations. In a reading class or social studies class, children read the parts, and a discussion follows. Again, it is not the purpose of the teacher to moralize, but to provide an open-ended experience. The children discuss among themselves ways in which such a situation might be handled, and thereby determine their values or help develop values.

Children in the upper grades especially enjoy these dramas and often write their own. Some commercial ones are available, most of which deal with teen-age problems.

Puppets

The effective use of puppets to develop values appropriate for living comfortably together was demonstrated in Chapter 1 when Mrs. Jackson, a middle school teacher, used puppets to settle the problem of breaking a school rule.

Puppets can sometimes be used very effectively for building healthy social relationships. A puppet show is a dramatization with puppets instead of people. The advantage in using puppets rather than people is sometimes very definite. If the problem to be acted out is one where children have developed strong guilt feelings, they may be reluctant to act their feelings before the class—or they may not put into the dramatization the emotional ingredients that appeared in the actual incident.

Puppets, therefore, become a projective technique. By getting down be-hind a table or in back of a puppet stage where faces cannot be seen, children will be better able to reproduce a scene because they, too, are seeing the puppet act out their emotions. This is more objective and often more realistic than the real-life drama.

The Open-ended Story

Another excellent technique for developing values is the use of the open-ended story, which deals with a social problem in the lives of the children. The story does not include a solution; it merely poses a problem. It can be used in the same manner as dramatization. After the story has been read, the children discuss possible endings.

Following is one sample of an open-ended story. It was written for use in the third or fourth grade. The discussion questions at the end will suggest how children, through empathy, come to understand each other's feelings and build values of human relationships.

AN OPEN-ENDED STORY

The Case of the Broken Tulips

All the children in the fourth grade were excited. Tomorrow they were going to have the Spring Festival, and today was the day they were going to decorate the gym for it!

Marcy could hardly wait! She was chairman of the decoration committee. She knew the gym was going to be beautiful. Mr. Sellers, her teacher, had met with her committee and they had made all the plans together. She thought about them all the way to school, and she could see the gym transformed into a garden just as they had planned it.

Marcy's mother had helped her a great deal. She had promised her that she might borrow the large lawn umbrella to be placed in the center of the gym.

Marcy and her committee planned to put crepe paper streamers from the tip of each point on the umbrella to the sides of the room. Each streamer was going to be a beautiful spring color. Mr. Sellers had given them some money from the P.T.O., and they had gone to the store and bought the crepe paper the night before. Marcy smiled as she thought of the beautiful pinks, the bright yellows, the soft blues, and the lovely violets in the crepe paper.

The children were going to hang huge murals of spring flowers on the walls of the gym. They had painted them in art class. Each one would be framed in green crepe paper. Then, most beautiful of all, they were going to bring the first spring flowers from their home gardens to bank around the base of the umbrella and around the refreshment stand at one end of the room. Marcy hoped that they could get enough flowers!

Mr. Sellers was giving directions on how they would work in the gym, when Marcy's mind drifted back to the reality of the fourth-grade room.

"After we get all the crepe paper and the paintings in place," he was saying, "you may bring the flowers from home. In this way, they will not get crushed and they will stay fresh until the festival. . . ."

Before Marcy could realize it, they were in the gym and everyone was working just as they had planned to do. At noontime Mr. Sellers called them together. "Boys and girls," he said, "you have done a wonderful job! Doesn't our gym look beautiful? All that remains is to put the flowers in the middle of the room and around the refreshment stand. When you go home for lunch I think it would be safe to bring them back."

Marcy was the first one back in the afternoon. She came with her arms loaded with flowers from her mother's garden. As chairman of the decoration committee, she eagerly accepted the flowers which each child brought and carefully arranged them at the base of the umbrella in the center of the gym. Long before the last child had returned from lunch, however, Marcy knew that there were not going to be enough flowers to do the job. In her imagination she had seen one big mass of color under the umbrella. Instead, there were individual bouquets. More flowers were needed to fill in the empty spaces.

Marcy could not keep the disappointment from her voice when she told Mr. Sellers that there were not enough flowers. "Well, Marcy," said Mr. Sellers, "the gym looks beautiful and even if we don't get more flowers I think it will be all right. However, if you feel that we need more, perhaps some of the children will be able to find some and bring them to school in the morning."

So Marcy went from child to child asking for more flowers. But their mothers had already given them most of the new spring flowers from their gardens and almost no one could promise to bring any more.

Marcy was so disappointed she did not feel like going to school the next morning. When she entered the room her greatest fears were realized. There were almost no new flowers waiting for her. She was about to resign herself to bitter disappointment when Angie Botts saved the day. Angie came into the room with her face beaming and her eyes sparkling. Her arms were loaded with red and yellow tulips. There were enough to do the job.

Marcy squealed with delight as she took the tulips from Angie. "See," Angie said, "now you can have it just like you wanted and I brought them to you, didn't I?"

Marcy hustled Angie off to the gym. In no time at all they had arranged the flowers around the base of the umbrella. Marcy praised Angie and told her how wonderful she was and how she alone had saved the Spring Festival from disaster.

Marcy could not understand why Angie had been so eager to please her. Certainly Angie was not one of her friends. In fact, Marcy and the girls had often made fun of Angie. She was not like the rest of the girls. She did not have nice clothes and she never belonged to the clubs or went to the parties that the other girls attended. Marcy ignored Angie most of the time, although Angie was always trying to give her something or to sit with her to eat her lunch on the days when they ate in the cafeteria. Marcy felt a little guilty as she watched Angie beaming at her while she arranged the flowers.

When they returned hand-in-hand to the fourth-grade classroom Mr. Garson, the principal, was talking to Mr. Sellers at the front of the room. They seemed to be very serious and the children were very quiet. Marcy and Angie took their seats.

Mr. Garson turned to look at the boys and girls. "Children," he said, "Mr. Sellers and I have a serious problem to discuss with you. Our good neighbor across the street, Mrs. Parsons, has just telephoned me. Someone has broken off all of her prize yellow and red tulips and all of the blossoms are missing. Mrs. Parsons noticed many of the children carrying flowers to school yesterday and today and she called me to ask if we might help her find out what happened to her favorite blossoms."

Panic seized Marcy's heart. From the corner of her eye she took a quick look at Angie. Angie was looking right at her, smiling. Her face glowed with happiness.

End

Questions for Discussion

1. What do you think happened next in the story?
2. Why was Marcy so anxious to have the gym look so well?
3. Why was Angie so anxious to please Marcy?
4. Do you think Angie took Mrs. Parsons' flowers?
5. If you think she did, do you think she knew it was wrong to take them?
6. If you think she didn't, why did Marcy feel panicky when Mr. Garson told the children about the broken tulips?
7. If Angie took the flowers, and she knew it was wrong, *why* did she take them?
8. Why did Angie like Marcy so well?
9. Can you think of a happy ending to the story?
10. On what basis do you choose your friends?
11. Have you ever wanted to be someone's friend and that person would not play with you?
12. Have you ever wanted a friend so badly that *you* would do anything to get one—even something you thought was wrong?
13. Is there something we could each do to help keep things like this from happening?
14. What things were very important to Marcy in the story?
15. What things were very important to Angie in the story?
16. Which were more important—Marcy's things or Angie's things?

17. What things were important to Mr. Garson?
18. What things were important to Mr. Sellers?
19. What things were important to the other people in the story?
20. What events were important to some but not to all the people in the story?

The Problem Story

Similar to the open-ended story is the problem story. The problem story poses a problem with a "What-would-you-do?" type of ending. Its purpose is to help children build values and make decisions and judgments.

Problem stories have been used successfully as early as the kindergarten. Shaftel and Shaftel write of the use of problem stories in their book, *Role Playing for Social Values: Decision Making in the Social Studies*[5]. This book will provide the teacher with many problem stories to use in the classroom.

Problem stories may be detailed, or so short they merely present a problem. In one sixth grade where considerable falsehoods were being told, the teacher used the problem story below. Her goal was to help children understand that social pressures sometimes force us into situations where we behave in unaccepted ways. The teacher recognized the telling of falsehoods as a symptomatic behavior for some unmet tension. In order not to put any one person in the spotlight, she used a story that was not involved with falsehoods but with stealing. In the discussion following the story, the children built up some concepts and understandings about correct social behavior. The teacher also helped build rapport with children by providing ways for them to meet their problems within her classroom.

A Problem Story: The Case of the Christmas Stocking

The children in Miss Anderson's sixth grade decided they would collect money to help support a school in a foreign country. This particular school was in a disaster area. The children wrote to the principal of the school, who sent them a list of supplies such as balls, paint, crayons, paper, and paste. The children were going to buy these articles with their money and send them to the school for Christmas.

They hung a Christmas stocking in the front of the room with a sign on it which said, "Fill the Stocking for Christmas," and then they brought their pennies and nickels to put in it.

One night Miss Anderson decided to count the money in the Christmas stocking. She counted eight dollars and ninety-six cents. On the following morning Miss Anderson reported to the boys and girls and complimented them on their good work.

After school that evening Miss Anderson went to the library to secure some

5. Fannie R. Shaftel and George Shaftel, *Role-Playing for Social Values: Decision-Making in the Social Studies* (Englewood Cliffs, N.J.: Prentice-Hall, 1967).

books for the children. As she returned to her classroom she met Helen, a sixth-grader from another class, coming out of her room.

"Why, Helen," said Miss Anderson, "what are you doing in my room? Can I help you some way?"

"No," said Helen, "I was just going by and saw your pretty bulletin board, so I came in to see it." And with that Helen darted down the hall.

Miss Anderson was puzzled. She entered the room and looked around. Her eyes picked up a piece of paper on the floor. It was the sign on the Christmas stocking, which had been knocked down. Miss Anderson went to the front of the room and, taking the sign from the floor, she started to pin it back on the stocking. Suddenly she was aware that the stocking seemed very flat compared with what it had been like earlier in the day. So Miss Anderson dumped the contents from the stocking onto her desk and counted it. There was exactly three dollars and sixty-five cents.

If you were Miss Anderson, what would you do?

The Problem Picture

Problem pictures are a projective technique that can be used to help children understand the world around them, and to better interpret the feelings and problems of others. Figure 8.2 is taken from the cover of a popular magazine.[6] It presents a social problem, with a sense of humor for some of the parties involved, but perplexity and confusion for other parties involved.

This picture gives the teacher an opportunity to build a discussion around a situation that involves a great deal of empathy and develops a better understanding of the behavior of all people.

Below is a conversation, written from recall, as it developed in a third-grade classroom. Mrs. Bond, the teacher, had been disturbed over some lunchtime conversations she had heard wherein the children in her class complained about their parents not giving them more privileges. She felt the picture had possibilities for developing appreciations for the role of the parent and the responsibilities that went with it.

Class Discussion

Mrs. Bond: Today I want to talk about a picture I found which I like very much. Are you all sitting where you can see the picture? When I show it to you, study it hard for a few minutes to make sure you understand what it is trying to say. This one picture is really made of three small ones and you will begin by looking at the top picture first. (*Shows picture.*) Who can tell me the story of this picture?

(*Many hands are raised.*)

Mrs. Bond: Bill, you tell me the story of this picture.

Bill: Well, it's about two boys who are having a pillow fight. They are in their bedroom on the third floor. Their father is way downstairs, but he hears them because they are yelling and screaming and making a lot of noise. So he goes upstairs to stop them, but they

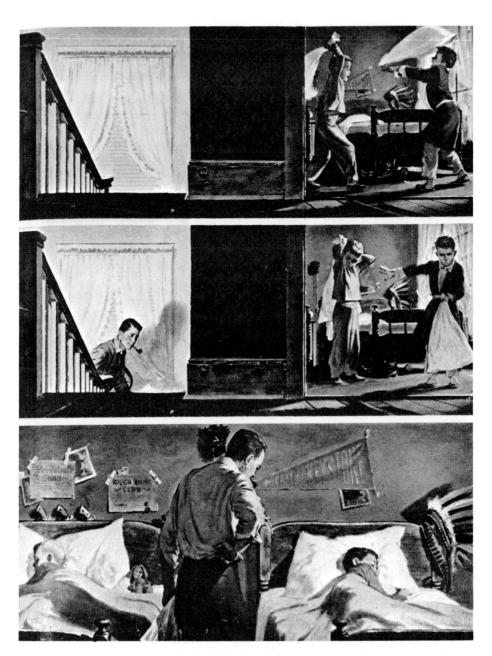

Figure 8-2. *The pillowfight.*

6. Cover by Tom Utz, reprinted with permission from *The Saturday Evening Post*, ©1955 the Curtis Publishing Co.

hear him coming. So when he gets up there, they pretend they are fast asleep.

Mrs. Bond: Well, that was good story, Bill. Does anyone have anything to add to the story?

Bob: Well, they aren't really asleep. They're just pretending.

Mrs. Bond: Why do you suppose they feel they must pretend to be asleep?

Joe: Because they'll get heck if they get caught.

Mrs. Bond: Why will they get heck?

Mary: Because they're being naughty!

Betty: They're supposed to be asleep and they know it!

Sally: I think their father is angry!

Mrs. Bond: Kevin, do you think the father is angry?

Kevin: Yes.

Mrs. Bond: Why?

Kevin: Because it's past the boys' bed-time and they're supposed to be asleep.

Mrs. Bond: Does this make *your* fathers angry?

Children: Yes, oh yes, it sure does.

Mrs. Bond: Do you think your fathers ever had pillow fights when they were little boys?

(Silence—Rudy volunteers)

Rudy: Well, I bet they did!

Mrs. Bond: I bet they did, too! Then I wonder why they get angry when their own little boys have pillow fights?

(another silence)

Bill: Because that's the way fathers are!

Mrs. Bond: You think all fathers are like that, Bill?

Kevin: Mine isn't.

Janet: Neither is mine.

Mrs. Bond: You two think only *some* fathers are like that.

Harriet: I think fathers don't like to be disobeyed.

Shawn: They want everybody to do what they want them to.

Eric: My father is always telling me to do something and if I don't he yells at me.

Mrs. Bond: You feel that fathers are all bossy at times. Is there a reason?

John: Well sometimes kids are bad and then fathers have to get tough.

Mrs. Bond: Let's look at our picture again. You said the father was angry because the boys were supposed to be asleep. You said fathers were bossy and that sometimes kids are bad. Do you think the boys in the picture are being bad?

Mary: No, they were just having fun.

Mrs. Bond: Then what is the father really mad about? What makes fathers angry besides the times when people don't do as they say?

Rudy: Maybe he's angry because he wants them to get their sleep and they are still awake.

Mrs. Bond: Rudy thinks the father is as much worried as angry.

Helen: Yes, I think he is worried.

Mrs. Bond: Look closely at his face. Make a face like it. Now make an angry face. Are they alike?

Bill: Something alike. I think the father is worried.

Harriet: He wants the kids to get to sleep.

Mrs. Bond: Can you think of any reasons why he wants the boys to go to sleep?

Joe: 'Cause—'cause they've got to get up in the morning to go to school, and they won't want to if they don't get to sleep.

Mrs. Bond: Joe thinks the father is worried that the boys won't get *enough* sleep.

Mary: Yes, that's it—the boys want to play, but the father knows they need sleep.

Mrs. Bond: You said that the father wasn't angry; that he was worried. You said that he really is concerned over the boys' health. Is he coming upstairs because he is angry at them or because he loves them a lot?

Mary: He loves them a lot. He is looking out for them.

Mrs. Bond: We said the father really acted as he did because he loved the boys a lot. Is that what we said when I first showed you the picture?

Bill: No, sometimes you don't see the whole story at first. You have to think about it.

Mrs. Bond: Did some of you change your idea of the story?

Children: Yes.

John: The father is really looking after the boys, because they aren't being sensible.

Mrs. Bond: Could we say that sometimes we don't understand what people do and maybe we should think about it?

Children: Yes.

It is interesting to notice Mrs. Bond's technique in using this picture:

1. She made sure the picture communicated the central idea to all the children.
2. She asked carefully planned questions to keep the children thinking and to keep the discussion going.
3. She did not moralize or force her opinions on the children. She *did* reflect their feelings and helped them to rephrase their statements of values.
4. She did not preach.

Bibliotherapy

Bibliotherapy is a technique that can best be used to help individuals adjust socially, although some teachers have had a great deal of success using this technique with groups of children. The teacher chooses a book for a child to read wherein the main characters have the same social or emotional problems as the reader. The theory is that the child will identify so closely with the main character of the story that he or she will apply the solution of the character to his or her own problem. A series of books dealing with the same or similar problems eventually help the children to see that their own problems are not insurmountable.

One example of the use of such a book is the case of a fourth-grade teacher who used Eleanor Estes' *The Hundred Dresses* to help a child who was rejected by her peer group. A second-grade teacher used *I Saw It on Mulberry Street,* by Dr. Seuss, for a child who had a vivid imagination that was not accepted at home. This was followed by Louis Slabodkin's *Magic Michael* and other such stories.

One modern writer whose books have a special appeal to children because they deal with the problems of children in a direct, understanding and humorous way is Judy Blume. *Are You There, God? It's Me, Margaret* deals with the problem of religion and young girls entering puberty. *Then Again, Maybe I Won't* and *It's Not the End of the World* deal with puberty, growing up and divorce. All of Mrs. Blume's books communicate with children and are excellent for use in bibliotherapy.

Some psychologists, librarians and teachers feel that the use of bibliotherapy can cause as much harm as good to a child. They contend that a child may read books in which other people solve problems similar to his or her own but that actually the circumstances may be quite different. The child may not be able to solve his or her own problem and consequently may become more frustrated and develop deeper feelings of inadequacy. To such children, literature may become unrealistic and the child may turn from it.

If bibliotherapy is to be used with children, it will take a careful and discerning teacher who selects books wisely for the child in question and who observes carefully to be certain that the material being read is helpful.

Group bibliotherapy is sometimes successful when it is carefully planned and used. If the social studies program is to deal with values and attitudes it cannot ignore such significant problems as birth and death. Many excellent books have been written for children which face these topics head-on and provide excellent opportunities for discussion in developing attitudes. Such books can be read to the class when death, for instance, is explored because of an experience such as the death of a teacher or a custodian which creates an emotional problem among the children. Or the teacher may hand one of these books to a child who is encountering such an experience in the family. One book on death, for example, is Judith Viorst's *The Tenth Good Thing about Barney.* The story deals with the death of a pet cat named Barney. It simply and beautifully presents the cycle of life in a manner which young children can understand. It is beautifully illustrated by Erik Blegvad and I have found older children enthralled by its universal quality. Another book which deals effectively with death is *My Grandson Lew* by Charlotte Zolotow. A discussion of this simple primary story is bound to help many children through a difficult time and assist them in forming positive attitudes toward death.

Other books today deal with all aspects of life in a frank but beautiful way. A generous supply of such books should supplement the textbooks of any classroom.

Filmstrip Situations

Some commercial filmstrips provide open-ended picture stories for helping children develop values, understandings, and appreciations. These filmstrips are accompanied by a recording. They present a series of pictures that illustrate a social or ethical problem. Then the recording is stopped, while the children discuss a solution to the problem. The filmed ending may then be shown if children and teacher care to see how the problem really worked out. This ending can of course, lead to further discussion. The *First Things: Values* series, by Guidance Associates, is an excellent example.

Make your own filmstrip.   Soak an old filmstrip in bleach for five minutes, then rinse it thoroughly in hot water. When it is dry, pictures can be drawn on it with a grease pencil or with a felt-tip pen. You can also type on it. When work is completed on the filmstrip, spray it with an affixative.

Film Problems

In Chapter 1 we met Mr. Arnold, a teacher in a middle school, who helped his students develop values through the use of the film *The Law and the People,* the presentation of Muhammud Ali's Supreme Court fight for his right to box. Films of this nature are very useful for developing values in children and helping them in making decisions.

Many such films are now available. Teachers will want to send for catalogs from major film companies to become familiar with the material currently available for classroom use.

One excellent resource is the National Film Board of Canada which has produced a series of films that provide problem situations useful in the upper grades for discussion purposes and for value building. This series is called "What Do You Think?" (distributed by McGraw-Hill). Other films which are excellent to use with this age group are available from various film distributors: "The Toymaker," "Boundary Lines," "The Magician," "Brotherhood of Man" and "Have I Told You Lately That I Love You?".

Textbook Exercises

Modern social studies textbooks are concerned with the development of values and attitudes in children and many provide exercises or suggest activities in value development. Samples of these exercises and activities appeared in the previous chapter.

Environmental Studies Cards

Stimulating and exciting kits for developing creativity are produced by Environmental Studies and published by the American Geological Institute and supported by the National Science Foundation. The purpose of the kits is to develop a human environment, one founded on mutual trust. As the accompanying booklet says, TRUST TAKES TIME. The kits contain a packet of cards each of which presents one concept related to feelings or knowledge and develops this concept by a variety of techniques. Each card presents the problem attractively on one side and then on the flip side a variety of approaches are used to develop the theme. Slogans are sometimes used, quotes related to the concept are given, and a section is reserved for THE ACTION, a box full of suggested activities for students to pursue in order to develop the concept. A MORE box which tells about it and a NOTESPACE section where a student may jot down notes of his or her discoveries complete the cards.

These cards deal specifically with building concepts and helping children understand their environment and themselves as a part of that environment. They are clever, challenging and beautifully packaged. They present a direct attack on creative development and can serve as an ideation source for teachers who wish to design their own cards. Each card is responsible for building attitudes, a result of a change in values.

Teacher-Made Task Cards

Just as many subject matter areas are currently designed so that children can teach themselves, cards or worksheets can be designed to help children in value and character development.

Some of these cards deal directly with the affective domain. Mrs. McBride, one teacher in an open school, planned a unit called KNOWING ONESELF with the entire group. She called it WHO AM I? and thought the children would gain a great deal by studying themselves as human beings. Cards like the following were planned and placed in a learning center designed especially to contain materials on the art of becoming a *human* being.

Once teachers have several task cards to use in one learning center, they may leave them in the center for a period of time and then change them. Often these cards may be exchanged with a different set from another teacher if the new set fits the needs of the children. Children who follow through successfully

DECISION MAKING

Task Card 1

Below is a problem. A decision must be made in order to solve it. Read the problem and decide how the story should end. Then answer the questions on the back of the card.

THE SWIM PARTY

More than anything else in the world Michael wanted to go to Jerry's swimming party. He was sure he was going to be invited. After all, he and Jerry were good friends and he had spent days in Jerry's back yard watching the big machines and the men dig the dirt, mix the cement and put in the tile, and set up the diving board. Jerry told him then how his father said he could have a Saturday afternoon swim party when the pool was finished, and they had more or less planned it together. But here it was, Thursday, and he hadn't had a telephone call from Jerry yet. Maybe Jerry was still angry over the little argument they had on Sunday afternoon and was just being mean to get even. When Michael saw him at school on Monday, Jerry had avoided him. In fact, Michael didn't see Jerry to talk to all week. It was not until Wednesday, in fact, that he knew anything about the swim party. Bill Adams sat at his table in the cafeteria. During their conversation Bill asked Michael if he was going to Jerry's swim party and told him how Jerry had called him last Monday afternoon. Michael was crushed to think he hadn't been asked. He purposely sought Jerry out but Jerry was very cool and never mentioned the party at all.

Friday came and still Jerry avoided Michael. All the guys seemed to be invited to the party but him. By the time school was out on Friday afternoon all anyone was talking about was Jerry's swim party. Michael felt humiliated, hurt and even angry. He told his mother about it and she felt badly, too. She suggested Michael call his cousin Jason who lived across town and invite him to go to the matinee of a good monster picture at the movie theater. Because Michael had spent most of his allowance, Mother even agreed to pay Jason's way.

Michael felt better having something to do. He called his cousin Jason at once, and Jason was excited about going to the movie. He said his dad would bring him to Michael's house. Michael's mother called while he was on the phone and said to invite Jason to a cookout in the back yard after the show so Michael did.

Michael felt better after he talked to Jason. He and his mother made plans for the cookout, but in the back of his mind he still had an unhappy feeling about not being invited to Jerry's party.

Saturday was a beautiful day—ideal for a swim party. Michael helped his mother set up the picnic tables on the patio. Then he got wood and charcoal and opened the folding chairs so everything would be ready for

Figure 8-3

the cookout. While he was sweeping off the flagstones, his mother came to the door. "Michael," she called, "telephone!"

Michael hurried into the kitchen and took the receiver. It was Jerry. "Hey, Mike," he said, "I guess I haven't seen you much this week. I just remembered to ask you to come to my swim party this afternoon. Can you make it?"

For a split second Michael almost said "Yes." Then many thoughts ran through his mind. What about Jason who was planning on the movie and the cookout? What about his mother who had gone to all the trouble of having the cookout for him and who was even putting up the money for Jason's ticket? Why was Jerry asking him at the last minute? Had someone else checked out? Had Jerry really just forgotten him? What would the other guys think if he went—he had told them just yesterday that he wasn't going to the swim party.

How did Michael answer Jerry?

DECISION MAKING

Task Card 1 (reverse side)

1. See if you can tell why you made the decision you did.

   Clues:
   a. Was it for the good of everyone in the story?
   b. Was it because of your own values?
   c. Was it because you felt you knew all the facts?

2. Ask a friend to read this card and see if he or she makes the same decision. Discuss your decision with your friend. If he or she agrees with you keep asking friends to read it until one disagrees with you— or makes a different decision. Talk it over.

Figure 8-3 (*continued*)

on a series of cards may work in a group to create a new [learning center] for another group of children. They can often teach the lessons they learned to other children.

Many task cards and work sheets are open-ended. There are no right or wrong answers. They cannot be graded, but they can be of help in aiding the teacher to evaluate and to better know each child, and to help each child know himself better.

In planning for learning cards in the centers it is important for the teacher to remember he or she must plan projects, questions and situations which place children at all levels of thinking; some activities should be planned to provoke analysis, synthesis and evaluation. Some should also be open-ended to encourage creative thinking. Some of the taxonomies can be of great help in planning.[7]

Figure 8-4

7. B. S. Bloom et al., *Taxonomy of Educational Objectives: Handbook No. 1, The Cognitive Domain* (New York: Longmans, Green, David McKay, 1956).

David R. Krathwohl et al., *Taxonomy of Educational Objectives: Handbook II, the Affective Domain* (New York: David McKay, 1964).

DECISION MAKING

Task Card 2 (reverse side)

Were you right?

Do you often make decisions when you have only one fact?

How many facts do you need in order to make decisions?

List all the reasons you can think of that explain why you made the decisions you did.

Why were you wrong?

Figure 8-4 (continued)

DECISION MAKING

Task Card 3

1. What is a decision?
2. Can you remember the last time you made a decision for yourself?
3. Can you remember the last time Mother or Father made a decision for you?
4. Can you remember the last time your teacher made a decision for you?
5. Is it possible for you to always make your own decisions? Why? Why not?
6. What do you need to KNOW to make a decision?
7. How do you need to FEEL to make a decision?
8. How do you need to THINK to make a decision?
9. What must you CONSIDER in order to make a decision?

DECISION MAKING

Task Card 3 (reverse side)

Who Can Make the Decision?

Buying shoes?
Doing household chores?
Choosing friends?
Where to go for a picnic?
How much to spend on a new car?
What book to read?
What time to do homework?
Where to spend summer vacation?
How to spend an allowance?

List all the facts you had to consider in making these decisions, like:
    money _____   _____

    other people _____   _____

_____   _____

List all the values you had to consider like:
    fairness _____   _____

    sportsmanship _____   _____

    responsibility _____   _____

_____   _____

Figure 8-5

DECISION MAKING

Task Card 4

Paying for Decisions

Have you made many decisions lately? Were they wise ones? Have you regretted some? Keep a record for a while and check yourself.

PAYING FOR DECISIONS

Decision	Consequence
April 12. Mom told me I couldn't go out both weekend nights and I'd have to choose between the movie on Friday or Janie's pajama party on Saturday. I chose the movie.	Poor decision. The movie was lousy and the kids had a blast at Janie's party. Everyone is talking about it today and I feel "out." I think close friends are more important than an old movie, and I think some of the girls are mad at me.

(Reverse of card plotted for more space to record incidents.)

Figure 8-6

SELF-CONCEPT

Task Card 1

How do others see you?
Make a photograph album of how you think others see you.
Include the following (use pictures from magazines as photographs):
At Home
With Friends
In School
With Relatives
Sitting Alone
On My _____ Team

Figure 8-7

SELF-CONCEPT

Task Card 2

Draw pictures showing how you look:

When you don't
get your way.

When you lose a
game of Bingo.

When your best
friend doesn't
speak to you.

When you get a
high grade on a
test.

Figure 8-8

SELF-CONCEPT

Task Card 3

Match the following phrases with the box that best suits you.

1. I won first prize in a contest.
2. My father scolded me.
3. I stayed out too late.
4. "You may go to the movies with your friend."
5. "You cannot go out with your friend."
6. I failed my math test.
7. The members of the team did not choose me.
8. A boy called me a bad name.
9. My mother kissed me.
10. My father kissed me.
11. My brother put his arm around me.
12. Everyone got a piece of candy but me.
13. My teacher told me I was pretty.
14. I didn't get home from school on time.
15. I won an airplane flight to Florida.
16. I inherited some money.

WELL I NEVER

dancing

nervous

I never do anything right!

So excited!

angry

Figure 8-9

Activities

Throughout this book we have seen how carefully selected, meaningful and purposeful activities can help children change attitudes and values.

A few years ago, a great deal of energy was expended on the so-called activity program of the elementary school. The activity movement was a great step forward in pedagogy. However, activity for activity's sake is no more valuable than knowledge for knowledge's sake. And some schools not only went activity-mad, they also incorporated into their programs activities that approached the ridiculous.

Behind the use of every activity should lie a clear-cut objective. Some general criteria for the selection of activities in the classroom follow. Activities and projects have significance and worth when they:

1. Have content of social importance.
2. Provide opportunities for children to gain deeper and more accurate understandings of the community in which they live.
3. Build sound attitudes toward people in differing groups.
4. Help boys and girls develop increased understanding of democratic values and traditions.

5. Provide opportunities for children to learn how to solve problems through critical thinking.
6. Provide opportunities for children to develop and retain social interests.
7. Help children learn to accept the fact that the world in which we live is changing rapidly and that change can be directed and controlled as intelligent people work together cooperatively.
8. Help children learn essential social studies skills, such as interpreting maps and globes and developing a sense of time and chronology.
9. Help internalize learnings.

On previous pages we have observed children engaged in worthwhile activities, all designed to fulfill a purpose and to meet an objective in the social studies program.

Check Sheets

Sometimes the values of children can be identified through the use of check sheets, questionnaires, value choices and other devices. The main value in such

---

CHECK SHEET

Sample 1

UNFINISHED SENTENCES

1. On Sundays, I like to _____

2. Something I would be willing to die for is _____

3. I like people who _____

4. People hurt me when _____

5. If I had two days to live _____

6. I feel good when people _____

7. If I had a lot of money _____

8. My favorite fun on Saturday is _____

9. The hardest thing for me to do is _____

10. If I were a teacher, I _____

Figure 8-10

CHECK SHEET

Sample 2

WHAT IS IMPORTANT TO YOU?

Below is a list of ten things most people like. Read the whole list. Then put a 1 in front of the one that is most important to you, a 2 in front of the one that is second in importance, and so on.

____ a happy, successful life
____ admired and liked by others
____ a world at peace
____ a world of beauty
____ a chance to do my thing
____ freedom (independence)
____ equality for everyone
____ friendship
____ freedom from worry
____ to be good in school work

Figure 8-11

CHECK SHEET

Sample 3

THINGS I LOVE TO DO[8]

Make a list of the ten things you love to do best.

1. _____
2. _____
3. _____
4. _____
5. _____
6. _____
7. _____
8. _____
9. _____
10. _____

M-F   L   N   A   P

Then put a check in the columns at the right using the following key:
M-F   If your mother and/or father also like to do it.
L   If you did it lately—within the past 6 months.
N   If it is a new activity.
A   If you like to do it alone.
P   If you like to do it with other people.

Figure 8-12

8. Sidney B. Simon, Leland W. Howe, and Howard Kirschenbaum, *Values Clarification* (New York: Hart, 1972).

materials is that a teacher may have the children fill out these forms for the purpose of better knowing a child, his value system and his system of priorities. A similar form filled out at the close of a unit designed to change values indicates the success of the strategies used.

Human Resources

Recently a group of *senior volunteers* has been added to the list of resources for the elementary school. The senior volunteer has a unique contribution to make to the school. Early retirement and increasing longevity both contribute to the availability of the older adult. Any senior volunteer can be used in the school. A background in education is not necessary, but can be helpful.

Senior volunteers go through a training program which prepares them to know their duties and to understand what they may legally do and not do while helping in the school. Some schools plan this training program with an administrator and a corps of teachers in charge. Senior volunteers have been of great help in gathering books for teachers, collecting pictures, sharing their own abilities and talents (playing piano or other musical instruments, hobbies such as patchwork quilting, etc.), helping individual children and such.

The senior volunteer fills in a grandparent-type relationship and this is encouraged. Fewer and fewer children today live with or see their grandparents, and a great sense of stability is lost. Bridges are built between generations and between the structures of society with education. School systems that need help in all sorts of tasks can do well by contacting local chapters of Senior Volunteers and soliciting the help of older people who are happy and willing to be of service. The organization is known as RSVP and is under the jurisdiction of ACTION, Washington, D.C. 20521. Their slogan is, "Aging is a matter of mind, and if we don't mind, it doesn't matter."

The sense of stability and the values which result when youth works with old age is one of the best techniques to help humans understand other humans.

Simulation Games

One highly creative development which has recently become popular is the use of simulation games which can be used to develop concepts and understandings in the social studies. These games also develop various values, understandings of human relationships, and the need for certain qualities such as punctuality, faith, trust and integrity. Many teachers have invented games in order to develop a complex concept in economics, for instance, on a simple level which can then be used to demonstrate to children exactly what happens when the rules and principles are applied in real life situations. Most of these games are constructed so that human elements enter into the dealings and human frailties and drives gum up the works as they often do in real life situations.

In teaching a unit on money, its value in society, how it is earned, how to invest it, etc., an excellent commercial game to play is "Monopoly." The goal of "Monopoly," as most people know, is to buy, rent and sell properties profitably.

Some samples of simulation games which have become popular with teachers who wisely use them to accomplish specific objectives are listed below.

The Stock Market Game, Western Publishing Co., Racine, Wisconsin

Careers (on fame, prestige, money and opportunities in a variety of careers), Parker Brothers, Box 900, Salem, Mass. 01970

Life (concepts explored are wealth, money, insurance and stock), Milton Bradley Co., Springfield, Mass.

Seal-Hunting (to understand Eskimo societies), Abt Associates, 55 Wheeler St., Cambridge, Mass. 02138

Market (economics), Abt Associates, above.

Economy (economics), Abt Associates, above.

Junior Executive (concepts of earning money, debts, lending and borrowing), Western Publishing Co., Racine, Wisconsin

Activity Cards

Some school systems write entire units built around the themes of prejudice, integrity, responsibility, compassion, etc., all of which are attitudes determined by certain values held by children.

One such unit contains activity cards for the student to work through. A sample of some of these cards follows:

ACTIVITY CARD 1

Objective: to promote initiative

1. Construct a telegraph in your classroom and send messages by Morse code.
2. Blockprinting is done in much the same way as printing by the first wood blocks made by Gutenberg. Make some block prints and see how easy it is to make a copy for everyone in the class in a short time. Compare this to the time it would take if one person had to make an original for everyone in the class.
3. You read in this chapter that people have always used the power of their minds to figure out better ways of doing jobs that have to be done. Make a list showing how each of these groups of people did this in the past: the Eskimos, Hopis, Mayas, Egyptians, Romans. Would this statement be true? The more people use the power of their minds, the greater is the civilization which results.
4. Make a list of all the tools your parents use at your house to help them do their jobs more easily.
5. Make a list of all the things you use during the day that help you to be more thrifty with your energy.

Figure 8-13

6. Years ago one person often invented or discovered something. Now most of our inventions and discoveries are made by many, many people working together. Why do you think this is so?
7. Years ago the geography of the country determined what people would do for a living. This is no longer completely true. List ways that people have learned to overcome their geography, such as making crops grow in the desert.

Figure 8-13 (*continued*)

ACTIVITY CARD 2

Objective: to develop the attitude of open-mindedness

1. There is much political unrest in some countries. Collect articles from the newspaper and read about the problems of one of those countries. Read different viewpoints of the same situation.
2. People often think of spaghetti as an Italian dish. Did this food really come from Italy originally? Find out about this. You may like to have a spaghetti dinner at school some day.
3. The Paleo-Indians were the first known people to come to what is now called America. Why, then, do we say that Columbus discovered America, and why did we name this land after Americus Vespucius? What might this great land be called if we had not named it after Americus Vespucius?
4. Some people have been labeled as men who have been born too soon. Some of them are: Thomas Jefferson, Robert Fulton and Benjamin Franklin. Read about the lives of these men and report to the class. Why did people say that they had been born too soon?
5. Visit a newspaper office and see how movable type is used in the printing of a newspaper. Do you think the invention of the newspaper changed life in the world? How?
6. Newspapers often say that teenagers are troublemakers and often run only those articles which show teenagers in trouble. Is this fair? List reasons why it is not. Think about all the teenagers you know when you do this.

Figure 8-14

ACTIVITY CARD 3

Objective: to promote critical thinking (Grade 6)

Here is a problem to discuss. First do what this tells you to do; then have a group discussion on the problem.

WHAT TO DO

We say that the United States is a democracy. What is a democracy? See your book. Collect newspaper clippings from your paper which show we are or are not a democracy.

A PROBLEM FOR YOU

Look at the news clippings you have collected. Are there some which describe people who are not equal or do not have equal freedoms?

There are some people who feel we are not yet really a democracy—that democracy is an ideal and we are working for it. But we have not reached it yet.

WHAT DO YOU THINK?

Find ways to support your beliefs. Remember, be critical thinkers!

Figure 8-15

ACTIVITY CARD 4

Objective: to develop appreciations

1. Make charts of the contributions made by each of the countries to the world. Include historical gifts such as the printing press by Gutenberg; democratic ideas from Switzerland; great men and women such as painters, inventors, composers, politicians; products which now come from these countries and other things for which they are famous.
2. Some great artists lived in Spain. You may enjoy looking at their pictures. In a book by Rockwell Kent called *World-Famous Paintings* you can find the pictures of these great painters and something about their lives. Look up these names and report on them: Murillo and Velasquez.
3. If you have people in your community who come from other countries, perhaps you can have them come in and tell you about their homeland.
4. If you live near a city where there is a Chinatown, plan a trip to visit it. Here you will see some of the beautiful Chinese art. You will learn about Chinese architecture and religion.

Figure 8-16

ACTIVITY CARD 5

Objective: to develop compassion

1. In many schools children march on Halloween to collect money for UNICEF. UNICEF is a branch of the United Nations which helps take care of children in other parts of the world. Two cents buys a quart of milk for some undernourished child. Can your grade plan some way to help other people this Halloween?
2. Instead of exchanging gifts in your classroom for the Christmas holidays, bring a gift for a veteran who is in a veteran's hospital (or a needy family, etc.) and decorate your tree with such gifts. Perhaps a committee could be chosen to deliver the gifts.
3. Make a list of all the things you find in your neighborhood that are there because people believe in being kind and good to each other. Would your school be one? Your parks? The Red Cross?
4. Philadelphia was a city founded on "brotherly love." Find out how it came to be.
5. How did the Constitution of the United States consider the fact that people might want to worship differently? How does it try to help people develop consideration for each other?

Figure 8-17

Media Tapes

One approach to developing values is to present the children with material which discusses values and their importance in making decisions.

Mrs. Hartness used the MEDIA MATERIALS tapes and the accompanying material with her students most effectively. These tapes dealt with the following topics: *What Are Values?, Supporting Value Statements, Recognizing Value Conflicts,* and *Actions and Values.*[9]

Summary

Values are beliefs; they are a means of judging the quality of actual behavior. Behavior is prompted by the set of values inherent in each individual. Every society has a set of basic values which cements the people together. Individuals have varying values which do not always conform to those of other individuals. The schools must expend energy and money toward identifying common values and making certain that they are perpetuated in the society. Through various types of sociodynamics and individualized material, the de-

---

9. Jerry K. Wald, Media Materials Inc., 2936 Remington Ave., Baltimore, Maryland 21211.

velopment of values has become a direct target for instruction in modern social studies programs. This is as it should be because values determine attitudes, appreciations and character.

To the College Student

1. Start to collect stories and plays that you may use in your classroom to build values, understandings, and appreciations.

2. Divide your class into groups and assign each group the job of demonstrating one of the valuing techniques described in this chapter. Or, create and demonstrate an idea of your own.

3. Team up with a friend; study each other over an hour's period, and then write down the values your friend appears to have from his or her behavior. Share your lists with each other and discuss the significance of overt behavior.

To the Classroom Teacher

1. The next time an appropriate social problem or a behavior problem arises in class, think of ways you can use it to develop a creative learning situation rather than trying to settle it at once by yourself.

2. Try some of the ideas in this chapter with your children.

3. Use an open-ended story dealing with some ethical problem and try to identify the values of the children in your classroom.

4. Ask a group of students to write a play of some problem recently experienced in school. Have them present it before the rest of the class. If you teach a primary grade, have them dramatize it without a script.

5. Plan a unit on RESPECT with emphasis on respect for other people's property and for public property with the objective in mind that your unit may discourage vandalism, a current national social problem.

6. How do you think your own attitudes, values and appreciations developed? Do you ever remember anyone "teaching" them to you, or were you expected to acquire them through the act of growing up? Make a list of all the ways you can think of that values are learned.

7. Make a card file of children's books that may be used for bibliotherapy. Be sure to read some realistic fiction by modern authors of children's books, especially the books of Judy Blume.

To the College Student and the Classroom Teacher

1. Write to the address below for a catalog of other social dramas. Also write to the National Education Association, Washington, D.C., for its "unfinished stories" series.

Put on one of these dramas for a [P.T.O.] meeting or for a college class, and conduct a discussion about it. (*Address:* Human Relations Aids, 1790 Broadway, New York N.Y.)

2. Make a collection of pictures that might be used to develop creative solutions to social or ethical problems.

3. Psychodrama is another use of a projective technique for helping individuals with personal problems. Find out what a psychodrama is. Perhaps someone from the psychology department will come to class and demonstrate the psychodrama.

4. Look up the topic "Projective Techniques" and discuss ways techniques other than those mentioned in this chapter can be used creatively to help children solve problems.

5. In the various taxonomies for thinking, the levels of thinking are described as memory, reasoning, judgment, analysis, synthesis, evaluation and creative thinking. Review the task cards presented in this chapter and identify all the levels of thinking described in the taxonomies.

Selected Bibliography

ADAMS, DENNIS M. *Simulation Games: An Approach to Learning.* Worthington, Ohio: Charles A. Jones, 1974.

ADAIR, MARGARET W., and PATAPOFF, ELIZABETH. *Folk Puppet Plays for the Social Studies.* New York: John Day, 1972.

BARKER, WAYNE. *Brain Storms: A Study in Human Spontaneity.* New York: Grove Press, Inc., 1968.

BELCH, JEAN (comp.). *Contemporary Games: A Directory and Bibliography Describing Play Situations or Simulations.* Vols. I and II. Detroit: Gale Research Co., 1973.

BELOK, MICHAEL, et al. *Approaches to Values in Education.* Dubuque: William C. Brown, 1973.

BROWN, J. A. *Techniques of Persuasion from Propaganda to Brainwashing.* Baltimore: Penguin Books, Inc., 1967.

CHESTER, MARK, and FOX, ROBERT. *Role-Playing Methods in the Classroom.* Palo Alto, Calif.: California Science Research Associates, 1971.

CRUMP, CLAUDIA and DUNFEE, MAXINE. *Teaching for Social Values in Social Studies.* Edited by Patricia M. Markun. Washington, D.C.: Association for Childhood Education International, 1974.

EBERLE, ROBERT. "Does Creative Dramatics Really Square with Research Evidence?" *Journal of Creative Behavior* 8, No. 3 (Third Quarter 1974): 177–182.

EBERLE, ROBERT. *Scamper: Games for Imagination Development.* Buffalo: DOK Publishers, 1971.

FRAENKEL, JACK. *Helping Students to Think and Value: Strategies for Teaching the Social Studies.* Englewood Cliffs, N.J.: Prentice-Hall, 1973.

GILLISPIE, PHILIP H. *Learning through Simulation Games.* Paramus, N.J.: Paulist-Newman Press, 1974.

GUNN, ANGUS M. "Educational Simulations in School Geography," in *Focus on Geography.* Washington, D.C.: National Council for the Social Studies Yearbook, 1970: 350–367.

HORN, ROBERT E., ed. *The Guide to Simulations-Games for Education and Training.* Cranford, N.J.: Didactic Systems, 1976.

KINGHORN, HARRIET. *Classroom and Workshop-Tested Games, Puzzles, and Activities for the Elementary School.* Englewood Cliffs, N.J.: Parker—Prentice-Hall, 1975.

LIVINGSTON, SAMUEL A., and STOLL, CLARICE S. *Simulation Games: An Introduction for the Social Studies Teacher.* New York: Free Press, 1973.

MAGER, ROBERT. *Developing Attitude Toward Learning.* Belmont, Calif.: Fearon, 1968.

MAIDMENT, ROBERT, and BRONSTEIN, RUSSELL H. *Simulation Games: Design and Implementation.* Columbus: Charles E. Merrill, 1973.

MARZOLLO, JEAN, and LLOYD, JANICE. *Learning through Play.* New York: Harper & Row, 1974.

MELANCON, HOWARD J. *Bulletin Board Ideas for Social Studies.* Minneapolis: Denison & Co., 1974.

METCALF, LAWRENCE E., ed. *Values Education.* Washington, D.C.: National Council for the Social Studies, 1971.

NESBITT, WILLIAM A. *Simulation Games for the Social Studies Classroom.* 2nd ed. New York: T. Y. Crowell, 1971.

PIERNI, MARY PAUL FRANCIS. *Creative Dramatics, Guide for Educators.* New York: Herder and Herder, 1971.

PURKEY, WILLIAM W. *Self-Concept and School Achievement.* Englewood Cliffs, N.J.: Prentice-Hall, 1970.

RATHS, LOUIS E.; HARMIN, MERRILL; and SIMON, SIDNEY B. *Values and Teaching: Working with Values in the Classroom.* Columbus: Charles E. Merrill, 1966.

ROKEACH, MILTON. *Beliefs, Attitudes and Values.* San Francisco: Jossey-Bass, 1968.

SHAFTEL, FANNIE R., and SHAFTEL, GEORGE. *Role-Playing for Social Values: Decision-Making in the Social Studies.* Englewood Cliffs, N.J.: Prentice-Hall, 1967.

TORRANCE, E. PAUL. "Sociodrama as a Creative Problem-Solving Approach to Studying the Future." *Journal of Creative Behavior* 9, No. 3 (Third Quarter 1975): 182.

WOODS, MARGARET S. *Wonderwork: Creative Experiences for the Young Child.* Buffalo: DOK Publishers, 1970.

Creative Teaching of Study Skills

Creativity is rarely a single flash of intuition: it usually requires sustained analysis of a great many observations to separate out the significant factors from the adventitious. A keen observer once said of Einstein that part of his genius was his inability to understand the obvious. Rejection of superficial explanations of one's own as well as of others is prerequisite to understanding. To reach a correct solution efficiently also requires unconcern for all except the truth. Science practiced to bolster a faulty hypothesis rather than to test it objectively is often worse than useless.

HENRY EYRING[1]

INTRODUCTION

No person can work successfully at a task until he or she has learned how to use the tools to complete it. An important part of a social studies program is to teach the tools (or skills) children need to perform the tasks at hand. These skills are also those needed for successful independent living in a democratic society.

Some educators will argue that the skills identified here are not all social studies skills—that many fall into the category of language arts. Bickering over the classification of skills is like watering flowers on a rainy day. The fact is that all the skills identified below are communication skills necessary for the development of independence and meaningful human relationships in living. Time devoted to classification arguments might better be spent on teaching since all children must learn their skills somewhere in order to complete the tasks they will confront in the social studies program.

1. Henry Eyring, "Scientific Creativity," in *Creativity and Its Cultivation,* ed. Harold H. Anderson (New York: Harper and Brothers, 1959): 3.

IDENTIFICATION OF STUDY SKILLS

When the teachers of Glendale outlined their objectives for social studies as reported in Chapter 2, these were the skills they felt were necessary for social living and individual growth in each child:

1. Skills in problem-solving.
2. Skills in critical and creative thinking.
3. Communication skills.
4. Study skills—
    a. Using *inquiry*.
    b. The ability to do research, to use reference materials.
    c. The ability to make oral and written reports.
    d. The ability to use basic research materials.
    e. The ability to use original sources.
    f. The ability to summarize and synthesize.
    g. The ability to select main ideas.
    h. The ability to read for details.
    i. The ability to plan.
    j. The ability to read and use maps, charts, graphs.
5. Group dynamics skills—
    a. The ability to listen.
    b. The ability to discuss issues.
    c. The ability to debate issues.
    d. The ability to take turns in discussion, to share viewpoints, to react intellectually rather than emotionally.
6. Evaluation skills—
    a. Group evaluation.
    b. Self-evaluation.

The teaching and learning of these skills can be a creative process accomplished largely by the method used in teaching. Conditions can be set for teaching them if a few basic principles for developing creativity are applied to the teaching act:

1. The experiences children have in developing these skills should be open-ended rather than fact-centered. Each skill learned or discovered should be applied at once to problem-solving.
2. Teachers can use techniques that are devised to evoke original behavior,

Figure 9-1. *Developing the skill of synthesizing.*

discovery, and unusual responses as well as the necessary common responses.

3. New skills should be utilized in varied situations so children can apply them to solve many problems; functional fixedness should not destroy their multipurpose use.

4. Skills are necessary to all functions of living and are learned to enable children to solve certain problems. They must become as automatic as possible and be learned as quickly as possible.

5. A full account of complete creative-artistic performance involves evaluative abilities and abilities that are not primarily creative. The learning of these abilities makes possible creation of other sorts. In setting conditions for creative teaching of skills, the teacher must provide for ways

these skills may be creatively applied, even though, in themselves, they are not creative acts.

6. The development of skills may contribute to the development of many intellectual factors: cognition, production, and evaluation.

7. The motivation of children to learning falls into two categories: children may be motivated by *content* or by *method* of teaching. When the material being studied is of high interest value, children often are eager to learn it, and almost no other motivation is necessary. This is generally true of material about the space age or dinosaurs. When the material being studied is not of such high interest value, yet is of importance to the children, motivation may be built through the use of an interesting technique or method for motitvation. A film or filmstrip, a puppet show, a stimulating question, a dramatization, a picture, a flannel-board presentation, a model, a diorama—all these create immediate involvement on the part of the children, and, when children become involved, learning can take place.

8. Skills development helps develop creativity in many ways. Learning skills of research and note-taking, for instance, leads a child toward independence in learning and independence is a quality of creative people. Learning skills of map-, chart-, graph-, and cartoon-reading enables children to initiate their own learnings. Creative children are able to initiate their own learnings.

9. The unit method of teaching calls for the learning of the above-mentioned skills in a normal and logical way. If the unit method is not used, the skills must be taught in lessons. It is essential that they be taught as tools and utilized by the child.

10. The learning of study skills gives children techniques to verify opinions and evaluate discussions, to synthesize, summarize, draw conclusions, and help in passing judgment and making decisions—all of which are affiliated characteristics of creativity.

11. Skills learning is as important as learning content or developing creativity. It is often necessary to take time out to learn skills so that content learning can move forward.

With a rapidly changing society and our knowledge explosion, we cannot expect children to acquire all of the knowledge they will need in order to live effectively in the space age. But we can teach them the skills they need to help them acquire knowledge and find solutions to problems after they leave school. Such skills should be identified and incorporated into the instructional program in the social studies.

Since the skills of problem-solving, developing critical and creative thinking, group dynamics and evaluation are discussed on other pages of this book, we will devote our discussion here to examples of ways the principles of creative teaching can be applied to the development of study skills.

DEVELOPING STUDY SKILLS

Working Through Inquiry

The current popularity of the *inquiry* method of teaching leads young students to believe that it is a new strategy of teaching. Actually it is not. Much of the inquiry technique has been used in the illustrations throughout this book.

Thomas and Brubaker define inquiry as follows: *the process individuals or groups go through in attempting to answer questions or to solve problems they consider worthy of their attention.* And teaching through inquiry or an inquiry approach means any mode of instruction that helps learners acquire skill in this process.[2]

These writers focus their definition on seven steps. The first two steps relate to goals or objectives, the next five to methods and materials of investigation, and the last one to evaluation.

Steps in the Inquiry Process

1. Identifying problems or questions to investigate.
2. Analyzing the issues into component parts representing subquestions.

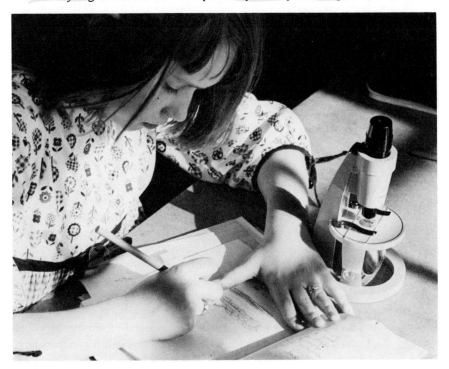

Figure 9-2. *Developing the skill of scientific experimentation and notation.*

2. R. Murray Thomas and Dale Brubaker, eds., *Teaching Elementary Social Studies: Readings* (Belmont, Calif.: Wadsworth, 1972): 276.

3. Planning who will collect what data, where and how to answer the subquestions.
4. Collecting the data.
5. Organizing the information.
6. Reporting the results.
7. Evaluating the success of the process.[3]

Many teachers call individual steps of this process "inquiry" and at times in the learning process each step or process can be legitimately used to meet the objectives of the lesson. But true inquiry utilizes all steps to complete the total process. In the chapter on Unit Teaching the steps for developing a unit are described and appear to be the same as the steps of the INQUIRY process.

Dewey defined the pattern of inquiry as common sense, and the scientific method.[4] Dewey also sets a pattern for inquiry as: 1) a felt difficulty, 2) institution of a problem, 3) suggestions and hypotheses, 4) abstract reasoning or systematic inference, 5) testing by action.

Dewey maintained that thinking in the human begins when the equilibrium of habitual action is disturbed. The initial step in inquiry is to see and feel that a situation requires inquiry. Dewey stated:

> [The principle of inquiry is violated] when emphasis falls chiefly on getting the correct answer. Then the recitation tends to become a guessing bee as to what the teacher is really after. The emphasis on getting the correct answer sets predetermined, fixed or narrow ends. The nature of the process is geared to the attainment of those ends. Inquiry is cut short, and the education derived is limited.[5]

Social studies teaching is teaching by inquiry.

Doing Research

The ability to do research through reading (and other methods) is a skill which all students need throughout their schooling. It is perhaps one of the most effective ways of answering problems. The basis for sophisticated research required for college study can be laid in the elementary grades.

Research skills do not just come intuitively: they must be taught. I have seen many well-meaning yet naive teachers decide to break away from the use of a single textbook by installing a fine selection of texts and supplementary books in the classroom, helping the children to identify a good set of problems that can be researched and then telling the children to go to it. Naturally, chaos resulted. Children had no idea how to work in groups, how to dig out material from the books supplied or how to make reports. A visit to Mr. Garrison's middle school room shows a creative and sensible approach to the problem.

3. Thomas and Brubaker, p. 280.
4. John Dewey, *Logic: The Theory of Inquiry* (New York: Holt, Rinehart & Winston, 1938): 101.
5. Dewey, p. 267.

Mr. Garrison launched a unit of work much in the same manner as other teachers reported in this volume. After questions for the unit were listed on a chart, Mr. Garrison helped the children classify the questions by topics: food, clothing, shelter, education, transportation, communication, protection, life styles, customs, history, politics and geography. He then suggested that the children plan a *way* to work. Since his students had been exposed only to traditional textbook teaching up to this point, they suggested exactly what they had been taught: that they read from their social studies books to see if they could find answers to the questions.

Mr. Garrison accepted the idea that this was one way to find answers but that there were also many other ways and some were more fun and more economical than this one. He told the class that he would like to show them some ways they might organize to do research in the coming week.

He first printed the questions on charts. The unit was on Africa, and he had collected excellent textbooks and supplementary books on Africa. The first day he put the questions dealing with the geography of Africa before the class. The children read the questions aloud. Because they were familiar with the textbook reading lesson, he gave each child a textbook.

Before the children started to read to find the answers to the questions, Mr. Garrison had them arrange their desks and chairs into two large groups. He then assigned seats at the two tables for all the children in the classroom. He told the children to read to see how many answers they could find to the questions on the chart.

Mr. Garrison had grouped the children so that his slower readers were at one table. While the other group was reading, he sat with this group to help them read. Some of the material he read to them so they would not fall too far behind the other group. When he noticed that many children from both groups had finished, he asked all the children to stop reading and to look at the questions. The children then answered the questions. Among them they knew all the answers. From the answers they gave, Mr. Garrison helped them to make an outline on the chalkboard. Together they wrote a report in three paragraphs from their outline.

Mr. Garrison summarized the work by saying, "Today we learned how to read a great deal of material to find several answers. We also learned how outlines help us and we learned how to make a written report from an outline. Tomorrow we will try something else."

The next day Mr. Garrison arranged the desks into five groups. He held a discussion at the beginning of his social studies period.

"Can you think of a way," he asked, "that we might look up *more* material today then we did yesterday in the same length of time?"

Charlie suggested that different groups might look up different answers rather than all the children looking up the same answers.

"A good idea," said Mr. Garrison. "Here is what we will do. I will number the groups. Groups One and Two will look up the answers to the questions on this chart. Groups Three, Four, and Five will look up the answers to the questions on this chart. I have put the page references on the charts and we will do the same as we did yesterday."

Figure 9-3. *Mr. Garrison's class experiments with working by committees.*

As soon as the children finished reading, Mr. Garrison again went through the questions on both charts, made an outline for each and then selected two capable children from each of the groups to write the report during their work period.

The next day the reports were read and evaluated. Mr. Garrison moved slowly and followed this procedure for three more days. At the end of the week he evaluated the work with the children. He pointed out to them that they had accomplished twice as much work the last day as they had the first day because two different topics were being researched in the same length of time. He reminded them that they had been more interested in each other's work and in each other's reports when they had worked and reported on *different* topics. He showed them that they had been learning from each other as well as from him.

The next week Mr. Garrison gradually led the class into working in three groups on the questions on three different charts, then to four groups, and by the end of the week each group was working on a different set of questions and writing a separate outline and report. The classroom was orderly, children were highly involved and highly motivated, and the unit was completed in this manner. Some children were even working alone on a chart and preparing a report for the class.

As soon as the children had organized the questions for study for their next unit, Mr. Garrison helped them classify the questions on charts and then asked them to sign up for the chart they would like to work on. The tables in the room were then grouped by committees and Mr. Garrison said, "During our last unit we worked in groups, but I think now we are ready to work in committees and this is quite different. What is a committee?"

The children discussed the concept of committee and reached this definition which Mr. Garrison wrote on the chalkboard. "A committee is a group of people that has a definite job to do."

The jobs of the committee were then listed as follows:

1. Each committee has a chairperson who:
   a. Assigns jobs to the group.
   b. Helps the group members.
   c. Brings together the group work.
2. Each committee has a secretary who:
   a. Makes a record of the group work.
   b. Writes any reports the group may need.
3. Each committee has members who:
   a. Do the jobs assigned as well as possible.
   b. Go to the chairperson for help in finding materials.
   c. Keep notes of their readings and give them to the secretary.

Mr. Garrison then explained that each committee would work on one chart of questions on which he had printed many references so they could use their textbooks along with other books. He then appointed the chairperson and secretary for each committee and they went to work. Mr. Garrison moved from committee to committee helping each to get organized.

Mr. Garrison's plan for developing group work in research worked effectively. Once the *structure* for working was established and children were comfortable with it, he taught them other things, such as how to take notes, how to outline, how to summarize and synthesize materials, and how to make informative and creative reports.

Mr. Garrison's strategy is not the only way to organize children for social studies research, but it is a good plan for it affords the children security each step of the way with enough risk-taking and open-endedness to allow for creative production.

Other Ways to Do Research

It is important to realize that all research skills do not necessarily require the skill of perfected reading as a prerequisite. Slow-learning children need not be deprived of a good social studies program because of their reading disability. Information can be obtained in many ways besides the textbook. It is important to notice that the skills of research, for instance, are stated as *reading, looking,* and *listening* for details. The concept of research with elementary-school children is to be considered broadly and must include many techniques for assembling and using material. All children can participate in many kinds of research regardless of intelligence or abilities.

The following list of suggested activities illustrates the variety of ways in which research can be conducted, skills developed and information obtained:

1. Make a list of all the things you would like to know if you were to visit a lumber camp. Now look at the filmstrip, *Life in a Lumber Camp*, and answer the questions you listed. (Grade 4)

2. Collect all the pictures you can find on life in Alaska and tell what you learned from studying these pictures carefully. (Grade 4)

3. Make a collection of all the things you can find that were made in Japan. (Grade 4)

4. Visit an ice cream factory and learn how ice cream is made. (Grade 4)

5. Make a list of all the materials used in building a house. (Grade 4)

6. Make a chart of all the ways nature spreads seeds. (Grade 4)

7. If you like Greek myths, make up a myth and talk it into a tape recorder. Play it for the rest of the children. (Grade 4)

8. Using the outline you made as you studied this chapter together, start a notebook on Africa. Find pictures, stories, maps, and clippings to go with your outline. (Grade 6)

9. Many Americans now are allowed behind the Iron Curtain. If you have anyone in your community who has been in Russia, invite him or her to speak to your class. Find out what freedoms children have in Russia. (Grade 6)

10. Look about your own town and see if you can find any churches or other buildings built in Gothic style. Do they have beautiful stained-glass windows? Ask someone to tell you how these windows were made. From where did they come? (Grade 5)

One group of sixth-graders made some startling discoveries about their community. They found the population was diminishing each year and set out to find the reasons why this was so. This led to a study of many things; among them were the lumber industry, soil erosion, local tax plans, financing, mortgaging, job opportunities, and local history. This group made a film of their findings and gave a Parents Night exhibit which helped stir the community to the point where a revival took place. School children, themselves, took on the project of replacing seedlings on the depleted hillsides.

Discovery is a part of the creative act—it may be the discovery of a problem or the discovery of a solution to a problem. It should be a part of all planned learning experiences.

New materials have been designed which will help many children develop certain research *and* study skills independently. These materials can be of great assistance to the teacher and children when properly used. Children can often be made aware of more advanced kinds of research than simply "looking up material" and gathering facts to arrive at solutions to a problem.

Making Oral and Written Reports

When children reach the point where they are capable of doing research by groups, and then individually, other members of the class want to hear about what they are doing and the things they are learning. Just as a teacher finds it necessary to "spoonfeed" the children into research skills, spoonfeeding techniques may be employed to lead the children to making creative, interesting and accurate reports.

A return to Mr. Garrison's classroom will show how he developed this skill in the children.

After the children had worked in groups doing research for a few days, each day eavluating their work at the close of the period, Mr. Garrison said, "Some of you have looked up the answers to almost all of the questions and are ready to make your outlines and write your reports today. Before you do this work I would like you to think of some interesting ways you can give your report to the rest of the class. It is going to be tiresome if we just read each report. If you can plan an interesting and different way to give it, you can write it so it is suitable for the way you will present it."

The children suggested many ways of giving a report and with Mr. Garrison's help they wrote these ideas on the chalkboard.

Some Ways We Can Give Reports

1. A TV panel show with questions and answers
2. A dramatization
3. Using charts and graphs
4. Giving it with pictures
5. Making it into a roll movie
6. Planning it like a television show, like a newscast or "You Were There" program
7. Making a tape recording of it
8. Using maps with it

The children met in their committees to decide on a way to make their report. As soon as one committee was ready to report the children listed criteria for making a good report. At the end of the report, the children evaluated it by checking it against each statement on the criteria chart. Over a period of time the reports steadily improved. Soon the children were able to organize and carry out committee work with a high degree of efficiency.

In this account of Mr. Garrison's activities we have seen how one teacher developed the *concepts* and necessary *procedures* for group work in conducting and reporting research.

Using Basic Research Materials

This is how Mr. Garrison developed the skill of using reference material in his language arts periods at the same time he was teaching research skills.

He used the encyclopedia as his main reference source. He placed a children's encyclopedia on a table before the group in the front of the room. The children had used encyclopedias but mainly on a trial and error basis. Mr. Garrison wanted all of them to know and realize the wonders lying between the covers of this set of books.

Mr. Garrison talked about the encyclopedia. He told the children how much he used it and what a help it was to him in his teaching. He informed them that he was going to teach them how to use it so they could enjoy all of its wonders, too. He informed them that there were many kinds of encyclopedias printed at various reading levels and that he would keep several in the room so that all of them might find one set to use.

After this motivation, Mr. Garrison used the following procedures:

1. He asked the children to each write on a slip of paper a question they had recently wondered about. "Or," he added, "put down a question about something you have been interested in for a long time."
2. Mr. Garrison collected the questions and read them. As he read them he asked the children to help him group the questions by topics. Mr. Garrison wrote the topics alphabetically across the chalkboard and placed the slips of questions under the appropriate topic.
3. "Now," said Mr. Garrison, "I can find answers to most of these questions in the encyclopedia. With our dictionaries we learned to look up words. In our encyclopedias we can learn to look up subjects or topics."
4. Drawing on the children's knowledge of alphabetizing and the dictionary, Mr. Garrison built these understandings:
    a. The encyclopedia, too, is arranged alphabetically.
    a. It is arranged by volumes rather than in one book like the dictionary.
    c. It, too, has guide words. Guide letters appear on the front of each book to tell you which book to choose. Guide words appear at the top of the pages to tell you the page on which to find your topic.
    d. Encyclopedias must be kept in alphabetical order so they are easy to use.
5. Mr. Garrison then passed out the encyclopedias so the children could use

them by two's. "Let's list what an encyclopedia tells us and what we can find in it," he said. This list resulted:

An Encyclopedia:
  a. Tells about subjects.
  b. Has pictures to help explain the subject.
  c. Has page numbers and a one-book index.
  d. Explains its abbreviations.
  e. Gives some pronunciations.
  f. Contains maps, graphs and charts.
  g. Some encyclopedias are also numbered.
6. Mr. Garrison then allowed the children, working by two's, to look up their topics in the encyclopedia. He spent some time allowing each child to tell the answer to his or her question if it could be found. He encouraged the children to give the answers in their own words. Copying from encyclopedias or other sources does not contribute to any of the objectives of the social studies program.

With repeated work on the encyclopedia and occasional reminders from Mr. Garrison, such as "I don't know that, but we can look it up in the encyclopedia," or "I think that's the answer but let's check it in the encyclopedia," the encyclopedia became a fascinating research tool for this grade.

Using Original Sources

Often children can have many creative experiences when they are taught how to use original sources in doing research. While studyiing the Civil War, Mr. Jones took a group of children to a neighboring university library where they brought home eyewitness accounts of some of the battles and events which the children had discovered in the library archives. These accounts were compared with more recent ones and great disparities were discovered. Excellent creative thinking as to why the accounts differed came out of the discussion. The children discovered that history tends to be embellished and sometimes distorted in the retelling.

Mr. Jones found a painting of the Battle of Gettysburg done shortly after the close of the war by an eyewitness. He then found an impression of the same battle painted by an artist twenty years later. He also found one that had been painted by a contemporary artist. The scenes were very different in many respects. In trying to decide why they were different, the children learned a great deal about accurate reporting and artistic license. The creative and critical thinking resulting from this experience were excellent.

A fourth-grade group discovered a great deal about their community when they decided to make a motion picture about it. Their study took them to places they had not known existed. One very exciting discovery was made when they surveyed a field outside of town to discover the geographical center of their state. They painted a pole, and, with the farmer's permission, planted it on the spot. On the top of the pole they hung a flag that said, "This is the geographical center of Alabama. It was discovered by the fourth grade." Each child then signed his or her name on the flag in crayon. This experience later took on additional significance when state surveyors, planning for a new highway to be built through the state, informed the children by letter that they had discovered their flag and that their measurements were off by only two feet!

Discovery can play a great part in developing research skills in children when the local resources of a community are used—parks, town records, an industrial plant, a survey of occupations, a visit to a farm or dairy, a study of local watershed and geography, an art museum, or an old graveyard.

Lacking material to interest his children in local history, Mr. Smith took them to an old graveyard that adjoined the school property. Children became interested in the inscriptions on the gravestones and eventually copied every one to bring back to school. They tried to trace local families by the names on the gravestones and to reconstruct local history. One very interesting discovery was made by a boy who noticed that many children had died at one specific period of time. Further research disclosed this to be the year when a great typhoid epidemic hit the community.

In promoting this type of research, the teacher plays a new kind of role. Instead of answering questions, he or she poses them.

Summarizing

In the taxonomies discussed in this book, synthesis is an important type of thinking. It is the ability to pull together material and to get from it those facts and understandings important to the reader.

Children's first step toward the ability to synthesize is to learn to summarize.

Mr. Garrison pointed out the need to summarize material collected when planning an oral report. He also explained to the children that a written report was actually a summary of the things they read.

He introduced the children to the principles of writing a summary by placing a collection of Norman Rockwell's family paintings before the class. He asked the children to study each picture carefully and to make up a sentence which told the main idea. When any child had created such a sentence he or she went and wrote it beneath the picture on the chalkboard. Betsy liked the painting where the doctor has a stethoscope on a little girl's doll. She wrote, "Betsy and the doctor are playing that her doll is sick."

Next Mr. Garrison taped a series of pictures in sequence that told a story on the chalkboard. The children were encouraged to look at each picture, then write one sentence about each that told the main idea as they had done previously with the single pictures. Their sentences were as follows:

Picture 1:   The taxpayers voted to build a recreation park in Centerville for the children.

Picture 2:   The park turned out to be beautiful and useful.

Picture 3:   Some adults and children did not take care of the park.

Picture 4:   Vandals ruined equipment in the park.

Picture 5:   The park was closed.

Mr. Garrison pointed out that all the main ideas of the pictures were here. "Now let's see if we can combine any of the ideas so we will not lose the meaning but will make the sentences shorter." They decided they could combine statement 1 with statement 2, and statements 3 and 4. When the five statements were rewritten, the following paragraph or summary of the pictures resulted:

"Taxpayers in Centerville built a beautiful, useful recreation park for the children, but it was closed because of improper care and vandalism."

Mr. Garrison thought that this was a good summary of the message portrayed by the pictures. "Can you tell me now what a summary is and how we go about making one?" he asked.

The children discussed his question and decided a summary was two things:

1. It was selecting all the main ideas from a story, report, or unit, and
2. Writing these ideas as simply and with as few sentences as possible.

To practice summary writing, Mr. Garrison asked each child to bring in his favorite comic strip from the evening paper for the next day's work. He had each child paste the comic strip at the top of a sheet of paper. Under each picture each child wrote the main idea of the picture. Then at the bottom of the sheets they combined the main ideas into summaries.

The papers were then placed on the chalktrays, were shared and each summary was evaluated by the remainder of the class. One series of sentences and the summary follows:

1. Charlie Brown tells Lucy he does not trust her.
2. Lucy screams at him to shame him because he does not trust her.
3. Lucy persuades him to kick the football.
4. He takes a long run and kicks.
5. Lucy removes the football and Charlie Brown falls flat on his back.

Summary: Charlie Brown, a trusting soul, believes that Lucy will hold the football for him to kick, but she betrays his trust again.

Mr. Garrison then applied all the principles and techniques the children had learned in a social studies text where the children read a section together on the discovery of gold in California, writing one sentence for each paragraph and then combining the paragraphs into a summary statement.

To practice summarizing, Mr. Garrison's students invented a game. In their rap groups, everyone who wished to say something first gave a condensed version of what the previous speaker said. This had to be approved by the first speaker before the second speaker could talk about what he or she wished.

EFFECTIVE WAYS TO STUDY

Gathering Facts and Knowledge

It is extremely important that children realize that there are many *ways* to study. The manner in which study skills are taught can contribute to creative development or destroy it.

Too often children are exposed to *one* way of attacking a problem. Day after day they approach social studies lessons by the *same* method of study. Motivation for study can be greatly enhanced when each unit of work (or at least part of units of work) is approached through a variety of study techniques. Use of the same approach to problem-solving or application of a skill *one* way may result in a fixedness in the use of that technique or skill which will prevent the learner from using it in other creative ways.

Textbooks *can* make a contribution here by suggesting to children ways to approach the units of work set up between their covers. Some textbooks are beginning to do this. In the introduction to each chapter, they *set conditions* for developing effective study habits and applying these new learnings in creative ways. But if the textbook does not do this for the teacher, it is imperative that the teacher expose the children to as many ways of study as possible.

The material on the following pages shows a variety of creative ways to develop study skills as teachers and children approach new units of work.

Primary Grades

In the preceding chapters we have discussed ways of helping primary children to study. Most of these have been centered around the following skills:

1. Helping children plan.
2. Helping children learn by experience.
3. Developing concepts by moving from concrete to abstract experiences.
4. Helping children to organize and schedule periods within a day as well as the entire day.
5. Building values, attitudes, and appreciations about study.
6. Setting the best environment possible to stimulate good study skills.
7. Learning skills of discussion, recitation, drawing, and reading.
8. Learning how to tackle problems.
9. Learning democratic procedures of operation and democratic ways of living together.

Intermediate Grades

Using the textbook in a variety of ways for studying has been discussed previously in this book (see Chapter 7). The use of unit teaching as a more dynamic and flexible method for developing study skills has also been discussed (see Chapter 5). To these techniques we can add others designed specifically to motivate children to learn a variety of ways to approach the *act* of studying. A creative teacher will use all these techniques (and more) to motivate children.

Following are examples of suggested approaches to developing study skills. They have been selected from textbooks or observed in classrooms.

1. Studying through anticipation.
2. Studying by finding facts to be used for critical thinking.
3. Using subheadings in a textbook as an aid to studying.
4. Using pictures as an aid to studying.
5. Using an outline as a way to study.
6. Developing group skills for studying.
7. Studying through the use of activities.
8. Self-study through the use of task cards.
9. Studying through the use of games.
10. Studying through audience-type motivation and group processes.
11. Studying by use of supplementary materials.
12. Studying by use of map skills.
13. Studying through reading and discussion.
14. Studying through the use of dramatization.

Studying through Anticipation

Following is an excerpt from a fourth-grade workbook:

A Way to Study

On the following pages are four stories about Indian boys and girls. They live in four different places: the Great Plains, the Southwest, the Northeast, and the Southeast. Make a list of things you would like to know about all four tribes. Then read each story to find the answers to your questions.

Other textbooks suggest ways to study; here is an excerpt from a sixth-grade textbook:

A Way to Study

After you have read this chapter about Egypt and China, you will want to know more about these strange lands far across the sea.

One way to study is to think up questions and then find the answers. After you have read this chapter think of all the things you still want to know about Egypt and China. Make a list of them. Then make a list of all the places you can go to get information. Get some of these materials at your library and look for the answers. There is a list of books that will help you at the end of this chapter.

One way to save time would be to have different people look for the answers to different questions and report to the class.

This is always a good way to study because you are looking for something definite.

Finding Facts for Critical Thinking

One way to study is to look for answers to questions already set up. This is practical, but not particularly creative, and children should be supplied with supplementary questions which require that they apply this new knowledge to thought-provoking situations. They will use convergent thinking for divergent processes.

Notice how Miss Parker provided for creative thinking by using newly learned material in the situation that follows. The children read about the Fall of Pompeii to answer "fact" questions of this nature:

1. How many days did it take to destroy Pompeii?
2. How long was Pompeii a city?
3. What unusual thing happened on August 24, 79 A.D.?
4. Why did the people die suddenly?
5. What caused Pompeii to disappear so suddenly?
6. How did the burying of Pompeii help us today?
7. How long did Pompeii remain buried and forgotten?
8. What were some of the things men learned about Pompeii after the stones and ashes were cleared away?
9. Why was the forum important in Roman cities?
10. About how large was the city of Pompeii?
11. What were houses like in Pompeii?
12. How were people able to discover what plants and flowers grew in Pompeii?
13. What did the people of Pompeii do for entertainment?
14. Did the people of Pompeii know how to read and write? How do we know?

At the end of the reading of the chapter in the textbook, Miss Parker and the children discussed the questions, reread material for specific answers, and then discussed these questions (Interpretation and drawing inferences):

1. Why do you suppose Pompeii was never rebuilt?
2. If men had understood about "dead" volcanoes in those days, do you think Pompeii would have been buried?
3. Make a list of all the things you can find in this chapter that the Pompeiians had learned to do.

Now answer these questions:

1. Did the people of Pompeii know as much about their world as the Egyptians? Would you say they had as great a civilization as the Mayas? How many of the things they did are we still doing today?
2. Did the people of Pompeii take advantage of their geography and their wonderful climate? Did they really understand their geography?
3. Pompeii is sometimes called "The City of Frozen History." Why do you think it is called this?
4. Is there still danger of Mt. Vesuvius erupting? If so, why has the city of Naples been built on the Bay of Naples near Mt. Vesuvius?

Using Subheadings

In another fourth grade the teacher divided the chapter on the Vikings into subheadings. Some textbooks are designed in this manner and can be used easily this way. The teacher put this material on the board as a suggested way for her children to gather material:

A Way to Study: The Vikings

Sometimes people can get ideas about what they are going to read by looking at the titles or names of the sections they are to read. Below are the titles of the sections in this chapter. Can you tell by reading them what this chapter is about? Can you also tell the order in which the chapter is going to be written?

Titles to Sections:
1. The Boat Mound
2. Graves Again
3. Who Were the Vikings?
4. The Sea-Warriors
5. Iceland Is Settled
6. Eric the Red
7. Leif Ericson
8. Vikings in America
9. The Sagas
10. The Ships

Using Pictures

For another chapter in the textbook, the teacher developed the skill of using pictures as an aid to studying.

A Way to Study: Leonardo da Vinci

Another way to study and learn about new places is to study pictures. You have had many pictures to study in this book. Up to now you have looked at them as you read the book. In reading this chapter, try this: Look at all the pictures first. Read the captions. Think about what each picture is telling you. Do they make you want to know more? Do they give you a clue as to what this chapter is about? Now read the chapter and fill in all the things that the pictures do not tell you about.

Using an Outline

Children can be helped to study when they are taught to follow an outline:

A Way to Study: (a sample)

This chapter is a long one but a very exciting one. One way to study long chapters is to see it in smaller parts. A chapter is sometimes written in "units." This means that an author writes about one idea and then goes on to another. All the ideas in this chapter are written about using energy but the different ways to use energy are put into units. Read these units and you will know what is coming. Units arranged like this are called an outline. After you read this chapter come back to the outline and see if it doesn't help you to remember all you have read.

Outline—Chapter 15

Unit I: The Secret of Man's Growth
    A. Man learns
    B. Man thinks
    C. Man has muscles and mind
Unit II. Early Man Makes Energy
    A. Energy through tools
    B. Energy from wood
    C. Energy from inventions and animals
    D. Energy from wind and water
Unit III: Man and Water Invent Energy with Steam
    A. Steam power
    B. Early uses of steam
    C. Steam power starts to work
    D. Thomas Newcomen invents a steam engine
    E. James Watt improves the steam engine
    F. The power of steam changes man's life
      (etc.)

A similar sixth-grade study situation would be as follows:

One way that people often use to study is to try to organize their ideas under main topics and then read to fill in the topics. Below is an outline of this chapter with the main topics and the subtopics. Read this chapter and then see if you can fill in all the details. You might do it alone or as a class.

  1. Introduction
       A. The meaning of democracy
       B. The origins of democracy in Greece
       C. Children in a democracy
       D. A controversial issue
  II. Characteristics of Democracies
       A. Government of the people
       B. Majority vote but minority rights
       C. Direct or representative participation
       D. Republican government
       E. Constitution
          (etc.)

Developing Group Skills

Textbooks could make children aware of the skills they will need to study and live together effectively, if they were designed as follows:

Chapter XX
Earth's Last Frontier, the Sea

A Way to Study
   In Chapter 4 you learned some ways of working together. You learned that people who live together must learn:

  1. To respect each other's rights.
  2. To share things.
  3. To cooperate.
  4. To listen to each other's ideas.
  5. To be polite and courteous.
  6. To find answers to problems.
  7. To look for information.
  8. To discuss problems.
  9. To plan carefully.

   In this chapter you will read about a new frontier: the sea. In the future men will have to depend a great deal on the sea. They will need to explore the sea as they are now exploring the air.

As you read this chapter, keep the ideas above in mind. Sometimes we study by looking for answers. Sometimes we study by thinking of problems. As we read this chapter, think of all the problems of living together that nations and peoples will need to solve as men explore and use the sea. List some at the end of each unit of study.

A follow-up of this chapter might help children build certain skills in this manner:

Some Problems to Think About

Take time to list problems you thought of as you read this chapter. Add them to the ones below. Take time to discuss ways you think they might be solved.

1. *To respect each other's rights*
   Problems:
   a. How will the nations work out ways to share the products of the sea?
   b. How will they get the gold and other minerals in the sea?
   c. What are some of the rules that people have already made up regarding rights at sea? What happens to an abandoned ship? Where is the sea open to the ships of all nations and where does it belong to the country which it touches? Are there traffic rules about speed at sea? How do ships avoid crashing into each other at sea?

2. *To share things*
   a. How will the nations be sure that each has its share of the sea's treasures?
   b. How will people learn to avoid the dangers of the sea?
   c. How will people *share* the gold from the sea?

3. *To cooperate*
   a. What are the best ways of taking treasures from the sea?
   b. Who will decide what are the best ways?
   c. How will poorer nations be able to get their share of the sea's treasures?
   d. What will Israel probably do with the method of freezing sea water to make it fresh if this method is economical?

4. *To listen to each other's ideas*
   a. What laws will need to be made about sharing the sea's treasures?

5. *To plan carefully*
   When we talk about the frontier of the sea we have to learn a whole new language. Here are some of the new words you learned in this chapter. They are strange and wonderful. Try them out on your friends. See if they know what they mean.

• fossil	• sea serpent	• nylon nets
• Charybdis	• snorkel	• bromine
• skin divers	• helmet	• Scylla
• bathysphere	• electro-fishing	• Atlantis
• echo sounder	• Maho	• aqua-lung
• diving barrel	• whirlpool	• squid

- aluminat
- albatross
- Odyssey
- trilobite
- decompression chamber
- Maelstrom

- pressure
- atomic submarine
- coelacanth
- flippers
- diving suit

- soundings
- diving bell
- bathyscape
- plankton
- magnesium

Using Activities

Here is a chance for your class to cooperate by working in groups and then sharing ideas. Have your class divide into three groups. Let each group do one of the following assignments, then report to the whole class:

A Way to Study (a sample idea)

Group 1: Dramatize the story of Ab.

Group 2: Make a chart of all the animals you can find that lived in the time of the caveman.

Group 3: Make a report on the Great Glacier. Read about it in books and tell the class what you have found.

Using Task Cards

In Chapter 6 the values of individualized instruction and self-learning were stressed. Units of work, modules, contracts and work sheets have been designed in such a manner that children can teach themselves many things by following the cards sequentially and working through the problems proposed on them.

We have seen how many teachers have taught knowledge and explored values through the use of work sheets, contracts and task cards. Many skills can be taught in this manner also. Following are some task cards which show how this concept has worked in certain selected situations. Most of the sample cards presented were designed by teachers although many commercially prepared cards are available.

Mrs. Fenner's upper age groups were studying about propaganda and its uses in changing behavior among people. One aspect of the study dealt with advertising. Here are some of the task cards Mrs. Fenner designed and used for independent development of critical thinking and the skills of classifying, observing, weighing evidence and drawing conclusions.

ADVERTISING

Task Card 1

Think of a product you would like to *sell*, or better yet think of a product you would like to *invent*. Then either write or tape a planned talk on these topics:

1. Tell about the product you want to sell.
2. Tell about yourself and why you are selling this product.
3. Examine newspapers and see how people tell about products.
4. Examine magazines and see how people tell about products and themselves.
5. On the back of this card is an ad for cereal. This is how General Mills tells about one of its products. How would you do it?
6. Listen to the commercials on any half-hour television show and keep notes on how different companies tell about their products.
7. What creative ways can you invent to sell your product?
8. Notice that advertising appeals to peoples' senses: sight, smell, taste, touch, sound. Can you design an advertising campaign for your product which will appeal to all senses?

Figure 9-4

PSYCHOLOGY OF ADVERTISING

Task Card 2

1. Why do people advertise in the first place?
2. Collect many favorite commercials from TV or from magazines and categorize them on the following chart.

Product	Co.	Type of ad	Appeal: Age Level	Sight	Smell	Touch	Taste	Sound

3. Advertisers appeal to the needs, wants and wishes of people as well as to the senses. Use your collection of ads and categorize them on the chart on the back of this card.

Figure 9-5

PSYCHOLOGY OF ADVERTISING

Task Card 2 (reverse side)

NEEDS AND WANTS CHART

	Ad	Company

1. The need to be loved by others
    mother
    father
    peers
    girlfriend
    boyfriend		

2. The need for approval		
3. The need to belong to a group		

4. The need to look well
    body
    face		

5. The need to be healthy		
6. The need to achieve—to hold worldly possessions		
7. The need to be attractive to others		

List some other human needs and find advertisements that fit them—categorize them as you have on this chart.

Figure 9-5 (*continued*)

← Use this task card and
see how it works

ADVERTISING

Task Card 3—Skills Building

HOW TO MAKE A LAYOUT FOR
NEWSPAPER ADVERTISING

Ask yourself these questions:

1. What is the *main idea* I want to put across? You can make your main idea stand out in your layout by:
   a. *Placement*—Give it the most important place in the layout.
   b. *Color*—Color it bright, or in a color different from the others in the layout.
   c. *Contrast*—Make it different in color, size, type of line, dimension or in idea from the rest of the material on the page.
   d. *Size*—Be sure that all the important words and ideas can be read at first glance.
   e. *Creativeness or Uniqueness*—An unusual idea will draw the consumer's attention at once. Think about unusual ideas and unusual ways to present it—like three dimensional materials, adding sound, playing on words, appealing to senses and needs.
2. Once you have your main idea, decide what printing will go on the ad. Make your printing eye-catching and be sure it is a part of the total design of the layout; it should not look as though it was tacked on as an afterthought.
3. Check the ad to make certain it contains all the information necessary to sell your product, such as a description of the product, where it can be purchased, unusual features about it, any necessary addresses and telephone numbers.
4. Make a rough sketch of your layout to determine where objects and lettering will be placed. Sometimes a good design can be obtained by laying blocks of paper on a background to indicate where the drawings go, and strips of paper to indicate where the lettering goes. The papers may be easily moved around to help you see the total design.
5. Sketch in the art work and the lettering. Then draw it carefully.
6. If your layout is to be duplicated, the drawing will need to be carefully transferred to a stencil or duplicating master. If it is to be printed, consult your teacher.

Figure 9-6

Following are a few task cards that show how some teachers have developed skills of observation and empathy through the use of a variety of unit topics.

ENVIRONMENTAL STUDIES

Task Card

STUDYING THE IMMEDIATE ENVIRONMENT
(Using all your senses and developing powers of observation)

- Mark off one square foot on any portion of your school yard that is still dirt, that is, not covered with blacktop. This is *your* square foot to observe and study carefully.
- Note all the things *above* the dirt: grass, insects, pieces of stick, stones, trash. List everything you see.
- Dig into the earth and note everything you see: insects, roots, soil, stones, moisture, etc.
- List all the things you *know* about this square foot of earth.
- Make a list of questions of all the things you still want to know about your square foot of earth.

Figure 9-7

BEHAVIOR EMPATHY CARD 1

Think about these questions:
1. When were you a cackling hen?
2. When were you a poor loser?
3. When were you a jolly green giant?
4. When were you king of the castle?
5. When was the last time you were a crybaby?
6. When were you a mean little kid?

Share some of these memories at group meeting today, if you wish.

Figure 9-8

BEHAVIOR EMPATHY CARD 2

Look around your school and observe how these behaviors are shown:

anger _____

courage _____

care _____

love _____

worry _____

happiness _____

joy _____

delight _____

sadness _____

pride _____

nervousness _____

fear _____

success _____

Draw a picture or plan a play with other people that will show the remainder of the group how you observed these behaviors. Use no names.
(By following this last direction you will demonstrate another behavior:
consideration.)

Figure 9-9

One teacher placed the chart opposite in her social studies center to
provoke an interest in emotions and how they are used. Of course, the children
wanted to know about it so the words were discussed and the children talked
about situations where this cycle occurred. Later the chart was used to plan
role-playing situations to present before the class.

Using Games

Many games have been invented in recent years which provide acute involvement on the part of children and which develop certain concepts in each of the
social sciences. Many of these games are complicated, but they put children in
various political, social and economic situations to the degree that they are
confronted on a small scale with the same judgments and decisions with which
national, state and local leaders are confronted. There is a section on these
games in the previous chapter.

Using Audience-Type Motivation and Group Processes

Another way to study is by the audience-type reading situation. This technique
is most effective when children are highly motivated to a topic and are eager

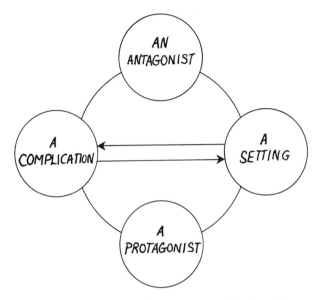

Figure 9-10. *What creates emotional behavior?*

for information. One such topic is outer space.

The study method suggested below not only helps children to gather information; it also develops values, appreciations, attitudes, and social skills previously discussed in other chapters.

A Way to Study: **Space Exploration**

This chapter tells much of what man knows now about outer space. These topics are discussed:

1. The History of Space.
2. Dreams of Space Travel.
3. Dreams Begin to Come True.
4. Dr. Robert Goddard: A Pioneer in Space.
5. How a Rocket Works.
6. Rockets Today and Tomorrow.

This chapter is very important to you because in your life outer space exploration will increase and we will find out many things we do not know at present.

It would be a good idea for you to read this chapter together. Discuss what you read. Then you will want to make a list of other questions you have about outer space. Group your questions under topics such as these:

1. The Astronauts: How They Were Selected and Trained.
2. The Satellites and What Happened to Them.
3. The Space Program for the Next Twenty Years.
4. Space Platforms: How They Will Work.
5. The Moon: What Life Is Like There.
6. What Makes a Satellite Stay in Orbit.

Then allow every member of the class to sign up for a topic to work on. All the boys and girls whose names appear under one topic will be a committee.
Each committee will meet and do these things:

1. Choose a chairperson.
2. Choose a secretary.
3. The chairperson will read the questions under the topic.
4. The committee will add more questions to the topic.
5. The committee will decide on ways to find answers to the questions.
6. Each committee member will be given a job—something to look up or something to do.
7. The committee will look for the answers to their questions.
8. They will discuss what they have found.
9. They will decide how to tell the rest of the class what they have found.
10. They will make an interesting report to the rest of the class. Some ideas:
    a. give a puppet show.
    b. make a play of the report.
    c. make a roll movie.
    d. have a panel discussion.
    e. have a quiz, TV, or radio show.
    f. make charts or use bulletin boards.
    g. have an exhibit.
    h. use shadow scenes.

Working on committees is one way to see how well you have learned to work together, to share ideas, to listen to other people, and to cooperate.

Using Supplementary Materials

Following is a suggestion that one teacher used effectively with supplementary material of interest to the children:

A Way to Study

1. Read the first part of the chapter together through the map study.
2. Then divide your class into five committees. One committee will work on each of the following topics:
   a. Pacific Islands
   b. The Mainland (Thailand, Burma, and Malaya)

c. The Philippine Islands

d. Australia

e. New Zealand

3. Each committee will meet around tables in the room, one in each corner and one in the middle. Each will appoint a chairperson and will study one part of the book together.

4. Each committee will plan a report to give to the whole class. Use maps, globes, pictures, dramatizations, shadow plays, or any other interesting way of giving your reports.

5. Each committee should then plan a test for the rest of the class to see if everyone understood the report. There should be a discussion of all the items missed on the test.

6. Have each committee meet again for a story time over a period of days. Get these books from the library and have someone in each group who reads well read to the rest of the committee, or take turns reading to each other.

Committee 1: Pacific Islands
Far into the Night, by Clare and George Louden (Island of Bali)
Call it Courage, (MacMillan), by Armstrong Sperry

Committee 2: The Mainland
(Thailand, Burma, Malaya)
Burma Boy, by Willis Lindquist
Anna and the King of Siam, by Landon (Globe Readable Classics)
Getting to Know Malaya, by Jim Breetweld

Committee 3: The Philippine Islands
The Picture Story of the Philippines, by Hester O'Neill

Committee 4: Australia
Australia, by Rafello Busoni
Australia, by Ferrine Moti and Nell Reppy

Committee 5: New Zealand
Down Under, by Mario James

Using Map Skills

Still another approach to study through the use of maps follows:

A Way to Study: (a sample idea)

In this chapter of your book you will have a chance to see how well you have learned some of the things you have been studying. You will be able to see how much you have learned about world geography and how well you can read maps. You will have a chance to see how well you think critically and share ideas. You will have a chance to see how well you can put certain facts you have learned to work for you.

To help you learn about Europe today, that continent has been divided into sections in this chapter. The authors grouped the countries in these sections because their climate is similar, the geography is similar, and the industries are similar. Each section may have more than one country in it.

To see how well you can use what you have learned, there are four maps on each section which will tell you many things about each country as it is today. The first map is always one that shows you the way the land looks from an airplane. From studying this map you will be able to see whether this section has plains, hills, or mountains. You will see what large rivers there are and the directions they flow. You will be able to see how near the equator each section is.

All this will help you in telling about the climate, the things the people do for a living, and the natural harbors where they will build seaports. It will tell you about the coastline and whether or not each nation is industrial or agricultural.

By using a scale of miles, you can see how far apart places are from each other.

Maps like these, which show the natural features of a country, are called *physical maps*.

The second map on each section will tell you about the man-made features of each section. A map like this is called a *political map*. From it you can learn about the great seaports, the riverports, and the inland cities. The star indicates the capital city.

You will also learn what the boundaries of each country are, whether they touch seas or other countries. You will be able to tell the size of each country compared to the other countries in that section. You will also be able to see, in some cases, why certain cities have become the site of great battles or the envy of other countries.

By the time you get to the third map in each section you will already know many of the things that people do for a living. You will know this because the geography and the climate of a country influence what people will do. This map will help you to check to see if you are right.

For instance, in countries where there is a rugged seacoast, we often find many seaports, and fishing is an important industry. In countries that are low and fertile there are generally good farms and rich grass growing, so farming and dairying are important industries. Often in rugged, mountainous countries we find excellent water power and minerals, so mining and manufacturing are great industries. After reading Map 1 you can guess at the industries of each country and the products that come from these industries. By looking at Map 3 you will be able to check your work. You will also be able to tell *exactly* what products come from the farms and the mills of each country. We will call this a *product and industry map*.

The last map on each section will tell you some new things. It is a map that will tell you some of the things this country does to help the rest of the world. It will tell you, too, how the rest of the world helps it.

You will want to know when you read Map 3, whether or not each country makes enough of anything to sell some to other countries. Goods that are sent out of a country are called ''exports.'' The prefix ''ex'' means ''from''—so this is easy to remember. Exports are goods going out from a port to other lands.

The prefix ''im'' means ''not''—such as *not* produced. Imports are goods that come into a country. These are the goods a country does not raise and has to buy to feed its people or to help them live comfortably.

Also, on the fourth map of the sections of Europe, you will often find a small inset map, which will show you other countries controlled by the countries in Europe. You will be able to tell how powerful each country is in the world today. We will call this a ''world relations'' map.

A good way to study this chapter will be for you to do it together, or in small groups. You will then be able to read the questions together and share ideas about the answers. You, with your teacher to help you, can share many ideas in answering the questions. And if you are in doubt about the answers or want to learn more than you find in the book, many references are given. You can turn back to the pages mentioned in the book and review what you already know about each country. Also you can find the books mentioned in the text and read many stories by yourself about each country. You will find lists of good books and films about each country in the pages at the end of the chapter. This is a good chance for you to see how well you can think, study, and share ideas.

Through Reading and Discussion

In a classroom of good readers the following is one good way to study:

This is a short chapter that will show you how people rose up against the kings, who were power-hungry, and secured more freedoms.

Because there are many new words and new ideas in this chapter, it is a good one to read together as a class. You could read each section silently with the idea that you will ask questions about it of your teacher and your classmates. After everyone has read each section, hold a discussion and allow all students to ask their questions.

Perhaps you can find pictures, books or films which show some of the events mentioned in this chapter.

Often the textbook can be used as a springboard for studying more specific areas as the following technique demonstrates.

A Way to Study

This part of the great human adventure is sad in many ways; many of the freedoms accomplished by people were lost. However, it is very exciting too. It was a very adventurous time. It was the age of knights and outlaws, of fairs and tournaments. It was the age of kings and romance.

There is so much written about this time that only a small part can be put in this book. This has been put in story form, which will make it easy for you to read together. Then you can look up material in other books and report to each other about these exciting times. Here are some things you may enjoy reading about in other books:

1. Who was Sir Lancelot? A great poet named Tennyson wrote about him in a book called *Idylls of the King*. It is a book of poems about knights.
2. Read about King Arthur the Knights of the Round Table.
3. What was the Holy Grail? Read about it.
4. How did a boy in a castle become a knight?
5. What went on at a tournament?
6. Who was Little John? Read *The Adventures of Robin Hood* and find out.
7. What weapons were used in the Middle Ages? How were castles stormed?

8. How were castles built in the Middle Ages? Were slaves used? Did they pile the stones like they did in ancient Egypt?
9. Choirs began in the Middle Ages. Can you find out how?
10. How was food preserved at that time?

Keep a list of all the other questions that come to mind as you read this chapter. It is true that learning about one thing often makes us want to know about other things. After you read this chapter you can look up the answers to your new questions. Use textbooks and encyclopedias.

Through Dramatization

Some study skills and other skills can be developed around an activity, as this textbook suggests.

A Way to Study

By now you have learned to work well on committees. You may feel you want to learn new ways of working together. Talk about this and decide *how* you want to study about the Romans. You might want to read about the Romans together and then give a television play in your classroom. You could use a large box and cut out a hole for a TV screen. You could have committees work on writing the scenes for your play. Perhaps you would like to make up a story about Marcus, a Roman boy, or Lenya, a Roman girl. Then you would need committees to work to find out about the kind of clothes the Romans wore, the kinds of food they ate, and what their houses were like. You could make scenery and show how the people lived. If you do not have much room in your classroom, you may want to make a puppet show or a marionette show instead. This will give you a chance to practice sharing ideas and working together.

Summary

Study skills taught in meaningful context and applied to problem-solving situations help children to function independently and to develop their creative powers. The degree to which this is accomplished is determined by the creative techniques utilized by the teacher in presenting these skills and providing practice for their mastery.

The component skills of creative development, such as problem-solving, critical thinking, organizational skills, the ability to perceive and synthesize, keen audio and visual perception, the ability to evaluate, the ability to verify opinions, the ability to pass judgments and make decisions, the ability to identify and define problems, flexibility of thinking, the ability to redefine and rearrange and to self-initiate learning are developed in the creative teaching of study skills. Good study habits can lead a child to independence in learning, a valuable asset.

To the College Student

1. Now that you have read this chapter, discuss it in terms of the shortcomings of your own training in study skills.

2. Stop at a gas station and pick up a road map. Look at it and ask yourself if you can read all of it intelligently. Very few schools teach the use of road maps. With the increase in our thruway, turnpike, and freeway systems, how important is a road map? How could you find ways to read the ones you brought to class?

3. Invite a geographer to bring samples of the maps that he or she uses.

4. Think of ways the suggestions for "Ways to Study" could be applied to your college classroom. Try some of them. Were they more motivating than regular textbook assignment-recite study techniques?

5. Brainstorming is a technique often used to promote critical thinking. Suppose you were a manufacturer presented with the problem of having one million hula hoops left in your warehouse after the hula hoop craze had subsided. Brainstorm the uses to which you might put these hula hoops so you will get back your investment.

6. Make a list of all the ways you see in which Telstar promotes communication. Now discuss all the creative ways you could use to develop these ideas with children.

7. List the times and places during one day where you rely on symbols, maps, charts and pictorial representation to communicate. Consider road signs, dorm direction signs, floor plans, road maps, charts, graphs, symbols on vehicles which make them easy to identify, books, classroom grades—everything. Pool your ideas to stress the need to be able to read symbols, maps and charts.

8. Find several instances in this book where the processes of INQUIRY are carried out.

To the Classroom Teacher

1. Try using the different ways of studying with your students as they are suggested in this chapter. In addition, try creating other ways of studying such as:
   a. Studying through the use of a motion picture.
   b. Studying through the use of a filmstrip.
   c. Learning to study by use of a television.

2. Think of all the ways you can teach children about maps by using modern materials (mock-ups, films, road maps, plastic maps, etc.) that will cut down on the time you usually spend on maps but which will, at the same time, do a more efficient job of teaching.

3. Have the children collect all the different *kinds* of maps and charts they can find. Then study them to see how well they can read them.

4. Make a list of all the resources that you could use in your neighborhood for "original" research as it is defined in this chapter for your social studies program. Start with your colleagues. Which ones have traveled and have pictures? What are their hobbies? Are there people in the community who churn butter, make patchwork quilts, shoe horses?

To the College Student and the Classroom Teacher

1. How well can you read a road map? a weather chart? a table of statistics? Think back over your own school experience to the point where you remember being taught these skills. Were you ever taught or did you just pick them up? One suggestion for using this chapter would be to divide your class into four committees, one for each of the following headings: study skills, research skills, using original sources, and map skills. Have each group meet and read together some of the ideas and illustrations presented here and then demonstrate each in some creative way before the class.

2. Make a collection of graphs and charts from newspapers and magazines which can be used with children.

3. Try to recall how you were taught the study skills discussed in this chapter. Was the method at all creative? Observe some good teachers and note how they develop study skills in their students.

4. Discuss this statement: The ability to do research, to outline, to summarize, to synthesize, to take notes, to select main ideas, to read for details and to make oral and written reports falls under the heading of the language arts and should not be discussed in a book about social studies such as this one.

Selected Bibliography

BEYER, BARRY K. *Inquiry in the Social Studies Classroom: A Strategy for Teaching.* Columbus: Charles E. Merrill, 1971.

ELLIS, ARTHUR K. *Teaching and Learning Elementary Social Studies.* Boston: Allyn and Bacon, 1977.

FAIR, JEAN, and SHAFTEL, FANNIE R. *Effective Thinking in the Social Studies.* Washington, D.C.: National Council for the Social Studies, 1967.

GOLDMARK, BERNICE. *Social Studies: A Method of Inquiry.* Belmont, Calif.: Wadsworth, 1968.

MASSIALAS, BYRON G. et al. *Social Issues Through Inquiry: Coping in an Age of Crisis.* Englewood Cliffs, N.J.: Prentice-Hall, 1975.

NELSON, JACK L. *Teaching Elementary Social Studies Through Inquiry.* Highland Park, N.J.: Drier Educational Systems, 1972.

RYAN, FRANK L. and ELLIS, ARTHUR K. *Instructional Implications of Inquiry.* Englewood Cliffs, N.J.: Prentice-Hall, 1974.

SCHAEFER, ROBERT J. *The School As a Center of Inquiry.* New York: Harper & Row, 1967.

SEIF, ELLIOTT. *Teaching Significant Social Studies in the Elementary School.* Chicago: Rand-McNally, 1977.

SMITH, JAMES A. *Creative Teaching of Language Arts in the Elementary School.* 2nd ed. Boston: Allyn and Bacon, 1973.

————. *Creative Teaching of Reading in the Elementary School.* 2nd ed. Boston: Allyn and Bacon, 1975.

URANEK, WILLIAM O. *Creative Thinking Workbook.* Lexington, Mass.: William O. Uranek, 1971.

10

The Skills of Group Living

Life should be better and richer for children and adults because of the kind of living and learning that goes on in the elementary school.

RAGAN AND MCAULAY[1]

INTRODUCTION

Membership in a democratic society demands of each individual certain skills for living in harmony with others. Therefore, in teaching for social living much stress is placed on social processes—the techniques for conducting group work that make it possible to live effectively together. Certain values must be developed in children for them to become effective, stable group members. A good social program develops these values by providing life situations in the classroom where use of these values becomes a common occurrence.

From an early age it is essential that children recognize *variance of opinion* so that they later will accept a *conflict of ideas.* All through life it will be necessary for them to *make choices,* and they must learn to *evaluate effectively and critically* in order to do this. In a democracy it will be necessary for them to *identify common goals* with their coworkers and yet maintain a degree of *flexibility*. Children will need practice so that they may learn to *discover and define problems,* and so that they will know when and *how to find facts* to solve these problems.

They will need to learn how to consider opinions, to be scientific in making decisions, to be able to communicate their own ideas; they will find it necessary to *assume leadership* or *fellowship* as the situation demands, and to *plan intelligent action*. In times of crisis they must know the value of morals. They

1. William Ragan and J. D. McAulay, *Social Studies for Today's Children,* 2nd ed. (Englewood Cliffs, N.J.: Prentice-Hall, 1973).

will need to know how to delegate and accept authority. They will need to know how to inspire others to work on a common cause and how to help reach consensus in community-school affairs. They will need to understand, above all other skills, that creative thought is valuable, and they will need to learn how to accept creative thought which differs from their own. They will also have to defend their own ideas when they know they are right and be unwilling to conform to group pressures. All of these and many more techniques must be developed for cohesive group living.

The children will also need to understand when to think intelligently and when to respond emotionally; when to conform and when they may be individual. Much creative behavior, for instance, calls emotional factors into play. This is especially true of that phase of the creative process in which insight or a break-through begins; ideas emerge, thoughts bubble to the surface. Afterwards, the ideas must be tested in the light of the intellectual; they must meet certain criteria and stand the test of logic. But the ideas could not have been attained through reasoning—creative thinking was required.

Emotional reaction may often have a decided effect on the decision-making mentioned in the paragraph above and on the behavior of the individual, especially if a person is reluctant to surrender his or her own ideas for better or more appropriate ones. Sometimes emotional reaction may interfere with sound decisions. In the classroom, children should be provided with experiences that will help them see how emotional behavior can be used as a constructive or as a disruptive force. One factor that indicates a creative child is that he or she is neither compulsively conforming nor compulsively nonconforming, neither emotionally controlled nor intellectually controlled. Each individual has the freedom to decide when to be either and bases his or her decision on the appropriateness of the situation.

CREATIVITY AND CONFORMITY IN GROUPS

Conformity is not a bad thing. If there were no conformity, schools could not run, traffic would not move, production lines would not function, and jobs would not be completed. The teacher's job is to teach when conformity is necessary and when it is not. More specifically, it is to be certain that in every instance where creativity can be developed the proper creative rather than conforming conditions are set for it.

BEHAVIOR MODIFICATION

A current topic of great interest which has to do with changing group and individual behavior is behavior modification. This is a form of control exercised over children in an attempt to change behavior to forms acceptable by groups, thus helping children to learn behavior which is acceptable and that which is

Figure 10-1. *A core for social living: the group rap session.*

not. The technique comes from the philosophy of B. F. Skinner and is founded on the doctrine of behaviorism.[2]

In behavior modification, children are placed in situations where they give an acceptable or correct response and are immediately rewarded with some pleasant factor—a piece of candy, a star, praise, etc. Since the reward is pleasant, the child repeats the act, is again reinforced with pleasantness and eventually performs in the manner by which he or she is assured of getting this pleasure. Behavior modification has worked well with children who have emotional or learning problems in helping them adjust to home and school life and to exhibit more acceptable behavior.

Too often the technique has been applied to normal children in an attempt to *control* behavior with less satisfactory results.

Winett and Winkler have empirically shown that nearly all classroom applications of behavior modification are directed toward making children sit in their seats, stop shuffling their feet, refrain from talking without permission and promote conformity to teacher rules and values which are often oppressive and paradoxical to creativity.

Behavior modification practices could, theoretically at least, be used to promote divergent thinking and feeling processes typical of a healthy personality

2. B. F. Skinner, *Beyond Freedom and Dignity* (New York: Alfred A. Knopf, 1971).

and essential to creative problem solving. Yet in practice to date the evidence indicates that it is used largely to mold "deviant" children to "obedient," "well-behaved," "teacher-pleasing," "disciplined" individuals.[3]

THE CLASS DISCUSSION

Discussion can contribute to creative development. It can also be used to help children understand those instances where conformity is necessary in order to develop democratic processes.

Much needs to be done in methods courses in teacher education institutions to improve the prospective teachers' skills in leading discussions. In most methods courses, a great deal of attention is paid to objectives, to theories of teaching which have their origins in philosophy and psychology, to various ways of working with students and to the tricks of the trade. Little attention is given to the problem of handling the content of instruction even though the *manner* by which this content is manipulated is closely related to what the student will learn from the discussion. There are several processes of discussion which have been identified. They need to be explored and understood so each may be used in developing logical discussions from which inferences may be drawn and decisions made. They are: defining, classifying, conditional inferring, explaining, comparing and contrasting, evaluating, designating, describing, stating, reporting, substituting and opining.

Levels of Thinking in Discussion

In recent years, various taxonomies have been devised which can be of help to the teacher in developing thinking processes on various levels as they pertain to discussions. Bloom's taxonomy identifies six levels of thinking skills:

1. Knowledge
2. Comprehension
3. Application
4. Analysis
5. Synthesis
6. Evaluation[4]

---

3. R. R. Winett and R. C. Winkler, "Current Behavior Modification in the Classroom: Be Still, Be Quiet, Be Docile," *Journal of Applied Behavior Analysis* 5, (1972): 499-504.

4. Benjamin S. Bloom et al., *Taxonomy of Educational Objectives: Handbook No. 1: The Cognitive Domain* (New York: David M. McKay, 1956).

   Benjamin S. Bloom, "The Thought Processes of Students in Discussion" in Sidney J. French, *Accent of Teaching* (New York: Harper & Row, 1954).

A teacher stimulates thinking by the type of questions he or she asks. Questions generally provoke thinking in one of the above areas plus the area of creative thinking. Some taxonomies state that there are four main types of thinking activities and they are: remembering, reasoning, evaluating or judging, and creative thinking.

Knowledge or memory questions are on the lowest step of the scale. A teacher asks, "Name the capital of North Dakota" or "Tell me the reasons for the War Between the States." In memory or knowledge questions the student simply parrots back to the teacher something that has been read and remembered. Teachers often ask too many questions of this type and students are challenged very little to practice other types of thinking.

Questions which evoke a knowledge answer are not always of the type that demand a recall of facts. They may ask for a knowledge of study habits, of trends and sequences, of classification or categories, or methodology, of criteria, of theory or structuring, of principles and generalizations. Such questions often seem more complex than a question which calls for a factual answer but actually they ask only for recall of something.

Memory is an important part of the learning process. It provides a factual foundation upon which other learnings can be based. The teaching of memory learning alone is insufficient, however. Higher forms of questions are required to provoke broader learning: questions which show reasoning, or in Bloom's taxonomy, questions whose answers show comprehension of what one has read or learned. Bloom identifies three types of comprehension behavior: 1) translation (putting an idea into another form of communication); 2) interpretation (explaining the meaning of something in ones' own words); and 3) extrapolation (making estimates or predictions based on understanding of the trends, tendencies or conditions described in the communication).

In a social studies discussion the teacher asks, "What do we mean when we call Philadelphia the cradle of liberty?" This is a comprehension question which requires translation of a formal definition into a concrete example. In another the teacher presents a cartoon of Benjamin Franklin standing on a dock ready to board a ship. In his hand is a snake which is coming apart into little pieces. Each piece is labeled after one of the colonies. Beneath the cartoon are the words "UNITED WE STAND." The teacher asks, "What does this cartoon mean?" This is an example of a comprehensive question calling for interpretation. A teacher shows the children a graph of population growth for the past ten years. The children note the trends and then predict the population for the next five years. This is comprehension through extrapolation.

Questions in the comprehension category require a student to know an abstraction well enough to be able to demonstrate its use when asked to do so. But questions in the *application* category go a step further. In *application* the student not only knows how to apply what is comprehended, he or she will do so in appropriate situations without being asked. Application problems demonstrate the principle of transfer of learning. A simple skill of the use of the application can be found in Figure 11-2 where we see that a group of boys have learned the skill of making paper mâché, have learned about the pyramids, and have applied one to the other to construct a model for classroom use.

Analysis questions are the type which help the student distinguish fact from hypothesis, identify conclusions and supporting statements, distinguish relevant from extraneous material, note relationships between facts, find evidences of the author's technique and purposes, etc. Bloom divides analysis into three types: 1) elements (where the student is expected to break down the material into its constituent parts); 2) relationships (to determine connections and interactions among the elements); and 3) organizational principles (the arrangement and structure which holds the whole thing together). Examples of questions which call for analysis responses in children are found in Chapter 9 which listed the questions about Pompeii.

Analysis questions call for decision making and judgment on the part of the children. A sample of an analysis question follows:

"Our textbook says that the main reason the Pilgrims came to America was for freedom of religion. I have here another textbook which says the main reason the Pilgrims came to America was the desire for land and the wish to set up their own form of government. Some of you have perhaps read other reasons. Now, let's get your views on which reasons are probably most correct. What do you think?"

Questions which call for synthesis require children to take many facts, generalizations and experiences and to organize them into a structure not present up to this time. Bloom indicates that this category most clearly provides for creative behavior on the part of the learner but cautions that this is not completely free creative expression since generally the student is expected to work within the limits set by particular problems, materials or some theoretical and methodological framework.

Since Bloom's publication much research has been conducted in the area of creativity and many researchers would place creativity a step above synthesis—and even above evaluation. High level creativity is more than a reorganizing of experiences: the student synthesizes all relevant experiences and comes up with something new—something that did not exist before.

Evaluation questions are concerned with making judgments about the value, for some purpose, of ideas, work, solutions, methods, material, etc. Generally these questions call for a combination of all the other thought skills. Reading a flo-graph on a participation chart as shown later in this chapter, or answering questions evaluating self as shown in this chapter as well, are examples of evaluation questions. Often evaluation questions are the beginning questions for a new process. Evaluation questions are always asked with distinct criteria in mind. Those criteria, as well as the decisions made, are determined *by the children*. An example is the children's evaluation of their oral reports as described in Chapter 9 when the product was checked against the criterion chart.

Questions which stimulate creative thinking are those which produce ideas, propose new solutions to problems, invent ways of doing things, etc. Samples of questions which provoke creative thinking are given throughout this book. Questions designed for creative thinking often trigger brainstorming sessions.

Since questions are tools by which teachers teach and without which they cannot teach effectively, careful planning of the questions used with children is essential.

Jones believes that creative thinking is a very high level of thinking and places it in a category by itself. She develops a diagram consisting of four categories that contribute to the total thinking process of the child: literal comprehension, interpretation, critical thinking and creative thinking.[5] She explains her categories as follows:

1. *Literal comprehension:* This is the level where teachers all too often elicit a response requiring the parroting of a fact just read and consider the task concluded. At this level, however, a child needs *intelligence, reading ability,* and *memory* in order to be able to perform the required task. It is a low level of thinking and requires no independent thinking.

2. *Interpretation:* At this level the child must add two new ingredients. The first is a *background of experience* upon which to draw. The second is the *ability to relate those experiences* to the task at hand.

3. *Critical thinking:* When a child is capable of performing these four enumerated skills, he or she can then draw a conclusion, make a generalization, or formulate a judgment. In order to do this the child must analyze a given situation. He or she must not only draw upon previous experiences, but must synthesize several experiences, evaluate them, discard extraneous ones, and, on the basis of these procedures, arrive at a conclusion that is satisfying as an answer to the problem. At the stage known as critical thinking, then, the child must exercise *intelligence, reading ability,* and *memory; have a background of experiences; be able to make associations; analyze,* and *synthesize;* and then *make judgments.*

4. *Creative thinking:* Jones, like the author, believes that creative thinking is the highest of all levels of human thought and worthy of placement in a separate category. In addition to the eight qualities mentioned above, the creative thinker must add to these one or more of the following: *imagination, emotion,* and *energy.* Jones says,

If a child has arrived at a judgment or a generalization or a conclusion through his ability to think critically, and if he then can add to this the highly individual ingredient, imagination, he can come up with an original, creative thought. If this original thought is one about which he feels strongly (has emotion), and if in turn his strong feeling overcomes his lethargy and causes him to exert energy in this direction, he produces original thinking.[6]

5. Virginia W. Jones, "Reading Comprehension and the Development of Thinking Skills" (Lincoln, Nebraska: The University Project) Mimeographed Bulletin, p. 3. Used by permission of the author.
6. Ibid.

In developing creative thinking, the questions are open-ended, and there is no right or wrong answer. Each child's answer is original for that child and should be accpeted.

Jones summarizes her taxonomy as follows:

1. Literal feedback
   a. requires intelligence, reading ability, memory
   b. requires that pupil parrot back words of text
2. Interpretation
   a. requires literal comprehension
   b. requires background of experiences, plus ability to make associations
3. Critical thinking
   a. requires literal comprehension
   b. requires interpretation
   c. requires the ability to analyze, to synthesize, to make judgments
4. Original thinking
   a. requires literal comprehension
   b. requires interpretation
   c. requires critical thinking
   d. requires imagination, emotion, and energy[7]

The type of thinking stimulated by questioning according to Jones' categories may be illustrated with questions taken from various discussions from the Bicentennial unit described in Chapter 5.

1. *Literal Comprehension:* Knowledge questions (literal comprehension of material read)
   a. Why did the Pilgrims leave England?
   b. Why didn't the Pilgrims stay in Holland?
   c. What were the names of the boats on which the Pilgrims sailed?
   d. How long was their voyage?
   e. At what place did they finally land?
   f. Who were the leaders of Plymouth colony?
   g. Describe the first winter in Plymouth.
   h. What was the real name of the Lost Colony?
   i. Who founded the Lost Colony?
2. *Interpretation:* (ability to relate background to a task at hand)
   a. Do we celebrate Thanksgiving today for the same reason that the Pilgrims celebrated it?

7. Ibid.

    b. Why were the log cabins in Plymouth built with steep, slanted roofs?

    c. Were the pioneer women following style when they wore long sturdy homespun skirts, or were there other reasons?

    d. From what you have read, list all the things you think might have happened to the lost colony.

    e. From this graph, tell the class the years when the wheat crop was the highest in the United States and tell us also how many bushels of wheat we can expect to produce next year barring a catastrophe.

3. *Critical thinking:* (ability to draw conclusions, synthesize, make generalizations, and form judgments)

    a. Did the *Mayflower Compact* have any relation to the *Constitution of the United States?*

    b. What do writers mean when they say that the New England states are the cradle of liberty in the United States?

    c. Economists tell us that some of the greatest industries in the United States today were started the first year at Plymouth. What would they be and can this be called a reliable statement?

    d. "Although the colony at Roanoke has been called the Lost Colony, the one product for which it became famous has kept its memory alive and has caused one of our greatest problems in this country today." What does this statement mean to you?

    e. Why doesn't the U.S. government ban the sale of cigarettes as well as banning the advertising of cigarettes on television, knowing that cigarettes are a health hazard to its citizens?

4. *Creative Thinking:* (ability to imagine and to react with emotion and energy)

    a. Write a diary as if you were a boy or girl living in Plymouth during the first winter.

    b. What kind of government might we have today if England had won the Revolutionary War?

    c. Tell about your adventures when you got into a time machine, turned the dial backward, and emerged during a Salem witch trial.

    d. Guernsey cows were first brought to Salem from England. Write a report on what life would be like in the colonies without cows.

    e. Write a story of your ideas of what happened to the Lost Colony: pretend you lived there at the time.

    f. Suppose you could go back in time and as a pirate sink the boat on which Sir Walter Raleigh was taking the first tobacco to England. What effect would this have on today's world and problems providing no one else transported tobacco from America to Europe?

To design good classroom questions and worthy classroom discussions, the teacher needs to begin by analyzing and planning the kind of thinking task to be set. Then he or she should fit the form and phrasing of the question or problem to this task. Precision and clarity in the wording of the question will focus thinking squarely on the task.

Discussion and Creativity

However, excessive premature structuring of the class discussion may act as a deterrent to creativity.[8] The teacher will remember that when discussion is used for creative purposes it should not be too heavily structured. It is also important to remember that the process is as important as the product when originality is being encouraged. The teacher will also keep in mind that the part he or she plays in the discussion will close or open the flow of ideas. The teacher's comments will help children to clarify what they have said or will reflect their feelings, but will not close issues. The questions will be open-ended in that they suggest new ideas rather than one set solution. The teacher will look for the uncommon response, the remote or unusual ideas, and the cleverness of responses to provide cues for leading the discussion forward toward creative production.

In creative discussion children are able to make use of a question: they examine it, think it through, and create answers of their own rather than coming up with a preconceived one.

The teacher will need to be aware that some research on group processes in its relation to creativity shows that groups have tremendous influence on individuals and individuals often conform to the opinion of group majority— even when the individuals are right.[9] Ability to be independent seems to be less possible under social pressures.[10] Yet independence in human beings is essential for creative production. Part of the teacher's job will be to help individuals who have unusual or different beliefs to stand their ground until proven incorrect. On the other hand, the teacher will help all group members to be tolerant of any one person's ideas until they are proven to be impractical for the situation.

Research also shows that we may expect greater descriptive social stress when classroom groups are divided heterogeneously than when they are divided homogeneously. Creative thinking is stimulated by social stress. It would seem then that heterogeneous grouping in a classroom might be more productive than homogeneous grouping.[11]

It is a fact that some "positive" tension is necessary as a condition to stimulate creativity. On the other hand, research has shown that excess stress may disrupt thinking and diminish productivity. This was referred to as "neg-

8. Barbara Biber, "Premature Structuring as a Deterrent to Creativity," *American Journal of Orthopsychiatry* 29 (1959): 280-290.

9. S. E. Asch, "Studies of Independence and Conformity: 1. A Minority of One Against a Unanimous Majority," *Psychological Monographs* 70, No. 416 (1956).

10. G. Moeller and M. J. Applezeig, "A Motivational Factor in Conformity," *Journal Abnormal Psychology*, 55 (1957): 114-120.

11. E. Paul Torrance, "Can Grouping Control Social Stress in Creative Activities?" *Elementary School Journal* 57 (December 1961): 139-145.

ative" tension earlier in this volume. Torrance has concluded that social stress may be controlled in the classroom to some degree by using various patterns of grouping.

Class discussions can serve other purposes. They may help children learn when to conform. Many class discussions may be directed toward convergent thinking or used as a problem-solving device. These discussions will differ from those directed toward divergent thinking or creativity.

The fetish for getting everyone to participate in a discussion can be overdone. Also, the fetish of discussion for discussion's sake is pointless.

How can a teacher control or evaluate problem-solving class discussion so it is worthwhile? In some classrooms children have learned to talk and talk—but they don't talk about much!

First of all, a class discussion must have a purpose—*and every child should be aware of that purpose*! In a classroom where chartmaking is encouraged, one chart might be entitled, "What Makes a Good Discussion" and may be used as a guide for the class. A review of this chart before each class discussion will focus the purpose of the discussion and the techniques for discussion more clearly. In a fifth or sixth grade such a chart might read as follows:

Discussions

1. What is the purpose of our discussion?
   a. Are we trying to settle an issue?
   b. Solve a problem?
   c. Make a judgment?
   d. Build an attitude?
   e. Share ideas?
2. How shall we go about our discussion?
   a. Who will act as chairperson?
   b. Do we need a secretary?
   c. Do we need an observer?
   d. Will we need follow-up committees?
   e. Consultants?
3. How will we conduct our discussion?
   a. Give everyone a chance to present his or her views.
   b. Stick to the problem at hand.
   c. Seek for facts when they are needed.
   d. Avoid arguments if possible.
   e. Do not interrupt. Be courteous.
4. Evaluation
   a. Was discussion well conducted?
   b. Did we accomplish our purpose?
   c. What are our next steps?

After each discussion is over, a quick check of the chart will serve as an evaluation device.

The teacher's role in a class discussion is that of guidance, the degree of which will vary with the topic under discussion and the types of children involved. In working toward a solution to a problem, the teacher may plan questions that are thought-provoking and which will keep the group from wandering off on a tangent.

In a discussion of any kind the teacher will need to be aware of his or her part in the discussion by considering the following: how questions are phrased, how questions are adjusted to individual abilities and styles of responses to answers. The teacher will structure discussions to the degree that he or she asks questions which continually stimulate the children and lead them from simple memory thinking to the higher levels of synthesis and creativity as proposed by Bloom.

In discussions whose goal is to develop creative solutions or invent some original idea, the teacher will take a less active part and will listen carefully to the contribution of each child, recognizing and lauding the original contributions all the children make.

Different kinds of questions for different kinds of guidance are necessary. A question such as, "What do we already know about such rules that will help us?" invites recall and previous knowledge. A question such as, "How would you feel if this were done to you?" invites emotional response and the power

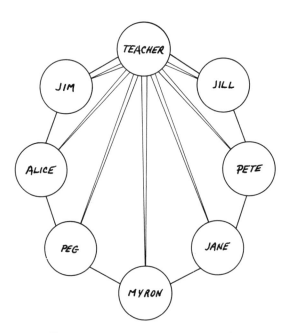

Figure 10-2. *A simple flo-graph will show a teacher if a group discussion is dominated by one person. This flo-graph shows that the "discussion" period was really a question and answer time.*

of empathy. And a question such as, "It seems that no one to this time has ever had this problem before, so what can we suggest as a solution?" calls for creative response.

There will be many discussions much more informal and unplanned than these imply. Nevertheless, the teacher functions in the same capacity. He or she keeps the discussion directed to a purpose; reflects individual and group feelings and clarifies the progress of the group by helping them verbalize clearly what they are thinking and facilitates communication.

In the lower grades, the informal discussion is more common than the more formal planned discussion, though, even at this level, there will be times when class discussions will be planned and group decisions made.

A teacher who has not conducted group discussions may be easily discouraged. He or she must remember it is difficult for the children until they practice, too. Greater success will be obtained if the first discussions are rather structured. Later the class will take over gradually. The teacher can preplan with a committee and delegate responsibility. One child can act as secretary and recorder to write down the important points. The teacher can serve as an observer, watching the group for participation, checking for arguments, for domination by one person, and other shortcomings.

Using a Flo-graph

It is well to have some check to be sure all children who want to are participating. The use of a flo-graph is helpful here, since it shows the teacher how the conversation is going. To insure worthwhile discussion, the environment is most important. Democratic discussions are encouraged when children and adults sit in an informal circle or at least can see each other. The teacher or chairperson presents the topic. Teachers may structure the first discussion by stating the job of the recorder or secretary, the observers, and the chairperson, and by designating each member of the group as a contributor. Leadership fluctuates with the flow of the contributions.

On a piece of paper, the teacher has a series of circles, one to represent each student. As they speak each child's name is written in a circle and then a line is drawn from it to the next person speaking, and so on. A supply of such sheets duplicated previously and kept handy makes the flo-graph comparatively easy to use. This graph clearly shows the number of people who have participated and the flow of the conversation. It does not attempt to record what was said—it is a measure of the dynamics of the group.

A flo-graph may be coded to give a teacher a more accurate picture of the kinds of participation within the group. Sometimes the child who talks a great deal appears to be taking a very active part in discussion and may seem to have a well developed concept of group dynamics. A closer examination of his or her contribution may reveal it to be merely questions or repetition of other members' contributions.

A suggested code is as follows:

C—contribution
RR—repeats what someone else has said
Q—asks a question
R—makes a response to a question

Using this code, a flo-graph was designed which looked like the one in Figure 10-3.

This graph reveals the following facts:

1. The part that each person played in the discussion is easily diagnosed.
2. The teacher asked two questions and gave two responses.
3. Jim asked two questions and repeated what someone else had said twice.
4. Alice asked two questions.
5. Peg asked two questions and answered one question.
6. Myron made a contribution and answered three questions.
7. Jane asked a question and answered one.
8. Jill made two contributions.
9. Pete made two contributions and gave one answer to a question.

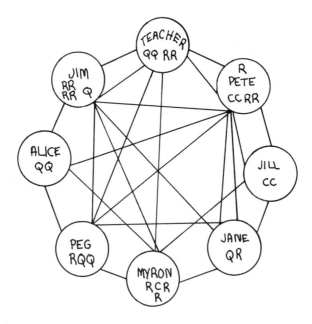

Figure 10-3. *A simple flo-graph will show the teacher if a discussion is truly a cooperative sharing of ideas.*

10. All members participated in the discussion, which moved from one
    person to the other very freely.

We now see, however, that some people ask questions or repeat what
others say. If this pattern continues repeatedly, the teacher knows which children
need help in developing discussion skills.

Using a Participation Chart

Some teachers use "participation charts" for recording the dynamics of the
discussion. A supply of duplicated sheets is kept available for instant use. This
helps them see again who the participants were and how the conversation
progressed. In case of a bottleneck, where two people get into an argument,
the teacher can stop the class and show the chart. The chart in Figure 10-4
shows, for instance, that in a fifth-grade class discussion between 9:05 A.M. and
9:10 A.M. Joe and Helen dominated the discussion. The rest of the class was
bored and discourteous. So the teacher stopped the discussion and showed the
chart, and a hasty evaluation put the derailed discussion back on the track.

THE PANEL DISCUSSION

Although panel discussions are not generally as effective as total group discussions, they have an important place in bringing problems and issues before a
group—especially a large group where total participation is impossible. In the
classroom, panel discussions may be used effectively, even in the early grades,
when problems of importance need to be brought before the group and both
sides of the issue discussed.

In a first and a second grade, for instance, a problem arose over the use
of the playground area that both groups were forced to share. In this case the
teachers wisely did not make the decisions for using the playground. Instead,
they used the *problem* to create a genuine learning situation. Each teacher
discussed the problem with her class independently. The problem was clarified
and stated simply. Each teacher helped her class determine the main points of
argument in favor of the class. Each tried to anticipate the problem of the other
group.

Representatives from each group were chosen to present the main arguments. A chairperson was appointed from an upper grade, and each group was
briefed in the techniques of a panel discussion. In a classroom assembly of the
two grades the chairperson stated the problem and each child on the panel
presented the arguments for his or her room. After all the children had spoken,
the chairperson led a discussion. Teachers helped the group to summarize the
points and guided the group into making a general decision to be applied and
tested on the playground.

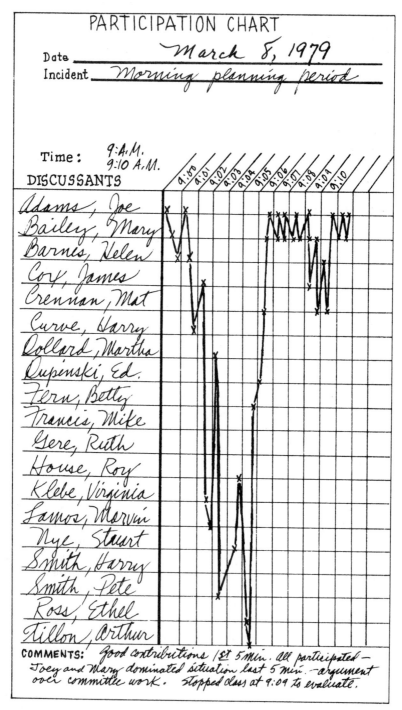

Figure 10-4. *A participation chart will help teachers and children follow the trend of discussion and will help to avoid deadlocks.*

These teachers were laying the foundations for effective use of panel discussions in upper grades. A panel discussion contributes some unique factors which a general discussion does not. It can be more carefully planned and thought through as groups anticipate the trend of discussion. It gives training in critical thinking since it calls for "projection" into the other person's mind in order to see his or her point of view. It gives each person (or side) a chance to state the problem and to present points before the general discussion takes place, thus economizing on time. And, hopefully, a panel discussion results in some creative solutions to problems.

Teachers using panel discussions for the first time should point out their value to the children to be sure that they understand the purpose of using this as a particular technique at this specific time. The children will need to learn the techniques for conducting a panel, which is equally as important as the subject-matter. At first the panel may be crude and faltering, but an evaluation of the technique, as well as the material covered, will help refine the process for later use.

There is much value in the meeting of people to express conflicting ideas and to make points relative to these ideas. In this instance, a group of people meets before an audience and each presents his or her case—generally about one topic. Individual preparation has gone into this situation, but there has been little group preparation. The motivation is present because the topic is generally one of current interest. This is more commonly known as a "symposium" than as a panel discussion. The panel discussion is better used by groups as a technique for arriving at a consensus about their own problems.

Also, it often lays the basis for debating, which is another effective group process even for intermediate-grade pupils.

Buzz Groups

We have seen how a teacher can effectively use buzz groups or rap sessions as they are currently called in the previous chapters.

Buzz groups or rap sessions are extremely valuable in instances where the class is too large to be handled effectively in a general discussion. They are also effective for smaller groups. In the classroom they can help the teacher who has a large number of children to find instances for using democratic procedures without losing control of the group.

Buzz groups can be used in many ways. A teacher beginning a unit may be overwhelmed by numbers of children who wish to put questions on the board. He or she is conscious of the value of independent contributions and of the dangers of crushing some children who do not often participate, yet physical limits often make it impossible to respond fully to the demands of the children. This situation can be controlled by dividing the class into buzz groups, where children just turn around and face each other in small groups and discuss the question at hand. In this instance the teacher may structure the buzz group by telling each group to choose a leader and then for the group to think of a list of ten questions they would like to have put on the board. At the end of ten or fifteen minutes, each leader reads his or her group's questions, which are put on the board. Duplications are checked to indicate the strongest interests of the class as a whole. In this manner, each child has had the opportunity to contribute, and a true opinion of the class interest is observed.

Teachers who do not have immediate success with buzz groups will perhaps need to structure them more carefully at first. They may meet with a committee of "leaders" and set up some criteria for conducting a group.

It is important in this instance that the leaders change frequently. It is also wise to discuss buzz groups and their purpose before using them with the entire group. As the mechanics are understood, the teacher will find children using buzz sessions fluently.

Teachers may use buzz groups in various ways. It is an effective method for getting issues before the class; it may be used for obtaining divergent ideas about a class problem; it may be a technique to use in discussing a report, an assembly program, or a sociodrama.

The term "rap" session often applied to discussion is not quite interchangeable with the term "buzz" group. A whole class may be involved in a rap session; a buzz group is generally a smaller group within the class.

BRAINSTORMING

A technique often used as a small group process as well as a large group process is brainstorming. This technique has been explained in Chapter 1 and demonstrated in many reports throughout this volume.

DEVELOPING EVALUATION SKILLS

Guilford has said that thinking factors fall into three general groups. There is a group of *cognition* factors, a group of *production* factors, and a group of *evaluation* factors. We become aware of a problem with which we are confronted, we produce something of our own because of this awareness, and we evaluate the product of our thought. He states that a total creative act involves all three of these aspects.[12]

Evaluation is a part of the creative learning process. It contributes to the development of creativity in that it keeps learnings from closing in and becoming complete. It provides the open-endedness to learning which is so essential to divergent thinking. By using evaluation, the teacher helps the group assess its acquired skills and learnings but immediately applies this assessment to new and more complex learnings.

Evaluation is wide in scope and may be applied to the individual, to the group, to the process, or to the total program; and since none of these can be

12. J. P. Guilford, "Creative Abilities in the Arts," *Psychological Review* 54 (1957): 110–118.

considered in isolation, evaluation must be concerned with all of the involved interrelationships.

Because evaluation is a part of the creative learning process, the teacher should help each child to evaluate himself or herself. The student may be evaluated in terms of any or all of the following: readiness, intelligence, achievement, social and emotional development, physical and mental health, creativeness, and special talents and abilities. Evaluation must also be concerned with the interrelationships of these factors.

Self-evaluation

In the Greek unit mentioned in Chapter 3, the children evaluated their own work through the use of evaluation cards designed so that they could tell their own progress by taking and checking their own test.

One of the advantages of writing behavioral objectives is that the terminal behavior is described in the statement of the objective and the child can often be given the responsibility of determining whether or not he or she has mastered the competency defined.

Take the following behavioral objective, for instance: As a result of this lesson each child will be able to read a bar graph as indicated by the test exercise on page 84 in the workbook *Graphs and How to Read Them*. The child will be expected to have 80 percent of the responses correct.

The fulfillment of the objective here can easily become the responsibility of the child if the teacher tells him or her at the onset of the lesson what is expected.

Self-evaluation can take place in the affective domain (those areas which deal with feelings, values, attitudes, etc.) as well as the cognitive domain (those areas dealing with knowledge and thought processes).

Children in all classrooms should have their own folders arranged in an easily accessible file drawer. In these folders they can place samples of their creative writing.

They can also keep samples of their handwriting, their arithmetic papers, and their teacher-made tests to study their own progress from time to time.

The techniques for self-evaluation are numerous. Children must be taught the value of all of them. Some methods which can be used effectively with children are given below.

Observation.   Children must be helped to be keen observers. Acute observation is the base of both the creative process and the scientific process. Sensitive observation may be applied to self-evaluation in the following way:

1. Did I do the job as well as I can?
2. Does the paper look as well or better than the others I have done?
3. Did I omit any parts of the exam?

4. Did I leave out any capitalization and punctuation?
5. Have I put away all my materials?
6. Did I omit any main parts of the outline?
7. What sort of impression did I make on the class?
8. Did I do the job assigned to me?
9. Have I found all the information necessary to make a complete report?
10. Am I able to read maps correctly?
11. Do I understand charts and graphs?
12. Do I get the point of this cartoon?
13. Do I get the main idea from this picture?
14. Does the filmstrip mean something to me?
15. Am I able to find the parts from a film for which the class is looking?
16. Does the diorama or exhibit tell me something?
17. Am I able to see the purpose in the bulletin board?
18. Was I able to get the right sequence of events in the television show?
19. To how many new uses can I put this information?
20. For what can I use this material?
21. How could I make that color with tempera paint?

A teacher must realize that observations by children (indeed, by many adults) are often accompanied by inaccuracy or emotion. Often children, like adults, see only what they *want* to see. Self-deception and distorted perception are common partners of faulty observation. The teacher's goal will be to continually refine accuracy in observation and reporting and will also guide the children to improve the accuracy of observations made in relation to their predictions.

Listening.   Listening can be used by children as an evaluation skill in situations such as the following:

1. Did I follow all directions carefully?
2. Did I hear all the main ideas?
3. Did I hear the plans for this period so that I know exactly what to do?
4. Did I understand the ideas Bill was trying to get across in his report?
5. Was I attentive when the announcement was made so that I know exactly what I am to bring and what my part is in the program?
6. Did I get the idea of the joke?
7. Was the musical background of the television show appropriate?
8. Did the consultant really tell us what we wanted to know about Alaska?
9. Was I able to fill in my notes from what the teacher told me?

Skills for the teaching of listening can be found in many language arts books. Children can evaluate many of their own activities by using listening as an evaluation skill.

Conferences.   Conferences may be held for evaluation purposes frequently. Self-evaluation on the part of the child may play a very important part in these conferences.

In Miss Stillman's fifth grade, the children helped to evaluate their own progress periodically through the conference technique. Two afternoons were set aside during the week when Miss Stillman scheduled a conference with each child. On these two days, Miss Stillman planned the daily program with her group very carefully so that all children were gainfully occupied during the conference periods. Usually each child planned the entire afternoon around assignments made by Miss Stillman, his or her own unfinished work, and work with special teachers and consultants.

Miss Stillman placed a conference table in the rear of the room where she could be somewhat removed from the class but where she could see all the children while she worked with one child at a time. As each child took a seat by Miss Stillman she opened that child's folder and read aloud the last report letter which had been sent home. After reading the letter, Miss Stillman asked such questions as these:

Miss Stillman: In your last report letter it said that you weren't doing as well as you could do in social studies, Johnny. I know Mother has been helping you at home. How do you feel about your social studies now?

Johnny: I know I'm doing better, Miss Stillman. I've had better papers.

Miss Stillman: Yes, you have. Let's look at your folder. My, these *are* good papers. I'm really proud of your progress, Johnny. I guess I'll have to say we've just about got this problem solved when I talk to your father and mother next time or when I send home your next report. Don't you think so?

Johnny: Yes.

Miss Stillman: John, there is one other thing mentioned here on which we were going to work. Last time we agreed we would try to help you to do a better job in group discussion. You interrupted all the time and did not wait your turn. How do you feel about that?

Johnny: I think I'm better. I've been trying hard.

Miss Stillman: Yes, I've noticed that. One thing that has helped is that you are stopping to think about what you plan to say and as a result you say more when it is your turn. I'm glad you have learned to organize. I'm proud of the way you have worked on that problem, too, Johnny. Now, tell me how you feel about the rest of your school work.

Johnny: Well, I think I'm doing okay in everything else. I like school.

Miss Stillman: I'm glad about that. How do you feel about your reading? Do you read much outside of school?

Johnny: No, I don't read much outside but I guess I'm doing okay in reading. I like to read.

Miss Stillman: I'm glad you like to read. That is the most important thing. But I am a little concerned about your reading. Johnny, do you remember some tests we took just about the time we had our play about Robin Hood? Well, I want to tell you why I gave you those tests. They showed me how well you *can* do. Now the tests you took in reading last week also told me something. They told me you are not doing as well as you can do. I'd like to suggest that you start taking books home to read. Days are getting shorter now and you won't be able to play outdoors as long and perhaps you can find some time to read each evening after dinner. I think that will help you.

Johnny: Okay.

Miss Stillman: How do you feel you are getting along with the other children?

Johnny: Fine.

Miss Stillman: Let's talk about your study skills. I've watched you work and I have a few notes here that I'd like to share with you. First of all I'd like to say I think you are a good worker. Your work is always done on time, and you work very well independently (*etc.*).

After these conferences Miss Stillman wrote summary reports of the children's progress to go home to the parents. Each child's letter was read to the child before it was sent home so that any unclear points could be discussed. When the letter went home, each child was able to discuss it with his or her parents. Miss Stillman used these letters as a basis of her conferences with the parents.

Conferences of this sort help the child to develop self-understanding and self-awareness. Self-awareness is a characteristic that must be exploited to develop creative people—self-awareness leads to self-realization. Roe has said, "You cannot be easily manipulated if you know more about yourself than your would-be manipulator does."[13] Self-awareness suggests an ability to look at one's self objectively.

In one school system, simplified conferences of this nature were held with kindergarten children. The conference was based on the checking of a series of stick-figure cartoons. One showed a child sharing with other children. The teacher asked the child, "Do you think you share well?" If the child said "Yes," and the teacher agreed, a check was placed in a little box drawn under the left side of the picture. If the teacher and child talked it over and felt that work was needed on this, a check was made in a box on the right side of the picture.

Conferences with children can be held for each subject. Through a series of questions the teacher helps the child learn the skills of self-evaluation. These

13. Anne Roe, "Man's Forgotten Weapon," *American Psychologist* 14 (1959): 263.

conferences need not always be formally arranged as in the case of Miss Stillman. They may well be the casual, informal type that takes place when a child hands in an assignment.

Rating scales. Children can be taught to use self-evaluating rating scales. The kindergarten picture-card mentioned above is really a simplified rating scale. Any device that puts judgments on a continuum may be classified as a rating scale, which may be used for group evaluation as well as for individual evaluation.

In a sixth grade where Mr. Salem was trying to develop good study skills among his boys and girls, they listed together what they considered to be good study habits. Once a month they rated themselves according to a scale they set up. Figure 10-5 shows Mr. Salem's rating scale.

In Miss Andrews' third grade, children evaluated themselves by using a rating scale which Miss Andrews drew and ran off on a duplicating machine. She used simple drawings which the children checked, as shown in Figure 10-6. Another class used the rating scale shown in Figure 10-7 to evaluate each person's work habits. Such rating scales can be used in a variety of ways to help children assess their own progress.

Teacher-made tests. Teacher-made tests serve two basic purposes: they tell the teacher how much the child has learned and how well he or she has taught. When tests are handed in, corrected, and the grades recorded, they do not really serve as an evaluation device. But if the teacher uses the test for further teaching or as a diagnostic instrument to help the individual child, it serves an evaluative purpose.

Teacher-made tests may help children evaluate their own progress when they are carefully corrected, when personal notes are written along the margins, and when they are used for individual conferences. They may also serve as a springboard for keeping personal charts and profiles from which each child can see his or her own growth.

Teacher-made tests are often more reliable than commercial tests because the teacher can construct the test to check the specific objectives set up at the beginning of a unit of study.

Teacher-made tests need not all be written ones. Teachers can be very creative in designing tests.

Thomas and Brubaker give the following eight criteria for the construction of teacher-made written tests:

1. The test items should focus only on the stated objectives.
2. The distribution of items on the test should reflect the teacher's belief about the relative importance of the various objectives.
3. The kind of test item a teacher selects to evaluate for an objective should be as appropriate as possible to that objective and to the developmental level of the pupils taking the test.

HOW WELL DO I STUDY? Name _____ Grade _____ Date _____ STUDY SKILLS	I DO THIS VERY WELL	I DO THIS WELL	I DO THIS FAIRLY WELL	I DO THIS POORLY
1. I FIND OUT WHAT I HAVE TO DO				
2. I GET MY MATERIALS READY				
3. I GO TO WORK AT ONCE				
4. I REMOVE ALL DISTRACTIONS				
5. I GET HELP WHEN I NEED IT				
6. I FINISH MY WORK ON TIME				
7. I PLAN FOR EXTRA TIME WHEN I NEED IT				
REPORTS—CONTENT				
1. I READ MY ASSIGNMENT CAREFULLY				
2. I DO ALL PARTS OF THE ASSIGNMENT				
3. I USE MATERIALS WELL				
4. I PLAN MY REPORT WELL				
5. I GIVE MY REPORTS WELL				
6. I AM ABLE TO HOLD THE INTEREST OF THE CLASS				

Figure 10-5. *A self-rating scale.*

4. Test items should be so constructed that the pupil understands the question asked or the problem to be solved. The type of answer desired should be clear to the child who knows the material.

5. The test should be organized so that the child sees readily what he should do and how he should do it. The mechanical aspects of the test—directions, item organization, answer system, and typography—should not hinder the accurate assessment of the pupil's skill and knowledge.

6. Items should discriminate between the pupil who has met the objectives and the one who has not.

Figure 10-6. *A self-rating scale.*

Name _____ Grade _____ Date _____

HOW WELL DO I WORK WITH OTHERS?

	ALWAYS	USUALLY	SOMETIMES	NEVER	NOT SURE
I TAKE PART IN ACTIVITIES					
I LIKE TO TRY OUT NEW IDEAS					
I VOLUNTEER FOR COMMITTEE WORK					
I WORK WELL WITH OTHERS					
I WORK WELL ALONE					
I SHARE MY IDEAS					
I LISTEN TO THE OTHER FELLOW'S IDEAS					
I AM COURTEOUS WHEN I WORK WITH OTHERS					
I STAY WITH THE JOB UNTIL IT IS FINISHED					
I KEEP MY TEMPER WHEN PEOPLE DO NOT AGREE WITH ME					

Figure 10-7. *A checklist for evaluating self in ability to work with others.*

7. The test should be corrected as objectively as possible. Without sacrificing objectivity, the correcting process should be as speedy and simple as possible for the person doing the marking.
8. Unless speed of response is a necessary aspect of the instructional goal, the pupil should have time to complete the test at his own work pace.[14]

Pupil-made tests.   In evaluating knowledge and some skills, pupil-made tests are appropriate for classroom use. They can serve as an evaluation device for the teacher as well as self-evaluation for the child. They also afford an opportunity for creative development.

In the intermediate grades children reveal what they are learning as much by the questions they ask as by the answers they give. It is on this premise that pupil-made tests are valuable.

In a fifth grade, Mr. Herring finished teaching a unit on the Middle Ages. He felt his students had learned a great deal. He talked with them about the things they had learned and asked if they knew of ways he could find out exactly what each person had learned. They suggested a test. Mr. Herring felt this was the opportunity for which he had been waiting to use pupil-made tests.

Mr. Herring set aside a period to teach the children about test-making. First he discussed with them the reasons behind testing; these were listed on the board. Then he asked the children to think of all the tests they had ever taken and asked them to think specifically about the kinds of questions they had answered. The following list resulted:

1. True and false.
2. Making choices.
3. Filling in blanks.
4. Matching.
5. Ending sentences.
6. Writing about a question (essay).
7. Choosing correct answers.

Using each type of question, the class proceeded to make up some samples from their Middle Ages unit. Mr. Herring then asked them if they felt they could make up a good test about the Middle Ages. The children were eager to try.

It was decided that all the people who had worked on various committees would meet together. They would review their reports for the class and then proceed to make up the following:

• 5 true-false questions
• 5 matching questions

14. R. Murray Thomas and Dale Brubaker, *Decisions in Teaching Elementary Social Studies* (Belmont, Calif.: Wadsworth, 1971), 499–534.

- 5 filling-in-blanks questions
- 5 sentences to be completed
- 5 multiple-choice questions
- 5 selection questions
- 1 creative application question

These were to be handed to Mr. Herring. He was to edit them, delete duplications, and make a composite of the remaining items.

Mr. Herring was well able to tell how much his group had learned by the questions that were submitted. Nevertheless, the test was duplicated, and each child took it. From it each was able to evaluate himself or herself in these ways:

1. Facts learned from the unit.
2. How well he or she had listened to reports.
3. How much had been learned from the unit as compared with other members of the class.
4. How well he or she had observed the exhibits, bulletin boards, etc.
5. How well he or she had studied.
6. How well he or she was able to select what the classroom committees felt were the main ideas.

Pupil-made tests may be constructed in a variety of ways and for a variety of purposes. They serve both teacher and children to good purpose in the evaluation process.

Standardized tests.   Standardized test results can be useful to children if they are used discreetly and with careful interpretation. If the rapport in a school is such that children can have the test interpreted in relation to their ability, these tests are very valuable in helping children evaluate their own progress from year to year. Profile charts of individual scores can be made yearly, using a different colored pencil from year to year on the same chart so that the child can see growth in the same area.

The danger in using achievement test scores with children is that grade-levels are used more than subject-age or growth-age. Half of any class will be below grade level if the group is a normal one. Therefore, in using achievement test profiles teachers should explain to the child that a certain line on the chart shows what he or she is capable of doing and the colored pencil shows what he or she *is* doing. When these lines are far apart they indicate a problem, which teaching and learning may correct. When the lines are fairly congruent (whether the child is up to grade level or not), it means he or she is performing normally according to his or her intelligence (even though the child may be two years below grade level).

Standardized tests often serve as an individual diagnostic device as well as a measuring device for pupils.

Graphs and charts.   Research shows that slow learning and average children learn best in cooperative environments, and that bright children tend to thrive under some competition. In all cases, self-competition is a stronger motivation than peer competition. Charts, graphs, and profile charts provide an excellent way for children to keep their own grades and scores and to have a long-term record of their progress. Continued encouragement and help from the teacher will keep the child striving to do better each week.

Self-evaluation stories.   Creative stories that children write about themselves and their feelings can be used as an evaluation technique. These topics are suggested:

- How I Feel about Tests.
- How I Feel about School.
- The Person I Like Most.
  (To these the following might be added:)
- What Am I Like?
- What Kind of Person Am I?
- How Good Am I in School?
- Me as a Speaker.
- My Self-Portrait.
- My Feeling about Arithmetic (or Spelling, Social Studies, etc.).
- What I Think about My Teacher.
- Things that Make Me Angry.
- People I Like in School.
- What I Thought about John's Report.
- My Book Report.

Simply by organizing his or her thoughts to write about such topics, a child is self evaluating. The value of writing in this fashion is enhanced if the child is not required to put his or her name on papers. The act of writing itself serves as a catharsis for the child, and the material that is written can be of great importance to the teacher.

Autobiographies, journals.   Autobiographies, journals, and other types of records help children to keep track of their activities from day to day and can be of great help in evaluation when reread at some later date.

Pupil files.   Pupil files have been mentioned as a means of keeping records for comparison of work from month to month. They can serve as a cache for keeping graphs, test records, profile charts, and other evaluative material.

One other use of the pupil file is that it serves as an informal method of communication from teacher to pupil. It is a simple matter for a teacher to write notes to the children when examining some of their work after school, either to give praise or to offer suggestions. These notes can be dropped in the file. If children are encouraged to look in their file folders each day, this can become an effective way of pupil-teacher evaluation on an individual basis. Teachers can often leave work sheets made by them or torn from a workbook with a note clipped on for a child who needs extra help. If the teacher also has a file folder in the drawer, children can be encouraged to drop finished material and informal notes into the teacher's file. This means a more orderly accumulation of materials for the teacher than having the material dropped all over the desk.

As teachers work with children and give them increasing responsibility and independence, together they will discover many ways for pupils to evaluate themselves. It is important to remember that the techniques must be chosen in terms of the goals to be evaluated, but that they must also be viewed in terms of numerous other criteria. Evaluation should serve as a steppingstone toward planning the next course of action. Objectivity aids in decreasing the degree of error in evaluation, so children should be made aware of objectiveness in their evaluation experiences. The technique must always be tested in terms of reliability—does it measure consistently what it purports to measure? Is it valid and is it practical? Can the children understand the directions and purpose for using it?

Group Evaluation

To establish a working rapport and to bring a group spirit into play, continual group evaluation is as necessary as continual individual evaluation. Consciousness on the part of the members as to their contribution to group progress is essential if group living is to be realized in a classroom.

Throughout this text, reference has been made to the evaluation procedures necessary to promote group growth. This evaluation is an integral part of the instructional program. Evaluation is the summarizing of evidence at a given point which gives proof of group growth and remusters forces into a new plan to move ahead.

Group evaluation of cognitive learnings and affective learnings is necessary in order to be certain that all objectives for humanized living are met. In the account of Mrs. Rogers' work with the teachers of Glendale described in Chapter 2, we saw these teachers defining acceptable behavior for the children and making provisions to check out each type of behavior by some means of evaluation. In the account of the Middle East bazaar described in Chapter 1, the teachers established objectives they hoped to meet and evaluated the results in terms of these objectives. In some instances competency lists are made and then tests for each competency are designed to determine whether each child has mastered it.

Different types of group evaluation should be employed for assessing different behaviors. In the puppet sociodrama enacted in Chapter 1, Mrs. Jackson took advantage of a teachable moment to develop some values in the children. Mrs. Jackson did not sit down and plan a lesson to build these values. However, she had worked on the committee of teachers who determined the values they felt should be developed during the year and had them so firmly planted in her mind that she was free enough and creative enough to use an "on-the-spot" situation to accomplish her goals. The fact that the children arrived at five different solutions to the problem was an evaluation in itself that her plan was successful. Notice also that Mrs. Jackson checked her lesson against the principles of creative teaching to determine whether or not the children had been subjected to the creative process.

Group evaluation is of necessity a cooperative process. The group sets an objective; it works toward that objective; and it evaluates in light of that objective. This may be done in terms of one period during the school day or for a semester or a year's work, depending on the objective or purpose being evaluated.

A second grade plans to attend its first assembly program in the auditorium. The teacher prepares the children so that they may meet this new experience securely. The trip is planned and each child understands: 1) the purpose of the trip and 2) his or her responsibility to the group on the trip. After the trip is over, the group evaluates in terms of its purposes.

Likewise, in launching a unit the group establishes long-term purposes and as the unit progresses they are evaluated to determine whether or not the purposes are being achieved. In this manner children learn to face their obligations to the class and, later, to the community.

The teacher may have objectives for the group which are not the objectives the group has for itself. One such objective, for example, might be to help each member of the group grow in ability to assume responsibility toward group procedure. In this case, the teacher provides opportunities for individuals to assume responsibility in group situations.

The teacher must evaluate the outcome of his or her planning. After the goals and objectives are clear, he or she must try to envision behavior patterns in the work of the children which show that the purposes are being attained. Anecdotal records are important for recording evidence of group behavior. From these records the teacher is able to plan the next step in meeting previously selected goals or establishing new group goals.

It is important whether it be the group's evaluation of itself or the teacher's evaluation of the group, that the evidence be gathered from many situations. The teacher will need to use many devices, and the group itself can use some individual and group techniques.

Sociometric Techniques

Each teacher should frequently make a sociogram of his or her group. Sociograms provide clues for grouping. When children do not seem to group themselves effectively, a teacher may discover the isolates, "rejects," leaders and cliques. Clues may be found for grouping; ideas for putting shy children on

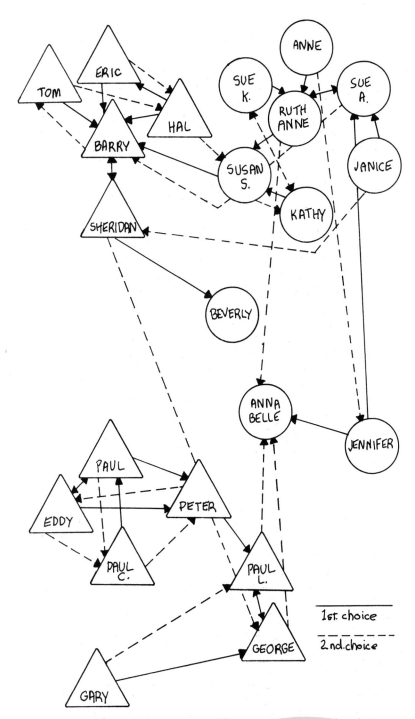

Figure 10-8. *A sociogram constructed for a ten-, eleven-, and twelve-year-old group readily shows the influence of the "gang" age and the "cliques" of the sexes.*

committees with children they like; ideas for helping isolates make friends in small groups. Later on, another sociogram will help the teacher see how the children are growing socially.

Personality tests also will assist the teacher in finding social and emotional areas where children need help.

Natural or Interest Grouping

Plenty of opportunity should be afforded children to work on committees and in groups of their own choice. At some time during the school day a child needs to feel comfortable with his or her friends. Opportunity for such grouping often presents itself in unit work and in sitting together for lunch or for other common interests.

The groups children choose naturally can provide the teacher with clues concerning their likes and dislikes and will help in discovering problems.

These ideas point up the numerous ways teachers may gather evidence to make decisions concerning their classroom groups and the small groups operating within the classroom group. No one device is more important than any other. Each is used to measure some phase of the group's work. *All* should be used if needed. After the required evidence is gathered it must be organized in useful form and interpreted in terms of the children's level of development.

REPORTING TO PARENTS

Teachers must not only teach group processes to children through classroom experiences, but must use group processes in the act of educating the parents of the children. "Reporting to parents" might be more accurately phrased "conferring with parents," for if the school situation is a good one, parents know what is going on. They meet with the teacher frequently to evaluate their child's growth process, but this is no more a report for parent than it is for teacher. It is a sharing of ideas and a formulation of plans for the child's formal education. That plan should include as many ideas and suggestions for work at home as it does work at school.

Too many schools still send home outmoded and uninformative report cards wherein a child is given a symbolic grade in the subject-matter areas and in various overt acts supposedly indicative of worthy character or personality traits. What this report hopes to do is of great doubt in the minds of many parents and many teachers. Schools that carry on a reporting system of this kind generally consider the "report" an end-product of a teacher's evaluation of a year's work. Actually it is really the beginning. If the report is to be of any value at all, it acts as a springboard for group processes between parent and teacher for mapping out a plan of action for a child. Evaluation is in a sense diagnosis.

Teachers need to know how the child acts at home, his or her interests and hobbies, attitudes, experiences, and home environment. Teachers, because of their indirect acquaintance with family problems, can bring an objective point of view to the study of the child. But parents, more emotionally related to the child, will bring the more subjective points of view which are necessary if teachers are to determine causes of behavior and help the child with his problems.

On the other hand, few parents today are capable of teaching their children all they need to know without professional assistance. Parents and teachers want the same things for every child—the best education. Often they travel parallel roads in achieving this goal with the child running confusedly back and forth between them. It is easier and more effective to join hands—child, parent, and teacher—and travel the main road together.

There are many problems and situations that will concern every parent. The teacher will want to discuss these problems with the parents. This need not be an additional burden on the teacher, for a room-mother and father will generally do the phoning and prepare some refreshments for the meeting. The teacher will not dominate the situation; this destroys the feeling that all are going to learn together. Rather he or she will act as guide and help the parents state the problems they want to discuss during the year or the activities they want to undertake. The teacher will suggest ideas and offer necessary information, but must make sure that it is also the parents' meeting and that the parents *feel* it is their meeting too.

For problems concerning the specific child, a parent-teacher or a parent-teacher-child conference will need to be held. A record should be kept of this conference. Some teachers make out a form which they check with parents and on which they write comments as the conference progresses. One such form is included as a sample. Each school will need to work out a form best suited to its needs.

The teacher slips a carbon under one form and clips another form under the carbon. In this way the parent has a copy to take home. This is an effective way of reporting.

No evaluation session is complete unless the next step for progress is planned in terms of decisions reached. On the conference sheet, or on a separate form, a plan for the child should be mapped out so that parents will not negate the work of the school nor will the school confuse the child by making demands on him or her that are different from those of the home.

Healthy home-school cooperation is essential if the modern school is to accomplish its objectives. Blocks, such as uncommunicative "report cards," must be removed to facilitate the learning process. Parents have a right to a part in their children's education. This must not be interpreted as meaning teachers should teach what parents think they should teach. It means, rather, that the job of education is that of teaching everyone, and parents can gain security and confidence in the school only when they have an opportunity to discover, understand, and participate in what the school is doing. The teacher can provide the opportunity for the parents to learn.

HILLSBORO CENTRAL SCHOOL

Parent—Teacher Conference

Donnelley, Jim   Grade 5

Name, Last   First

Date of Conference — June 8, 1979   Age 10

SKILL AREA	STRONG AREA	DOES VERY WELL	DOES WELL	FAIR WORK	DOES POORLY	WEAK AREA—NEEDS HELP	COMMENTS ON PERSONALITY ADJUSTMENT, WORK HABITS, STUDY SKILLS, EMOTIONAL, SOCIAL AND PHYSICAL GROWTH
Creative Arts	X						
Language Arts							
Reading		X					
Writing				X			
Spelling				X			
Grammar				X			
Oral Expression		X					
Written Expression			X				
Social Studies	X						
Science	X						
Arithmetic Skills		X					

We discussed Jim's academic work. He is above average as a student. Mrs. Donnelley was concerned about Jim's sudden aggressiveness. He is becoming defiant at home. No signs of this in school however. We talked about the possibility of his behavior changes being a characteristic of his age—the need for peer approval as against parental approval. His striving for independence (see next page)

COMMENTS ON SKILL AREAS	SUGGESTED WAYS TO HELP AT HOME
Jim loves art work — his language arts are only fair due to his rapid physical growth, in part, which makes him clumsy at writing. He needs motivation for reading. I am going to let him chair a science committee which he likes very much	Mrs. Donnelley took home the booklet "How Children Develop." We thought we might change Jim's home chores. His lack of responsibility may be due in part to boredom. He will tend the furnace instead of making his own bed for awhile — also help his father in the

USE ADDITIONAL SHEETS FOR COMMENTS, CARBON OF REPORT GOES HOME WITH PARENT, ORIGINAL IS PLACED IN CUMULATIVE RECORD FILE

Figure 10-9. *A report form used with parents.*

CREATIVE EVALUATION

Since creative development is the main topic of this series of books, a word must be said about its evaluation. Until recently, most creative growth in children was recognized and evaluated through the observation of the teacher and other adults who worked with children.

Since the intelligence test does not evaluate creative giftedness, many researchers are currently engaged in developing tests that *do* measure creativity. While many of these tests have not as yet been validated or checked for reliability, some are currently available for use and have been effective up to this point. Teachers can add to the knowledge being gathered about these tests by using them with their classes and reporting their work to the authors of the test. Many have high reliability, such as the Torrance Tests of Creative Thinking, and may be used to help teachers detect creative potential as well as the results of their creative teaching with children.

Summary

Group dynamics can be an agent for the developing of creativity among individuals and for building the necessary attitudes for accepting creative people and creative ideas. Many techniques for using group dynamics creatively have been discussed in this chapter. Among them is evaluation.

Evaluation is a very essential and integral part of the learning process. It is wide in scope and may be applied to the individual, the group, the process, or the program. It is that part of the learning process which lets us know where to start and to what degree we have been successful. It is recognized that while present-day techniques and methods of evaluation may be in keeping with today's knowledge regarding these matters, there is still opportunity for the improvement and refinement of both. And in the meantime, the existing evaluative practices with their admitted shortcomings are far superior to human judgment alone.

To the College Student

1. Make up evaluation check lists or self-evaluation sheets to use in your college class.

2. Think of all the ways you can where a sociogram would be of advantage to use in a college class (a flo-graph, a participation chart). Try some out in your class discussions and analyze the functions of each member of the class.

3. With your instructor, plan a series of classes using his or her topics but employing each of the techniques suggested in this chapter for developing social competence: the discussion, buzz groups, a panel discussion, and other democratic processes. Evaluate each class session in relation to its value against the lecture system. List advantages and disadvantages of each type of class.

4. Brainstorm the following topics:
   a. Ways I Can Make History Interesting to My Fifth and Sixth Grade Students.
   b. Ideas I Can Use to Develop Creativity in a Unit on Canada.
   c. Field Trips I Can Take in My Town to Build Necessary Concepts of Man's Interdependence in Second Grade Students.
5. Plan a series of questions built around the taxonomy suggested on page 302 which will demonstrate each type of thinking on each level of the taxonomy.

To the Classroom Teacher

1. Try using some of the evaluation devices suggested in this chapter, especially that of encouraging your students to help you make up a test. Think of ways you can evaluate children other than those mentioned here.

2. Examine your program and note what devices you are using each day to: 1) help your pupils evaluate themselves and 2) help you evaluate your instructional program. Are they adequate? If not, determine which of the techniques discussed in this chapter you could begin to use.

3. Set up some evaluation criteria against which you can rate yourself as a teacher. Use it from time to time. Does an awareness of the objectives of good teaching as you have spelled them out on the evaluation sheet tend to improve your teaching?

4. In Chapter 1 there is an evaluation sheet with which teachers may check themselves in terms of their *creative* teaching. Check yourself with this sheet to determine your own effectiveness as a creative teacher.

5. Examine the questions and problems taken from textbooks in Chapter 7 and rank them in types of thinking according to Bloom's taxonomy for cognitive thinking.

To the College Student and the Classroom Teacher

1. Take half a class of children and demonstrate the use of a funnel to them by using colored water, a pitcher, a funnel, and a can with a narrow opening. After the experiment, place the objects on a table before the group. Have the other half of the class return to the room, and ask *all* the children to write as many uses as they can think of for the objects on the table. Give them three minutes. Then compare the responses by *number* of items, *unusual uses* of responses and *variety* of items. If the group that did not see the demonstration has more responses and has come up with more ways to use them, you will have demonstrated the principle of functional fixedness.

2. New tests have been designed which predict creativity. Send for some and administer them to your class. Before you score them make lists of the children who you feel are most creative in your classroom. Then check your judgment against the test scores. How well can you identify creative children through observation?

3. Are there differences in the following terms? Discuss them or use the dictionary to observe what each means:

- evaluation
- appraisal
- testing
- marking
- reporting to parents
- judgment
- measuring

4. Set up a good rating scale for a student-teacher cooperating-teacher situation. Decide how you could use it most effectively.

5. Using the levels of questions from Jones' adaptation of Bloom's taxonomy as stated in this chapter, go back to Chapter 7 and classify some of the textbook questions and exercises there according to her criteria.

Selected Bibliography

BERG, HARRY D., ed. *Evaluation in the Social Studies.* Washington, D.C.: National Council for the Social Studies, 1965.

BROWN, FREDERICK G. *Measurement and Evaluation.* Itasca, Ill.: F. E. Peacock, 1970.

BUCHANAN, L. J., and LINDGREN, H. C. "Brainstorming in Large Groups as a Facilitator of Children's Creative Responses." *Journal of Psychology*, 1973, p. 83.

CARPENTER, HELEN M., ed. *Skill Development in Social Studies.* Washington, D.C.: National Council for Social Studies, 1963.

CHAPIN, JUNE R., and GROSS, RICHARD E. *Teaching Social Studies Skills.* Boston: Little, Brown, 1973.

GLOVER, JOHN A. *Behavior Modification: Enhancing Creativity and Other Good Behaviors.* Pacific Grove, Calif.: Boxwood Press, 1975.

HUNKINS, FRANCIS P. "The Influence of Analysis and Evaluation Questions on Achievement in Sixth Grade Social Studies." *Educational Leadership* 25 (1968), 326–332.

———. *Involving Students in Questioning.* Boston: Allyn and Bacon, 1976.

———. *Questioning Strategies and Techniques.* Boston: Allyn and Bacon, 1972.

THORNDIKE, ROBERT L., ed. *Educational Measurement.* 2nd ed. Washington, D.C.: American Council on Education, 1971.

TORRANCE, E. PAUL. *Role of Evaluation in Creative Thinking.* University of Minnesota: Bureau of Educational Research, 1964.

11 Curriculum Relationships and Challenges

Neglecting man as the central focus of study in our educational program has been a grave omission indeed as our multiplying troubles now prove—to what real meaning is knowledge related? What true values govern the use of factual learning, material treasures, and the genius of scientific achievement? . . . The main thrust of new education is the realm of man, individually and socially. . . . It is the age of humanity which will seek the self-knowledge needed by every individual in the conflict and struggle of a multi-ethnic world . . . will apply values to knowledge and release the creativity in every individual, too often stifled in the classroom.

EWALD NYQUIST[1]

INTRODUCTION

It is this author's view that social studies should not be compartmentalized or limited to subject matter objectives. The goal of humanistic, creative social living is difficult to attain without including most of the other subject matter and skill areas of the curriculum, for the social studies is really the means by which the objectives of the elementary school are realized, and consequently the core of the elementary school curriculum.

The criteria for judging the creative qualities of the elementary school program are:

1. Does the student *initiate* inquiry or only inquire along lines set by others?
2. Is there opportunity to *exhibit* and *take responsibility for* successive evidences of creativity, even though the created items are not "distin-

1. Ewald Nyquist, "The Age of Humanity or Aquarius and the Rebirth of Love," speech presented at the Division of Humanities and the Arts Statewide Conference, Albany, N.Y., Spring 1970.

guished"? That is, does the student learn to take satisfaction in *small evidences* of creativity?

3. Are there opportunities for the student's original work to be judged according to *individual progress* rather than according to group norms?

4. Is there time in the program for a substantial investment of time in *idiosyncratic specialization*? By this I mean unusual interests which do not necessarily lie within the standard academic disciplines, *e.g.*, the history of boating on the Missouri River, the role of herbs in human affairs, homemade musical instruments, the changing patterns of the comic strips, etc. *Already is incorporated in music classes*

5. Is there evidence that the progressive changes during the academic year are toward *greater diversity of talent* rather than toward greater conformity?

A program that would score well on these five items would be skewed toward creative teaching.

SOCIAL STUDIES AS A CORE TO CURRICULUM DESIGN

Because social studies deal with the development and understanding of human relationships, there are few areas of the elementary school curriculum which do not fall under this classification. When the time comes for the elementary teacher facing twenty-five children to translate objectives into strategies in situations ranging from self-contained classrooms to open schools, he or she will do it in the most efficient, economic and appealing way possible. The teacher will be forced to integrate, correlate and individualize for the good of each child.

The social studies is a natural place to begin to design curriculum. Each of the subject matter areas and skills development areas of the elementary school curriculum can enrich the social studies content, and each social studies unit can provide enrichment, motivation and enlightenment for the study of the other subject matter and skills development areas. The social studies can justifiably be the core of the elementary school curriculum. It is in many schools. When it is, evaluation in the social studies includes evaluation in other content and skills areas.

SOCIAL STUDIES AND CHILDREN'S LITERATURE

A philosophy concerning the use of children's literature with the social studies was stated in Chapter 7.

With beautifully written historical fiction and biographies for children so plentiful, it is incredible that more attention has not been given to the teaching of social studies through the use of children's literature.

Figure 11-1. *Literature as an impetus for social studies. Dale, Mike and Richard studied Egypt after reading* Bright and Morning Star *by Rosemary Harris.*

In the realm of children's literature, there are literally thousands of books now being written which deal with almost every topic found in any social studies curriculum outline. These are not simply information books; many are books of fact and some are fictionalized history or current events. But they are written and illustrated by some of the finest writers and illustrators of children's books in the world. When children become involved with these books, they are exposed to high standards of art and writing and to some of the finest stories ever told.

Social studies texts, it has been pointed out, deal largely with information, concepts, generalizations and summaries. Their chief value lies in their use as reference material for children who can read well, as the excerpt in Chapter 7 shows. A social studies text simply imparts knowledge but to really understand an issue, an ethnic group, a culture, or a country, children must *feel* the issue. What, for instance, did it *feel* like to be a pioneer girl facing the wilderness in the westward movement? Middle school girls and boys *know* after reading books such as Caroline Brinks' *Caddie Woodlawn*, Laura Ingalls Wilder's *Little House on the Prairie*, and a host of others built around the same time in history. What did it *feel* like to be poor and Black in the south in the early nineteenth century? William Armstrong's magnificent Newbery Award winning book *Sounder* tells you how it feels. What is more, he makes you *feel* the despair, rage, hopelessness and pain of the characters in his book—he helps the reader to *feel* the issues, to empathize—a *human* approach.

By reading the factual description of Peru as derived from a text book and comparing it to the poetic account from Ann Nolan Clark's *Secret of the Andes* as presented in Chapter 7, the reader will understand what I am saying here—the response of the reader is quite different in reacting to the two passages.

The author once taught a unit on United States history completely through the use of children's literature. One of the activities of the unit was checking the authenticity of the novels read against the true factual material read. The tests given as part of the evaluation showed the children were able to separate fact from fiction because of the discussions held comparing the types of books read. In fact, this type of approach afforded the author the opportunity to teach for critical thinking, creative thinking, analytical thinking and emotionalized reading.

SOCIAL STUDIES AND THE CREATIVE ARTS

Dr. Ewald Nyquist, former Commissioner of Education of New York State, wrote the following:

> We believe that a special opportunity exists in the humanities and the arts to provide the leadership needed for a true educational renaissance in our school system. We believe especially that literature, drama, music, the dance and other visual arts can help young people to relate to one another, and to the universe, with a new sense of excitement, concern and reverence.[2]

The creative arts and the performing arts are wedded in helping humans relate to one another in Dr. Nyquist's statement. Since dance, art, music, drama and architecture are all means of communicating, they can be of great assistance in developing human relationships.

Music

In studying any country for whatever objectives in a social studies unit, for example, it is very important if children are to understand other cultures that they get the "feel" of the people as well as facts about the culture. Often the "feel" gives children deeper insights than the facts. The feel of a country is imparted by the creative products of the people. The history and glory of a country is remembered more through its creative artists than through its warriors.

Music, one of the creative products of humans, is perhaps the only universal language in the world. It expresses the common emotions of humankind in a manner so unique that it is understood everywhere. The instruments and type of scale vary from country to country, thus giving the music of each country a special quality of its own. A contrast will be noted, for instance, in the Queen's Own Band of London and the Gamelin (oriental orchestra composed of bells, gongs, flutes, drums, etc.) of Indonesia. Each is a reflection of the culture in which it originates. Hearing it helps the listener to feel better acquainted with the people it represents. Each tells the children that life is different and environments are different but that all may be expressed through the common medium of music.

Music used in social studies units not only enriches, it explains. The music of the history of the United States is perfect for the time and life styles it reflects.

2. Ibid.

Corseted women in long full silk and satin dresses over layers of petticoats, and men in tight silk breeches, high collars, powdered wigs and buckled slippers were not likely to invent music which requires almost complete freedom of body movement such as rock and roll. The stately, dignified gavotte and the minuets danced at the time with foot tapping to show off pretty slippers, swirling to accent the flowing of fabric and the peeking of petticoats, and raised hands with fingers touching to display imported lace and jeweled fingers are the perfect dances for the life style of the plantation owner or the city dwellers of George Washington's time. This type of music is best created with stringed instruments and the delicate tones of the harpsicord.

Musical instruments rise and fall in popularity according to the type that best expresses the life style of the day. The Swiss are experts at playing bells because bells were important in keeping track of their livestock that roamed the Swiss mountains. In some herds, each animal had a bell with a different tone and lonely goatherds amused themselves making tunes from the bells.

The music of the pioneers was a break away from that of the plantation owner. It became reflective of the sounds of the rolling wagon wheels, the clomping of horses hooves, the shout of the wagonmaster. Nights were spent around campfires singing and dancing. Because harpsicords, harps and other instruments were delicate, bulky and difficult to transport and required too much room, the fiddle became popular.

Every country of the world has its own music, and children are denied a great heritage when it is isolated from social studies. Vienna is not Vienna without its waltzes; Poland is not Poland without its polkas; Switzerland is not Switzerland without its yodeling; Africa is not Africa without its drums and veldt songs; and the United States is not the United States without its jazz. And today is not today without all of these types of music easily available to everyone yet with a distinct type of music of its own. Contrast all of the above with girls and boys in jeans dancing to the modern sounds of electric guitars, basses, drums and synthesizers. The music, like the times, is vigorous, full of movement made possible by freedom from bulky clothes, the beat and the rhythm of the frantic living of the times. The lyrics infer the problems and life styles important to youth. In music and lyrics can be found the sounds of the times expressed in new and exciting ways by the use of electronics.

Nearly every community contains ethnic and cultural groups which could be used as resources when the teacher is teaching various social studies topics. Most of the parents or townspeople who could share their culture with the children will be able to play their music or will have some recordings of it.

Church choirs in each community afford an opportunity to tape some of the great music of the past and present. In units which explore the religions of the world, religious music can be used to motivate the children to an interest in all religions. The lives of great composers can also be introduced this way.

Unless music is integrated with the social studies, many songs and dances of the past and of other countries or areas will never be understood or appreciated by children. Ethnic music is what it is because of the particular situations in which it was born. The terrain and geography of the country are in it, the history of the people is in it, the clothing worn at the time it was written dictates its tempo to a great degree, the materials accessible in the environment determine to some degree the instruments that could be made to create the sounds. When music is used as part of the study of a country, children can better understand the Bavarian folk dance, the Irish jig, the American folk song, the Indian lullaby, the Spanish flamenco, American country and folk music and the German drinking songs. They understand the music because they better understand the country itself and the character of the people produced by that country.

The use of music in the social studies curriculum is not restricted to the study of history and geography of foreign countries. Many creative teachers find units with which they can correlate music or use it to demonstrate a way of communication.

Music can be used to set the mood for a choral poem or a play. One group of teachers in an open school situation encouraged the children to write their own music to accompany their choral recitations and their skits in a television play on POLLUTION. Another group collected and used all the marching songs of the civil rights groups in studying RIGHTS. Mr. Platt, who was involved in a unit on EMOTIONS, used music to show how people expressed emotions in a variety of ways—his children collected and listened to songs expressing love, joy, anger, bitterness, sadness, happiness, depression, defeat and triumph.

Miss Walters, an upper primary teacher, used music in a unit on transportation with such songs as "Casey Jones," "Up, Up and Away," "Wagon Wheels," "The Air Force Song," "Come, Josephine, in My Flying Machine," "Old Man River," "A Bicycle Built for Two," and others.

Music has become a part of the life style of every child in our land today. Many children own their own transistor radios, and these radios appear to be glued to one ear. The children hear music on television; it is thrown at them through loud speakers in stores and public buildings; it is used as a background to set the mood for all motion pictures; it is found on buses, airplanes, taxis and automobiles. Even young children often have their own record collections, play a musical instrument, and own a portable phonograph or stereo. These accessible and rich resources afford one of the best means of bringing understanding to any social studies unit.

Hickok and Smith list many resources and activities for correlating music and social studies which will be of help to the teacher in *Creative Teaching of Music in the Elementary School,* one of the books of the Allyn and Bacon Creative Teaching Series.[3]

Dance

All that has been said about music above can be applied to teaching the various dances of the world to children. Music and bodily movement are inseparable.

---

3. Dorothy Hickok and James A. Smith, *Creative Teaching of Music in the Elementary School* (Boston: Allyn and Bacon, 1974), pp. 282-299.

Communication can take place among people through bodily movement as well as through verbalism—or through music.

Dancing has its roots in the distant past. People throughout the world have danced to express feeling and to communicate ideas. Dance is another international language. It is a natural expression of the inborn creative drive of every individual. It plays a more dominant role in our civilization with each passing year. In 1975, for instance, the one area of entertainment in the United States that took in the most money at the box office (including plays and major sports events) was *ballet*.

A dance is a movement put to a pattern. It is a "movement" history of the epics of the world, an expression of the feelings of man, a record of his fantasies. It is a form of expression that can be employed easily as a means of developing creativity. In an accepting, permissive atmosphere, the dance, like music, may be utilized to develop divergent thinking processes.

Children in the primary grades learn to interpret sound and music and learn to create pattern and rhythm as a result of listening to music. After children have had a great deal of time to experiment with bodily movement put to music, they enjoy learning dances that other people have created. At the young age level, simple dances such as "Looby Loo," "I Put My Left Foot In," primary folk dances, and song dances such as "Brother, Come and Dance with Me" are enjoyed. Their own creative representation should not be dominated by the traditional forms, however.

From this point on the dances of other cultures are greatly enjoyed. Because of their imaginative minds, however, little children do not restrict their dances to imitation of people. They are airplanes, trains and bicycles, providing a new media for expression in transportation units. They can be animals or machines at the drop of a hat, enhancing the experiences provided by any unit. Because of their creative imaginations, they can be almost anything at any time.

Children in the intermediate grades will enjoy the folk dances of other countries and the folk dances of their own country. They will "feel" the way of life in England while winding a maypole to the happy music of "Country Gardens"; they will "feel" their blood leap and pound when they do the Virginia Reel to fiddle music or try American square dances, or "feel" the dignity of the minuet as they literally march through the dainty steps.

One middle school group interested in the Mayan ruins at Chichen Itza came across some authentic music taken from a book kept by a Spanish priest which is one of the few authentic records left of the Mayans. As part of their studies they recreated a ceremonial dance with the music, and with their knowledge of the Mayas made costumes and props to go with the dances. Since they could find no hollow stones to strike such as those which lined the Mayan Highway to the Well of Sacrifice, they used hollow metal pipes, sawed off to a variety of lengths to create the sound of the music as they thought it might sound.

Children can come to understand what dances do for people in other cultures and what they communicate. They can learn that these dances constitute part of the folklore of that country. However, the learning of these dances, the creative products of a culture, does not develop the creative powers of the children learning them. They do serve the purpose of showing them a multitude of ways that thoughts and feelings can be put into movements, and from these movements they may create new patterns of movements of their own. The children should also understand that the success of performing a folk dance, or a classical dance such as the ballet, lies in learning it so well and copying the movements of the original dance so accurately that each dancer's movements are highly synchronized with the others. This is not at all like the creative dance in which they put their own ideas for movement into new patterns. The former develops convergent thought processes; the latter develops divergent thought processes. The contrast in the two processes may be likened to the two kinds of workbook exercises in social studies where one exercise instructs the child to draw a chart or graph exactly like the one on the preceding page and the other tells the child to write a story telling what he would find should he land on the moon.

Children can experience the joy of creating dances for any number of situations related to the social studies. One group of fifth and sixth grade students, involved in a unit on RECREATION, worked with their music and gym teachers to create a football dance. The gym teacher took the boys to see a group of male dancers. The boys were then interested in taking the dramatic and comic movements of the football game and assembling them into a pattern while the music teacher worked out some music to accompany the patterns.

The girls in this classroom became interested in dance after seeing the presentation by the boys so the teacher put the two groups together when their next unit was introduced—Indians of North America. They combined to create an Indian dance with the pattern of the dance fashioned after life in an Indian village as they had studied it. Peaceful music provided the mood for the opening of the dance where the squaws sat in a circle occupied in carrying out the many village activities of daily living. One pounded corn into meal, one wove a blanket, another sewed buckskin, and another scraped a deerhide. The peace of the village was broken by the arrival of a messenger who brought the news that the braves were returning from war. The braves entered in full war dress with stories of their conquests, which each told with elaborate gestures. A war dance followed to celebrate the victory. The dance ended with the braves going off to hunt as the day ended and the women calmly went back to their work.

Creating a dance is a problem-solving process. The creative result is a pattern of movements and both the process and the product can be creative. Performing an existing dance is a problem-solving process, but neither the process nor the product is creative. Both concentrate largely on imitation.

Social studies can be greatly enriched and topics better understood when the children dance as other people danced or when they create dance interpretations of their own. In the refinement of developing creative dances the principles of elaboration, alteration, expansion, flexibility, originality and fluency may be applied.

Hickok and Smith provide many suggestions for the use of dance with the social studies.[4]

4. Ibid., pp. 163-183.

Art

All social studies programs and art programs have at least one common objective: to make the child aware of his or her immediate and remote environment.

Classroom units, holidays, special occurrences, and exciting events often become subjects of children's paintings. At all ages children use art to show their growing sense of design, their changing emotions, and their maturing visual skills.

As the subjects of the children's painting change, so do their techniques and abilities. Clay modeling becomes a popular form of art expression. Large painting, as on friezes or scenery for a play, gives the child a different feeling of space, area and paint. Sewing, weaving, fresco painting, and puppetmaking all have their place in providing a child with creative outlets using varied media. If these media are available most of the time in the classroom, some day the

Figure 11-2. *Zelda and Zimmy resulted from a primary study of Halloween customs, and stories about them became the base of an introductory reading program.*

child will "discover" them and the techniques for using them. The joy of finding new art forms will provide a motivation for work.

Some suggestions for correlating art with social studies to meet certain specified objectives follow:

1. Illustrate phases of history (How did you feel when you won the battle of Yorktown?), and use the illustrations for wall murals, bulletin boards, scroll movies, or scrapbooks.

2. Make get-well cards for students who are ill at home or who have been hospitalized.

3. Make clay maps, salt and flour maps, or papier mâché maps. They can become art objects when painted and embellished with pictures of products of a given area, historical events, or homes of famous people.

4. Make puppets for presenting historical and current social problems (What problems are caused by water pollution?).

5. Build dolls, forts or models (an adobe hut, for instance).

6. Use shadow plays to present current problems. (Tell the story of pollution in this country with colored lights and shadows).

7. Make dioramas depicting historical events, countries as they are today, or problems such as slums, pollution and poverty.

8. Make stuffed toys (What kind of animal would you create to put in our Koo-Koo Zoo?).

9. Design holiday decorations (What have you always wanted to put on a Christmas tree that your parents wouldn't let you?).

10. Make masks from as many materials as possible (paper bags, paper plates, papier mâché, aluminum foil, and clay molds).

11. Make mobiles (Show your impressions of ski jumping or swimming at the Olympic games).

12. Construct posters in two or three dimensions for advertising plays, puppet shows, etc.

13. Take photographs for various topics in social studies.

14. Make tabletop mock-ups of social studies projects.

15. Create flannelboard stories or reports.

16. Draw cartoons of political issues.

17. Plan slogans, designs, etc., to promote political issues.

18. Construct kites, models of wigwams, kayaks, etc.

19. Paint scenery for plays and puppet plays.

20. Design silly machines and explain what they do.

21. Make and decorate kites of any shape that will fly.[5]

5. John E. Ritson and James A. Smith, *Creative Teaching of Art in the Elementary School* (Boston: Allyn and Bacon, 1975), pp. 240-244.

SOCIAL STUDIES AND MATHEMATICS

Social studies and mathematics are often closely related because children can apply and extend their mathematics skills and concepts in social studies units. While studying about the family or the community, for example, primary age children can enrich their understanding of the concepts of more and less, and relative size, shape, and position. They can conduct surveys to determine which of the children's families have more or less children than others, do map work to explore the size and location of their homes, neighborhoods, and communities, and observe the shapes of their classrooms, schools, and communities.

Primary children can also read and construct simple maps, charts, and graphs related to what their families do when they spend time together, where they go and how far they travel while on vacations, as well as find the shortest distance between two places such as home and school.

The social studies program provides many opportunities for children to practice estimating distances between places of production and consumption. These and similar experiences with maps enable children to become comfortable with reading and understanding various units of measurement such as foot, yard, mile, meter, and kilometer. Older children often become quite skilled in using map scales to calculate distances and in conceptualizing relationships between maps and the real world. The creative potential of the learners is realized when treasure maps of imaginary lands are constructed and when children compute alternative ways to travel while on field trips. Many meaningful mathematics problems need to be solved as children determine how much time it will take to get to the places they will visit on their trips.

Mathematical understandings are enhanced when children calculate distances and time changes by using latitude and longitude. The importance of climate can be better understood when they figure elevations on maps and important relationships become clear as they compare maps that show amounts of rainfall, length of frost-free seasons, longitude and latitude, and types of crops grown.

Interpreting numerical data about population size, density, distribution, and mobility presented in absolute numbers and in percentages strengthens mathematics abilities.

Investigating imports, exports, cost, profit, loss, and a host of other economics-related understandings also builds mathematics skills.

A greater awareness of people around the world can be gained as children compare calorie consumption in various nations. A personal sense of belonging to the human species can be facilitated as children read and prepare recipes from various countries or ethnic groups. There is no human activity which is more fun than eating together! Practice with addition, subtraction, multiplication, division, and fractions becomes a natural and necessary part of the social studies unit when children decide what ingredients are needed, how much to buy, and how much the ingredients will cost. Comparative shopping, in which children must relate dollars and cents to grams, ounces, pints, and liters, improves mathematics skills as well as economic understandings.

The integration of social studies and mathematics is essential if children are to understand history. A sense of chronology, which is based on number sequence, can be learned as children read and construct time lines, called number lines in the mathematics program, that depict important historical events.

Another example of how social studies and mathematics were combined effectively is shown in the picture (Fig. 11-3) and the account below of a study of oceanography made by some middle school children.

These children became fascinated with bathyspheres and made a huge purple papier mâché bathysphere of their own. Mrs. Gelwicks, the teacher, used the bathysphere as a springboard for a spin-off unit on math.

Children would step to the back of the S. S. Aardvark as they named the bathysphere, take a seat, gaze out of the portholes, imagine the classroom was a deep sea, and settle down to solve some nautical problems.

Navigating, it was found, was much easier once you learned to solve tricky problems using fathoms and knots. All the children received the opportunity to work on some of the fifty sea-related math problems put on task cards at the desk inside the S. S. Aardvark.

Children also used the bathysphere for reading purposes.

Figure 11-3. *Social studies and mathematics: the S.S. Aardvark.*

SOCIAL STUDIES AND THE LANGUAGE ARTS

The language arts are generally regarded as the tools for learning although some aspects of the language arts, such as children's literature and creative writing, can well be defined as disciplines with their own bodies of content.

As tools of learning, the language arts become the tools necessary for the teaching of social studies. Many times in this volume, the reader has seen how the skills of reading, research, chart-making, letter-writing, composition, story and poetry writing, outlining, summarizing, note-taking, report-making, oral expression, reference usage and a host of other skills have made possible the fulfillment of a social studies unit.

One aspect of the language arts which has not been discussed at any length is the creative aspect—where children do their own creative writing. Teachers who are sensitive to the creative drive in children will find many ways to develop this drive using social studies content. Reports resulting from reading research may be very creative, or children may be inspired by the reports of other children and in the proper setting may write poems of the following nature:

What America Means to Me

America is a free country
You say anything you please!
You worship as you please.
You speak what you think is right.
In America you do anything you like.
Some people think you can break laws like: killing, shooting, breaking windows,
*   stealing, robbing.*
These are easy rules to follow,
But everything else you can do.
You can go to school and get an education instead of someone saying, "Get
*   out, this is just for rich people." Or if you're walking on the sidewalk no*
*   one stops and tells you to walk in the street.*
Nobody really knows what the Statue of Liberty means.
I think it means this:
This is the land of the free. The land of Good Will—where all people are treated
*   equal.*
For no man is different, the rich or the poor.
God bless America the land of the free.
Where all men are treated equal and fair.

— Peter
Grade 6

A CHALLENGE FOR THE FUTURE

"The most precious commodity of any society is its children."

This often quoted cliché should be expanded to read: "The most precious commodity of any society is the creativity of its children." For while conformity and an ability to conform are necessary ingredients for the purpose of gluing a society together and keeping its wheels oiled, it is the *creative* aspects of each personality which, if properly developed, will produce the unusual, unique and different ideas that will move society forward and lead humans into better relationships and to whatever happiness they find in their lifetimes. The child born into the democratic society of the United States stands a greater chance of fulfilling his or her destiny than in any other place on earth—but only if that child understands the world through knowledge and interpretation of it; only if he or she possesses the skills and techniques needed to take an active part in it; only if certain attitudes, values, and appreciations are held toward it; and only if the child's mind has been stimulated to its *fullest* development so that knowledges, skills, values and appreciations can serve to build a better life for himself or herself and all of humankind.

To develop any mind to its fullest, as Guilford has pointed out, we must now direct our attention to the *creative potential* in each individual by considering the development of those *divergent* thinking processes that were so neglected in the past. If the creative potential of each individual could be released, what a dynamic force would be set free to cope with the problems of a troubled world!

Part of this can be done by a reassessment of the social studies program, the preservation of methods that now produce creative acts, and the implementation of new methods that will develop the potential and understanding for creative and aesthetic living together.

When the concept of creativity is applied to social studies teaching, individualism and individual worth in a democratic society take on a new dimension. And the teaching of the social studies, if it is to accomplish its goals, must take on new dimensions also.

Social studies programs throughout the country need to be revamped in terms of our new understandings. The creative teachers of the nation will use the new concept and come up with ideas much more creative than those presented here. Teacher education institutions will also need to revamp methods courses in social studies so that new, young teachers can develop their own creativity and realize its fulfillment in their own teaching.

Creative teaching can be a dynamic force in developing the character of the nation. Creative teaching knows no limits in developing an exciting, stimulating approach to learning.

This book has only scratched the surface. But at least it *is* a start in the right direction.

Summary

Three types of learning constitute the core of the social studies program:

1. The development of understandings: this means children must learn certain knowledges and facts, they must develop concepts and generalizations and arrive at basic principles.
2. The development of attitudes: this means they must develop a set of values, they must learn to accept other people, become a responsible citizen, develop traits and characteristics such as responsibility, concern for all people, respect for others' rights, love of country.
3. The development of skills: this includes ability to think creatively and critically, to solve problems, to read maps, charts and globes, to use reference materials, to plan, to organize, to evaluate.

Each of these learnings calls for different types of evaluation. The types of evaluation used to assess progress among children in such vast areas of understanding and growth cannot be limited to any one type of evaluation—it is, rather, a challenge to the ingenuity of all teachers and curriculum builders to use and devise varied and appropriate evaluation techniques for the aspect of development being evaluated. The social studies encompasses all areas of the curriculum and the total objectives of any social studies program cannot be fulfilled if the children do not have mathematical skills for computing, language arts skills for communicating, creative arts skills for feeling and expressing, and creative skills for fusing, synthesizing, inventing and relating to the environment.

The End Product

Does creativity lead to happiness and more enjoyment of life?

The answer obviously depends to a large extent on your personal definition of "happiness." There is fairly general agreement of the meaning of "creativity"—the ability to use our imagination to generate new and relevant ideas. Happiness, on the other hand, is not so simple to define. But every definition we can think of leads us to believe that while creativity cannot guarantee happiness, it certainly can help. . . .

The creative person is not just the great artist, or writer or inventor. He is the individual who uses his imagination to find effective solutions to his day-to-day problems. His creativity helps him avoid boredom, overcome his disabilities and laugh at life. He is likely to have more financial security, self-confidence and satisfying personal relationships. In our opinion, he is a happier person.[6]

A happy person is generally an effective citizen.

6. Gordon A. MacLeod, "Does Creativity Lead to Happiness and More Enjoyment of Life?" in *Have an Affair with Your Mind,* Angelo M. Biondi, ed. (Great Neck, N.Y.: Creative Synergetic Associates, 1974).

To the College Student

1. One of the most valuable references you can have in your teaching is a file of children's literature. Explore some children's books by having each member of your class bring one to class each day to read or to review. Have each member find out something about the author and the books he has written. Each class member can take notes on these reports on a 3×5 card. Star the books which are especially appropriate to use in your social studies program. Circle the names of those which seem especially appropriate to develop some creative aspect of a child's behavior.

2. There are many children's magazines on the market and many inexpensive children's books that suggest social studies topics. Bring some samples to class. Assess them for their literary value—which can you classify as literature?

3. Read appropriate sections of Park and Smith, *Word Music and Word Magic* (Boston: Allyn and Bacon, 1977), and compare some children's books with the criteria listed there for literary value. Also check some children's textbooks against these criteria. Are there any textbooks of literary value?

4. Try to recount some impressions you received of people and places by reading children's books when you were in elementary school. Did you, by chance, read Frances Hodgson Burnett's *The Secret Garden*? What impressions did you get of England because of it? Did you read *Wee Gillis* by Robert Lawson and Munro Leaf? How about *David Copperfield* by Charles Dickens or *Heidi* by Johanna Spyri? Were the impressions you received supported by what you read in your textbooks or were they purely imaginative?

5. Read *Island of the Blue Dolphin* by Scott O'Dell, a Newbery Award book, and discuss all the ways in which it could be used in the classroom in connection with various areas of the curriculum, especially the social studies.

6. Collect specific stories from children's literature which lend themselves to interpretation through puppetry, dramatization, dance, pantomime, shadow plays and music and which can also tell something about developing understandings of a given time or place. Have various committees present their ideas to the class. Evaluate them.

7. Plan a social studies unit which you could teach in its entirety through children's literature.

8. Conduct a survey in your campus school or a school which works with your college on the preferences of children in your community for books and illustrations. Design a simple sheet for children to check books they like best, and another for the pictures they like best. Tabulate these to find class preferences, if any. Note whether children choose color illustrations over black and white. How much does the community environment influence children's choices, do you suppose? Which books are related to social studies topics?

9. If you have access to groups of children from different subcultures, choose a book and try reading it to a group of children in each of these subcultures. Take *Johnny Tremain* for instance: read it to a group of children in a typical middle-class suburban community, to a group in an inner-city school of the same age, and to a group of the same age in a rural school. Also try books such as *It's Like This, Cat; A Quiet Place; Spring Is a New Beginning*, and others. Note the reactions of the children. Do they react the same in each group? Would you say that some books have appeal for all groups? Which ones are popular in some groups and not in others? Does this activity violate, to a degree, the philosophy expounded in this chapter?

10. Read some children's books and categorize them under the following headings to show which needs the book might meet:

- security need—general
- spiritual security need
- need to belong
- need to love and be loved
- need to achieve, to be respected
- need for change
- need for aesthetic satisfaction

To the Classroom Teacher

1. Construct an evaluation sheet which will serve as a check for selecting the more creative children in your classroom. List all the behaviors on the left side which indicate creative behavior as you have come to recognize it in this book and leave room on the right side to check the degree to which you have seen the behavior displayed in each boy and girl.

2. Make a collection of books (with the aid of your school librarian) which would be suitable to use in your social studies program. Star the ones on the list which can also be used to develop creativity.

3. From your collection of books in No. 2 above, design a curriculum where you will use these books to develop values, character, understanding, attitudes, skills and knowledge for all your social studies units this year.

4. In planning your next unit, use the *Periodical Guide to Children's Literature* to see how many ways literature can be used in correlation with social studies, science, arithmetic, and the creative arts.

5. Collect specific stories from children's literature that lend themselves to: a) the building of values, b) the solution of children's problems, c) the development of appreciations, and d) the development of empathy.

6. Conduct a survey in a school to determine which are the favorite subjects of children. How does social studies rate? Ask the children to write a paper on why they do or do not like social studies.

7. Meet with your music and physical education teachers and plan as many ideas as you can for integrating music and dance into your next social studies unit.

To the College Student and the Classroom Teacher

1. Review this book and find instances among the many units and accounts cited as illustrations of classroom practice which show the development of creativity through: oral expression, listening, social living, writing, construction, audiovisual materials, conversations, human relationships.

2. Einstein said, "Imagination is more important than knowledge." Discuss this quote for its full meaning. Do you agree with it?

3. Make a list of all the experiences you remember from your art and music classes where your creativity was squelched rather than developed.

4. Make a list of all those areas in the curriculum where you feel creativity cannot be developed; that is, where convergent thinking processes are the only processes which can be effectively employed.

5. E. Paul Torrance in his book *Guiding Creative Talent* (Englewood Cliffs: Prentice-Hall, 1962), states that the following behavior is necessary in teachers to establish creative realtionships: genuine joy or pride in the creative powers of pupils; the sort of relationship which does much to build self-esteem in individuals; genuine empathy; a creative acceptance of limitations and assets rather than the use of them as vulnerable areas by which to gain control of the individual; a search for the truth about a situation rather than an attempt to impose group consensus or individual opinion; permissiveness; a friendly environment.

   Discuss this statement. If you were the chairperson of a department of elementary education in a college of education and you believed very strongly that your graduates should possess these qualities, what experiences would you plan to incorporate into your teacher education program that would insure their development? Just previous to graduation time, how would you evaluate each student to be certain he or she has developed these behaviors?

6. Discuss the following open-ended situations:
   a. What could you do to prepare a group of inner city children for a book like *Sounder*?
   b. What techniques can a classroom teacher use in general to motivate children to read books?
   c. Does a motion picture about a book tend to add to or detract from the book?

Selected Bibliography

CHAMBERS, DEWEY. *Children's Liteature in the Curriculum.* Chicago: Rand McNally, 1971.

DURKIN, MARY C., and ELLIS, KIM. *Taba Program in Social Studies. People in Change.* Reading, Mass.: Addison-Wesley, 1975.

EDWARDS, JEANNE. *Creative Crafts.* Grand Rapids, Mich.: Zondervan, 1970.

HICKOK, DOROTHY, and SMITH, JAMES A. *Creative Teaching of Music in the Elementary School.* Boston: Allyn and Bacon, 1974.

KING, EDITH. *The World: Context for Teaching in the Elementary School.* Dubuque: William C. Brown, 1971.

MUESSIG, RAYMOND H., and ROGERS, VINCENT R. *Social Science Seminar Scenes.* Columbus: Charles E. Merrill, 1965.

National Council for the Social Studies. "Notable Children's Trade Books in the Field of Social Studies," *Social Education* 39, No. 3 (March 1975), 172-176.

PRATT-BUTLER, GRACE K. *Let Them Write Creatively.* Columbus: Charles E. Merrill, 1973.

RITSON, JOHN, and SMITH, JAMES A. *Creative Teaching of Art in the Elementary School*. Boston: Allyn and Bacon, 1975.

RUSSELL, JOAN. *Creative Movement and Dance for Children*. rev. ed. Boston: Plays, 1975.

SMITH, JAMES A. *Adventures in Communication: Language Arts Methods*. Boston: Allyn and Bacon, 1972.

————. *Creative Teaching of Language Arts in the Elementary School*. Boston: Allyn and Bacon, 1973.

————. *Creative Teaching of Reading in the Elementary School*. Boston: Allyn and Bacon, 1975.

————, and PARK, DOROTHY M. *Word Music and Word Magic: Children's Literature Methods*. Boston: Allyn and Bacon, 1977.

TOOKEY, MARY E. "Developing Creative Thinking through an Interdisciplinary Curriculum," *Journal of Creative Behavior* 9, No. 4 (Fourth Quarter 1975), 267–276.

WALSH, HUBER M., ed. *Anthology of Readings in Elementary Social Studies*. Washington, D.C.: National Council for the Social Studies, 1971.

WESTCOTT, ALVIN M., and SMITH, JAMES A. *Creative Teaching of Mathematics in the Elementary School*. Boston: Allyn and Bacon, 1967.

Index